LANDMARK
FILMS

LANDMARK FILMS

The cinema and our century

William Wolf
with Lillian Kramer Wolf

Library of Congress Cataloging in Publication Data
Wolf, William.
Landmark films: the cinema and our century.

Bibliography: p.
Includes index.
1. Moving-pictures—History. 2. Moving-picture producers and directors—Interviews. 3. Moving-picture actors and actresses—Interviews. I. Wolf, Lillian Kramer, joint author. II. Title.
PN1993.5.A1W59 791.43'7 79-14817

ISBN 0 448 23172 7 (U.S. and Canada only)
ISBN 0 7092 0875 8

Filmset in England by SX Composing Ltd., Rayleigh, Essex.

Printed and bound in the United States

Designed by Colin Lewis

In the United States
Paddington Press
Distributed by
Grosset & Dunlap

In the United Kingdom
Paddington Press

In Canada
Distributed by
Random House of Canada Ltd.

In Southern Africa
Distributed by
Ernest Stanton (Publishers) (Pty.) Ltd.

In Australia and New Zealand
Distributed by
A.H. & A.W. Reed

For Julie, Karen, Ann, Jay,
Ian, Robert, Jonathan,
and Sarah Elizabeth

Contents

Acknowledgments

Landmark Films would never have materialized without my diligent collaborator, Lillian Kramer Wolf, and I am incalculably grateful not only for her skills as researcher and editor, but for her insights, encouragement, and stamina during the lengthy period in which the book dominated our lives.

Our indebtedness to those whose interviews, conversations, or background information have contributed to *Landmark Films* has been expressed in the Author's Note. We would also like to convey our thanks to the companies and institutions that were of immense assistance in arranging screenings and providing research and production material, or photographs: American International Pictures, Avco Embassy Pictures, Buena Vista, Cinema 5, Columbia Pictures, The Film Society of Lincoln Center, The India Consulate, The Italian Cultural Institute, Janus Films, The Japan Society, Metro-Goldwyn-Mayer, The Museum of Modern Art Film Stills Archive, New Yorker Films, Paramount Pictures, Reggane Films, The Swedish Information Service, The Toho Company, Twentieth Century-Fox, Unifrance Films/The French Film Office, United Artists, Universal Pictures, Donald S. Velde, Yeah, Inc., The Walter Reade Organization, Warner Bros., and especially, the indispensable Film Study Center of the Museum of Modern Art and the Research Center of the Library of the Performing Arts at Lincoln Center.

Many individuals, including persons at the aforementioned companies and institutions, have helped facilitate this project. We are most grateful to Paul Baise, Marion Billings, Mary Corliss, John Dartigue, Dick Delson, Edward Epstein, Jerome Epstein, Jerome Evans, Nicole Farny, Sandra Faux, John Friedkin, Bernard Glaser, Jay S. Harris, Stephen Harvey, Vicky Horsford, Mike Hutner, Robin Katz, Bill Kenly, Joanne Koch, Ruth Pologe Levinson, Wynn Loewenthal, Arlene Ludwig, Ronald Magliozzi, Yvette Mallet, Peter Meyer, Paul Myers, Vérité Moszynski, George Nelson, Al Newman, Stanley Newman, Richard O'Brien, Katzuto Ohira, Harry Reems, Raymond Rohauer, Reid Roosfelt, Donald Rugoff, Suzanne Salter, Buffy Shutt, Charles Silver, John Skouras, Jillian Slonim, Burt Solomon, John Springer, Lawrence Steinfeld, Anne Thompson, Catherine Verret, Bill Werneth, Randi Wershba, Charles Woerter, and

Mary Templeton – for the care with which she typed the manuscript.

We also wish to thank the writers and publishers of books, articles, and reviews quoted in the text.

Finally, we extend our appreciation to David Lubell, our agent and attorney, and to those with whom we have worked at Paddington Press who believe that a book is more than a commodity – John Marqusee, Janet Marqusee, Catherine Carpenter, Martin Greenwald, Sukey Howard, Lanning Aldrich, Karen Moline, Colin Lewis, and Piers Murray Hill.

W.W.

Author's Note

Landmark Films is predicated on the recognition that cinema, in existence for so short a time, has achieved unique importance in our lives. Much has been written extolling film as the art form of this century, in contrast with its beginnings when it was generally denigrated as lowbrow entertainment for the masses. The extraordinary proliferation of film books, the ever-increasing number of courses in universities and high schools, and the attention paid to film criticism attest to this reversal of attitude. Nevertheless, even among the most enlightened, there remain those who would deny cinema the capacity for artistic and intellectual depth associated with literature and the theater, and who begrudgingly persist in trying to limit its role to that of light entertainment.

A symptomatic comment, which riles me all the more because I am an admirer of his wit and political perspicacity, is Russell Baker's statement in the *New York Times* of February 17, 1976. In a column censuring Lina Wertmüller's *Seven Beauties* (which, incidentally, I believe he misinterpreted), he contended: "Even at their best, movies probably can never be more than entertainments for the child imprisoned in the oldest of us." *Potemkin, Grand Illusion, Citizen Kane, The Seventh Seal, 8½, The Sorrow and the Pity,* and yes, *Seven Beauties* – to name a few of the selections in this book – are illustrative of film as art rich in content.

To avoid misunderstanding, I would like to stress that *Landmark Films* is not a compilation of great films, although many are that; it makes no attempt to include all great directors; it is not about stars or genres; it does not aspire to be a history encompassing each significant milestone, movement, or period in the evolution of film. My endeavor is to provide perspective on certain films that have had special impact on the medium as art or entertainment; have achieved stylistic or content breakthroughs; set major trends; influenced our lives or molded our attitudes; conveyed the spirit of an era; represented important currents in society; served as focal points for national debates on mores, language, or lifestyles; broken taboos or barriers; expanded our horizons; or advanced new forms of expression. Each film chosen satisfies one or more of these criteria. I begin with *The Birth of a Nation* as the landmark that dramatically signaled film's potential.

In that the art of cinema is international, the scope of this volume is also international. However, as an American living in the United States, my viewpoint inevitably reflects a measure of domestic bias, some of which is offset by my good fortune in having a collaborator who is English. Perhaps the future will yield landmarks from parts of the world not represented here – one watches eagerly for further developments in Germany, where a new generation of filmmakers that includes Rainer Werner Fassbinder, Werner Herzog, and Wim Wenders is commanding international respect; in Latin America, where cinema is showing healthy stirrings as evidenced by the films of Cuban director Tomàs Gutièrrez Alea; and in Africa where the work of Senegalese filmmaker Ousmane Sembène raises expectations. Political change in Spain may stimulate a fruitful era of filmmaking, and there is also promise in the extensive film activity in Canada, Australia, and other countries.

I would like to express my warmest thanks to all whom I have interviewed for *Landmark Films:* Woody Allen, Robert Altman, Ralph Bakshi, Constantine Costa-Gavras, Alfred Hitchcock, Gene Kelly, Marcel Ophuls, Arthur Penn, Joseph Strick, Melvin Van Peebles, and Lina Wertmüller. I am likewise indebted to Charlie Chaplin, Stanley Kubrick, and Satyajit Ray, whom I interviewed for magazine and newspaper articles from which I have excerpted. I have also drawn upon my conversations with many individuals through the years for quotations or background information. Among them: Lindsay Anderson, Bibi Andersson, Robert Benton, David Brown, John Cassavetes, Gerard Damiano, Jules Dassin, Robert Downey, Federico Fellini, Giancarlo Giannini, Jean-Luc Godard, Paulette Goddard, William Goldman, Richard Heffner, Dennis Hopper, Joris Ivens, James Ivory, Sidney Lumet, Marcello Mastroianni, Ismail Merchant, Toshiro Mifune, David Newman, Jack Nicholson, Eleanor Perry, Frank Perry, Robert Redford, Claude Renoir, Alain Resnais, Bert Schneider, Robert Sumner, Hiroshi Teshigahara, François Truffaut, Liv Ullmann, Barbara Van Dyke, Willard Van Dyke, Max von Sydow, and the late Herbert Biberman, Vittorio de Sica, Peter Foldes, Boris Karloff, Buster Keaton, Walter Reade, Jr., Edward G. Robinson, Roberto Rossellini, and Luchino Visconti. I am deeply grateful to all whose comments have contributed to *Landmark Films*.

A procedural point: Unless otherwise noted, the year given for a film is, insofar as can be ascertained, the year of its première.

Finally, it is my hope that these pages will communicate my enthusiasm for film, and that the views expressed in the spirit of sharing ideas and opinions will stimulate the reader to further thought, exploration, and debate.

WILLIAM WOLF
New York City

Newsclips

Following the assassination of the Archduke Franz Ferdinand of Austria–Hungary at Sarajevo on June 28, 1914, Europe rushes into war.

1,198 DIE AS GERMAN SUB SINKS LUSITANIA
—May 7, 1915

Albert Einstein, having promulgated his Special Theory of Relativity in 1905, sets forth his General Theory in 1915.

UNITED STATES DECLARES WAR ON GERMANY
—April 6, 1917

BOLSHEVIKS SEIZE POWER IN PETROGRAD
—November 7, 1917

In February 1918, progress in rights for women occurs in the United Kingdom when women over thirty are permitted to vote in Parliamentary elections . . . In March the first signs of the Spanish influenza pandemic that will kill 21,640,000 are detected.

WAR OVER—ARMISTICE SIGNED AFTER 10 MILLION DEAD, 20 MILLION WOUNDED
—November 11, 1918

THOUSANDS ARRESTED IN PALMER RAIDS AGAINST ALLEGED RADICALS IN 33 US CITIES
—January 2, 1920

LEAGUE OF NATIONS BECOMES OFFICIAL AS PART OF TREATY OF VERSAILLES —January 10, 1920

The 18th Amendment banning the manufacture, sale, or transportation of alcoholic beverages in the United States takes effect in January 1920 . . . US women get vote under 19th Amendment in August . . . *Ulysses*, by James Joyce, appears in 1922 and sets the literary world talking.

MUSSOLINI MARCHES ON ROME —October 28, 1922

1914-1929

TOMB OF TUTANKHAMEN OPENED —February 16, 1923

TOKYO AND YOKOHAMA DEVASTATED BY EARTHQUAKE —September 1, 1923

The Ku Klux Klan, reorganized in 1915, continues racist rampage including lynchings and floggings, and in 1923 claims five million members . . . In 1924, Lenin dies . . . Britain gets its first (minority) Labour Party government . . . In 1925, John T. Scopes convicted in Dayton, Tennessee, for teaching Darwinian theory . . . A new book, *Mein Kampf*, by Adolf Hitler, is published in Germany . . . George Bernard Shaw awarded Nobel Prize . . . Alban Berg writes *Wozzeck* . . . Josephine Baker charms Paris in *La Revue Nègre*.

GENERAL STRIKE IN BRITAIN —May 4, 1926

GERTRUDE EDERLE FIRST WOMAN TO SWIM ENGLISH CHANNEL —August 6, 1926

US Secretary of Commerce Herbert Hoover demonstrates potential of television in 1927, appearing on first transmission linking Washington and New York.

LINDBERGH LANDS IN PARIS AFTER SOLO TRANSATLANTIC FLIGHT —May 21, 1927

SACCO AND VANZETTI, MAINTAINING INNOCENCE, EXECUTED DESPITE WORLDWIDE PROTESTS —August 23, 1927

BABE RUTH HITS 60TH HOMER —September 30, 1927

Women in United Kingdom break another barrier in 1928 and finally obtain equal voting rights with men . . . Penicillin discovered . . . On St. Valentine's Day, 1929, Al Capone mob guns down fourteen members of Bugs Moran gang in a Chicago warehouse.

STOCKS PLUNGE, WALL ST. PANICS —October 29, 1929

1915

The Birth of a Nation

The Birth of a Nation glorified the Ku Klux Klan. The "renegade" Gus (Walter Long) is lynched.

Art and Racism

IT IS DISTURBING to begin a book with *The Birth of a Nation,* but history has its demands. Film scholars rightly recognize David Wark Griffith's Civil War epic as the pioneering work that expanded the potential of the film medium and accorded motion pictures status as an art form. But Griffith's artistic triumph also stands as the most racist major film made in the United States. That Griffith could insist throughout his life that he did not perceive the film as anti-Negro illustrates how deeply ingrained racial prejudice is. The artistry of Griffith applied to such maleficent purpose typifies the painful contradictions in American life.

Those who have not seen *The Birth of a Nation* may wonder whether its content is really so revolting. It is. The film involves far more than its gross racial slurs and stereotypes. It does no less than glorify the Ku Klux Klan as the savior of the South. It condones a lynching, extols "Aryan birthright," sees white womanhood imperiled by a black menace, arouses fears of miscegenation, and views the Reconstruction period in a manner so prejudicial that it borders on hysteria. The good Negroes are the "Faithful Souls" who love their masters. The bad Negroes are those goaded by the carpetbaggers into harboring delusions of grandeur about their right to vote and govern. "We shall crush the white South under the heel of the black South," declares one typically inflammatory title. "Ku Klux Klan, the organization that saved the South from black rule," proclaims another. White actors in blackface are minstrellike caricatures. A disclaimer that the film is "not meant to reflect on any race or people of today" is an empty gesture. *The Birth of a Nation* contains poignant antiwar sentiment, but that aspect is dwarfed by its racism.

Despite the obnoxious content, there is no escaping the position of the film as a giant in the realm of technique. Griffith's genius lay in synthesizing an array of technical skills and approaches still in their infancy to tell his story and churn emotional excitement to a degree unlike anything hitherto engendered by film. His picture was over three hours long, in itself audacious for the time, and audiences were astonished that filmgoing could be so momentous an event.

The Birth of a Nation was not the first epic. Spectaculars with big sets and large casts had been made by Italian directors. There had been *Quo*

Vadis? (1912) and *Cabiria* (1913), both of which interested American filmmakers. Griffith saw his opportunity for an epic in the Reverend Thomas Dixon, Jr.'s flagrantly antiblack novel, *The Clansman,* from which he made *The Birth of a Nation.* It was by no means the first racist film. Lawrence Reddick, in a 1944 article reprinted in *Black Films and Filmmakers,* edited by Lindsay Patterson, pointed to many such films including the *Rastus* series, with titles like *How Rastus Got His Turkey* and *Rastus in Zululand, Coon-town Suffragettes,* and *For Massa's Sake,* "the story of a devoted slave who wishes to be sold in order to pay for the gambling debts of his master."

The story of *The Birth of a Nation,* which begins in 1860, focuses on two families, the Stonemans of Washington D.C. and the Camerons of Piedmont, South Carolina. Austin Stoneman (Ralph Lewis) is leader of the House of Representatives and the character is clearly a travesty of Thaddeus Stevens, the influential radical Republican leader and dedicated foe of slavery. Stoneman has a daughter, Elsie (Lillian Gish), and two sons, Phil (Elmer Clifton) and Tod (Robert Harron). Stoneman's aide, Silas Lynch (George Siegmann), is a mulatto, as is his housekeeper-mistress, Lydia Brown (Mary Alden). The Stoneman sons visit the Camerons in Piedmont, and Phil falls in love with the elder Cameron daughter, Margaret (Miriam Cooper). Her brother Ben (Henry B. Walthall) sees a daguerreotype of Elsie Stoneman and is enchanted by her. The outbreak of the Civil War puts the families on opposite sides. Ben and his brothers, Wade and Duke, go off to fight for the Confederacy. Ben survives, but the other Cameron sons and Tod Stoneman die. Ben, known as "The Little Colonel," has been condemned to death by the North and lies wounded in a hospital where, in one of those coincidences dear to the ways of movieland, Elsie is working as a nurse. Ben's mother (Josephine Crowell), anguished over his impending fate, visits Lincoln, "The Great Heart," and persuades him to spare her son.

Now the plot grows headier. After Lincoln is assassinated, Stoneman sends the villainous Lynch to Piedmont to agitate Southern blacks to rise up and oppress the whites. Lynch is elected lieutenant governor. The blacks are portrayed as crazed with power, an uncouth mass who shun work, sit shoeless in the legislature, and abuse the "faithful" Negroes who prefer the good old days of subjugation. Ben, having recovered and returned home, organizes the Ku Klux Klan to save the South. He gets the inspiration for the KKK garb when he sees white youngsters covering themselves with sheets to frighten a group of black children. The Klan is outraged when Flora Cameron, also referred to as Little Sister (Mae Marsh), jumps off a cliff to "the opal gates of death" in fear of Negro "renegade" Gus (Walter Long), who is pursuing her. Ben and the Klan hunt Gus; he is caught, summarily given "a fair trial," and lynched.

Leading black militia in his effort to take over the South, Silas Lynch seizes Elsie, intending to force her into marriage and make her queen of his "black empire." The Klan now rides to the rescue, and Griffith turns the ride into an action-crammed, intense experience. White supremacy is restored; the blacks are crushed and disenfranchised; and love between Ben and Elsie, and Phil and Margaret, symbolic of the reconciliation of North and South, prevails. The film ends fancifully with a tableau of Christ signifying everlasting peace.

Today, Griffith's techniques are taken for granted. They have even become clichés because of their familiar use and abuse. But at the time they accounted for much of the impact of *The Birth of a Nation*, along with its unusual length and explosive subject matter. Griffith used the embryonic film language of the early part of the century with imagination and sophistication. Crosscutting proved to be particularly effective in augmenting the drama; by piecing together film from the different scenes, and cutting back and forth between them, Griffith imbued the picture with suspense and excitement. As the Ku Klux Klan rode to the rescue, he alternated between shots of the Klan and shots of the endangered Elsie to accelerate the action to a fever pitch. The rhythm he brought to film is an important legacy. Griffith also attained new levels of camera flexibility, moving further away from the stationary camera to the judicious use of long shots to encompass the movement of large numbers of people, and close-ups to reveal intimate expressions. He also heightened the sense of drama with tracking shots, following the action with the camera. Flashbacks today have become a very overworked device, sometimes employed creatively, more often clumsily. When Griffith resorted to a flashback to make a point in telling his story, he was on still unrefined terrain.

Especially striking was Griffith's use of the iris. In one portion of the darkened screen a refugee family is isolated within a small circle of light that gradually enlarges to show Sherman's army and the widespread destruction that caused the people to flee. It is a tour de force, relating individuals to the carnage and dramatizing the sense of futility in the warfare between North and South. The manner in which Griffith panned the camera to capture the sweep of action gives a further sense of size and grandeur to the film. His use of the fade-out as a means of punctuation is another example of the range of vocabulary at his command. Antedating Cecil B. DeMille, Griffith employed hundreds of extras to maximum effect, making it seem as if he had thousands. As for his actors, Griffith taught them to perform more realistically, toning down the ludicrously exaggerated gestures and emotions that were the norm in silent films. With remarkable skill and wise choices, Griffith forged the foregoing elements into a surging spectacle that could manipulate emotions. It was a display of virtuosity never before accomplished in film. *The Birth of a Nation* began a new era of cinema.

The cost of Griffith's film was $100,000, then a figure that raised eyebrows. Griffith did considerable research to provide accurate visual detail; for example, he paid meticulous attention to recreating the scene at Ford's Theater for the assassination of Lincoln. The director, who used no shooting script, would carefully rehearse his actors before a take. Lillian Gish, in *The Movies, Mr. Griffith and Me,* wrote that the only scene shot in more than one take was the tragic instant when Little Sister plunges to her death. Griffith's casting was not entirely successful. Gish is bright, charming, and realistic, but Marsh looks awkward and silly. The leading men are good within the context of the character clichés. Some casting of interest: Raoul Walsh plays John Wilkes Booth, Erich von Stroheim is seen falling from a roof, Donald Crisp is General Ulysses S. Grant, and Eugene Pallette is a Union soldier.

Amid much fanfare, the film premiered as *The Clansman* in Los Angeles on February 8, 1915, and as *The Birth of a Nation* in New York on March 3, 1915, at the then-high cost of two dollars a ticket. Audiences were impressed, but diverse reaction was swift, and angry controversy swelled. The National Association for the Advancement of Colored People battled vehemently against exhibition of the film, which was exacerbating racial hostilities. The Ku Klux Klan, long dormant, was reactivated in the light of the noble role in which it had been cast. Reviews appearing in the Atlanta newspapers in December 1915 give some idea of the enthusiasm many white Southerners had for Griffith's accomplishment and for the viewpoint expressed. Ward Greene in the *Atlanta Journal,* describing the "land of the lost cause [lying] like a ragged wound under a black poison" wrote: "Loathing, disgust, hate envelop you, hot blood cries for vengeance." Thrilled by the burning cross and the rescue by the Ku Klux Klan ("that's when you are lifted by the hair and go crazy"), he dismissed any charge of prejudice, asserting: "The picture does every credit to the negro race, [and] lauds those faithful old black people whose fealty to their masters led them to dare the anger of mistaken fanatics...." In the *Atlanta Constitution,* Ned McIntosh, deeming the film more educational than hours of studying books, declared: "You sicken at the sight of an attempt to enforce marital racial equality. Again and again the unbearable hideousness of Reconstruction is borne in upon you." To him, the Ku Klux Klan is rescuing "women and homes and civilization from an unspeakable curse."

The Birth of a Nation played for twelve years in the South, where on occasion, to advertise its arrival, white-hooded horsemen would ride down the street. Box-office gross is difficult to ascertain, as many bootleg prints are said to have been in circulation; the film may have grossed as much as $50 million over the years. Protests raged and pickets demonstrated, as in Boston when it opened there in April 1915. Some one thousand blacks demonstrated at the State House, appealing to the governor of Massachusetts to bar the film. Griffith fought consistently against attempts at censorship. This was only right, as banning any work violates freedom of expression. But the attacks on *The Birth of a Nation* were evidence of the widespread antagonism it caused.

Griffith, a Southerner whose father was a Confederate colonel, was born in Kentucky in 1875. His family was poor, and while growing up he worked at odd jobs for the *Louisville Courier* and in dry goods stores. As a young man, he was interested in acting and joined a stock company as Lawrence Griffith. Drawn to New York in search of a career as a playwright, he was unsuccessful in this aspiration. However, New York was the center of film activity. Griffith met Edwin S. Porter, whose *The Great Train Robbery* (1903), a one-reeler, has earned a place in film history as the first significant motion picture to tell a story. Porter rejected a scenario that Griffith had written, but hired him as an actor in the film *Rescued From an Eagle's Nest* (1907). The following year, Griffith began working at the Biograph Studios, located on Fourteenth Street. There Griffith met Billy Bitzer, the cameraman with whom he was to have a long professional relationship, beginning with the first film Griffith directed, *The Adventures of Dollie* (1908). When Griffith moved to California after he left Biograph, he persuaded Bitzer to join him. Bitzer's camerawork on Griffith's films deserves a central place of honor as they shared in the development of their avant-garde techniques, some of which they tried out in films prior to *The Birth of a Nation*. Bitzer, as quoted by Iris Barry in her monograph *D.W. Griffith,* published by the Museum of Modern Art in New York, recalled: "All through the following sixteen years that I was at his side he always was not above taking advice, yes, even asking for suggestions or ideas. He always said to me, 'Four eyes are better than two.' "

By 1910, Griffith was filming in California during the winter months. In those early days, when the customary length of a film was one reel, pictures were ground out like sausages. Griffith had made approximately three hundred by 1911, his first two-reeler being *Enoch Arden*, released that year. His total output before *The Birth of a Nation* was almost five hundred, including the excellent *Judith of Bethulia* (1914), his last film for Biograph and America's first four-reel feature.

With the profits from *The Birth of a Nation,* Griffith financed his next epic, *Intolerance,* which cost $2.5 million and was released in 1916. Griffith interwove four stories, one modern, the others set in Judea, medieval France, and Babylon. This time the subject was bigotry through the ages. Lillian Gish was "The Woman Who Rocks the Cradle," suggesting the unifying theme of eternal motherhood. For the Babylon portion, Griffith built the largest and most elaborate set that had ever been constructed. Bitzer went up in a balloon to photograph the panorama, achieving the effect of later-developed crane shots. Techniques were further refined and

Griffith's spectacle, with its cast of thousands, was the talk of the film world. In 1919, Lenin arranged to have it shown throughout the Soviet Union; Russian director Sergei Eisenstein would later speak of its influence upon him. An impression exists that *Intolerance* was Griffith's atonement for the views of *The Birth of a Nation*. Gish maintained that such statements were "completely untrue," and that Griffith saw no reason to apologize. "*Intolerance*, on the contrary," she wrote, "was his way of answering those who in his view were the bigots."

The influence Griffith has had on film is profound, and his works have been studied with fascination and admiration by succeeding generations of filmmakers. But in harsh practical terms he was consistently occupied with the burden of financing. *Intolerance* was a commercial failure, and Griffith's ambitious project pitted him against those who preferred more conservative filmmaking. In 1919, he, Douglas Fairbanks, Mary Pickford, and Charlie Chaplin formed United Artists to guarantee themselves maximum freedom and to keep the profits of their work, instead of letting the established studios reap the gains. Eventually, under mounting financial pressure, Griffith had to sell his interest in the company.

Griffith's films following *Intolerance* included *Hearts of the World, True Heart Susie, Broken Blossoms, Way Down East, Dream Street, Orphans of the Storm, America, Isn't Life Wonderful, Sally of the Sawdust, Abraham Lincoln,* and *The Struggle*. *Abraham Lincoln,* in sound and released in 1930, had a scenario by Stephen Vincent Benét and starred Walter Huston as Lincoln. It was the last of Griffith's films to be well-received. A year later, *The Struggle,* dealing with the evils of drink, was panned. It was his final effort. He was not to be successful in the sound era, in company with so many stalwarts of the silent days.

The sadness of Griffith's sinking into oblivion after having made such contributions to the development of filmmaking has haunted those who care about what happens to creative people once they are no longer in vogue. There have been accounts of Griffith, isolated and without much money. In 1940, the Museum of Modern Art presented a retrospective of his work, an event that briefly brought him renewed attention. Eight years later, he died at the age of seventy-three. In 1975, the U.S. Government issued a ten-cent commemorative postage stamp in recognition of his contributions as a moviemaker.

That year, director Rouben Mamoulian summed up the feelings of many when he went before a national board meeting of the Directors Guild of America to urge a monument in Griffith's honor, and reminded the Guild that when Griffith died there was not enough money to put a marker on his grave and the Guild had paid for the tombstone. "This giant of the screen," Mamoulian said, "virtually single-handed, transformed the peep-shows of nickelodeons and the primitive, funny shorts into a fine art. . . . It would be no exaggeration to call him the father of the art of motion pictures. His accomplishments transcend our national boundaries. Every country on this earth is in his debt. We, the directors, owe him even a greater debt. He was the first to cut a path through a jungle of difficulties and thus made it easier for us to try to follow in his giant footsteps. He was the first to assert the creative independence and value of a director, to demonstrate the dignity and the responsibility inherent in our profession. He left us a noble heritage indeed; that of imagination, courage, persistence, and inspiration.

"What thanks did Griffith get? The last many years of his life were tragic and cruel: no fitting homage from his nation, no position of honor from Hollywood. Discarded by the very industry he ennobled and enriched, he died alone, poor and unsung."

THE BIRTH OF A NATION
USA (Epoch Producing Corporation) 1915

Cast

Elsie Stoneman . . . . Lillian Gish
Hon. Austin Stoneman . . . . Ralph Lewis
Phil Stoneman . . . . Elmer Clifton
Tod Stoneman . . . . Robert Harron
Lydia, Austin Stoneman's housekeeper . . . . Mary Alden
Margaret Cameron . . . . Miriam Cooper
Flora Cameron . . . . Mae Marsh
Flora as a child . . . . Violet Wilkey
Ben Cameron . . . . Henry Walthall
Mrs. Cameron . . . . Josephine Crowell
Dr. Cameron . . . . Spottiswoode Aiken
Wade Cameron . . . . André Beringer
Duke Cameron . . . . Maxfield Stanley
Mammy . . . . Jennie Lee
Gus . . . . Walter Long
Silas Lynch . . . . George Siegmann
Jeff, the blacksmith . . . . Wallace Reid
Abraham Lincoln . . . . Joseph Henabery
Gen. U.S. Grant . . . . Donald Crisp
Gen. Robert E. Lee . . . . Howard Gaye
Sen. Charles Sumner . . . . Sam de Grasse
John Wilkes Booth . . . . Raoul Walsh

and Elmo Lincoln, Olga Grey, Eugene Pallette,
Bessie Love, William de Vaull, Tom Wilson

Running time..195 minutes
Produced by..D.W. GRIFFITH
Directed by ....D.W. GRIFFITH
Adapted by ........................D.W. GRIFFITH, assisted by FRANK WOODS; based on the novel and the play *The Clansman*, with additional material from *The Leopard's Spots*, by REV. THOMAS DIXON, JR.
Assistant Director ....GEORGE SIEGMANN
Cameraman.............. G.W. BITZER, assisted by KARL BROWN
Music arranged by.......................JOSEPH CARL BREIL and D.W. GRIFFITH

1922

Nanook of the North

Nanook.

Reality on Film

MUCH HAS HAPPENED to the documentary form since the appearance of Robert Flaherty's vivid film of the Eskimo's struggle for survival, but *Nanook of the North* is still capable of impressing a contemporary audience. Its naturalistic purity, sense of discovery, drama of perilous daily existence, and reflection of Flaherty's immersion in his subject matter transcend time. It is easy to grasp why Robert Sherwood, a film critic before he became famous as a playwright and screenwriter, wrote in *The Best Moving Pictures of 1922–23*:

> There have been many fine travel pictures, many gorgeous "scenics," but there is only one that deserves to be called great. That one is *Nanook of the North*. It stands alone, literally in a class by itself. Indeed, no list of the best pictures of the year or of all the years in the brief history of the movies, could be considered complete without it.

Frances Taylor Patterson, writing in the *New Republic* when the film was released, observed: "It may be said to be the first photoplay of the natural school of cinematography." *Nanook of the North* was the first feature to present reality with such dramatic immediacy, intimacy, and eloquence. Its release heralded thrilling new possibilities for turning the movie camera on the world in which we live.

The concept of photographing "real life" was not new; the filming of familiar subjects was an obvious course. At the first public demonstration of the Lumière Cinématographe at the Grand Café in Paris on December 28, 1895, *Workers Leaving the Lumière Factory* was a typical one-minute experimental presentation. By 1912, newsreels were being shown by Pathé, Fox, Universal, Hearst, and Paramount. In Russia, after the revolution, Dziga Vertov developed his kino-eye theory about photographing truth and made his noted Kino-Pravda series. The later term *cinéma vérité* stems from Vertov's designation of his work. In 1921, *Mannahatta*, a one-reeler about New York City inspired by a Walt Whitman poem and made by still photographer Paul Strand and painter Charles Sheeler, gave impetus to the documentary genre, although the first use in English of the word to describe such a film was by John Grierson, in reviewing Flaherty's second film,

Moana, in the New York *Sun* in 1926. Grierson, himself to become a leading pioneer in documentary film production, took the term from the French word *documentaire*.

Flaherty was one of those rare persons who deserve to be referred to as a larger-than-life character. Of Irish descent, he was born in 1884 in Iron Mountain, Michigan, the son of an adventurous man who became owner and operator of an iron-ore mine. When the mine failed, Flaherty's father turned to gold exploration. Young Flaherty's life revolved around his father's various enterprises and expeditions. It included a formative two-year period at Rainy Lake, Ontario, where the youth learned much about nature from neighboring Indians.

"Even in my teens," Flaherty recalled in a 1949 BBC interview, "I went on prospecting expeditions with my father, or with his men, often for months at a time, traveling by canoe in summer and by snow-shoe in winter. It was sometimes in new country that hadn't been seen before, the little-known hinterland of Northern Ontario. We mapped it and explored it, or at least my father and his men did. I was just an extra."

When his father became a consulting engineer for the Canadian firm of Mackenzie and Mann, a pivotal opportunity arose for Flaherty. In 1910, Sir William Mackenzie engaged him to explore the Nastapoka Islands off the east coast of Hudson Bay for possible deposits of iron ore. Flaherty's filmmaking was a by-product of his exploring career, and might never have happened had Mackenzie not suggested that he take a movie camera along on a subsequent trip to the Belcher Islands.

Flaherty's first attempt to film Eskimo life ended in disaster when he dropped a cigarette on the negative. Seventy thousand feet went up in a flash, and Flaherty had to be hospitalized because of burns he received trying to put out the fire. It was a terrible disappointment, but he had enjoyed his introduction to filmmaking, and hoped to go back to Hudson Bay to try again, this time drawing upon the knowledge gained in his first experience.

"It took several years before I could persuade anyone to finance such a film, for none of the picture people would listen to our idea," Flaherty wrote in an article that appeared in the February 1951 issue of *Screen Director*. "Who wanted to see a picture of people so utterly crude as the Eskimo?" Eventually, Revillon Frères, a Paris fur company, agreed to finance the film in exchange for a credit line; since Revillon was expanding its trade in the Hudson Bay region, it was interested in the project as a promotion.

Today a unit venturing to a remote location has the advantage of years of collective experience, modern equipment, and plane service to fly the film back to laboratories for immediate processing. Flaherty, preparing to work in 35° below zero weather, took along two Akeley cameras, which he had found were best suited to the cold. "I also took with me the materials and chemicals to develop the film, and equipment to print and project it," Flaherty continued in his report in *Screen Director*. "My lighting equipment had to be extremely light because I had to go by canoe nearly two hundred miles down river." The Eastman Kodak company provided him with developing gear and appropriate instructions, and he had a printing machine that fastened on a wall. His drying room was heated by a stove burning soft coal.

Flaherty thought he could make a more dramatic film by concentrating on one Eskimo family. He had heard about Nanook, leader of the Itivimuits and known throughout the Ungave Peninsula as a skilled hunter, and decided to name Nanook "my chief man." Writing in his book *My Eskimo Friends,* Flaherty noted: "Besides him, and much to his approval, I took on three younger men as helpers. This also meant their wives and families, dogs to the number of twenty-five, sledges, kayaks, and hunting impedimenta."

The film with which Flaherty came away involves viewers in the life of his subjects, and vigorously and poignantly captures the forbidding environment, the vast expanse of snow and ice, the bitter cold, and the scant prospect of finding food. The perpetually desperate plight of Nanook and his family becomes the dramatic core of the film. We make friends and sympathize with them, visit their habitat, go with Nanook on his expeditions for food, and leave the theater looking at our own environment with a new frame of reference. Pictorially, the work of Flaherty is astonishing considering the circumstances under which he labored. The frozen landscape, the seals and the walrus, the dogs, the action scenes, and the close-ups of Flaherty's Eskimo "stars" all gain in impact because of the filmmaker's sensitivity and talent for composition.

Despite the relentless hardships, Nanook manages to seem confident and good-natured, uncomplaining and stoic. One observes the children and wonders how long they will survive. We see Nanook teaching his small son Allee the rudiments of hunting. His wife, Nyla, looks after the children, and chews his boots to soften them so that he can put them on. Nanook, his rugged face denoting years of battling the elements, assumes the traditional male role, meeting the dangers that come with his status.

Particularly memorable is the walrus hunt, in which Nanook sneaks up on a group of walrus on shore, wounds one with his harpoon, and with the aid of other Eskimo, struggles mightily to prevent the hulking creature from slipping away into the sea. Its mate valiantly tries to pry the fatally wounded walrus from the harpoon. Another engrossing sequence occurs when Nanook demonstrates how he fishes through a small hole in the ice. He harpoons a seal and pulls it up through the hole. Ever present on these expeditions is the harrowing threat that, should he fail, the family will face starvation.

In another fascinating portion, an igloo is built for temporary shelter. Flaherty removed part of it to shoot interior scenes, which in a strict sense is cheating on the concept of pure documentary. But his motive was to show how his subjects lived, and the liberty taken was in the interest of truthful portrayal. The scene within the igloo shows the primitive haven in contrast with the oppressive cold outside. The terror of hunger is also implicit at feeding time for the ferocious dogs, who testily snap at the food tossed to them – a portent of how dangerous they could be if their meals were not forthcoming.

The film has its charming lighter moments. Flaherty brought along a phonograph and records, and footage shows Nanook intrigued by these alien items. He suspiciously examines the phonograph and tries to bite off a piece of a record. (The record that amused the Eskimo most, Flaherty later reported, was Caruso singing the prologue to *I Pagliacci.*)

Although Flaherty's purpose was obviously to convey what he saw, the dramatic and emotional appeal of his material and the visual beauty of his scenes combine to raise the work from travelogue to art form. As Sherwood wrote, "Here was drama, rendered far more vital than any trumped-up drama could ever be by the fact that it was all real." The explorer, having turned filmmaker, successfully explored new terrain in the motion picture medium.

When Flaherty returned with *Nanook,* he encountered predictable distribution difficulties. Paramount and other companies looked at it, but did not consider it commercial. French-controlled Pathé finally undertook to distribute it. The film, booked into the Capitol in New York, received a favorable reception, prompting Jesse Lasky to recognize that Paramount had been wrong to reject it. Lasky decided to back Flaherty in another project. This time Flaherty went to Samoa and took along his wife Frances, their three daughters, and his brother David. Out of this trip emerged *Moana*. Frances Hubbard Flaherty collaborated with her husband on the script, direction, and photography for *Moana,* and was to work closely with him in the future. Despite initial enthusiasm at Paramount, Flaherty was asked to make substantial cuts. When the film opened in New York at the Rialto in February 1926, the advertising approach pandered to sensationalism and Flaherty's serious work was promoted with the slogan, "The Love-Life of a South Sea Siren." Later, when another film with Flaherty was being considered, Hollywood producer Hunt Stromberg is said to have urged, "Let's fill the screen with tits."

Flaherty had now become a filmmaker first, an explorer second. As such, he was faced with the problem of raising money for his work and walking a tightrope between what he wanted to do and the compromises pressed upon him. Arthur Calder-Marshall, in his biography, *The Innocent Eye,* contended that the transition to filmmaker resulted in a veering away from the qualities that made Flaherty's early work so disarming. Flaherty's joint venture with German director F.W. Murnau, famed for *Nosferatu* (1922) and *The Last Laugh* (1924), was a painful experience. Their collaboration on *Tabu* (1931), another South Seas film, degenerated into conflict about ideas and intent; Murnau prevailed, making the film his, not Flaherty's.

Flaherty's significant British period began in 1931 when Grierson invited him to direct the documentary *Industrial Britain* for the Empire Marketing Board. Following this, Michael Balcon of the Gaumont-British Picture Corporation sent him to the Aran Islands in Galway Bay, where he filmed his famous *Man of Aran*, released in 1934. He then journeyed to India, this time under the auspices of Alexander Korda, to make *Elephant Boy* (1937), based on Rudyard Kipling's *Toomai of the Elephants*, which he codirected with Zoltan Korda. Sabu played the part of Toomai. Returning to the United States at the invitation of Pare Lorentz, then head of the U.S. Film Service, Flaherty, with Helen Van Dongen as editor, made *The Land* for the Agricultural Adjustment Commission. The film, which showed the plight of farmers during the Depression, was controversial, and the United States Department of Agriculture refused to release it. *The Land* had only limited showing domestically, and the State Department prevented its distribution abroad. Flaherty's last complete film, produced for the Standard Oil Company of New Jersey, and edited by Van Dongen, was the noted *Louisiana Story* (1948), which received a British Film Academy award. In 1949 he started, but never finished, an analytical film of Picasso's *Guernica*.

Flaherty died at the age of sixty-seven in July 1951, six months after the Screen Directors Guild held a retrospective of his work at the Museum of Modern Art in New York. His memory is honored by International Film Seminars, evolved from the Robert Flaherty Foundation, where films "that draw their inspiration from life and reflect the spirit of Robert Flaherty's explorations" are viewed and discussed.

The documentary genre is now far more complex and varied than in the day of "the initiator of the naturalist tradition in cinema, . . . the high priest of the spontaneities," as Grierson, who acknowledged Flaherty's influence on his own work, called him. The many who have contributed in various ways to its development include Alberto Cavalcanti, Walter Ruttmann, Joris Ivens, Henri Storck, Leni Riefenstahl, Helen Van Dongen, Pare Lorentz, Willard Van Dyke, Ralph Steiner, Humphrey Jennings, Basil Wright, Arne Sucksdorff, Lindsay Anderson, Paul Rotha, Edgar Morin, Jean Rouch, Chris Marker, Richard Leacock, D.A. Pennebaker, Allan King, Albert and David Maysles, Frederick Wiseman, Marcel Ophuls (see *The Sorrow and the Pity*), and – if one includes television – Edward R. Murrow and Fred Friendly.

A reappraisal of *Nanook of the North* would be incomplete without reference to what happened to Nanook himself. Two years after its release, he starved to death on one of his frequent hunting expeditions. By then, the film was widely known and Nanook's face familiar in many parts of the world. News of his death was even reported in the Chinese and Japanese press. The knowledge that Flaherty, in these stark moments of man versus environment, was previewing Nanook's fate intensifies the drama and underscores the authenticity of his milestone in the growth of cinema.

NANOOK OF THE NORTH
USA (Pathé) 1922

Cast

NANOOK
NYLA
ALLEE
CUNAYOU
COMOCK

Running time . . . . 60 minutes
Produced by . . . . REVILLON FRÈRES
Directed by . . . . ROBERT J. FLAHERTY
Scenario by . . . . ROBERT J. FLAHERTY
Photography by . . . . ROBERT J. FLAHERTY
Film Editor . . . . ROBERT J. FLAHERTY
Assistant Film Editor . . . . CHARLES GELB
Titles by . . . . ROBERT J. FLAHERTY and CARL STEARNS CLANCY

1925

Potemkin

The massacre on the Odessa steps.

International Impact

THE EFFECTS OF THE Russian Revolution are still being felt – in the arts as in the social and political spheres. One of the most influential films ever made, Sergei M. Eisenstein's extraordinary *Potemkin,* was an outgrowth of the upheaval in Russia. Building upon the earlier accomplishments of his mentor, D.W. Griffith, Eisenstein used montage with new virtuosity, illustrating how film could promulgate political ideas with hitherto unequaled fervor: revolutionary cinema for revolutionary goals.

Potemkin became a virtual textbook that is still studied today. The film stirred those politically attuned to its content and made some authorities fearful enough to ban it. Its international impact was formidable. Even though cinematic strides were evident in many countries, eyes turned to the work of Eisenstein.

Potemkin (also known as *Battleship Potemkin,* or *The Armored Cruiser Potemkin)* has as its source the story of the sailors' revolt of June 1905. The mutiny took place in the context of the events of that year. A demonstration in front of the Czar's Winter Palace in January had been ruthlessly suppressed; Russian troops were being defeated in the war with Japan; there were widespread strikes; and the year culminated in the unsuccessful December uprising.

As the film begins, two sailors, Matyushenko and Vakulinchuk, are talking. "We, the sailors of the *Potemkin* must stand in the first lines of the revolution with our brothers, the workers," proclaims the title. An early scene shows the seamen's cramped, wretched living quarters. The men are asleep in hammocks. The boatswain inspects them, pushing the hammocks aside roughly, and for no reason, hits the bare back of a young, sleeping sailor with a piece of rope. The sailor weeps in humiliation. On the surface everything is as usual, but there is an underlying air of unrest. The men surround a carcass of rotting meat; the ship's doctor peers at it through his pince-nez. He sees the maggots crawling all over it, but declares that they are not maggots, merely dead fly-eggs that can be washed off in salt water. Vakulinchuk protests that Russian prisoners in Japanese hands are better fed, but the officers will brook no complaints. The atmosphere is seething.

A bugle sounds. All are summoned on deck. The commander asks those satisfied with the food to step forward. He then pronounces that the rest will be executed. Matyushenko tries to incite the men to prevent the slaughter. Nineteen dissidents are rounded up and covered with a tarpaulin. A marine firing squad is assembled and ordered to shoot them. Vakulinchuk pleads with the marines not to shoot. "Brothers!" he cries. Cut to the stern face of the commanding officer, to the other officers, to the firing squad with poised rifles, to the cringing mass under the tarpaulin – back and forth, back and forth. Eisenstein's use of montage makes the suspense unbearable. The marines do not fire. The condemned men are freed and the revolt gathers force. Frame upon frame records the mutiny and the confusion. The doctor is thrown overboard; a close-up shows his pince-nez caught in the ropes.

Vakulinchuk is killed, but the men have won. They put their comrade's body in a barge and take it to Odessa harbor where it lies in state. The people of Odessa, first only a few, then steadily increasing in numbers, come to view the body; they bring the sailors food; their anger and anguish visibly mount. The adroit alternating of fantastic shots, at times abrupt, at times lingering, creates an exciting rhythm that accentuates this crescendo of humanity in motion. The sequence climaxes in the most renowned scene in cinema history – the massacre of the citizens of Odessa by Czarist troops. The soldiers relentlessly advance down the steps, their rifles aimed at the civilians, who try to retreat. But the soldiers show no mercy and fire into the crowd. There is panic. People desperately try to escape the gunfire. The steps are littered with the dead and the wounded. Close-ups accentuate the horrified reactions. A woman is shot in the face, blood streams from an eye. A boy is shot; his mother carries his body in her arms, going up the steps toward the soldiers. A carriage with an infant in it bumps down the steps, careering out of control. Eisenstein cuts back and forth between close-ups of the people, the soldiers, the carriage, building impressions of the sickening scene.

The final "act" (the film is divided into five parts) is the confrontation between the *Potemkin* and the naval squadron sent to quell the rebellion. The *Potemkin* runs up a signal: "Don't fight us – join us!" The suspense mounts. Will they fire? More close-ups convey the tension. The sailors of the squadron do not fire. The exultant crew of the *Potemkin* and their fellow-seamen wave to each other in comradeship symbolizing the growing force of unity and revolution, and the *Potemkin* passes through the squadron. In reality, the *Potemkin*, short of fuel and food, put in to the Rumanian port of Constanza and surrendered to the authorities. Some of the men escaped, some were executed, the rest exiled or imprisoned.

What set film buffs of the 1920s aflame was Eisenstein's startling use of montage to tell his story, fire the emotions, and project revolution as an answer to oppression. In *Potemkin,* he used different kinds of montage with a grace and rhythm not previously seen. Through his choice of shots and their juxtaposition, Eisenstein achieved heightened intensity and movement, and as a result, was able to deeply involve the viewer in the actions and emotions of the characters, as well as in the larger political viewpoint. His skill in using these techniques charged his films with excitement and made him a man from whom to learn. Eisenstein became known as a theoretician and teacher as well as a practitioner.

A key to Eisenstein's thinking is found in the following statement from his book, *Notes of a Film Director:* "In one of my articles I compared [my] method of treating close-ups with the figure of speech known as synecdoche. I think both depend on the ability of our consciousness to reconstruct (mentally and emotionally) the whole from a part." The doctor's pince-nez caught in the rigging triggers an instant association with their owner, his arrogance, the class differences, the anger of the men at his contemptuous approval of rotten meat as fit food, the justice of his fate, and perhaps, even an element of pity.

Eisenstein gains similar mileage by photographing parts of an object and editing these shots into a rapid series, creating a stronger, more significant impression than could have been achieved with one shot of the entire object. This occurs when the young sailor who was hit with the rope looks at a plate from which an officer has eaten, reads the inscription, "Give Us This Day Our Daily Bread," and throws the plate down in a fury. In the space of seconds, fragmentary views of the plate in motion augment the sailor's outrage at the disparate treatment of the officers and the men, at the maggoty meat, and at his earlier humiliation.

Potemkin is replete with sequences that project the viewer from the specific moment to broader understanding. The cruelty on the deck of the ship connotes the callousness with which all attempts at protest were crushed in Czarist Russia. The growing procession of mourners passing the body of Vakulinchuk suggests the gathering strength of the proletariat throughout the country, and the martyrs of the Revolution. The carnage on the Odessa steps indelibly stamps the Czarist regime with brutality, not only against the people of Odessa, but against others under its rule. When the film ends with the *Potemkin* sailing freely past the other ships of the squadron, the scene symbolizes the 1905 Revolution as a whole and as the prelude to the October Revolution of 1917.

David Mayer in his detailed analysis, *Eisenstein's "Potemkin,"* made a cogent observation on the director's ability to bend time and circumstance with overpowering effect through his rhythmic use of montage. Citing the Odessa steps sequence, Mayer described how the steps, although not unusual in themselves, under Eisenstein's camera eye

> . . . are transformed into a never-ending series of stone slabs down which the citizens of Odessa flee with no chance of escape from the massed

Czarist rifles above. In this sequence, Eisenstein distorts real time, stretching each harrowing moment into an eternity of peril. People flee endlessly down endless steps.

Eisenstein's use of montage involves various kinds of conflict that produce drama and tension. There is conflict between close-ups and long shots, conflict between an event being depicted and time on screen, and even conflict within a shot itself.

"Typage" is Eisenstein's term for another key aspect of his work. He delighted in casting non-professionals. Not satisfied with the actor who was to play the doctor, he gave the part to a workman on the set. For the role of the ship's priest, he found an elderly, bearded gardener who was supplied with a white wig. (In the famous scene where the priest falls down the stairs with his back to the camera, Eisenstein doubled for the gardener.) With few exceptions, the actors in *Potemkin* were unknowns. (Fellini works somewhat similarly, often relying upon non-professionals with faces that strike him as unusual or right for what he wants.)

Sergei Mikhailovich Eisenstein was born in Riga in 1898. His father's family, of German-Jewish origin, had converted to Christianity because of anti-Semitism. At first Eisenstein entered his father's field, engineering, which he studied in St. Petersburg until he joined the Red Army in 1918 to fight in the Civil War. Eisenstein credited the Revolution with giving him the feeling of freedom to break with the father-son tradition and "take my fate into my own hands." In *Notes of a Film Director,* he described how, when the war was over, he went to Moscow and "plunged headlong into the theater world." He joined one of the new workers' theaters, the Proletkult, where his talent for draftsmanship was put to use in designing sets that won acclaim for original theatrical ideas, and where he had the opportunity to work with famed director Vsevolod Meyerhold.

This was a time of passionate excitement and argument in arts circles and Eisenstein was caught up in the enthusiasm for new concepts and methods. (Given the chance to direct, he staged the play *Gas Masks* in a gasworks.) He was fascinated by the cinema; so was Lenin, who regarded film as the art of the masses and believed in its future, both as an art and as a weapon for revolution.

Eisenstein, offered the opportunity to work on a film, accepted with alacrity. His first venture, *Strike* (1925), like *Potemkin*, deals with events before the Revolution. A worker accused of stealing hangs himself, and his co-workers strike, only to be brutally crushed by the police. This film marked the start of Eisenstein's collaboration with outstanding cinematographer Eduard Tisse, who was to work with him on all his films.

Following *Strike*, Eisenstein was chosen to make *Year 1905*, which was to be included in a commemorative program marking the twentieth anniversary of the events of that year. In the summer of 1925, Eisenstein, together with Nina Agadzhanova Shutko, prepared a massive scenario in which the story of the *Potemkin* occupied only half a page. Filming started in Leningrad, but the need for more sunlight sent Eisenstein southward to Odessa and Sevastopol. Eisenstein explained in *Notes of a Film Director* that it was then that he decided to concentrate on the single episode of the mutiny as "the emotional embodiment of the whole epic of 1905." The battleship *Potemkin* no longer existed but her sister ship, *The Twelve Apostles,* was moored in the Bay of Sevastopol, where it served as a mine dump. Eisenstein had the upper quarters rebuilt with plywood, in accordance with the *Potemkin* blueprints. Filming on the open sea was done on the cruiser *Comintern* and one scene made use of a miniature in a swimming pool. The Odessa steps sequence was not planned. "Neither the original script nor the montage drafts provided for the shooting scene on the Odessa steps," he wrote. "The idea flashed in my mind when I saw the steps."

The film was completed in three months, with Eisenstein working day and night on the editing to have it ready for the December 21st commemorative event at Moscow's Bolshoi Theater. Although reaction was generally favorable, and a gala public showing was held in January at the First Sovkino Theater, Sovkino executives were later chastised by the poet Mayakovsky for not having given *Potemkin* the best possible distribution. Its foreign acclaim eventually led to its enhanced prestige at home, a situation that is not unusual.

Abroad, *Potemkin* quickly generated enormous enthusiasm, as well as controversy. Since little was known about Soviet film, there was immense curiosity. Léon Moussinac, in *Sergei Eisenstein*, wrote: "At that stage in the life of cinema, the French première of *Potemkin* was a thunderbolt which takes on, in retrospect, exceptional historical importance." Celebrated theater director Max Reinhardt predicted: "After viewing *Potemkin* I am willing to admit that the stage will have to give way to the cinema." In the United States, the picture was previewed in New York in the autumn of 1926. After its December première, *New York Times* critic Mordaunt Hall, although wary of the political content and the manner in which the director had weighted it, acknowledged: "The fact remains that it is a production in which the director displays a vivid imagination and an artistic appreciation of motion picture values." Later in his review he observed: "One of the bits of real art in this feature is . . . the early morning of the day following the mutiny. Here there are glimpses of the Port of Odessa – fishing smacks in a mist and other scenes which truly impress one with the inactivity of dawn. Then it becomes gradually lighter and things begin stirring. . . ."

There were far more enthusiastic reviews. Evelyn Gerstein, writing in the *New Republic,* felt the full sweep of the work:

> It has movement, tempo, rhythm, compositional beauty. Technically superb, it has no hollow virtuosity. . . . Eisenstein has a musician's feeling for tempo; his rhythms throughout are amazing, flexible, trenchant, cumulative. It is impossible to imagine the terrific power there is in the slow, steady rise of the guns, or the crazy speeding of the baby carriage down those hundreds of steps, into infinity.

After an initial ban, *Potemkin* had a triumphant year's run in Germany, where the unexpected size of the Russian fleet, implied by the film, led to questions in the Reichstag. (Eisenstein had used newsreel clips of a foreign navy.) The British Board of Censors, fearing *Potemkin*'s revolutionary sentiments, at first relegated it to film clubs. Eisenstein described this Censor Board in his memoirs: "One of them is blind and probably deals with the silent films; another is deaf and so gets the sound films; the third one chose to die during the very period that I was in London." In France, public showings were not permitted until the 1950s.

Eisenstein's next film was *October* (1927), released abroad as *Ten Days That Shook the World*, and partly based on the book by American journalist John Reed. By then, Stalin was in the ascendancy and Trotsky had been expelled from the Communist Party and was to be exiled. Accordingly, Eisenstein was forced to edit out lengthy sequences relating to Trotsky's role in the October Revolution. This was only the first of the political difficulties the director was to have.

Meanwhile, capitalist Hollywood had become enviously aware of the work of this filmmaker of the Revolution. David O. Selznick, then a young producer at MGM, saw *Potemkin* and recommended that its technique, "entirely new to the screen," be studied "in the same way that a group of artists might view and study a Rubens or a Raphael." Eisenstein, too, was anxious to come to the United States (he was especially interested in the new sound techniques) and did so in June 1930 at the invitation of Paramount. His visit aroused anti-Communist and anti-Semitic attacks, but many were eager to meet him. He had the opportunity to talk with D.W. Griffith in New York City, and in Hollywood, became friendly with King Vidor, Robert Flaherty, Josef von Sternberg, Walt Disney, and above all, Charlie Chaplin.

Several projects were discussed with Paramount but none materialized, including the proposed filming of *An American Tragedy*. Eisenstein had prepared a scenario of the Theodore Dreiser novel at Paramount's request. It was approved by Dreiser, and praised by Jesse Lasky, whereupon instead of proceeding with the film Paramount severed Eisenstein's contract. The script may have been too socially conscious for Paramount, but Lasky later admitted that the studio had been bombarded with protests against Eisenstein's presence in Hollywood, and implied that was the real reason the arrangements were terminated. *An American Tragedy* was subsequently filmed by von Sternberg in 1931, a version disavowed by Dreiser. Later it appeared in another guise under the title *A Place in the Sun* (1951), directed by George Stevens.

One story perhaps sums up Eisenstein's abortive Hollywood sojourn. According to Ivor Montagu, who accompanied him on the trip, titan Sam Goldwyn met with Eisenstein and, through the "interpreter" (Montagu) the Russian did not need, said, "Please tell Mr. Eisenstein that I have seen his film *Potemkin* and admire it very much. What we should like would be for him to do something of the same kind, but rather cheaper, for Ronald Colman."

Hollywood was clearly not the place for a revolutionary genius. Eisenstein's next stop was Mexico, where he went in December 1930 to shoot *Que Viva Mexico!* with the financial backing of Upton Sinclair and others. He and Sinclair had a stormy disagreement and the filming was interrupted. Considerable footage had been shot, but Eisenstein was precluded from editing it himself as Sinclair had the negative, and it was eventually edited by various people into films of different length. When he saw some of these films years later, Eisenstein was very upset and disowned them.

In April 1932, a disheartened Eisenstein returned home. There had been many social and political changes during his absence and he was subjected to further humiliation. In 1937, encountering virulent ideological attacks on his first sound venture, *Bezhin Meadow,* he had to publish an autocriticism in which he promised the cultural commissars "to rid myself of the last anarchistic traits of individualism in my outlook and creative method." Boris Shumyatsky, who as director of the Soviet Film Office led the attacks on Eisenstein and prevented him from completing *Bezhin Meadow,* was himself removed from his post a short time later. Writer Isaac Babel, who had collaborated with Eisenstein on the film, suffered a worse fate – he became a victim of Stalin's purges and perished in prison in 1941.

The criticism leveled at Eisenstein hampered his creative opportunities, but he continued throughout with his teaching at the Institute of Cinematography. However, when the Soviet Union felt increasingly threatened by Nazi Germany, he was asked to make a film about the Teutonic invasion of Russia in the thirteenth century. The result was his celebrated epic *Alexander Nevsky,* scored by Prokofiev, which contains the battle on the ice, one of the memorable sequences in cinema. When it made its appearance in 1938, the deep patriotism of Eisenstein's masterpiece was much praised and appreciated. Ironically, it was soon to be withdrawn, during the period of the Nazi-Soviet non-aggression pact. Eisenstein gained further respect with *Ivan the Terrible, Part I* (1944), and further vilification with *Ivan the Terrible*, *Part II*, filmed in 1945. *Part II* was criticized as "politically unsound," and was not shown in the Soviet Union until ten years after his death. Eisenstein had intended to make *Ivan the Terrible, Part III,* but his initial work on the film was destroyed and by the time he was permitted to continue he was too ill. As for *Bezhin Meadow,* the official story is that the footage was destroyed when the Mosfilm Studios were bombed during World War II. A half-hour compilation has been made from pieces of film found in Eisenstein's home and from production stills.

In 1948, shortly after his fiftieth birthday, Eisenstein, who had developed a heart condition, died. The political troubles heaped upon him were particularly painful as he had been a passionate believer in the Revolution. Indeed, it was this very commitment that inspired his art.

Eisenstein's story is a sad reminder of the fate of filmmaking in the Soviet Union. The glorious days of Eisenstein, Pudovkin, and Dovzhenko gave way to a fallow period of ideological conformity. In the 1950s, there seemed to be some forward motion with films like *The Cranes Are Flying* (1957) and *The Ballad of a Soldier* (1959), which attempted to deal realistically with Soviet life. One can point to other examples with a measure of individuality, and a few worthy films have been made from literary classics, but a pall has settled over Soviet filmmaking. Most discouraging and upsetting is the role Soviet power played in stifling the exciting advances in Czech cinema, illustrated by such pictures as *The Shop on Main Street, Closely Watched Trains, . . . And the Fifth Horseman is Fear,* and *The Fireman's Ball,* before leading Czech filmmakers were driven into exile after the 1968 Soviet invasion. Some good films have come out of other Communist countries, including Poland and Hungary; in Yugoslavia, the most promising and prominent director, Dusan Makaveyev, best known for his *WR – Mysteries of the Organism,* was subjected to criticism and had to work abroad for a time. The New York Film Critics Circle passed resolutions in 1975 and 1976 supporting appeals by filmmakers from many countries on behalf of Soviet director Sergei Paradjanov, whose *Shadows of our Forgotten Ancestors* had won prizes at sixteen film festivals. He had been condemned in 1973 to five years in a hard labor camp on charges of "homosexualism" and "blackmarketeering." Paradjanov was released in 1978, having served his full sentence.

Today, it is almost impossible to find a print of *Potemkin* in the form in which Eisenstein made it. The film has been doctored in so many ways: by cuts, messages added, and various unauthorized musical scores. (The sole score authorized by Eisenstein – although when he heard it, he evidently complained his film had been turned into an opera – was that of Austrian composer Edmund Meisel for the Berlin première.) In the United States, apparently only the Museum of Modern Art has prints of the original silent version.

Potemkin stands as a turning point in cinema. It also sadly evokes the plight of the artist, too often an outsider in his own country, and the betrayed dream of the Revolution that began with such high aspirations. Eisenstein wrote in *Notes of a Film Director:* "I was truly inspired while making *Potemkin.* And everybody knows that a man who has once experienced the ecstasy of creating will probably never be able to free himself from the domination of art." As for the significance of that art, perhaps documentary filmmaker John Grierson expressed it best on BBC Television in 1970. Calling Eisenstein "the greatest master of public spectacle in the history of the cinema," he added: "But he was also very much of a man who reacted to all the forces of his time, and especially to the great new world of industry and technology; and in his art he sought to mirror the colossal power and resources of this world."

POTEMKIN
(Bronenosets Potyomkin)
USSR 1925

Cast

Vakulinchuk	ALEXANDER ANTONOV
Matyushenko	MIKHAIL GOMOROV
Commander Golikov	VLADIMIR BARSKY
Chief Officer Gilyarovsky	GRIGORI ALEXANDROV
Petty Officer	A. LEVSHIN
The doctor and the priest	NON-PROFESSIONALS
Extras in crowd scenes	SOVIET NAVAL CREWS and INHABITANTS OF ODESSA
Other walk-ons	MEMBERS OF THE PROLETKULT THEATER

Running time	86 minutes
Produced by	GOSKINO
Directed by	SERGEI M. EISENSTEIN
Scenario	SERGEI M. EISENSTEIN, based on a larger scenario by EISENSTEIN and NINA AGADZHANOVA SHUTKO
Photography by	EDUARD TISSE
Edited by	SERGEI M. EISENSTEIN
Assistants	GRIGORI ALEXANDROV, MAXIM STRAUCH, MIKHAIL GOMOROV, ALEXANDER ANTONOV, A. LEVSHIN

Art Director . . . . VASSILI RAKHALS
Titles . . . . NIKOLAI ASEYEV
Music . . . . Originally without music,
EDMUND MEISEL's score for the Berlin
première was the only one authorized
by Eisenstein.

1927

The General

Buster Keaton in The General.

Zenith and Fade-out

HE HAD HIS BACK turned as he stood on the set, a dingy little room denoting the lonely dwelling of a man trying to shut out the world. He moved his shoulders and you knew it was Buster Keaton. Then he turned. At sixty-eight, his face was deeply lined, his paunchy body contrasting with the trim physique of his peak movie-making days, but his eyes unmistakably those expressive, penetrating eyes so endearing to Keaton devotees. He was performing in *Film*, written by Samuel Beckett, and the great comedian's life was nearing its end. Beckett stood close to the camera watching, while director Alan Schneider explained to Keaton the movements he wanted.

"I really don't know what this is all about," Keaton said to me when the scene was over and he had taken refuge briefly in a makeshift dressing room. A squat hat of the species that became his trademark rested askew on his head. "I just do what I'm told. Maybe *they* know what it's about." There was a wry note in his voice, but he seemed pleased that someone wanted him to play the part and satisfied that he was doing what was expected. It was a far cry from his commanding position during the days of *The General*, but at least his last years had been marked by a comeback from the neglect he had suffered. This was the summer of 1964; a year later he would be honored by the Venice Film Festival.

The General holds a paradoxical position in film history. It represents the highest craftsmanship of Keaton, one of the great comedians of the silent era, which was graced by magnificent talent such as that of Charlie Chaplin, Harold Lloyd, Harry Langdon, Laurel and Hardy, and in France, Max Linder. *The General*, Keaton's masterwork that embodies all that made him a director and performer of such perfection, epitomizes the artistry of which silent films were capable. Simultaneously and ironically, it symbolizes the fade-out of the silent epoch. It was cruel and wasteful that Keaton, at the summit of his filmmaking, should soon find his career in descent, not because he lacked the talent to adapt to sound, but because the bureaucratic studio system could not countenance the kind of independent, creative, largely improvisational art at which he excelled. Like the old Civil War engine he once loved in *The General*, he was about to become a relic.

The idea for the film came from a book by William Pittenger, *The Great Locomotive Chase*, the story of twenty Union raiders (Pittenger was one of them) who went behind Confederate lines to hijack a train in Atlanta. The daring escapade ended in their capture; some of the men were executed, the rest imprisoned. Keaton, with Clyde Bruckman as co-storywriter and co-director and aided by scriptwriters Al Boasberg and Charles Smith, centers the story on Johnnie Gray (Keaton), an engineer devoted to his locomotive, The General. When war breaks out, he wants to enlist in the Confederate army, but is rejected because he is more valuable to the South running the train. He tries unsuccessfully to join up under another name. Angry and despondent, he warns, "If you lose this war, don't blame me." The love of his life, Annabelle Lee (Marian Mack), thinks he is a coward and refuses to let him speak with her again until he is in uniform. Later, when his train is seized with Annabelle Lee aboard, Johnnie goes after it with the relentless, unshakable determination that recalls the traditional Keaton character of his other films. Nothing will defeat him. Always, he presses steadily onward toward his objective with single-minded resolve. In the end, of course, he is a hero, destined to live happily ever after with his girl and his engine.

Keaton was known for doing his own stunt work. For example, when spurned, Johnnie sits on the crossbar of an engine wheel that begins to move when the fireman decides to take the engine into the roundhouse. Johnnie rotates with the wheel, a potentially dangerous stunt. Keaton relived the moment in the article "Keaton at Venice" by John Gillett and James Blue in *Sight and Sound* (Winter 1965/1966):

> I was running that engine myself all through the picture: I could handle that thing so I was stopping it on a dime. But when it came to this shot I asked the engineer whether we could do it. He said: "There's only one danger. A fraction too much steam with these old-fashioned engines and the wheel spins. And if it spins it will kill you right then and there." We tried it out four or five times, and in the end the engineer was satisfied that he could handle it. So we went ahead and did it. I wanted a fade-out for that sequence: although it's not a big gag it's cute and funny enough to get me a nice laugh.

The genius of Keaton in *The General* is that he created a Civil War epic through the medium of comedy, with the humor so carefully restrained that the film never loses its drive as action drama. Keaton ambitiously and cleverly blended sight gags and whimsical situations with narrative and character development. The gags and comedy ideas range from Keaton's personal confrontations with humans or objects to more elaborate sequences. Johnnie's showdown with a cannon is pure Keaton. As he pursues The General with another engine, he becomes involved with a cannon, conveniently at his disposal in the spirited atmosphere of the film. He wants to fire at the enemy, but the cannon has other ideas. Its barrel drops so that

Johnnie is the target. Johnnie and the engine round a bend just in time, swerving from the line of fire. Later, Johnnie finds himself behind enemy lines and enters the house where Annabelle Lee is being held prisoner. Hiding under a table, he overhears the Union military plans. He rescues his lady in distress, and a reverse chase begins, with Johnnie the pursued as he makes for Confederate lines to warn of the impending attack. Keaton's ability to stage large-scale sight gags is gloriously evident. In one scene, a locomotive plunges into a river far below when the bridge that it is traversing collapses. And when Johnnie is struggling to operate another cannon, he has new problems aiming at the enemy. But never mind. The shot that goes awry hits a dam, unleashing a torrent of water on the Union soldiers.

Never did Keaton look more appealing. The close-ups reveal a handsome and serene, indeed a beautiful face, and he knew how long to have the camera dwell on it. But while his own performance cannot be overpraised, his talent for directing gives the film special distinction. It has a rhythm, beauty, and grace that makes it more satisfying than most silents. Keaton would have preferred to make *The General* in the South, but only in Oregon could he locate the exact narrow-gauge track for the period engine he had found. The photography is particularly accomplished, much of it resembling authentic pictures from the Civil War era. The content also holds interest. Although a Southerner is the hero in this one-man battle against the Union, no significance is attached to his allegiance. That aspect does not really matter; the passions of war recede into the background insofar as the audience is concerned.

Keaton was not one to make involved explanations about how he achieved his artistic effects. He did not profess to be a theoretician. Raymond Rohauer, in his introduction to the Film Classics Library's reconstruction in book form of frames from *The General,* recalled having asked Keaton why he thought the film was so flawless. Disappointed at not receiving a satisfactory answer, Rohauer observed, "Only much later did I realize that if Keaton had been able to explain it to me, very likely he wouldn't have been able to make the picture in the first place."

Born in 1895, Joseph F. Keaton started as a child performer in his parents' vaudeville act. Young Buster, so named by family friend Harry Houdini when the boy fell down a flight of stairs as an infant, was thrown about the stage by his father in their comedy routine. That was his early basic training in physical humor and he learned to fall without being hurt—at least, not often. His schooling was confined to the vaudeville houses; he had no opportunity for a formal education.

Keaton became successful as a vaudevillian, a profession that yielded many top comedians, including Chaplin. His contact with films began in New York in 1917 when he visited the studio of Joseph Schenck, where Roscoe "Fatty" Arbuckle, one of the funniest men of the screen and a clever comedy director, was working. The hefty Arbuckle invited him to do a scene. Keaton refused at first but, fascinated by the filmmaking process, succumbed and did some comedy bits. That was the beginning. Moving enthusiastically into the medium, he soon became a star making two-reelers with Arbuckle. Later that year they left for California, where, in 1920, Keaton was able to make his own films through the Keaton Studio (on premises formerly occupied by Chaplin), operated by Schenck, his future brother-in-law. Schenck took care of business dealings, with Keaton on a weekly salary of $1,000 plus a percentage. Keaton was free to concentrate on the creative side.

Among Keaton's cleverest comedies is *The Playhouse* (1921), a two-reeler in which he plays virtually all the parts with the aid of multiple exposure. Another gem is *Sherlock, Jr.* (1924); here Keaton as a movie projectionist identifies with the sleuth on screen and steps into the film action. *The Navigator* (1924), one of Ingmar Bergman's favorites, has Keaton and a young woman adrift on a deserted ship. *Seven Chances* (1925) pits him against problems of another kind, the need to find a bride by a deadline or forfeit an inheritance. Predictably, he is chased by a throng of women who all want to snare him.

After he made *The General*, a commercial as well as an artistic hit, Keaton should have had years of success ahead. He did make more silent pictures: *College* (1927) and *Steamboat Bill Jr.* (1928), under his independent production set-up, and *The Cameraman* (1928) and *Spite Marriage* (1929), for MGM. Keaton regarded his going over to MGM at the persuasion of Schenck as the greatest mistake of his life. Chaplin foresaw the consequences and warned Keaton not to do it. The institutionalization of filmmaking left no room for the kind of maverick individuality on which people like Keaton and Chaplin thrived. Keaton was not the businessman Chaplin was, and whereas Chaplin was able to retain his independence and make the pictures he chose, Keaton became a prisoner of the studio system and was crushed by it. The practice of having everything scripted undermined his intuitive approach.

It was not the technology of sound that rendered Keaton obsolete; he could surely have found ways to turn sound to his advantage had he been able to continue making pictures with the freedom he required instead of working in the mold. Apart from professional difficulties, he was increasingly mired in personal problems including battles with alcoholism. For a long period his story was one of decline, and when Keaton earned renewed accolades and was honored at the 1965 Venice festival, he remarked that it came thirty years late.

A bright spot was Keaton's heartwarming appearance in a comedy sequence with Chaplin in the latter's *Limelight* (1952). Their music hall act in the film is a duet to be treasured. On a less inspiring level, Keaton worked through the years doing minor parts in numerous films. Among those in the 1950s and 1960s were *Sunset Boulevard, Around the World in Eighty Days, It's a Mad, Mad, Mad, Mad World,* and *A Funny Thing Happened on the Way to the Forum.* Evoking memories of *The General,* he starred in a promotional film, *The Railrodder,* produced by the National Film Board of Canada, in which he traversed the Canadian railroads in a handcar. American International Pictures put Keaton into several of its beach pictures, further evidence of what he had to accept in order to work. He also made many appearances on television and earned substantial sums for doing video commercials. But no matter what he was able to achieve in the way of exposure and earnings, the decimation of his career as a filmmaker was an irretrievable loss. Here was a great director, as well as a great performer, but the world of cinema had been deprived of his creative gifts.

The General, which stands as the supreme achievement of Keaton's career, is the crossroads picture that indicates the vast capability both of the man at the zenith of his skills, and of the art of silent filmmaking. It is as sophisticated in its comic realm as Carl Dreyer's *The Passion of Joan of Arc* (1928) is in the dramatic sphere. But silent films were doomed, and so was Keaton's directorial career.

The new appreciation for *The General* and his body of work in the last decade of his life, and especially the interest among students, demonstrated to Keaton that his films would endure. With the Venice festival, he had become an international celebrity again. The press sought to interview him and the critics began to reappraise his contribution to cinema. Five months later he died at the age of seventy.

THE GENERAL
USA (United Artists) 1927

Cast

Johnnie Gray . . . . BUSTER KEATON
Annabelle Lee . . . . MARION MACK
Her father . . . . CHARLES SMITH
Her brother . . . . FRANK BARNES
Captain Anderson . . . . GLEN CAVENDER
General Thatcher . . . . JIM FARLEY
A Southern General . . . . FREDERICK VROOM
Three Union Generals . . . . JOE KEATON
MIKE DONLIN
TOM NAWN

Running time....................................90 minutes
Produced by..................BUSTER KEATON PRODUCTIONS, INC.
Presented by............................JOSEPH M. SCHENCK
Directed by ....BUSTER KEATON and CLYDE BRUCKMAN
Story by..................BUSTER KEATON and CLYDE BRUCKMAN,
based on *The Great Locomotive Chase*
by WILLIAM PITTENGER
Adapted by ....AL BOASBERG and CHARLES SMITH
Photography by ....DEV JENNINGS and BERT HAINES
Technical Director ....FRED GABOURIE
Lighting Effects ....DENVER HARMON
Film Editor ....SHERMAN KELL
Assistant Editor.............................HARRY BARNES
Make-up ....FRED C. RYLE

1927

The Jazz Singer

Historic sequence in which Al Jolson talked is interrupted when the cantor shouts "Stop!" Eugenie Besserer as Mama Rabinowitz.

The Sound Revolution

"WHO THE HELL WANTS to hear actors talk?" cracked Harry Warner after being conned into seeing and hearing a demonstration of sound films at the Bell Telephone Laboratories in New York City. According to Jack Warner in his autobiography, *My First Hundred Years in Hollywood*, his brother Harry was fascinated by the process, but solely as a means to provide musical accompaniment to films for the "small theater guys who can't afford an orchestra or any kind of an act. Or even a good piano player!" Just over two years later, on October 6, 1927, *The Jazz Singer*, using the Vitaphone synchronized sound system, opened at the Warner Theatre in New York City. Contrary to some impressions, it was only a part-talkie, and that part probably accidental, but it caused a sensation. Artistically, *The Jazz Singer* is an excursion into sentimentality and grows more archaic with the years. Historically, it was the catalyst that propelled movies into the sound age.

The particular vehicle for this auspicious occasion was acquired by Warner Bros. the year before for $50,000. Samson Raphaelson's Broadway play had starred George Jessel, who was to have been the lead in the film. However, much to what must have been his later chagrin, he and Warners could not agree on money, and Al Jolson was signed. *The Jazz Singer* is pure camp, with such titles as "God Made Her a Woman and Love Made Her a Mother," and racially offensive, with Jolson in blackface. The story begins, to quote the studio synopsis, in "The Ghetto – a city within a city – gray-bearded worshipers, raucus shysters, gay children, devout women, a pushing, yelling, seething civilization living in New York City's most congested area." This is where Cantor Rabinowitz (Warner Oland of subsequent Charlie Chan fame) and his family live. The cantor wants his son Jakie to continue the family tradition of five generations by succeeding him as cantor of the Orchard Street synagogue. Jakie has other ideas. At every opportunity he sings the popular music of the day. When the cantor learns Jakie is appearing in a beer garden, he is furious. Jakie runs away. Ten years later, out of work after roving the vaudeville circuits as a blackface performer, he drops into Coffee Dan's, where many of the diners are professionals who are invited to perform. Jack Robin, as Jakie is now known, sings, much to the pleasure of Mary Dale (May McAvoy), herself a performer. She helps him with his career and they fall in love.

Jack, now very successful out of town, has a chance to star on Broadway. He has been secretly corresponding with his mother (Eugenie Besserer), who is heartbroken at the family rift, and on his father's birthday, he visits his parents. The cantor is unbending and will not forgive him. Jack's show is scheduled to open – of all nights – on the eve of Yom Kippur, the most sacred of holy days to the Jewish people. At home, Cantor Rabinowitz lies gravely ill and cannot sing the traditional "Kol Nidre." If only his Jakie would return. Mama goes to see Jack, whom she finds rehearsing in blackface. At first she does not recognize him, then she implores him to hurry to the synagogue. After much soul-searching, and a confrontation with Mary and his producer, Jack hearkens to the call of his people above the call of Broadway. He makes his dying father happy by singing "Kol Nidre" (in whiteface). Virtue has its rewards – the show is postponed. Jack still has his chance to open on Broadway and is a smash hit; Mama is at the theater to hear him, meets Mary, and happiness abounds.

Even today, it is possible to feel the excitement 1927 audiences experienced when Jolson talked, which occurs on two occasions. (The full text of the dialogue can be found in Harry M. Geduld's book *The Birth of the Talkies: From Edison to Jolson.*) The first is at Coffee Dan's, after Jolson sings "Dirty Hands, Dirty Face." Responding to the applause, he says, "Wait a minute, wait a minute. You ain't heard nothin' yet! Wait a minute, I tell you. You ain't heard nothin'. You wanna hear 'Toot Toot Tootsie'? All right, hold on." Then to the band: "Now listen, play 'Toot Toot Tootsie' – three choruses. In the first chorus, I whistle. . . ."

The talking interlude that has the strongest impact takes place when he returns home, after his long absence. He plays the piano and sings Irving Berlin's "Blue Skies," during which he turns to his mother with a cascade of affectionate banter:

JACK: Did you like that, Mama?
MAMA: Yes.
JACK: I'm glad of it. I'd rather please you than anybody I know of. Oh, darlin' – will you give me something?
MAMA: What?
JACK: You'll never guess. Shut your eyes, Mama. Shut 'em for little Jackie. I'm gonna steal something [laughter, after which he kisses her] I'll give it back to you someday too – you see if I don't. Mama darlin' – if I'm a success in this show, well, we're gonna move from here. Oh yes, we're – we're gonna move up in the Bronx. A lot of nice green grass up there. A whole lot of people you know. There's the Ginsbergs, the Guttenbergs, and the Goldbergs. Oh, a whole lot of Bergs. I dunno 'em all. And I'm gonna buy you a nice black silk dress, Mama. You see, Mrs. Freedman, the butcher's wife, she'll be jealous of you.

Jolson continues his chatter, and sings more of "Blue Skies," until the cantor enters and shouts "Stop!"

Film history was made. The easy, intimate conversation between Jack and his mother was apparently ad-libbed by Jolson while he was recording "Blue Skies," and it has an almost cinéma vérité realism startlingly different from the title-punctuated acting (even good acting) of silent films. The magnetism for which Jolson was famous on stage was suddenly evident, in contrast with his broad performance in the rest of the film. The public's fervent response guaranteed that dialogue films were imminent, with the corresponding revolution in acting and filmmaking techniques.

Experiments with sound and film had been conducted virtually since the very beginnings of cinema, not only in the United States, but in France, Germany, Britain, and other countries. Early efforts were linked to the phonograph, invented in 1877, the Vitaphone synchronized sound system being a perfected outgrowth of these pioneering attempts. Later, sound-on-film systems were evolved – optical sound that, almost immediately, supplanted sound-on-disk, and magnetic sound that, in turn, supplanted optical sound. Silent films were rarely silent. It was usual for them to be accompanied by live music, and sometimes, by narrators. There were even sound effects, known as traps. Some theaters had large orchestras, some just a lone piano player. Scores were often composed especially for a film, frequently by leading composers such as Camille Saint-Saëns, Arthur Honegger, Darius Milhaud, and Dmitri Shostakovich.

The logical development for film would seem to be the provision of recorded music to replace live accompaniment, but the major Hollywood movie companies were not interested in the experimental sound shorts that Bell Laboratories demonstrated to them in 1924. Warner Bros., formed the year before, were not then considered important enough to be invited. Their eventual connection with Bell stemmed from their decision to build a radio station on the studio lot. Many film companies either owned radio outlets or used radio to advertise their product, and Warners wanted such ready access. In his autobiography, Jack Warner contended that the radio station "was almost directly responsible for the fantastic upheaval which took us from a net income of $30,000 for the first eight months of 1927, to a staggering profit of $17,000,000 for a similar period only two years later."

Western Electric, like Bell a subsidiary of American Telephone and Telegraph, was responsible for building the station, and KFWB began to transmit in 1925. Benjamin Levinson, Western Electric's supervisor in Los Angeles, suggested to Sam Warner that he take a look at Bell's sound shorts. Warners, in financial straits and more open to new ideas than the older and richer movie companies, were so impressed with Bell's method of recording sound on disks for synchronization with film that they leased the system from Western Electric (with subleasing rights) and named it Vitaphone.

Now heavily overcommitted financially, they concluded that they had no choice but to go all out with Vitaphone. *Don Juan*, starring John Barrymore, was already under way in Hollywood when Warners decided to record synchronized music for the film. The recording sessions were held at Warners' Vitagraph studios in Brooklyn, and when the lack of soundproofing there made recording impossible, at the Metropolitan Opera House, which was not much better.

Don Juan, and a program of musical and operatic shorts, premiered August 6, 1926, at the Warner Theatre in New York City. First, the audience was treated to another novelty. Will H. Hays, president of the Motion Picture Producers and Distributors Association, appeared on screen and addressed the audience through the Vitaphone system. The synchronization was impressive and the accomplishment was enthusiastically applauded. The shorts, including Giovanni Martinelli singing "Vesti la giubba" from *I Pagliacci* and Mischa Elman playing Dvořák's "Humoresque," followed, and then the feature. Warners' gamble was so successful that they made extensive plans for the further use of Vitaphone and the acquisition of more theaters. After *The Jazz Singer* the following year, the company made another Jolson film, *The Singing Fool* (1928), a "part-talkie," and *The Lights of New York* (1928), which lasted about an hour and was the first "all-talking" film.

The reaction of the Hollywood Big Five (MGM, Universal, Paramount, First National, and Producers' Distributing Corporation) was, initially, to join forces in an attempt to isolate Warners and ignore the new technology, then to seek other sound systems so that they would not be compelled to sublease Vitaphone. William Fox of the Fox Film Corporation had already bought a sound-on-film system he called Movietone and he entered into a reciprocal agreement with Warners. Regular Fox Movietone Newsreels were started on October 28, 1927, as a result of the enormous world-wide interest in Movietone's news shorts on Charles Lindbergh and Mussolini.

By the end of 1927, there were less than two hundred theaters equipped for sound films; two years later there were nine thousand, with many more waiting for orders to be filled. Once the movie companies realized the inevitability of sound, the rush to convert their studios and theaters bordered on hysteria, and frantic arrangements were also made for sound to be added to silent films already in production. The new development had major financial implications for the industry; the huge expense entailed and the dealings involving patent rights forced the studios to turn to banks and corporations, which ultimately resulted in their losing control to outside interests.

Visually, the advent of sound was a temporary step backward from the achievements of the silent film. The cumbersome early methods of housing the camera so that the noise it made was not recorded retarded its mobility.

(The zoom lens was a long way off.) The problem of extraneous noise was acute. Morrie Ryskind, who wrote the screen adaptation of the Marx Brothers picture *The Cocoanuts* (1929), filmed at the Paramount studios in Astoria, New York, recalled in an interview with Richard Anobile in *The Marx Bros. Scrapbook*: "If a fly buzzed on the set, it sounded like an airplane." Harpo Marx, in his autobiography *Harpo Speaks!*, reminisced how director Robert Florey would laugh so hard at the brothers' antics that the producer made him direct from inside a glass-enclosed booth so that his laughter would not be heard on the soundtrack. In the scene in which the Marxes handle blueprints, the crackling noise was so obtrusive that the blueprints had to be soaked in water before the scene could be shot properly.

Frank Capra recollected in *The Name Above the Title*:

> Shooting your first sound picture was an étude in chaos. First of all, no one was used to being quiet. Shooting of silent scenes had gone on with hammering and sawing on an adjacent set, the director yelling at actors through a megaphone, cameramen shouting "Dim the overheads!" . . . "Slower on the dolly!" . . . while everybody howled if the scene was funny.
>
> Suddenly with sound we had to work in the silence of a tomb. When the red lights went on, everyone froze in his position – a cough or a belch would wreck the scene. It was like a quick switch from a bleacher seat at Ebbets Field to a box seat at a Wimbledon tennis match. To the nervous snit of the non-stage silent actors – over having to memorize lines for the first time – the funereal hush added the willies. They shook with stage fright.

Much has been written about the peril confronting film stars. (The musical *Singin' in the Rain* has this situation as its plot premise.) Some survived handily. "Garbo Talks!" was the slogan heralding the star's appearance in *Anna Christie* (1930). Others courted disaster when they spoke, and images crumbled when voices did not match. Correspondingly, those with effective voices had the advantage. The inventiveness of silent comedy suffered because the stress was now on dialogue. That, in turn, brought new opportunities, but ended what has come to be known as the golden age of comedy. For many comic performers, it was the beginning of a downward spiral.

For many years, talkies were to rely heavily on adaptations of novels and plays. Classics were popular – and had the added advantage of being free as they were in the public domain. The studios immediately turned to writers who were more skillful with spoken dialogue, and most veteran title and story writers for the silents lost their jobs. S. J. Perelman, one of the new imports to Hollywood, recalled in a 1961 article in *Show* magazine the scene in 1931, when he was co-writer on the Marx Brothers' *Monkey Business:*

> ... At the studio where Johnstone [Will B.] and I were now applying ourselves to the script ... the two of us were quartered in a ramshackle warren of tan stucco that housed thirty or forty other scribes. They were all in various stages of parturition, some gestating gangster epics and horse operas, others musical comedies, dramas, and farces. Few of them were writers in the traditional sense, but persuasive, voluble specialists adept in contriving trick plot situations. Many had worked before the advent of dialogue, in silent pictures; they viewed the playwrights, novelists, and newspapermen who were beginning to arrive from New York as usurpers, slick wordmongers threatening their livelihood, and rarely fraternized.

Another repercussion was felt in the international market, about eighty percent of which had consisted of Hollywood product. American films were still dominant, but the introduction of sound gave impetus to domestic film industries. Whereas silent films were universally understood and needed only foreign titles, spoken dialogue presented an obvious barrier. Solutions to the problem included making several language versions of a film, superimposing subtitles, and dubbing.

Silent films had reached a high point in their ability to express ideas and drama visually (Erich von Stroheim's *Greed*, 1924; Abel Gance's *Napoléon*, 1926; Carl Dreyer's *The Passion of Joan of Arc*, 1928; and of course, *Potemkin*, are only a few of the examples that can be cited), and the creative community was divided on the merits of sound. Some felt that it would spoil what was being accomplished, and was grating and unnecessary. D.W. Griffith, however, was an enthusiast. Commenting at the time (as quoted by Geduld) he said:

> Talkies, squeakies, moanies, songies, and squawkies. ... But whatever you call them, I'm absolutely serious in what I have to say about them. Just give them ten years to develop and you're going to see the greatest artistic medium the world has known. Just think: you can get all the movement, the swing, the rhythm and the drive of the best of the old silent pictures into them. There you have your appeal to the eye. And added to this you have the human voice. And music, the one perfect art. You can combine the features of the picture, the opera, the legitimate theatre. As for the picture part of it, it will be superior to the painter's art, for it will be alive. ...

In 1928, Russian filmmakers Eisenstein, Pudovkin, and Alexandrov issued their manifesto, emphasizing as the desired aim "an orchestral counterpoint of visual and aural images." Unfortunately, the concentration on sound was such that there was a tendency to ignore the visual aspect of filmmaking. Japanese director Akira Kurosawa, as quoted by Donald Richie in *The Films of Akira Kurosawa*, lamented in retrospect: "Ever since the silent film gave way to the talkie, sound has interfered with the image – and at the same time this flood of sound has become largely meaningless."

Alfred Hitchcock remarked to François Truffaut, in the latter's book *Hitchcock*:

> Well, the silent pictures were the purest form of cinema; the only thing they lacked was the sound of people talking and the noises. But this slight imperfection did not warrant the major changes that sound brought in. In other words, since all that was missing was simply natural sound, there was no need to go to the other extreme and completely abandon the technique of the pure motion picture, the way they did when sound came in. . . . When we tell a story in cinema, we should resort to dialogue only when it's impossible to do otherwise. I always try first to tell a story in the cinematic way, through a succession of shots and bits of film in between. It seems unfortunate that with the arrival of sound the motion picture, overnight, assumed a theatrical form.

Ingmar Bergman observed during a 1975 seminar under the auspices of the American Film Institute's Center for Advanced Film Studies: "I think when the silent picture died and the sound picture came, the silent picture was in a development, in a marvelous development. But now we have sound, and we have to combine the sound and the picture, and they have to work together and live together, and I think that is a marvelous medium. I think we can do a lot with the soundtrack. I am a little bit worried about music, electronic or conventional music, because I have the feeling that film in a way is rhythm. Music, at the beginning, as Stravinsky said, is also rhythm. They are both unintellectual suggestions. I think it's dangerous to use real music, but to use sounds, different sounds – concrete or synthesized sounds – is very interesting, and I think we have just begun to do what we can do with sound and picture together. And that is fascinating."

The concern that motivated the studios was not that of Griffith, Eisenstein, Kurosawa, Hitchcock, and Bergman. The technology that took over following the release of *The Jazz Singer* was viewed as a means to boost profits. Sound was a gimmick to draw people into theaters, and the emphasis was placed on that, rather than on the artistic commingling of the aural and the visual. Commercially, talkies came at the right time for the Hollywood studios; they made the film business less vulnerable when the stock market crashed in 1929 and the world economy plunged into a state of disaster.

THE JAZZ SINGER
USA (Warner Bros.) 1927

Cast

Jakie Rabinowitz (Jack Robin) .... AL JOLSON
Jakie Rabinowitz as a boy .... BOBBY GORDON
Mary Dale .... MAY MCAVOY
Cantor Rabinowitz .... WARNER OLAND
Mama Rabinowitz .... EUGENIE BESSERER
Moishe Yudelson .... OTTO LEDERER
Harry Lee .... RICHARD TUCKER
Levi .... NAT CARR
Buster Billings .... WILLIAM DEMAREST
Dillings .... ANDERS RANDOLF
Doctor .... WILL WALLING
The Agent .... ROSCOE KARNS
Chorus Girl .... MYRNA LOY
with the participation of CANTOR JOSEF ROSENBLATT

Running time .... 89 minutes
Produced by .... WARNER BROS.
Directed by .... ALAN CROSLAND
Adaptation by .... ALFRED A. COHN, from the play
by SAMSON RAPHAELSON
Photography .... HAL MOHR
Editing .... HAROLD MCCORD
Titles .... JACK JARMUTH
Sound .... GEORGE R. GROVES
Assistant Director .... GORDON HOLLINGSHEAD
Musical Director .... LOUIS SILVERS
Music .... "Blue Skies" by IRVING BERLIN;
"Mammy" by SAM LEWIS, JOE YOUNG,
WALTER DAVIDSON;
"Toot Toot Tootsie, Goodbye" by GUS KAHN,
ERNIE ERDMAN, DAN RUSSO;
other popular songs; cantorial and classical music

Nine black men accused of rape near Scottsboro, Alabama, on March 25, 1931, a case that becomes a cause célèbre.

KIDNAPPED LINDBERGH BABY FOUND DEAD
—May 12, 1932

BONUS MARCHERS IN WASHINGTON ATTACKED BY POLICE AND US TROOPS, TWO KILLED
—July 28, 1932

Hitler named new German chancellor in January 1933 . . . Franklin D. Roosevelt becomes president in March, telling Depression-ridden America: "The only thing we have to fear is fear itself" . . . Prohibition is repealed in December.

JOHN DILLINGER SHOT DEAD LEAVING CHICAGO THEATER **—July 22, 1934**

MAO TSE TUNG FORCES BEGIN THE LONG MARCH
—October 16, 1934

WAGNER ACT GUARANTEES US LABOR COLLECTIVE BARGAINING RIGHTS **—July 6, 1935**

1930-1939

In 1936, General Francisco Franco launches civil war against Spanish Republican government . . . Bruno Richard Hauptmann, avowing innocence, is electrocuted for murder of Lindbergh baby . . . Jesse Owens jars Hitler's Aryan supremacy theory by winning four gold medals at Berlin Olympics . . . Edward VIII abdicates British throne to marry American divorcée Wallis Simpson . . . Auto workers in Flint, Michigan, stage sitdown strike in crucial labor battle.

GERMAN PLANES DESTROY GUERNICA —April 26, 1937

HOUSEWIVES ENTITLED TO SALARY DECLARES ELEANOR ROOSEVELT —May 12, 1937

TEN KILLED, HUNDREDS INJURED AS POLICE ATTACK STRIKING STEELWORKERS IN CHICAGO —May 30, 1937

BESSIE SMITH DIES IN MISSISSIPPI CAR CRASH —September 26, 1937

1939 World's Fair opens in New York . . . Ten million still unemployed in United States . . . Freud dies . . . Soviet Union and Germany sign ten-year non-aggression pact.

HITLER INVADES POLAND —September 1, 1939

ENGLAND AND FRANCE DECLARE WAR ON GERMANY —September 3, 1939

Grandfather of The Godfather

WESTERNS, WITH THEIR ritual of violent action between good guys and bad guys, have been a film staple not only because they make for uncomplicated, colorful entertainment, but because they spring from American frontier lore indigenous to the national experience. Western lawlessness gave way to urban lawlessness, which, spurred by prohibition, became a fertile, logical subject for films. Gangster warfare between rival mobs for the domination of bootlegging and the allied rackets of prostitution and gambling drew national attention. The mobster emerged as the new hero in another popular formula for story-telling: ambition, success, and inevitable death. The American gangster film is more than a genre; it is important as a manifestation of a cancerous condition. It mirrors the growing role organized crime has played, with the ultra-sophisticated power of the Mafia reflected in the two *Godfather* films, and in the headlined stories of the 1970s that revealed the CIA's use, during the Kennedy administration, of gangland figures in plotting to assassinate Fidel Castro.

Hollywood was quick to sense the entertainment potential in gangster violence, and Mervyn LeRoy's *Little Caesar*, presented to the public by Warner Bros. as a flimsily disguised characterization of Al Capone, was the landmark sound film that became the model. Such fare was not new; Josef von Sternberg's silent *Underworld* (1927) and Lewis Milestone's *The Racket* (1928) were among the many films of the genre in the 1920s. But the advent of sound provided new trappings. Now bullets could talk. The incessant noise of the machine guns, the chilling screech of brakes, the sound of chases through city streets, dramatically impressed upon the public the blessings of sound. The gangster film was a made-to-order answer to the need for new ways to attract the public to the theaters despite the desperate Depression conditions following the stock market crash of 1929. The industry was increasingly apprehensive about a situation in which there were five million unemployed in 1930 (the year in which *Little Caesar* was made), nine million in 1931, and thirteen million in 1932, by which time there had been nearly six thousand bank failures.

The distinctive, wide-mouthed, squat face of Edward G. Robinson became a household image, and the sound of his voice turning "yeah" into "nyeahhh" was imitated throughout the land by comedians and children. It was similar when James Cagney came snarling along as the hood Tom Powers in William Wellman's *The Public Enemy* (1931), another Warner Bros. triumph that solidified the genre. Robinson, playing Caesar Enrico Bandello, was an immediate star and so was Cagney.

The contemporary impact of *Little Caesar* was articulated by Richard Watts, Jr., then the young critic of the *New York Herald Tribune:*

> From *Little Caesar*, W.R. Burnett's much-admired novel about the rise and fall of a homicidal gang chieftain, comes the truest, most ambitious and most distinguished of all that endless series of gangster photoplays which have been inundating us in recent years. So many pictures celebrating the adventures of America's most picturesque banditti have been manufactured and their formula has become so stale that it is difficult to believe that a fresh and distinctive work on the subject is currently possible. But *Little Caesar*, by pushing into the background the usual romantic conventions of the theme and concentrating on characterization rather than on plot, emerges not only as an effective and rather chilling melodrama, but also as what is sometimes described as a Document. Chiefly, though, it is made important by the genuinely brilliant performance that Edward G. Robinson contributes to the title role. . . . *Little Caesar* is the first of the gangster pictures to capture any of that realistic sense and that menacing, rather shocking credibility that Edward Dean Sullivan gets into his books about Chicago crime. The viewpoint of the photoplay is strikingly effective. As closely as the censors will permit, it adopts something of the manner of Fielding's *Jonathan Wild* and permits us to see how its hero-villain sees his career as a triumph of integrity, character, and good old ambition, as proof that hard work, earnestness of purpose, and an avoidance of bad habits will carry the worthwhile fellow to the top. It has irony and grim humor and a real sense of excitement, and its significance does not get in the way of the melodrama.

Robinson (his real name was Emanuel Goldenberg) began his career at nineteen in the theater; ten years later, in 1923, he went to Hollywood and had already appeared in a series of gangster roles before *Little Caesar*. He almost did not get to play Rico as he was not the director's first choice. Picture Clark Gable riddled with bullets asking incredulously at the film's finale, "Mother of Mercy, is this the end of Rico?" Gable had been appearing on stage in Los Angeles in John Wexley's anti-capital punishment play, *The Last Mile*, a highly praised death row drama. According to Jack Warner, he was LeRoy's preference for the part, but when Warner saw Gable's screen test, he decided that his ears protruded too much and ordered that the film be made with Robinson. Gable soon went to MGM.

The action in *Little Caesar* is tough and uncompromisingly brutal, moving with the certainty of a Greek tragedy. The opening message, warning that those who live by the sword will perish by the sword, sets the required moral tone and forecasts the outcome. The film begins with the hold-up of a gas station by Rico and his crony Joe Massara (Douglas Fairbanks, Jr.). Rico realizes that he is small-time stuff and longs for the notoriety the Chicago big boys like Diamond Pete Montana (Ralph Ince) are getting. He heads for Chicago, where he pushes his way into the gang of Sam Vettori (Stanley Fields), who bestows upon him the name "Little Caesar."

The film chronicles Rico's ruthless rise to the top. He supersedes Vettori and so impresses "The Big Boy" (Sidney Blackmer), the top man in the Chicago underworld, that he is designated to take over from Diamond Pete. We know from the code of the period that Rico cannot possibly enjoy the rewards of crime without retribution. His arrogance leads to his downfall, and he ends as a fugitive. When he is finally gunned down, the story has come to its inevitable conclusion. More fascinating than the plot is the characterization. Rico, although able to kill without compunction, is something of a moralist. In the era of speak-easies, he shuns liquor. He believes in clean living to keep fit and to enable him to concentrate on getting ahead. Only when he is on the way toward destruction does he begin to drink. He has no interest in women; they are a distraction from the important pursuits.

Little Caesar, even when measured against today's more demanding standards, is extremely well-made. It is taut, brittle, and involving. The violence crackles with realism and produces a sense of terror with its matter-of-fact killing. A vivid recreation of Chicago's underworld, it remains one of the best crime films ever made. It was top box office, and as *Variety* put it, "caught the public appetite for underworld stories at its height." Its violence also prompted a torrent of complaints. It was as if *Little Caesar* itself were the cause of gangsterism, and if such films were not made, the gangs would disappear. Censorship was a persistent threat, with various local boards determining what should or should not be shown and imposing cuts. As Stephen Farber pointed out in his excellent book, *The Movie Rating Game*, the legal ruling that prevailed until 1952 was a 1915 Supreme Court decision that denied movies the kind of freedom of expression recognized for the printed word on the ground that they were "a business pure and simple . . . a spectacle or show." As a result, the film industry, vulnerable to criticism and the actions of censorship boards, moved toward the self-regulation that has been its byword and in 1930 the Motion Picture Production Code was established. It was not stringently enforced at first, but the gangster films, along with films then considered sexually racy, increased demands by pressure groups for a crackdown. In 1934, the Legion of Decency of the Catholic Church was formed and became an all-powerful force that the film companies felt constrained to appease. Joseph Breen, a Catholic, became head of the industry's Production Code Administration, and internal censorship was a fact of life, with a Code seal necessary for the release of each film.

In these days of relative permissiveness, one forgets the extensive limitations prescribed by the Production Code of 1930. For example, films were not supposed to "lower the moral standards" or show sympathy "to the side of crime, wrongdoing, evil or sin." There were to be no details as to the methods of crime, and criminals were not to be seen killing lawmen, including bank guards and detectives. To placate the protesters against screen violence, filmmakers affixed various versions of crime-does-not-pay platitudes. But even with the "heroes" coming to a bad end, there was a sense of audience identification with them that could not be expunged.

Robinson, as Rico, had charismatic vitality, as had Cagney in *The Public Enemy*. Paul Muni, playing a part also modeled on Al Capone in Howard Hawks's *Scarface* (1932), gave another memorable performance. Eventually, an outcome of the backlash was a concentration on G-man pictures, which took the spotlight from the gangster and transferred it to the FBI, then busy building its image under the control of J. Edgar Hoover. Cagney himself turned government agent on screen in *G-Men* (1935), and Robinson joined the law in *Bullets or Ballots* (1936). This did nothing, of course, to diminish the violent action. As for the youngsters of America who were to be shielded from evil influence, a popular hobby of the thirties was collecting cards contained in packages of chewing gum. These cards, in addition to featuring baseball players, also displayed the leading criminals of the decade and the G-men who captured them. As in the movies, all bases were covered.

Fortunately for Edward G. Robinson, he was not irrevocably typed by the Rico role although he did play a similar part in *Key Largo* (1948), which made a comment on the role of the gangster in the post-World War II period. Robinson filled a wide range of roles with professional expertise in pictures that included *The Amazing Dr. Clitterhouse* (1938), *Confessions of a Nazi Spy* (1939), *The Sea Wolf* (1941), *Double Indemnity* (1944), *House of Strangers* (1949), *A Boy Ten Feet Tall* (1962), and *The Cincinnati Kid* (1965). Encountered at Hadrian's Villa outside Rome on location for a crime comedy, *The Biggest Bundle of Them All* (1968), the actor spoke with satisfaction of his long career and joked about the heart attack from which he had recovered, saying, "I'm lucky to be still working." Robinson, who died in 1972, also became known as an avid art collector and connoisseur. In retrospect he ranks among the best and most colorful of Hollywood character actors.

Mervyn LeRoy, who elicited such a good performance from Robinson, has been a prolific director whose films have covered a wide range of subjects. Among the strongest examples of social conscience films produced in Hollywood, where the species has hardly been in overabundance, is *I Am a Fugitive From a Chain Gang* (1932), which starred Paul Muni as a victim of society who is subjected to the terrible conditions of prison chain gangs rife in the South at the time. A few of LeRoy's other films are *Gold Diggers of 1933*, *Five Star Final*, *Madame Curie*, and *Thirty Seconds Over Tokyo*. He also produced *The Wizard of Oz*.

The prison story, another popular category of the 1930s, also offered the possibility of mixing action-filled drama and social problems. These films were populated by vindictive wardens, stool-pigeons, innocent men wrongly incarcerated, and faithful or unfaithful wives and mistresses. Much has been written straining to discover social significance in films dealing with crime and prisons. More often than not, Hollywood was merely exploiting story potential. The film industry was catering to the public's fascination with crime, a fascination extending to various countries where people looked with amusement, interest, and occasionally horror at such American film product. (Filmmakers elsewhere developed their own versions of Chicago.) Always, there were efforts to find new approaches. In 1949, James Cagney appeared in his most effective crime film since *The Public Enemy*, an extremely violent movie called *White Heat*, with emphasis on the criminal as psychotic.

By the time Francis Ford Coppola's two *Godfather* epics reached the screen, the role of crime and the public's awareness of it had changed drastically. The criminal superstructure was viewed as a power comparable to that of government and big business, operating nationally and internationally and relying upon the collusion of officials in high places. Crime films had become much more intricate in style, and what could be shown had broadened enormously as moralistic rules were pushed aside. But just as *Little Caesar*, the grandfather of the modern crime film, was a target of angry criticism, *The Godfather* set off a clamor against its abrasive use of violence. Apart from such specifics as strangulation and a horse's head placed in someone's bed, it was attacked for glorifying crime and criminals – now shown as ordinary family folk when away from their daily business.

Coppola was being realistic, abandoning the clichés and portraying people instead of cardboard figures. Rico was a rounded character, too, but times were different. Big crime had now grown respectable. Poor Rico. Had he survived Chicago, he might have attained a nice, quiet life of power in the suburbs, living out his latter years in a bourgeois home filled with television sets on which he could watch historic pictures like *Little Caesar*. Occasionally, he might even be called upon to render a "patriotic" service, like arranging a murder contract for the CIA.

LITTLE CAESAR
USA (First National) 1930

Cast

Caesar Enrico Bandello (Little Caesar) ...... EDWARD G. ROBINSON
Joe Massara .... DOUGLAS FAIRBANKS, JR.
Olga Strassof .... GLENDA FARRELL
The Big Boy .... SIDNEY BLACKMER
Police Sgt. Flaherty .... THOMAS JACKSON
Pete Montana .... RALPH INCE
Tony Passa .... WILLIAM COLLIER, JR.
Arnie Lorch .... MAURICE BLACK
Sam Vettori .... STANLEY FIELDS
Otero .... GEORGE E. STONE

Running time .... 77 minutes
Production Company .... WARNER BROS.
Produced by .... HAL B. WALLIS
Directed by .... MERVYN LEROY
Adaptation and dialogue by ..... FRANCIS E. FARAGOH, based on the book by W.R. BURNETT
Photography .... TONY GAUDIO
Art Director .... ANTON GROT

1931

Frankenstein

Boris Karloff in the role that made him famous. The monster's tenderness toward the little girl (Marilyn Harris) evokes audience sympathy.

Pacesetter for Horror

IN 1931, WHEN THE very real monster of the Depression had engulfed the United States, the most famous and durable of horror films was released. Universal Pictures, which already had a reputation for films that frightened, hit upon a profitable diversion that appealed to audiences, made a star of Boris Karloff, and prompted seemingly endless spinoffs. Affection for the film and its monster continues, as evidenced by the satirical *Young Frankenstein* of Mel Brooks and the campy *Andy Warhol's Frankenstein*. The 1931 *Frankenstein* endures as a horror classic and a reflection of society's long-standing infatuation with the macabre.

The premise of the story, which was taken from Mary Wollstonecraft Shelley's 1818 novel, is even more relevant today. The transplanting of human organs snatched from fresh corpses, done in hospitals instead of spooky laboratories, and the creation of life in test tubes, are reminiscent of Dr. Frankenstein's obsession with using parts of bodies to produce a new being. The film holds up admirably in this age when contemporary horror films are geared more toward shocking an audience by being explicit than by developing an aura. Scenes today grow increasingly gory, as the blood flows freely and in color, and even dismemberment is graphically depicted.

There is a refreshing naïveté to the 1931 *Frankenstein*. The disastrous consequence of tampering with the unknown is a beloved cliché of the horror genre. Henry Frankenstein (Colin Clive), a young scientist, and his assistant, the dwarf Fritz (Dwight Frye), raid graveyards and gallows for bodies. Fritz steals a brain from the laboratory of Dr. Waldman (Edward Van Sloan) unaware that it is abnormal. Frankenstein infuses his creature with life by means of his electrical equipment and brings forth a monster of incredible strength. The monster kills Fritz, who has been taunting him, and later kills Dr. Waldman. Escaping, he encounters a little girl; she befriends him but he inadvertently drowns her. The irate villagers mobilize. Frankenstein searches for the monster, who seizes him and carries him to an old mill. The scientist narrowly escapes death and the monster is trapped in a fire set by the villagers.

Another difference between this kind of old-fashioned horror film and the blood-thirsty entertainment of today is that *Frankenstein*, for all of its efforts to shock, carries a note of compassion. Although the sensitivity of Mary

Shelley's novel is diluted in the film, the monster still evokes pity; this contributes to the film's durability and raises its level above horror pictures lacking sympathetic qualities. The tender sequence with the little girl is particularly well done. Similarly, in the *King Kong* of 1933 – and even in the inferior 1976 remake produced by Dino de Laurentiis – audiences' feelings for the gorilla escalate the film beyond special effects and terror. In the 1975 *Jaws*, the shark is an instrument of pure horror.

A 1974 exception is writer-director Larry Cohen's *It's Alive!*, which manages to stir up considerable sympathy for a monster baby who murders doctors and nurses as soon as it is born. The city organizes to capture the baby, but because its abnormality is the result of pills its mother has been taking, and the drug manufacturer wants to hush this up, the audience is led to be compassionate toward the creature and its frantic parents.

Denis Gifford's *Movie Monsters* reminds us how many such categories there are – the monster, the golem, the mummy, the zombie, the vampire, the werewolf, the cat, the ape, the beast, the brute, the mutant, the mask. While the public's fascination with horror as entertainment continues to intrigue students of behavior, one might also wonder about the psyche of those who create horror stories. Writing in the *New York Review of Books,* March 21, 1974, Ellen Moers traced the anxieties of Mary Shelley, "a woman who, as daughter, mistress, and mother, was a bearer of death," and raised questions of how close her creation of the monster was to her own traumas, and perhaps to her vision of herself. Mary Shelley's mother, the remarkable Mary Wollstonecraft, died giving birth to her. She herself at seventeen had an illegitimate daughter by Percy Bysshe Shelley and that child died a month later in March 1815. The next month she was pregnant again. Her father, the philosopher William Godwin, would have nothing to do with her when she ran off with Shelley. In the following year, during which she began *Frankenstein*, her half sister, Fanny Imlay, committed suicide at twenty, and Shelley's wife, Harriet, pregnant by another, drowned herself. In the very month of Harriet's suicide, Shelley and the once again pregnant Mary were married.

Moers asserted in her article:

> Surely no outside influence need be sought to explain Mary Shelley's fantasy of the newborn as at once monstrous agent of destruction and piteous victim of parental abandonment. "I, the miserable and the abandoned," cries the monster at the end of *Frankenstein.* "I am an abortion to be spurned at, and kicked, and trampled on. . . . I have murdered the lovely and the helpless. . . . I have devoted my creator to misery; I have pursued him even to that irremediable ruin."

The novel's route to the 1931 screen version was by means of a play by

Peggy Webling in 1930. There had been previous plays, the first shortly after the appearance of the novel, which also spawned numerous burlesques, including one staged in 1849 and another in 1887. The adaptation of the Webling play occurred against a background of extensive interest in horror reflected in the early product of cinema. A film version of *Frankenstein* had already been released in 1910 by the Edison Company. In 1915, another reincarnation, *Life Without Soul,* appeared. In Germany, where horror films proliferated, the film considered a pillar of the genre and of the German expressionist period – Robert Wiene's *The Cabinet of Dr. Caligari* – appeared in 1919. *The Golem*, previously filmed in 1914 by Henryk Galeen and Paul Wegener, was remade in 1920, and F. W. Murnau made *Nosferatu*, his famous version of Bram Stoker's *Dracula*, in 1922. In the United States, John Barrymore starred in *Dr. Jekyll and Mr. Hyde* (1920); Universal presented *The Phantom of the Opera* (1925), starring Lon Chaney, and *The Cat and the Canary* (1927), and had made its *Dracula*, starring Bela Lugosi, just before *Frankenstein.*

The original intention of producer Carl Laemmle, Jr., was to have the film written and directed by Robert Florey (who co-directed the Marx Brothers in their first film, *The Cocoanuts*, released in 1929). But British director James Whale wanted to undertake the project and received the go-ahead from Laemmle. Whale was a favored newcomer who had achieved acclaim for his production of R.C. Sherriff's play *Journey's End* in London and had also directed the film version. He had also been hired by Howard Hughes to direct dialogue for *Hell's Angels.* Whale later directed such films as *The Invisible Man, The Road Back*, and *The Man in the Iron Mask*.

The adaptation from Webling's play was by John L. Balderston, with screenplay by Garrett Fort and Francis E. Faragoh; Robert Florey had done the original treatment. The film, eventually to gross more than $12 million, was made on an investment of $250,000. Bela Lugosi, the original choice to play the monster, balked at doing the part, reportedly because he was not happy about having to wear the cumbersome make-up. He did assume the monster role in *Frankenstein Meets the Wolf Man* (1943).

Who *would* play the monster? During lunch at the Universal studio commissary Whale saw Boris Karloff and suggested that the actor test for the role. Karloff had been struggling for recognition on stage and screen for twenty years. The British actor, born William Henry Pratt, reached Hollywood in 1917 by way of Canada and the northwestern part of the United States. By 1931 he had already appeared in some sixty films. In that year he was in sixteen films apart from *Frankenstein,* including a role as a prison trusty in *The Criminal Code* that he had already played successfully on stage.

Karloff's portrayal was as much contingent upon the wiles of make-up man Jack Pierce as upon his own ability to communicate terror and pathos while encased in the make-up and costume. Pierce, who had turned from a baseball career to work in films, had to find a way to make Karloff look like a seven-foot six-inch monster. In a *New York Times* interview in 1939, when he was working on *Son of Frankenstein,* Pierce spoke at length about his methods, and described his extensive research into everything from surgery to burial customs:

> My anatomical studies taught me that there are six ways a surgeon can cut the skull in order to take out or put in a brain. I figured that Frankenstein, who was a scientist but no practicing surgeon, would take the simplest surgical way. He would cut the top of the skull off straight across like a potlid, hinge it, pop the brain in and then clamp it on tight. That is the reason I decided to make the monster's head square and flat like a shoe box and dig that big scar across his forehead with the metal clamps holding it together.
>
> Those two metal studs sticking out at the sides of the monster's neck have puzzled folks no end, so I'd better explain them. They are inlets for electricity – plugs such as we use for our lamps or flatirons. Remember, the monster is an electrical gadget. Lightning is his life force. So Karloff has not only spent 864 shooting hours in three pictures with those big bolts plugged into his neck but he carries a five-pound steel spine – that you can't see – to represent the rod which conveys the current up to the monster's brain.
>
> Here's another thing. I read that the Egyptians used to bind some criminals hand and foot and bury them alive. When their blood turned to water after death, it flowed into their extremities, stretched their arms to gorilla length and swelled their hands, feet and faces to abnormal proportions. I thought this might make a nice touch for the monster, since he was supposed to be made from the corpses of executed felons. So I fixed Karloff up that way.
>
> Those lizard eyes of his are rubber, like his false head. I made his arms look longer by shortening the sleeves of his coat, stiffened his legs with two pairs of pants over steel struts and by means of asphalt-walker's boots gave him those Newfoundland dogs. I cover Karloff's face with blue-green greasepaint which photographs gray. I blacken his finger nails with shoe polish. It takes me four hours to build him up every morning and two hours to tear him down every night. I figure I've heaped some 5,400 pounds of make-up on him as the monster in the past seven years.

Each of Karloff's size 24 boots weighed 21 pounds. Besides all this, the actor had to endure the irritation and pain the make-up sometimes caused. The transformation process began everyday at six A.M. and shooting continued until about seven in the evening. He would then be de-monsterized and go home, only to face the procedure again the following morning.

The steps taken to hide this information from the public while *Frankenstein* was being filmed demonstrates that the tactics of studios have not changed much over the years. It was good publicity to wait until the monster was unveiled on screen. Forty-four years later Steven Spielberg, the director of *Jaws*, released by the same studio, carefully concealed his mechanical sharks, now products of technology rather than the insights of a make-up artist.

For the special effects crucial to the scene in which the monster is given life electrically, the studio turned to Kenneth Strickfaden, who had started with experiments in his workshop at home and had graduated to movie special-effects man. He created the original laboratory equipment for the film. When Mel Brooks was making *Young Frankenstein,* Strickfaden, then seventy-eight, was living in Santa Monica, California; Brooks enlisted his aid in recreating the ambience for the satirical film in which Gene Wilder, instead of Colin Clive, fashions his monster, played by Peter Boyle.

The promotion campaign undertaken by Universal when *Frankenstein* was ready for release stressed its gruesomeness, or at least what passed for gruesomeness then. *Frankenstein* became a hit from the outset. *Variety* reported strong business in Detroit, Chicago, Washington, Boston, New York, and other cities, and used such descriptions as "the wallop of the season," "started big and getting bigger," and "the biggest money-maker in the country." Word-of-mouth was everything a press agent could desire. Adults and children dared their friends to see the film amid warnings that it was unbearably frightening. In some cases the film was advertised as "strictly for adults." Stomping around with arms outstretched became a popular imitation, whether by youngsters or comedians. Boris Karloff became the star of the hour, and he was now one of the top actors at Universal.

By 1938, it was rerelease time, and *Frankenstein* and *Dracula* were paired on a bill that drew huge throngs. The combination of *Frank* and *Drac* brought a sometimes hysterical response from people fighting to get into crowded theaters. The *New York Times* reported:

> At the Victory Theater in Salt Lake City the house was sold out by 10 o'clock in the morning. Four thousand frenzied Mormons milled around outside, finally broke through police lines, smashed the plate glass box office, bent in the front doors and tore off one of the door checks in their eagerness to get in and be frightened. The manager rented an empty theater across the street, bicycled the reels to it and in twenty minutes had it packed to the gunwales, with the street still full of frustrated phobiaphiles clamoring for admission.

This enthusiasm was repeated throughout the country.

The films that followed *Frankenstein* are numerous enough to require a scorecard. The titles themselves reflect the ingenuity at exploiting the bonanza. Among them are *Bride of Frankenstein*, which James Whale also directed; *Son of Frankenstein; The Ghost of Frankenstein; House of Frankenstein; Abbott and Costello Meet Frankenstein; I Was a Teenage Frankenstein; The Revenge of Frankenstein; Frankenstein – 1970* (made in 1958); *Frankenstein's Daughter; El Infierno Del Frankenstein* and *El Testamento Del Frankenstein,* both made in Mexico; *The Evil of Frankenstein; Frankenstein Conquers the World; Frankenstein Meets the Space Monster; Jesse James Meets Frankenstein's Daughter; Frankenstein Created Woman; Frankenstein Must Be Destroyed; Horror of Frankenstein; Dracula vs. Frankenstein; Frankenstein* (for television); *Frankenstein: The True Story* (for television); and *Frankenstein and the Monster From Hell.*

The numerous actors who played the monster or a version of him include Lon Chaney, Jr., Glenn Strange, Christopher Lee, David Prowse, Gary Conway, Michael Gwynn, and Bo Svenson. Karloff dropped the characterization after doing *Son of Frankenstein*, his third in the Universal series, but he had a partial encore in 1967, providing the voice of the monster in *Mad Monster Party*. Also, in 1958, he played Victor Frankenstein, a descendant of the fictional scientist, in *Frankenstein – 1970*. Much confusion has persisted between Frankenstein and his monster; many erroneously refer to the monster as Frankenstein.

Karloff's name became synonymous with horror films, one of his best being *The Mummy* (Universal, 1932), which traded on the mystique of exploring ancient tombs, with Karloff coming back from the dead. But no matter how many other kinds of parts the actor did in films, on the stage, or on television, the role with which he was identified was that of the Frankenstein monster. It had made him famous and earned him considerable sums of money, but in a sense it also imprisoned him. Although many considered him a fine actor, his ability was never fully explored.

Meeting Karloff in real life was an event. In 1941, when he was appearing on Broadway in *Arsenic and Old Lace*, student groups would sometimes go backstage and he would invite them on the set after the performance. The youngsters would be struck by his warm smile and kindly manner. He had the reputation of being very gentlemanly and totally different from his chilling screen image, and he was particularly pleased to receive hundreds of letters from children expressing empathy with the monster.

"They seem to understand," Karloff said in a 1951 interview, "that he was the victim of something beyond his control. He was bewildered and afraid. It was his great strength and panic which made him dangerous." Concerning *Frankenstein*'s success, the actor speculated: "People lead humdrum lives. The monster gave them a release. It titillated nerves and the palate to pretend there's something behind the door or in the closet."

Frankenstein looms as a welcome relic of a less jaded age in which a Karloff in monster clothing and make-up could impress the public as the last word in horror. Although the desire for vicarious thrills and chills is unabated, it takes a lot more to frighten those who have grown accustomed to watching the evils of the world paraded on television in their homes. Perhaps that accounts in part for the current escalation of morbid visual horror in films of the genre. Ever more bizarre ways must be found to shock the chill-seekers.

A forceful comment on what has happened since Karloff first played the monster was expressed in Peter Bogdanovich's *Targets*, the last film in which Karloff appeared before his death at eighty-one in 1969. Karloff plays Orlok, a horror-movie star, who wants to quit because he is fed up with his parts and feels they are out of date, as the modern world is filled with atrocities much greater than those concocted for the screen. He is persuaded to make an appearance at a drive-in theater to promote the opening of his latest film, and it coincides with the rampage of a berserk young man who has become a random sniper, killing and terrorizing people on the highway and then at the drive-in. While his horror image is on screen, Orlok bravely moves forward to confront the killer, who is patently representative of a world gone mad. Reality has become the greater horror.

FRANKENSTEIN
USA (Universal) 1931

Cast

Henry Frankenstein .... COLIN CLIVE
Elizabeth .... MAE CLARKE
Victor Moritz .... JOHN BOLES
The Monster .... BORIS KARLOFF
Dr. Waldman .... EDWARD VAN SLOAN
Fritz .... DWIGHT FRYE
Baron Frankenstein .... FREDERICK KERR
The Burgomaster .... LIONEL BELMORE
Little Maria .... MARILYN HARRIS
Father .... MICHAEL MARK

Running time .... 75 minutes
Presented by .... CARL LAEMMLE
Produced by .... CARL LAEMMLE, JR., with E.M. ASHER as Associate Producer
Directed by .... JAMES WHALE

Adapted by .... JOHN LLOYD BALDERSTON from the play by PEGGY WEBLING, based on the novel by MARY WOLLSTONECRAFT SHELLEY
Screenplay by .... GARRETT FORT and FRANCIS E. FARAGOH. Additional dialogue by ROBERT FLOREY
Scenario Editor .... RICHARD SCHAYER
Cinematographer .... ARTHUR EDESON
Special Effects .... JOHN P. FULTON
Make-up .... JACK P. PIERCE
Film Editor .... CLARENCE KOLSTER
Supervising Film Editor .... MAURICE PIVAR
Art Director .... CHARLES D. HALL
Sets .... HERMAN ROSSE
Electrical Properties .... KENNETH STRICKFADEN
Technical Assistant .... DR. CECIL REYNOLDS
Recording Supervision .... C. ROY HUNTER
Musical Theme .... DAVID BROEKMAN

1933

Duck Soup

Rufus T. Firefly gets help running Freedonia

Comedy Breakthrough

"ONCE YOU SEE THE Marx Brothers, you can never look at the world in the same way again," observed Woody Allen, from his own prestigious position forty-three years after *Duck Soup*'s release. "Whenever you view any kind of phenomenon you frequently think to yourself, 'My God, what a perfect chance for the Marx Brothers to come in here.' It's hard to look at an opera or anything serious without thinking of them. *Duck Soup* is probably the best talking comedy ever made. It's the best Marx Brothers picture – the fastest moving, no sentimentality, none of those added love stories. It just comes off perfectly."

Although many think *A Night at the Opera* their funniest film, others have come to agree with the assessment that *Duck Soup*, the last film they made before being pressed into a more conventional (for them) mold by Irving Thalberg at MGM, represents the Marx Brothers at their purest. Screen comedy of the absurd reaches its height in this surrealist freewheeling film that best exemplifies the unique contribution of the Marx Brothers, a phenomenon in themselves. The Theater of the Absurd owes a debt to the Marxes (Eugene Ionesco once remarked that the three most important influences on his work were Groucho, Harpo, and Chico), and they have inspired our leading contemporary funnymen. When Mel Brooks uses such sight gags as the appearance of the Count Basie band in the middle of a desert in *Blazing Saddles*, he is working in the tradition of the anything-goes comedy of the Marxes; a Latin American revolution depicted with abandon by Woody Allen in *Bananas* is akin to the lunacy of the warfare unleashed in *Duck Soup*'s mythical Freedonia; television's "Laugh-In" program, which during its better moments brought relatively inventive humor to that medium, was in the vein of the Marxes; the Monty Python brand of comedy is another descendant.

The Marx characters that emerged in their professional lives were extensions of personalities already manifested in their growing-up days in New York. The family was continually strapped for money and summoned its collective ingenuity to devise ways of hiding from the landlord when the rent was due. Chico hustled a buck any way he could and became addicted to gambling. Harpo had a knack for getting in and out of trouble. Groucho was the intellect, but not above buying the family day-old bread for four cents and pocketing the extra penny from the nickel his mother gave him. Minnie Marx, an undaunted stage mother, was intent on turning all her sons into show business stars. Gummo, pushed into the vaudeville life that Minnie had mapped out, realized it was not his calling and escaped by joining the army in World War I. Zeppo replaced him in the act and survived through *Duck Soup*, his last film, and the end of his uncomfortable adjunct status.

Important in launching the Marx Brothers on their vaudeville career was their uncle Al Shean, of Gallagher and Shean fame. ("Positively, Mr. Gallagher." "Absolutely, Mr. Shean.") It took more than a decade for them to become top vaudeville attractions. In 1915, they played the fabled Palace. The historic move to success on the Broadway stage occurred on May 19, 1924, when the Marxes opened in a musical, *I'll Say She Is*, causing powerful critic Alexander Woollcott to comment in the *Sun*:

> As one of the many who laughed immoderately throughout the greater part of the first New York performance given by a new musical show, entitled, if memory serves, "I'll Say She Is," it behooves your correspondent to report at once that that harlequinade has some of the most comical moments vouchsafed to the first nighters in a month of Mondays. It is a bright colored and vehement setting for the goings on of those talented cutups, the Four Marx Brothers. In particular, it is a splendacious and reasonably tuneful excuse for going to see that silent brother, that shy, unexpected, magnificent comic among the Marxes, who . . . is known to the adoring two-a-day as Harpo Marx.
>
> Surely there should be dancing in the streets when a great clown comes to town, and this man is a great clown. He is officially billed as a member of the Marx family, but truly he belongs to that greater family which includes Joe Jackson and Bert Melrose and the Fratillini brothers. . . . Harpo Marx, so styled, oddly enough, because he plays the harp, says never a word from first to last, but when by merely leaning against one's brother one can seem richly and irresistibly amusing why should one speak?

Other influential critics, including George S. Kaufman, Heywood Broun, and George Jean Nathan took up the Marxes with enthusiasm, and soon they were favorites in intellectual circles, with Harpo becoming a member of the Round Table set at the Algonquin. They subsequently had two more Broadway successes, *The Cocoanuts* and *Animal Crackers*, and while appearing in the latter, made their first film, a screen version of *The Cocoanuts* (1929), shot at the Paramount studios in Astoria, New York. They filmed during the day and rushed to Broadway for their evening curtain. *Animal Crackers* (1930) was also filmed in Astoria. The Marx Brothers moved to Hollywood for *Monkey Business* (1931) and *Horse Feathers* (1932), the hits that preceded

Duck Soup. With *Horse Feathers*, they made the cover of *Time* magazine, indicating the extent to which they had become national celebrities.

The arrival of sound was perfect for the Marx Brothers. It brought drastic changes in film comedy; repartee, gag lines, and situations depending upon dialogue came into their own. It was a time in which W.C. Fields and Mae West could thrive, and the Marx Brothers could shower audiences with their outrageous puns and non sequiturs. Eventually, formula situation comedy was to become the mainstay of film humor, but in the early years of the sound era, greater experimentation was prevalent. *Duck Soup* abounds with freedom of comic expression, and is so refreshing in its decimation of authority and pomposity.

Groucho, as Rufus T. Firefly, has been made ruler of Freedonia by the wealthy Mrs. Teasdale, who wields the purse strings and the power and is played by the grand lady of Marx pictures, Margaret Dumont, noticeably absent from their two previous films. The scene is a ballroom. Guards, ballet dancers scattering flowers, and singing guests enliven the party at which the new leader is to be honored. The chorus sings: "He'll make his appearance when/The clock on the wall strikes ten." Firefly is late. Music. Trumpets. No Firefly. Cut to a scene of Firefly asleep in bed. Awakened by an alarm clock, he removes his nightshirt; his dress clothes are underneath. He slides down a pole at the foot of the bed. Cut back to the ballroom as Firefly makes his entrance slithering to the bottom of the pole.

It doesn't take long for the Dumont-Groucho repartee to take wing:

MRS. TEASDALE: The future of Freedonia rests on you. Promise me you'll follow in the footsteps of my husband.
FIREFLY: How do you like that? I haven't been on the job five minutes and already she's making advances to me. Not that I care, but where is your husband?
MRS. TEASDALE: Why, he's dead.
FIREFLY: I'll bet he's just using that as an excuse.
MRS. TEASDALE: I was with him to the very end.
FIREFLY: Huh! No wonder he passed away.
MRS. TEASDALE: I held him in my arms and kissed him.
FIREFLY: Oh. I see. Then it was murder. . . .

When song breaks out, in a style reminiscent of Gilbert and Sullivan (favorites of Groucho), Firefly warns: "The last man nearly ruined this place/He didn't know what to do with it. If you think this country's bad off now/Just wait till I get through with it."

The arch villain in the film is Trentino (Louis Calhern), of the rival power, Sylvania. Chicolini (Chico) and Pinky (Harpo) are his spies. Pinky is also Firefly's "chauffeur." Chicolino later becomes his secretary of war. They

The enemy captured; Margaret Dumont, Harpo, Louis Calhern, and Chico

also sell hot dogs and peanuts and harass a lemonade vendor, played by Edgar Kennedy, famed for his slow burn. The Marxes ridicule government, dictatorship, protocol, international relations, patriotism, warfare, and just about everything having to do with the social order. Firefly presides over what passes for a cabinet meeting. The minister of war, before resigning indignantly, demands: "Gentlemen! Gentlemen! Enough of this. How about taking up the tax?" Firefly answers: "How about taking up the carpet?" The minister insists on taking up the tax. Firefly: "He's right. You've got to take up the tacks before you take up the carpet."

The manner in which nations become embroiled in war is satirized by Firefly's running battle with Trentino, the fate of their countries dependent upon insult and honor.

> TRENTINO: I'm sorry we lost our tempers. I'm willing to forget if you are.
> FIREFLY: Forget? You ask me to forget? A Firefly never forgets. Why, my ancestors would rise from their graves and I would only have to bury them again. Nothing doing. I'm going back to clean the crackers out of my bed. I'm expecting company. . . .
> TRENTINO: I am willing to do anything to prevent this war.
> FIREFLY: It's too late. I've already paid a month's rent on the battlefield.

When he slaps Trentino with his gloves, it means war. The picture suddenly erupts into song led by the cabinet ministers. A boisterous number, "Freedonia's going to war!," spoofs efforts to whip the population into a patriotic hysteria that will make everyone willing, even eager, to die for his country. "Oh, hi-de, hi-de, hi-de, hi-de, hi-de, hi-de-ho/To war, to war, to war we're gonna go. . . . They got guns/We got guns/All God's chillun got guns. . . . Oh, Freedonia/ Oh donya cry for me/ We're comin' round the mountain/ With a banjo on my knee." Firefly sends Pinky on a Paul Revere ride: "Tell 'em the enemy comes from afar/ With a hey nonny-nonny and a ha-cha-cha." Pinky's ride comes to an early conclusion when he sees a girl undressing.

The war is virtually fought indoors, at Firefly's headquarters and in a farmhouse kitchen. Firefly, dictating a wireless message:

"The enemy has captured Hills 27 and 28, throwing thirteen hill-billies out of work. Last night two snipers crept into our machine gun nest and laid an egg. Send reinforcements immediately. Send that off collect."

As shells explode in the background, Firefly handles a suggestion that trenches be dug: "Dig trenches? With our men being killed off like flies? There isn't time to dig trenches. We'll have to buy 'em ready-made. Here, run out and get some trenches."

Matters are no saner at Trentino's headquarters. Trentino: "Chicolini, your partner's deserted us, but I'm still counting on you. There's a machine-gun nest near Hill 28. I want it cleaned out." Chicolini: "All right, I'll tell the janitor."

Firefly is told he is shooting his own men. Firefly: "Here's five dollars. Keep it under your hat. Never mind. I'll keep it under my hat."

Pinky parades with a sandwich board: "JOIN THE ARMY AND SEE THE NAVY." When Mrs. Teasdale appears, Firefly commands, "Remember, you're fighting for this woman's honor, which is probably more than she ever did." Other typical dialogue adding to the general insanity:

> FIREFLY: Now, go out in that battlefield and lead those men to victory. Go on, they're waiting for you.
> CHICOLINI: I wouldn't go out there unless I was in one of those big iron things that go up and down like this. What do you call those things?
> FIREFLY: Tanks.
> CHICOLINI: You're welcome.

Duck Soup contains the famous scene, devised by director Leo McCarey, in which Chico and Harpo disguise themselves as Groucho to confuse him when he looks in a mirror. Woody Allen cited the scene as a prime illustration of how it is possible to get away with something so outlandish: "No one for one second has ever thought, 'My God, a guy would know that he's not in a mirror.' I've done jokes like that myself in many pictures – in *Bananas*, for instance, where we go in and order 800 sandwiches. Instinct tells me I can get away with that. But it is really funny only in the context of a fairly well constructed thing. It ruins the jokes when they become chaotic in an unplanned way."

While the Marx comedy of *Duck Soup* is anarchic in effect, it obviously took careful planning and meticulous construction for it to work. The screenplay by Bert Kalmar and Harry Ruby, with additional dialogue by Arthur Sheekman and Nat Perrin, is particularly good, as are the Kalmar-Ruby songs. McCarey, whose previous experience with comedy included directing Laurel and Hardy, was praised by Groucho as the only first-class director the Marxes ever had. (For a short span – before being fired – the prolific Herman J. Mankiewicz was on the film as supervisor.)

Just how satirical did the Marx Brothers mean to be in *Duck Soup*? There are differences of opinion on this point. Many knowledgeable about comedy, including Woody Allen, and certain of those who worked on the film, dismiss the idea that it was intended as political satire. Of course, audiences and critics often find elements in films that may not have been specifically contemplated. Some critical comment when the film was released assumed that it was deliberate political satire. Richard Watts, Jr., in the *New York Herald Tribune*, expressed the "fear that American experts at satirical farce are not at their best when mocking the frailties of dictatorship. Perhaps they are not bitter enough. Possibly they strive too definitely to retain their good disposition." Groucho has credited McCarey with giving *Duck Soup* an anti-war slant and Mussolini evidently got a message as he banned the film. (Marx Brothers films were banned in Nazi Germany because the Marxes were Jewish.)

Unfortunately for the Marx Brothers' artistic growth, *Duck Soup* was not very popular – yet another instance of creative talent going far beyond what the public is prepared to accept – and their contract with Paramount was not renewed. However, Irving Thalberg of MGM made the Marxes an offer; he was convinced that a coherent story, a love interest, and music, were ingredients that would make their pictures much more appealing to audiences. This was a turning point for the Marxes. Very funny pictures resulted, notably *A Night at the Opera* and *A Day at the Races*, but the channeling of Groucho, Harpo, and Chico into formula films stifled their ingenuity. *Duck Soup* held the promise of a range far greater than the Marxes were to achieve. As funny as they have been (even in the worst of their subsequent films), they did not develop new comic patterns and stretch their aims. That they had broader aspirations can be surmised from a complaint that Groucho voiced in a 1946 interview with Mary Morris in *PM*: "The movies don't recognize any real heavies in the world. You don't dare make a joke that implies anything wrong with Franco. The poor public is smothered under tons of goo."

Duck Soup not only tells us everything about what the Marx Brothers were, and something about what they might have been; as the quintessential comedy of the absurd in cinema, it is an inspiration to those comedy film-makers who wish to escape conformity and follow where their particular talents lead. The irreverence in *Duck Soup* is not likely to go out of style; this liberated comic way of seeing the warped world has lasting appeal as each generation has its sacred cows to ridicule. The more preposterous the world becomes, the greater the need for the anarchic comedy of the Marx Brothers as expressed in *Duck Soup*.

DUCK SOUP
USA (Paramount) 1933

Cast

Rufus T. Firefly .... GROUCHO
Pinky .... HARPO
Chicolini .... CHICO
Bob Roland .... ZEPPO
Mrs. Teasdale .... MARGARET DUMONT
Vera Marcal .... RAQUEL TORRES
Trentino .... LOUIS CALHERN
Lemonade Vendor .... EDGAR KENNEDY
Zander .... EDMUND BREESE
Secretary .... VERNA HILLIE
Agitator .... LEONID KINSKY
Judge .... GEORGE MACQUARRIE
Secretary of War .... EDWIN MAXWELL
Prosecutor .... CHARLES B. MIDDLETON
Minister of Finance .... WILLIAM WORTHINGTON

Running time .... 68 minutes
Directed by .... LEO MCCAREY
Screenplay by .... BERT KALMAR and HARRY RUBY. Additional dialogue by ARTHUR SHEEKMAN and NAT PERRIN
Music and lyrics by .... BERT KALMAR and HARRY RUBY
Director of Photography .... HENRY SHARP
Art Direction .... HANS DREIER and WIARD B. IHNEN
Edited by .... LEROY STONE
Musical Director .... ARTHUR JOHNSTON

1934

It Happened One Night

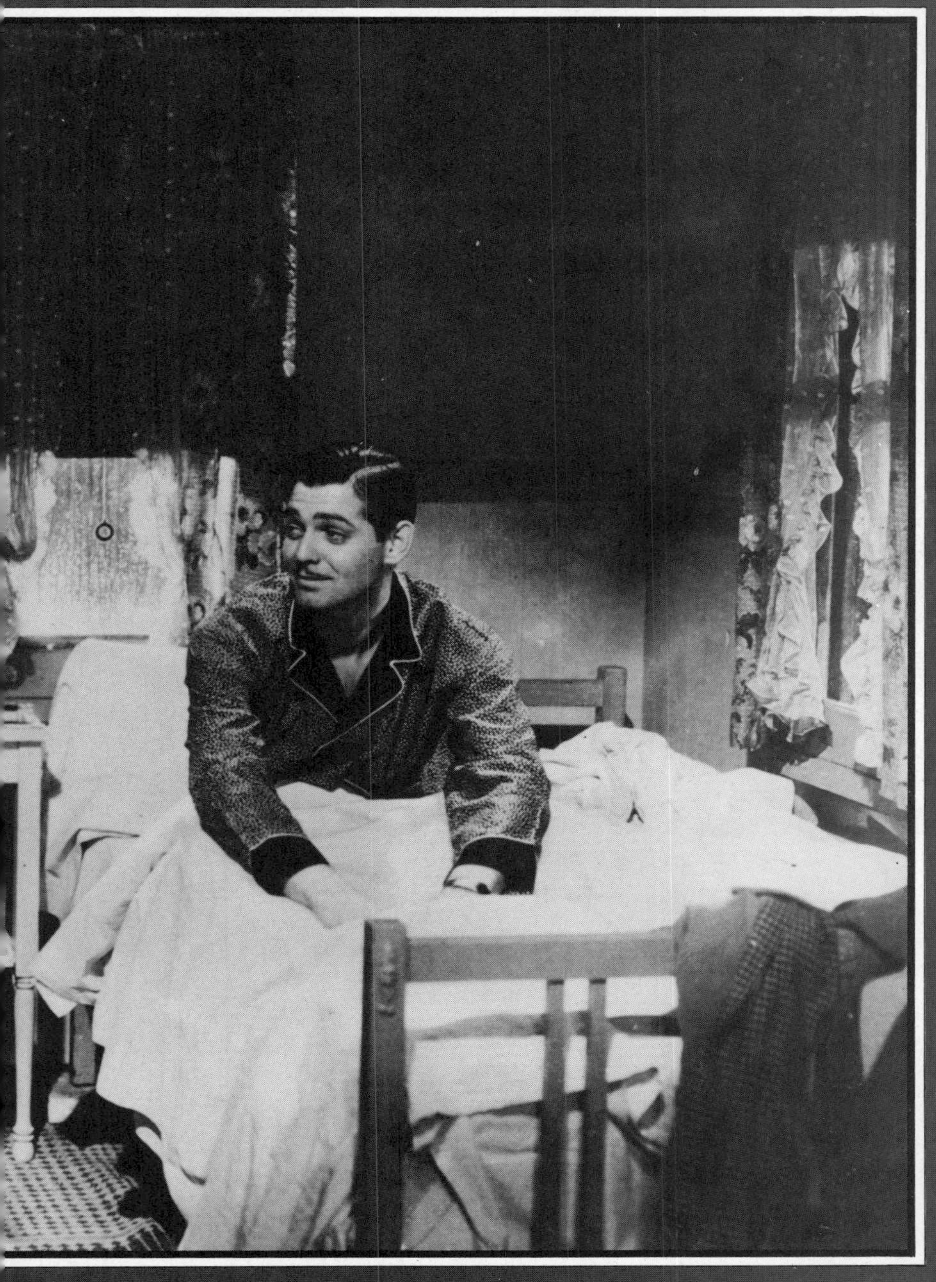

The Walls of Jericho. A blanket temporarily separates Claudette Colbert and Clark Gable in It Happened One Night.

Sex and the American Dream

PUT A MAN AND A WOMAN who have just met into a motel room with a blanket hanging up to separate them, and you have sexual titillation. Make the girl rich and spoiled, and the guy a working-stiff reporter, and you have class conflict. Pepper with comedy while tearing down class barriers along with the blanket, and you have light-hearted sex appeal mixed with an affirmation of the American dream. The combination proved to be particularly potent in 1934, when the Depression had badly shaken the myth of equal opportunity for all, and audiences were receptive to entertainment that would serve as a distraction.

It Happened One Night became a landmark that set the important "screwball comedy" pattern and forecast how Hollywood comedies would treat sex and society for many years to come. Be daring, even a bit risqué; be satirical, even a little caustic about the well-heeled or the establishment. But always be sure it is in the spirit of harmless fun and that sexual mores and the social or political structures are not shaken too aggressively. Even better, fashion plots and characters to minimize differences and send audiences home feeling euphoric.

Calling these comedies "very much a response to the Depression," Andrew Bergman pinpointed their essence in *We're In the Money:*

> They created an America of perfect unity: all classes as one, the rural-urban divide breached, love and decency and neighborliness ascendant. It was an American self-portrait that proved a bonanza in the mid-thirties.

With the proliferation of talkies, there was room, indeed a need, for an added style of comedy – humor that depended not upon the irascibility of W.C. Fields or the rampaging of the Marx Brothers, but upon sparkling dialogue and screwball situations involving people with whom audiences might identify, if only through wish fulfillment. Director Frank Capra, screenwriter Robert Riskin, and stars Clark Gable and Claudette Colbert found exactly the right property in *It Happened One Night.*

Capra, born in Sicily in 1897, came to Los Angeles with his family when he was six. His upward climb included writing *Our Gang* comedies for Hal

Roach and working as a gag writer for Mack Sennett. Capra co-directed Harry Langdon, one of the funniest of the silent comedians, in *Tramp, Tramp, Tramp* and directed him in *The Strong Man* and *Long Pants*. The first time he directed Claudette Colbert was in *For the Love of Mike* (1927), a flop. Before *It Happened One Night*, Capra and Riskin already had such hits as *Platinum Blonde* (1931), with Jean Harlow, and *Lady for a Day* (1933), which won four Academy Award nominations, but no Oscars. The next year, *It Happened One Night* made an unprecedented sweep of all five major honors, garnering Oscars for best picture, director, actress, actor, and writer. That did not happen again until the 1975 awards, when *One Flew Over the Cuckoo's Nest* won the same five honors.

The path of *It Happened One Night* had not been easy. Capra had a difficult time convincing Harry Cohn of Columbia to let him make the film. Cohn's advisers thought it would be just another of the bus pictures with which the market had been saturated since cross-country bus travel became popular. *It Happened One Night* was based on a magazine story titled "Night Bus," by Samuel Hopkins Adams. Capra changed the title to avoid the vehicular stigma and also adopted key story changes suggested by his friend, ex-reporter and writer Myles Connelly. It was Connelly's idea to have the heroine behave like a brat because she was bored with being an heiress, and to make the hero a newspaperman instead of a long-haired Greenwich Village painter.

Production was marked by antagonism between Gable and Colbert, and between Capra and Colbert. Prior to Colbert's being signed, her role had been turned down by Myrna Loy, Miriam Hopkins, Margaret Sullavan, and Constance Bennett. Robert Montgomery had refused the male lead. Clark Gable was cast because MGM titan Louis B. Mayer was in the mood to punish him by lending him to Columbia, which at that time was tantamount to exile. Resentful, Gable arrived at Capra's office drunk. Colbert agreed to play the part only after being offered $50,000, twice her normal price, with the pledge that the film would be shot in four weeks, otherwise she could leave, whether it were finished or not.

Viewed today, after the revolutionary changes in filmmaking, *It Happened One Night,* with its bubbling pace and flirtatiousness, seems charmingly naïve. Peter Warne (Gable), a reporter just fired in a rift with his editor, heads back to New York from Miami in a Greyhound bus. Traveling incognito in the bus is Ellie (Colbert), on the run from her millionaire father (Walter Connolly), who wants to break up her entanglement with playboy King Westley. Plot complications mount rapidly: At a stopover en route Ellie's luggage is stolen. Peter, who has recognized her and sees his chance for a scoop in chronicling her "Mad Flight to Happiness," comes to her assistance; they spend the night in an auto camp. Back on the bus, Ellie is accosted by an inquisitive traveling salesman (Roscoe Karns). Peter frightens him off and he and Ellie flee. They hitch a ride and their benefactor steals Peter's luggage; Peter retrieves it, takes the car, and they spend a night in a second auto camp. By now, the seeds of movie romance have been sown. At first, Peter is condescendingly protective, exasperated by Ellie's rich-girl attitudes. She is rebellious, but comes to admire his outlook, which makes her yearn inwardly for a more down-to-earth life. Predictably, despite their incessant bickering, they are increasingly attracted to one another. But, because of a misunderstanding, Ellie leaves Peter, returns home, and prepares for a lavish church wedding to her playboy, with her father now resigned to the marriage. Peter follows. The self-made millionaire thinks the reporter is after money. He learns different, and admires Peter's integrity. With her father's connivance, Ellie runs from the ceremony to join Peter and off they go.

At the time of its release, this frolic was considered brazen. Having Colbert and Gable share a twin-bedded room was a tease. Capra had wanted Colbert to partially undress in camera view, but she refused. Instead, Ellie drapes her undies on the blanket they have hung up as a room divider. Audiences and Peter found this sexy. In the famous hitchhiking scene, Ellie shows Peter how to get a ride by lifting her skirt and baring her leg. Colbert originally refused to do this scene and a chorus girl was brought in as a substitute. Vanity changed Colbert's mind when she decided her own leg was prettier. Colbert and Gable are beautifully abrasive in their love-hate relationship. She prances around in his pyjamas, he looks appealing with his boyish grin and bared chest. The crisp, often witty dialogue adds spice. The film ends when they are married and honeymooning in a motel. Again a blanket separates them. But this time "The Walls of Jericho" come tumbling down to the sound of a trumpet.

The symbolic ending sent audiences home giggling. It was mischievously suggestive in view of the Motion Picture Production Code, which was saddled with such restrictive clauses as: "In general, passion should be treated in such a manner as not to stimulate the lower and baser emotions"; "Undressing scenes should be avoided, and never used save where essential to the plot"; "The treatment of bedrooms must be governed by good taste and delicacy."

The response at Columbia to *It Happened One Night* was dismal. Nor was there anything in the critics' reactions to forecast its success. But the public responded enthusiastically. The title itself was sexy. The performances of Gable and Colbert were the talk of the country and people went to see them expecting a risqué love story and a good laugh. An idea of how popular the film was can be deduced from the state of alarm in the undershirt industry. When Gable took off his shirt, the sight of his bare chest inspired a nation of emulators, and undershirt sales reportedly dropped.

Capra had succeeded in giving the film spontaneity, excitement, and an air of realism. The auto camps, the bus travel, and the road scenes had a look of authenticity that greatly appealed to a public saturated with pretense. The scene that most demonstrates the director's ingenuity is that in which the passengers in the bus sing "The Daring Young Man on the Flying Trapeze." Capra used numerous cameras to shoot this singing session from various distances and angles, obtaining an improvisational ambience that registers on screen as a rollicking, realistic interlude. Capra was now in a position of power. He became one of the most prestigious directors in Hollywood, known for his socially aware comedies, and his name was billed above the title before it became fashionable to think of the director as a superstar. His subsequent films include: *Mr. Deeds Goes to Town* (1936), *Lost Horizon* (1937), *You Can't Take It With You* (1938), *Meet John Doe* (1941) – all with Robert Riskin as screenwriter; *Mr. Smith Goes to Washington* (1939), *Arsenic and Old Lace* (1944), *It's a Wonderful Life* (1946), and *State of the Union* (1948).

The inspection of some features of *It Happened One Night* can be instructive as to changes taking place in the 1930s. The role of Ellie, as played by Colbert, was consistent with a more balanced portrayal of women in a decade when women were perhaps least maligned on screen. To be sure, they were still subject to the clichés of the day involving "the fallen woman," marriage, and the incompatibility of a career and marital bliss. But they were shown holding down jobs, and were not merely appendages or playthings. The vacuous vamps and flappers of the 1920s had been deflated by Mae West's saucy, irreverent spoofing of sex sirens; *I'm No Angel* (1933) was an example. Stricter Production Code enforcement occurred in a backlash. Molly Haskell speculated in *From Reverence to Rape* that the Code, despite its evils,

> was probably at least as responsible as the Depression for getting women out of the bedroom and into the office. . . . Women were no longer able to languish in satin on a chaise longue and subsist on passion; they were forced to do something, and a whole generation of working women came into being.

Colbert's heiress certainly did not have to work, but she exhibited a good measure of independence, at least a susceptibility to the real world, and was a lively match for the hero.

It Happened One Night is closely bound to Hollywood's preoccupation with the battle of the sexes. Hollywood films have not been known for depth in man–woman relationships. The emphasis is usually on getting into bed rather than what happens after the couple have been there. Even when standards were radically altered in the 1960s and 1970s, films like *Bob and Carol and Ted and Alice* (1969), with its hints at switching partners, and *I Will, I Will . . . For Now* (1976), with couples enrolling at a sex clinic, have been shallow and coy in the context of their own time periods. The portrayal of man and woman as sparring antagonists in *It Happened One Night* is a framework from which neither film comedy nor life has been extricated.

A similar tendency toward surface-skimming can be observed in the comedy's approach to class distinctions. One may argue that *It Happened One Night* is only meant as good fun, but the notion that rich or poor, it doesn't matter, had an anesthetizing effect in the thirties. Capra's *Mr. Deeds Goes to Town* and *Mr. Smith Goes to Washington* posed questions about moral and ethical standards, but did not demand basic change. However, those who dismiss these films as bland are unfair. The Senate's anger at *Mr. Smith Goes to Washington* demonstrated that Capra had scored satirical points. Harry Cohn was pressured by Joseph P. Kennedy, then Ambassador to Britain, to refrain from distributing the film abroad for fear that it would damage the reputation of American institutions. Under Capra's prodding, Cohn held his ground. Nevertheless, measured against the state of the country and the world, such socially conscious comedies were mild.

The fondest memories of 1930s comedies derive from their ability to entertain and from the marvelous performers who made them sparkle – Cary Grant, Katharine Hepburn, Greta Garbo, Carole Lombard, Marlene Dietrich, James Stewart, Irene Dunne, Gary Cooper, Myrna Loy, William Powell. But, in addition, the mixture of man–woman relationships with the prevailing mores and myths serves as a mirror-image of what America was like during the period. Even what was glossed over or left out offers clues to that image. Capra's *It Happened One Night*, as well as reflecting its era, was the trend-setter that established a formula for entertaining audiences in the arduous decade of Depression and social upheaval.

IT HAPPENED ONE NIGHT

USA (Columbia Picture Corporation) 1934

Cast

Peter Warne .... CLARK GABLE
Ellie .... CLAUDETTE COLBERT
Alexander Andrews .... WALTER CONNOLLY
Shapeley .... ROSCOE KARNS
King Westley .... JAMESON THOMAS
Danker .... ALAN HALE
Bus Driver .... WARD BOND
Lovington .... WALLIS CLARK
Henderson .... HARRY BRADLEY
Reporter .... CHARLIE BROWN
Auto Camp Owner .... HARRY HOLMAN
Auto Camp Owner's wife .... MAIDEL TURNER
Zeke .... ARTHUR HOYT

Running time .... 105 minutes
Produced by .... FRANK CAPRA
Directed by .... FRANK CAPRA
Screenplay by .... ROBERT RISKIN, based on "Night Bus," a story by SAMUEL HOPKINS ADAMS
Photography .... JOSEPH WALKER
Film Editor .... GENE HAVLICK
Music Direction .... LOUIS SILVERS
Art Direction .... STEPHEN GOOSSON

The 39 Steps

"A handcuff, after all, isn't it a form of eroticism really?" – Alfred Hitchcock. Pamela (Madeleine Carroll) and Richard Hannay (Robert Donat) in The 39 Steps.

Contributions of a Suspense Master

"I REMEMBER ONE SUNDAY I was looking at the television and a very unusual silent film was on," Alfred Hitchcock remarked in our conversation of March 1976, on the eve of the release of his fifty-third film, *Family Plot*. "There was a scene with a baby in a pram. The baby suddenly stood up and fired a gun and shot a man across the street. I've had that idea for about twenty years, but have never found a reason for doing it. The way I was going to do it was that the baby stands up, shoots a man, settles down again, and then about an hour afterward you find a midget taking money from the boss who had commissioned the murder. I thought it was an amusing idea."

For fifty years Hitchcock has been dabbling in such ideas, usually molded into a pattern that has made his name synonymous with suspense to an international public. Many cinemaphiles, while also delighting in Hitchcockian entertainment, view his contributions as going far beyond that role. He is considered one of the most influential figures in filmmaking, because his technique, based on the principle of finding the best visual means of telling a story, provides inspiration and know-how for those eager to learn from the master. *The 39 Steps*, while not the first success of the British-born director, represents the best of his work at home before he diminished his country's meager film scene by taking his corpulent talent to Hollywood. The tale, about a ring of spies, contains the hallmarks of Hitchcock's style, later even more astutely developed in films such as *Psycho*. The enthusiastic reception of *The 39 Steps* was the turning point that sped Hitchcock on his way to a position of world renown and influence difficult to measure fully.

French director François Truffaut, a foremost disciple, told an enthusiastic audience who had come to join the Film Society of Lincoln Center in honoring Hitchcock in New York on April 29, 1974, that when he gets ready to shoot a scene, he thinks of the obvious way, and then speculates on how Hitchcock might film it. Truffaut also wrote in the introduction to his important interview book *Hitchcock:*

> The examination of Hitchcock's directorial career, ranging as it does from his silent movies in Great Britain to his current color films in Hollywood, is a richly rewarding source of discovery. In Hitchcock's work a filmmaker is bound to find the answer to many of his own

problems, including the most fundamental question of all: how to express oneself by purely visual means.

Hitchcock has harped on this point, as he did when talking about *Family Plot*. "What a lot of picture makers fail to do is to visualize what's on screen," he complained. "If you send a picture out with too much dialogue, people are not looking at a picture. They are paying their money to come and have a good read. My scripts are not readable. They demand that you visualize the words on the paper." Hitchcock saw a similarity between *Family Plot* and *The 39 Steps*, which he described as "a combination of melodrama with comic overtones."

Hitchcock, who was born in 1899, grew up as a Catholic in predominantly Protestant England, and attended a Jesuit school, where caning was accepted punishment. His home life was also stern. Some have traced his preoccupation with films of anxiety to childhood experiences, such as the time his father induced a police officer to "arrest" five-year-old Alfred and lock him in a cell for ten minutes as a punishment. The director's first film was a murder story, *The Pleasure Garden*, shot in Germany and released in 1926. *The Lodger*, on a pet theme, the wrong man accused, appeared in the same year and was hailed as the best British film made so far. *Blackmail* (1929), his first talkie, was a part-sound film also shot as a silent. Hitchcock's greatest triumph before *The 39 Steps* was his first version of *The Man Who Knew Too Much*, starring Leslie Banks, Edna Best, and Peter Lorre, made in 1934.

It is enjoyable to look at *The 39 Steps* again and trace the Hitchcockian touches that have since become familiar. The story concerns an innocent bystander who suddenly finds his life in peril, another favorite theme. It is spiced with other characteristic ingredients such as murder, scenes in unusual places, spies, strange encounters, action on a train, chases, comic relief, tricks to involve an audience, and the use of a device such as handcuffs to keep quarrelsome characters together. Hitchcock displays his ability to keep the pace tense, fast, and exciting. A young Canadian, Richard Hannay (Robert Donat), watches the strange act of Mr. Memory in a London theater. Mr. Memory, based on an actual music hall entertainer named Datas, is a human encyclopedia who answers questions from the audience. A man is killed, turmoil breaks out, and a mystery woman, Miss Smith, asks Hannay for help. She tells him of her connection with a dangerous spy ring. While taking refuge in Hannay's flat, Miss Smith is murdered. Her protector is in deep trouble; his life is threatened by the spies, bent on eliminating him because of what he knows, and the police logically consider him their prime suspect. Hannay has learned from Miss Smith that the spy ring operation is centered in a village in Scotland, and that its leader has part of a little finger missing. This offers Hitchcock one of his relished opportunities to control his audience, now conditioned to look for the hand with the missing finger. Hitchcock mischievously increases the suspense by lavishing camera attention on innocent hands.

The film is one long chase. The pursued Hannay heads for Scotland. On the train he meets Pamela (Madeleine Carroll) for the first time. She is skeptical of his story, but circumstances will later link her fate with his. After they fall into the hands of the spies, they are handcuffed together. When they escape, Hitchcock makes the most of the handcuff gimmick. Hannay, with Pamela still joined to him, takes refuge in an inn despite her objections. There is a droll, sexy scene in which she removes her stockings while his hand follows her movements. The director also makes use of handcuffs in *The Lodger*, *Saboteur*, and *The Wrong Man*. Hitchcock elaborated on this during a television interview with Richard Schickel in *The Men Who Made the Movies* series:

> I've always thought that the handcuff thing was almost a kind of a fetish. If you notice, any press photographer around a courthouse will try to get the picture of the man in handcuffs. There's some strange appeal that it has, and just in the same way the man who is handcuffed tries to cover them up. . . . It's almost a symbol of reduction, as it were, to the lowest form. . . . That's why in *The 39 Steps*, used in a different context as a comedy thing, it nevertheless had a fascinating effect on audiences – the fact that the man and woman were handcuffed together. And it sort of brought out all kinds of thoughts in their minds; for example, how do they go to the toilet was one natural, obvious question. . . . I think it relates more to sex than to anything else.

He made the same point in our conversation: "A handcuff, after all, isn't it a form of eroticism really? Why did people, when they photographed Patricia Hearst, show the chains around her?"

Hitchcock uses another scene of implied sexuality in a farmhouse when Hannay is befriended by the farmer's wife (Peggy Ashcroft). She finds him attractive and tries to help him. Implicit in her glance is a sexual yearning, but he is hungry only for food. Hitchcock is also keenly aware of how much audiences enjoy comic relief. Hannay and Pamela are tracked to the inn by the spies. The woman innkeeper accepts Hannay's story that they are trying to hide for romantic reasons, and in an amusing scene she turns away the pursuers.

The film's pace is derived from economical storytelling and progressively exciting developments leading toward the climax, which occurs in a music hall where Mr. Memory is again performing. Hitchcock knows that when a bizarre incident takes place in public it is more fascinating than it would be in private. In *The 39 Steps*, it is Mr. Memory who represents the key to the "MacGuffin," the device Hitchcock uses to hold his stories together. In it-

A tense moment for Hannay and the farmer's wife (Peggy Ashcroft)

self, a MacGuffin may be trivial. Here it is the formula for building a certain airplane engine that Mr. Memory has memorized. Hannay shouts from the audience, "What are the thirty-nine steps?" Mr. Memory, true to character, cannot help but blurt out the answer. "MacGuffins are best for spy stories," Hitchcock recalled in reflecting on *The 39 Steps*. "I was followed by the FBI for three months when I was learning about uranium 235 to use as a MacGuffin in *Notorious*."

The casting of Madeleine Carroll illustrates Hitchcock's theory about the kind of woman he likes to put in his films. Ingrid Bergman, Joan Fontaine, Grace Kelly, Eva Marie Saint – these are not women who flaunt sexuality. In Truffaut's interview book, Hitchcock stated his thoughts on the subject:

> Sex on the screen should be suspenseful, I feel. If sex is too blatant or obvious, there's no suspense. . . . I think the most interesting women, sexually, are the English women. I feel that the English women, the Swedes, the northern Germans, and [the] Scandinavians are a great deal more exciting than the Latin, the Italian, and the French women. Sex should not be advertised. An English girl, looking like a schoolteacher, is apt to get into a cab with you and, to your surprise, she'll probably pull a man's pants open.

A Hitchcockian principle of major importance is to let the audience in on the basic facts instead of springing a surprise ending. He has evolved the theory that mystery is not the way to achieve suspense. As he explained it: "I don't believe there's enough suspense in a mystery story. I think that concealing the facts from an audience doesn't create any emotional impact. You can only give an audience emotion if you give them facts to warrant that emotion." Thus, in *The Man Who Knew Too Much* (which he remade co-starring James Stewart and Doris Day), he lets the audience know that a diplomat is to be murdered in a concert hall (again, a public place) at the exact moment in the music when a clash of cymbals will muffle the shot. He builds suspense brilliantly as the audience waits for that moment while the race is on to prevent the murder.

The astute director frequently conceives of ways to focus audience attention where he wants it. If he wants the audience to watch the glass of milk, presumably containing poison, that Cary Grant is taking to his wife in *Suspicion*, he places a light in the glass to exert a visual pull on the spectator. In *The Lady Vanishes*, a mickey has been slipped into a drink. Hitchcock uses two oversized glasses through which he photographs Michael Redgrave and Margaret Lockwood and thus increases audience awareness of the importance of the glasses.

A viewer not conversant with the methods of filmmaking may be unaware of Hitchcock's techniques while succumbing to their effect. Hitchcock knows how to set up his audience psychologically, and combine his camerawork with his skills at montage to create maximum impact. The shower sequence in *Psycho* (1960) has come to be considered his *pièce de résistance*. Before we get to the grisly murder, we are led on a red-herring plot maneuver when Janet Leigh absconds with $40,000. We cannot conceive of her early death, since we assume that larceny is the main theme, and we also think it unlikely that one of the stars would disappear from the film so soon. We are, therefore, particularly vulnerable to the unexpected jolt of the terrifying stabbing sequence. The stabbing is made to look realistic and brutal, an effect Hitchcock accomplishes through montage. By juxtaposing seventy-eight pieced-together segments of film in forty-five seconds, he makes you think you have watched the knife piercing the woman viciously and repeatedly. *Psycho*, with its other horrific elements, significantly escalated screen violence, and quite understandably caused protest.

Hitchcock's visual technique has grown in sophistication since the making of *The 39 Steps*. An example from *Frenzy* (1972) indicates why there is so much to learn from his films. The killer escorts an unsuspecting victim to her flat. They go inside and the door shuts. A less creative director might have had the woman scream, or have shown details of the terror inside. Hitchcock, with the kind of scene that draws applause from a knowing audience, backs his camera away from the door, down the stairs, out of the house, and across the street in a long virtuoso take. This graceful, uninterrupted withdrawal is a striking visual farewell that seals the woman's fate.

His comments on a sequence from *Family Plot* gave further insight into his thinking. "One tries to improve upon the visual in order to create emotion. In the scene in which there is an attempt on the lives of our two principals, the heavy has released the brake fluid of their car, which is coming down the mountain. Here I do something that won't be discerned by the audience: When they start the car, I allow only the photographing of the windshield. But as the motion of the car increases and they can't stop, I eliminate the foreground altogether and show only the road ahead – the winding road, the hairpin bends, the passing cars. This is what would happen in real life. You would see only the road." Hitchcock was right in his strategy; this scene has elicited appreciative applause.

These are the touches that have earned him the admiration of other directors. Truffaut's French New Wave colleague Claude Chabrol is also among Hitchcock's disciples. Even the great Ingmar Bergman, while dismissing Hitchcock's films in terms of intellectual content, admitted to being impressed by his technique. Hitchcock is one of those rare artists of whom it can be said that each new film causes a stir of anticipation while earlier films continue to be popular whenever they are shown. His signature appearance is less an act of ego than a personal greeting to the faithful.

Devotees will argue about which films they prefer, but my preferences include *The 39 Steps*, *The Lady Vanishes*, *Foreign Correspondent*, *Suspicion*, *Notorious*, *Strangers on a Train*, *Rear Window*, *The Wrong Man*, and *North by Northwest*. There was a regrettable decline with *The Birds*, *Marnie*, *Torn Curtain*, and *Topaz*, with *Frenzy* breaking the downward pattern. In Hitchcock's illustrious career, the best of his work stands as more than enough achievement for any one man. But in another sense it is unfortunate that a man of Hitchcock's creativity and influence on the medium was not also inclined to deal with more significant subject matter. Hitchcock brushed aside such criticism: "A cobbler should stick to his last. Why didn't Agatha Christie write music? No, I'm a thriller maker."

Hitchcock contended that he derived most satisfaction from working out a script with a writer in such detail that he could maintain his reputation for shooting scenes in one or two takes. "I don't call it writing," he observed. "I call it making a picture on paper. In fact, I will go so far as to say that when the script is finished I wish I didn't have to make it into a picture. I have already had my enjoyment."

Providing entertainment seems to give Hitchcock more gratification than the influence he has had upon cinema technique or the adulation accorded him. At a news conference in 1947, he said: "I aim to provide the public with beneficial shocks. Civilization has become so protective that we're no longer able to get our goosebumps instinctively. The only way to remove the numbness and revive our moral equilibrium is to use artificial means to bring about the shock. The best way to achieve that, it seems to me, is through a movie." The landmark that gained him international renown, *The 39 Steps*, thoroughly reflects his desire to have fun with his audience.

Hitchcock, while highly valued as a pioneer, will also be remembered as the affable, playful individual who could delight in telling an audience gathered to honor his friend Truffaut: "I'm afraid I have a rather unpleasant announcement to make. A botulism has been found in the punch."

THE 39 STEPS
GREAT BRITAIN (Gaumont-British) 1935

Cast

Richard Hannay .... ROBERT DONAT
Pamela .... MADELEINE CARROLL
Miss Smith .... LUCIE MANNHEIM
Professor Jordan .... GODFREY TEARLE
Mrs. Jordan .... HELEN HAYE
Crofter .... JOHN LAURIE
Crofter's wife .... PEGGY ASHCROFT
The Sheriff .... FRANK CELLIER
Mr. Memory .... WYLIE WATSON

Running time .... 87 minutes
Produced by .... MICHAEL BALCON, with IVOR MONTAGU as Associate Producer
Directed by .... ALFRED HITCHCOCK
Screenplay by .... ALMA REVILLE and CHARLES BENNETT, with additional dialogue by IAN HAY; based on the novel by JOHN BUCHAN
Director of Photography .... BERNARD KNOWLES
Film Editor .... DEREK N. TWIST
Music .... LOUIS LEVY
Sets .... OTTO WERNDORFF and ALBERT JULLION
Costumes .... J. STRASSNER
Sound Engineer .... A. BIRCH

1936

Modern Times

Paulette Goddard and Charlie Chaplin in Modern Times.

Depression and Depersonalization

"I WORKED DAMNED HARD on the set to make a film, and everything I did was *con amore*, with my heart and soul, and with a terrific enthusiasm," reflected Charlie Chaplin at nearly eighty-three, almost four decades following the release of *Modern Times*. As he sat in his spacious home in Vevey, Switzerland, in February 1972, shortly before his triumphant return to the United States after a twenty-year political exile, he added: "One might say that my work had invention."

Modern Times, a perfect example of the inventiveness in which Chaplin justifiably took pride, also makes a definitive comic statement about the plight of man in our century. It sums up hilariously and wisely the despair of the Depression-ridden thirties and the merciless reduction of modern man to a cog in the wheels of alleged progress. Chaplin's Tramp had to contend with forces that harassed him. In *Modern Times* the conflict assumes proportions of universality going beyond his previous encounters. The Tramp becomes a symbolic figure for the individual in a more complicated age, with neither machinery nor authority to be trusted, and love and optimism even more desperately needed to strive for a better tomorrow. The career of Chaplin is a landmark unto itself; *Modern Times* expresses the combination of the comic skill that made him the most renowned film personage throughout the world, and the intelligence that extended his film talent to embrace concepts defining the precarious position of mankind.

Jean Renoir called Chaplin "the master of masters, the filmmaker of filmmakers." In his autobiography, *My Life and My Films*, Renoir, reminding us that Chaplin has done everything in his films, "script, direction, setting, production, performance and even the music," asserted: "His films are not only examples of perfect unity, but all his work is one. One may say indeed of Chaplin that he has made only one film and that every facet of that film is a different enactment of the same profession of faith." Jean-Luc Godard, in *Cahiers du Cinéma* of December 1963-January 1964, wrote: "He is beyond praise because he is the greatest of all. . . . one says Chaplin as one says da Vinci – or rather Charlie, like Leonardo."

The most moving passages in Chaplin's book, *My Autobiography*, concern the appalling poverty of his childhood in London. His parents were both vaudevillians, and he first appeared on stage at the age of five. Part of his childhood was spent in the Lambeth workhouse. His mentally ill mother was institutionalized for many years, and Chaplin's description of her existence is heartrending. In 1910 he journeyed to the United States as a member of a Fred Karno troupe. His film career is said to have started as a result of Mack Sennett and Mabel Normand seeing him in a Karno show. Subsequently, Sennett made him an offer to become a performer at Keystone, where he began in 1913 at $150 a week. "Mack Sennett was a great influence on me," Chaplin remembered at Vevey. "He would laugh at the things I did. I would think, 'well, that isn't very funny.' But he would think it was, and he gave me a lot of confidence."

Chaplin's success was extraordinary. He quickly became an international star, and by 1917 was earning more than $1 million a year. His pictures, such as *Tillie's Punctured Romance, The Tramp, The Pawn Shop, Easy Street, The Cure*, *The Immigrant*, *A Dog's Life*, and *Shoulder Arms*, kept audiences screaming with laughter and wanting more. His first feature, *The Kid* (1921), made a child star of Jackie Coogan. *A Woman of Paris* (1923), a sophisticated drama starring Edna Purviance and Adolphe Menjou, was acclaimed by the critics, but the public outside of the major cities was cool toward a Chaplin film that was not what they expected and in which he did not appear. (Rereleased in 1978, it was revealed to be an insightful, subtle masterpiece far ahead of its time technically and in its attitude toward women.) The Tramp returned in *The Gold Rush* (1925), which earned him $2 million personally and has endured as one of the most beloved comedies ever filmed. Chaplin's financial independence enabled him to retain his individuality and make the kind of films he preferred. By preserving control over the bulk of his work, he could determine rerelease policies, and when he left the United States under political persecution, he was in a strong financial position. The wealth he amassed, in contrast with the pitiful poverty of his beginnings, is something he never quite believed. Looking out of the windows of his living-room, he said, with amazement in his voice: "It's very nice to finish up in this luxurious place – for a poor boy, coming into all of this. It's very nice, very comfortable. I'd hate to be old with no money."

Making *Modern Times* as a silent film, except for music and effects and Chaplin's brief double-talk song, took nerve on his part. Even *City Lights* (1931) was daring in that respect, for talkies were obligatory by then. "I remember that I said I wouldn't talk and I didn't talk – and then I was like the rest," Chaplin remarked. "I felt that talk was revealing. I don't believe in revealing too much. I like the mystery in things. I remember reading about the reaction to *Modern Times*. They said I had a very husky voice."

Modern Times was made against the background of national despondency caused by the Depression. The assembly line symbolized to Chaplin a society that regarded man as a piece of machinery to be used and discarded. His genius impelled him to place the Tramp in the epicenter of 1930s poverty and depersonalization, and to beleaguer him with an avalanche of misadventures. Even before its release the picture became controversial. What was Chaplin up to now? There were reports that he was making a film containing left-wing propaganda, and it was eagerly awaited by admirers and detractors alike.

The foreword to the film announces: "*Modern Times* is the story of industry, of individual enterprise – humanity crusading in the pursuit of happiness." Apart from the eating of his shoe in *The Gold Rush*, nothing in Chaplin films is as remembered as the factory scenes of *Modern Times*, with the assembly line speed-up and automatic time-saving feeding contraption. Images rush to mind: Chester Conklin caught in the complex machinery, with Charlie feeding him during the lunch break; Charlie trying to eat corn-on-the-cob offered by a machine that goes berserk; Charlie tightening bolts on the line until his motions become reflex actions that he cannot stop, not even in the street when a woman with large buttons on her coat approaches. In the oppressive world of Chaplin's factory, there is also prophetic use of a giant television screen on which the workers can be monitored in Big Brother fashion.

Chaplin's Tramp in *Modern Times* is forever at the mercy of his natural enemy, the law. It was a time of strikes, of battles for the right to belong to a union and bargain collectively, a time of political demonstrations by the masses of unemployed. Charlie sees a flag fall from a truck. Being a good Samaritan, he picks it up and chases after the truck to return it, and as a protest parade rounds a corner, he is suddenly running in front holding the flag. He is arrested as a radical leader.

When he meets Paulette Goddard as the Gamin, they become two against the world. The shack in which they live is their island of happiness, even though it looks like one of the Hooverville shacks of the down-and-out in the Depression. Goddard, perfectly complementing Chaplin in her role, finds a job as a dancer in a cabaret, and in turn, gets Charlie hired as a waiter. He is called upon to substitute for a singer. The public at last would have the opportunity to hear the voice that remained silent on screen during more than two decades of stardom. Chaplin provides a delightful outpouring of double-talk:

La spinach or la busho, cigaretto toto bello,
Ce rakish spagoletto, Ce le tu la tu la trois.
Senora de la tima, voulez-vous la taxi-meter,
Le jaunta sur la seata, Je le tu le tu le waaah.

The film also contains the neatly-executed, funny sequence with the blindfolded Charlie on roller skates moving closer and closer to the exposed edge of a balcony. Survival is the theme coursing through the film, which retains for its characters a glimmer of hope no matter how grave the day may seem.

Paulette Goddard recalled in 1976, during a conversation we had: "Charlie was the greatest acting teacher I have ever known. He would get up, show you how something should be done, do it all beautifully himself, and you knew exactly what he wanted and did it. There has never been anyone like him and there never will be."

A similarity has been noted between *Modern Times* and René Clair's satirization of assembly-line society in *A Nous la Liberté* (1931), and there were accusations that Chaplin had appropriated the idea. Tobis, the producers of Clair's film, had, according to Basil Wright in his excellent and comprehensive book, *The Long View*, "fallen into the hands of Dr. Goebbels, who caused an action to be taken out against Chaplin for plagiarism." Clair was compelled to be a prosecution witness, but he turned the occasion into an *hommage* to Chaplin, acknowledging that he had stolen plenty from him. The case was withdrawn. Chaplin gave his version of his film's origins in *My Autobiography*. He had been thinking of ways to achieve realism on the screen, and had also envisioned Goddard as a gamine whose relationship with the Tramp could offer lively possibilities for comedy. Then he remembered a conversation he had had with a reporter on the *New York World* who was interviewing him. Hearing that Chaplin was to visit Detroit, the reporter told him how industry was luring men from the farms and giving them jobs on a conveyor-belt system that made "nervous wrecks" of them.

"It was that conversation that gave me the idea for *Modern Times*," Chaplin wrote. "I used a feeding machine as a time-saving device, so that the workers could continue working during the lunch time. The factory sequence resolved itself in the Tramp having a nervous breakdown. The plot developed out of the natural sequence of events. After his cure, he gets arrested and meets a gamine who has also been arrested, for stealing bread. They meet in a police patrol car packed with offenders. From then on, the theme is about two nondescripts trying to get along in modern times. They are involved in the Depression, strikes, riots and unemployment. Paulette was dressed in rags. She almost wept when I put smudges on her face to make her look dirty. 'Those smudges are beauty spots,' I insisted." Chaplin dated his feeding machine idea to 1916 when he had considered making a feature about a trip to the moon that was to have been a satire on progress.

There is a body of opinion that ascribes Chaplin's most successful work to his silent period, particularly his shorts. Critics of *Modern Times* foreshadowed the disenchantment with Chaplin that began when he became more ambitious, as he did in moving outward in the thirties, forties, and fifties, toward films that attempted to comment on the great problems confronting mankind. Even many of his admirers maintained that he was becoming too pedantic and drifting away from the qualities that had made him unique.

Surely the opposite is the case. Chaplin, having mastered comic pantomime and aware of the new needs of the age of sound, explored ways of improving upon his art and making it more significant. The outstanding films he has given us in his later period confirm his greatness; his lesser achievements are but other facets of a genius not willing to adapt to what was popular or facile. *The Great Dictator* (1940) is an uproarious put-down of Hitler, Mussolini, and the theory of the Master Race. A celebrated scene in cinema is Chaplin, as Adenoid Hynkel, dancing his inspired comic ballet with a balloon representing the world he hopes to conquer. Playing two roles, as Hynkel and as a look-alike Jewish barber, was an idea of pure genius. Chaplin told me that he would not have used slapstick comedy in the scenes involving the beating of Jews had he known of the extermination camps: "Nobody knew at that time what was being done in these camps. Afterward, I saw the ovens and said, 'I don't believe it.' Had I known, I couldn't have done the picture the way I did." At the end of *The Great Dictator*, Chaplin makes his impassioned plea for a better world. At the time, there were those who insisted that it was too long and propagandistic. More likely, people did not want to face reality. The speech is not long, but a beautiful conclusion, in keeping with the film as a whole.

When Chaplin made *Monsieur Verdoux* (1947), he was also criticized for his theme of a murderer who kills individual women for their money, in contrast with those who make huge fortunes through mass killing in war. Verdoux's verbal fencing with a priest attempting to console him before execution also drew hostile comments. As political persecution tightened about Chaplin, the film was picketed and its distribution impeded. *Verdoux* is Chaplin's deepest, most philosophical film, combining wonderful comedy with irony.

Limelight (1952), a supreme mixture of humor, romance, and wistful reflection on life, was the last film Chaplin made in America. He had been castigated as a womanizer, rebuked for not becoming an American citizen, and called a Communist. When he sailed for Europe in 1952 during the McCarthy tempest, he was told he would have to prove his good moral character before he could return. His next film, *A King in New York*, released in Europe in 1957 but withheld by Chaplin from commercial showing in the United States until December 1973, was the only feature film of the period to grapple with McCarthyism, satirically or otherwise. Amazingly, although made so close to the actual hysteria, it is remarkably lacking in acrimony and again reveals Chaplin's gift for perspective. His turning a fire hose on the Congressional investigating committee washes away tyrants everywhere in one swoosh. This underrated film, while flawed, has much comic brilliance and bears reevaluation.

"I didn't do it with any bitterness," Chaplin reflected. "It has a very good performance by my son Michael and there's a lot of good stuff in that picture.

If a picture gives the opportunity for invention, I'll take it, and I don't care what the hell the consequences are. We made fun of a lot of things, like progressive education. The story naturally veered toward this young chap whom the FBI was trying to pressure to inform on his parents. But I wouldn't accept any ideas unless there was great comedy in them. I'm not a pamphleteer. I had great fun, and that's the only thing I'm interested in."

Chaplin insisted that he had no ill will toward the United States: "I'm introspective, and I thought, 'well a war [Korean] was going on and they were terrified of communism.' The FBI people asked why I followed the party line. I said: 'If you tell me what the party line is, I'll tell you whether I follow it or not.' They couldn't believe that I wasn't a Communist. Oh yes, I was sympathetic to anybody who was hard up and needed help. That's all my politics ever got into."

By 1972, the political climate in the United States had changed and some small amends were proffered for the maltreatment Chaplin had received. He was invited back to New York by the Film Society of Lincoln Center, which staged a gala to salute him, and he received a special award from the Academy of Motion Picture Arts and Sciences in Hollywood. Chaplin talked to me of making another film, to be called *The Freak*, for which he was writing a screenplay about a man who discovers a creature, half-woman, half-bird. When the aged director, who had difficulty getting in and out of a chair, suddenly flapped his arms rapidly to show the fluttering of the bird-woman's wings, the movements were delightfully reminiscent of the young Charlie. Even though production of the film was subsequently announced as a future Chaplin project, it was clear that he was too feeble for another hurrah, and that the last film in Chaplin's career would be *A Countess From Hong Kong* (1967), which starred Sophia Loren and Marlon Brando. He died Christmas Day, 1977.

Just as *Modern Times* was a silent in the age of talkies, *Countess* was at odds with its time, having been made in the typically simple, old-fashioned Chaplin manner when it had become customary to film on location and use intricate camerawork, jump cuts, and frenetic editing effects. Chaplin, perhaps sensing the needs of the individual in this frenzied world, had made a romantic film that said love was all that mattered. Most critics tore into him vituperatively. Andrew Sarris was one of the few who shared my feelings. He wrote in the *Village Voice*:

> *A Countess from Hong Kong* is far from Chaplin's past peaks, but one scene with a momentarily irrepressible butler (Patrick Cargill) in Sophia's bedroom is as comically exhilarating as anything Chaplin has ever done. Chaplin might have been more modern, of course. He might have read selections from *Lady Chatterley's Lover* at five dollars a throw. Better still, he might have displayed footage featuring Chaplin

directing Loren and Brando in *A Countess from Hong Kong* and called the whole shebang *8o½*. Unfortunately, Chaplin will die as he has lived, an unregenerate classicist who believes in making movies he can feel in his frayed lace-valentine heart.

Chaplin's insights in *Modern Times* are equally applicable to humanity trying somehow to muddle through a new era in perpetual peril from forces it cannot or will not control; today, the Tramp would also be confronted by the threat of obliteration by nuclear weaponry, over-population, mass hunger, and environmental destruction. Silent *Modern Times* still speaks to us while it makes us laugh. And who cannot use that dash of vintage optimism we feel as the Tramp and his lady walk arm in arm and full of hope down the long road toward the unknown.

In 1972, Chaplin himself no longer had that streak of optimism. "When you see the size of the earth, you know there'll be another war sooner or later, when somebody will try to grab something, and it's a depressing thought – well, when that's on, I'll be all through."

MODERN TIMES
USA (United Artists) 1936

Cast

A Worker	CHARLES CHAPLIN
A Gamin	PAULETTE GODDARD
Café Proprietor	HENRY BERGMAN
Big Bill	STANLEY J. SANFORD
Mechanic	CHESTER CONKLIN
Burglar	HANK MANN
Sheriff Couler	STANLEY BLYSTONE
Company President	ALLAN GARCIA
Convicts	DICK ALEXANDER, FRANK MORAN
Chaplain	CECIL REYNOLDS
Chaplain's Wife	MYRA MCKINNEY
Governor	LLOYD INGRAHAM
Addict	LOUIS NATHEAUX
Workman	HEINIE CONKLIN

and MURDOCH MCQUARRIE, WILFRED LUCAS, EDWARD LE SAINT, FRED MALTESTA, SAM STEIN, JUANA SUTTON, TED OLIVER, EDWARD KIMBALL, JOHN RAND, WALTER JAMES

Running time....................................85 minutes
Produced by..............................CHARLES CHAPLIN
Directed by ....CHARLES CHAPLIN
Story and screenplay by.....................CHARLES CHAPLIN
Photography by...............ROLLAND TOTHEROH, IRA MORGAN
Assistant Directors ....CARTER DE HAVEN, HENRY BERGMAN
Art Directors ....CHARLES D. HALL, J. RUSSELL SPENCER
Music by...................CHARLES CHAPLIN; LEO DANIDERFF
"Je Cherche Après Titine"
Music Arrangers................EDWARD POWELL, DAVID RAKSIN
Music Director ....ALFRED NEWMAN
Production Managers ....ALFRED REEVES, JACK WILSON

1937

Grand Illusion

Left to right: Erich von Stroheim as aristocratic Colonel von Rauffenstein, Pierre Fresnay as Captain de Boeldieu, Jean Gabin as Maréchal.

The Great French Cinema

JEAN RENOIR'S masterpiece, *La Grande Illusion,* the work of a genius of cinema, vividly epitomizes the achievements of a noble period in the history of film. Audiences becoming attuned to the idea of film as art were deeply affected by the level of maturity of the great French films of the thirties. Depth of character, concern with basic problems of life, and truthful portrayal of the human condition made these films much more vital than the finest Hollywood product. *La Grande Illusion* not only represents this heritage but is the best antiwar film ever made.

Fittingly, it was in France, where the Lumière brothers had their pioneer showing in 1895, that cinema received early recognition as an art form. Ciné-clubs and art houses that supported independent, avant-garde films existed in the early twenties, when cosmopolitan Paris was pulsating with new ideas in the arts. Renoir began his film career during this exciting era, as did Spanish director Luis Buñuel, who, with Salvador Dali, made the daring *Un Chien Andalou* (1928) and *L'Age d'Or* (1930) in France. Another distinguished director emerging from the twenties was René Clair, whose films, including *An Italian Straw Hat* (1927), *Sous les Toits de Paris* (1930), *Le Million* (1931), *A Nous la Liberté* (1931), and *Le Dernier Milliardaire* (1934) displayed his talent for inventiveness and satire.

Among other important directors of the 1930s was Jean Vigo, who died at the age of twenty-nine, but left us his brilliant *Zéro de Conduite*, which soon after its 1933 release was banned until 1945, and *L'Atalante* (1934). Marcel Pagnol was another creative force, and he is fondly appreciated for the trilogy starring Raimu, *Marius* (1931) and *Fanny* (1932), which he wrote, and *César* (1936), which he also directed, as well as *La Femme du Boulanger* (*The Baker's Wife*, 1938) and *La Fille du Puisatier* (*The Well-Digger's Daughter,* 1940). Marcel Carné, in collaboration with writer Jacques Prévert, directed the haunting *Le Quai des Brumes* (1938) and *Le Jour se Lève* (1939), and eventually, during World War II, made one of the all-time greats *Les Enfants du Paradis* (1945). In the 1930s, Julien Duvivier was acclaimed for *Un Carnet de Bal* (1937) and *La Fin du Jour* (1939); Jacques Feyder for *La Kermesse Héroique* (1935); Jean Cocteau for *Le Sang d'un Poète* (1932). It is impossible to speak of the development of cinema without looking back with reverence and affection to this wonderful French epoch.

There were, of course, other films about the Great War before *La Grande Illusion,* including Lewis Milestone's persuasive, American-made *All Quiet on the Western Front* (1930), which deserves its place of honor. In Renoir's charming, eloquent, and informative autobiography, *My Life and My Films,* published in 1974 when he was eighty, the director recalled one of the reasons he made *La Grande Illusion:* "Excepting *All Quiet on the Western Front,* I had not seen a single film giving a true picture of the men who did the fighting." Renoir's film, a high point in humanist storytelling, went far beyond the "war is hell" theme. Although concerned with the horror and ironies of war, and the futile waste of lives, *La Grande Illusion* probed class allegiances and divisions. It exposed the crumbling social strata of the period, dealt with self-defeating nationalism, anti-Semitism, and outmoded concepts of military honor. Renoir, apprehensive over the prospect of another war, sought solutions in the rearrangement of society and the good will that could exist among individuals. In this age of threatened nuclear obliteration, the film glows with the optimism of a period in which it was easier to believe that feelings of brotherhood could surmount international barriers and prevent war.

An encounter Renoir had during World War I provided the story idea for *La Grande Illusion*. Having been wounded in the leg, he was transferred from the trenches to a flying squadron and became a pilot. Once, when he was in danger of being shot down by the Germans, a Major Pinsard, an ace fighter-pilot, came to his aid. In 1934, they met again by chance, when Renoir was on location shooting *Toni*. Pinsard's subsequent war experiences were remarkable. He had been shot down seven times over enemy territory, had been imprisoned seven times, and had escaped seven times.

In the film, written by Renoir and Belgian screenwriter Charles Spaak, two French officers, Maréchal (Jean Gabin), a former mechanic, and Captain de Boeldieu (Pierre Fresnay), are shot down in combat and captured. The commander of the German squadron is haughty Colonel von Rauffenstein (Erich von Stroheim), who looks upon war as a game of honor among men. He treats his prisoners with the courtesy due the heroic vanquished by the gallant victors, according to the gentlemanly rules. Renoir quickly gets at the heart of class similarities and differences through von Rauffenstein's obvious affinity with de Boeldieu, an aristocrat and career officer like himself.

Maréchal and de Boeldieu are interned in a camp inhabited by French, Russian, and British prisoners of diverse backgrounds and class. Renoir's prison scenes are extraordinary. He succeeds in evoking the impatience, the boredom, the feeling of being in limbo, and the longing of the incarcerated for their home environments. Through the relationships, the various antagonisms surface. In its simplest terms, *La Grande Illusion* is an escape film, within which format Renoir gives expression to his profound observations.

The one hope of the Frenchmen is to escape, and it takes them months of grueling work to dig a tunnel. They are transferred to a maximum security prison before they can put it to use.

The commandant of this fortress is none other than von Rauffenstein – himself in a sense confined there because terrible combat injuries preclude his being on active duty. He still serves his country, although he finds his new role repugnant, and he maintains the class bearing in which he takes such pride. In de Boeldieu he finds a kindred spirit, a bond of breeding and culture. De Boeldieu has more in common with his enemy than with his fellow Frenchmen. A new plan for escape is conceived, and a Jew, Rosenthal (Marcel Dalio), is in the scheme along with Maréchal and de Boeldieu. Here again, in their relationship, Renoir focuses on the class and cultural differences, the implicit anti-Semitism, and also on the need to submerge such differences to pursue a common goal.

De Boeldieu realizes that he represents a world for which there is no future, as the new democratic society that is taking shape will be for men like Maréchal and Rosenthal. To enable them to flee, he volunteers to create a diversion and climbs to the top of a turret. Von Rauffenstein pleads with him to come down, reluctantly shooting him when he refuses.

Next, Renoir is concerned with the relationship of Maréchal and Rosenthal, who succeed in getting away. As they trudge across the snowy countryside, Rosenthal, whose foot is injured, lags behind. Maréchal turns against his comrade, berates him for being a Jew and a burden, and leaves him. He thinks better of it, however, and returns. Cold and hungry, they continue their trek, happening upon a farmhouse. The film's most poignant portion now begins. The lonely widow of a German soldier (Dita Parlo) allows them to stay with her, and she and Maréchal develop a mutual affection. In this interlude the couple are left to their own feelings, uncomplicated by war, national boundaries, ideas of honor, and loyalties. The film gives us an inkling of what could be. But this does not last. Maréchal and Rosenthal, drawn by their ties to home, must move on, and the tension mounts as they make their way toward the Swiss frontier and safety. A German patrol comes along, and for a moment it looks as though the Frenchmen will die. However, they cross the border in time and the Germans do not shoot out of respect for territorial legalities. The men are safe at last.

The film is a work of rare perfection with its understatement, incisive characterizations, muted tensions, and excellent performances. Gabin plays his role with the kind of quiet virility that became his trademark; Fresnay and Dalio are superb. As for von Stroheim's von Rauffenstein, his bearing, aloofness, and style are overwhelming. Renoir revered von Stroheim as a brilliant director who had been battered by the commercial pressures of Hollywood, where his independence, extravagance, and obstinate refusal to be standardized made him an outcast. Reverence for von Stroheim did not

Von Stroheim as von Rauffenstein, prison commandant

make it easier for Renoir to work with him. They argued; the dispute upset them both to the point of tears, and Renoir swore he would rather abandon the film than quarrel with someone for whom he had so much respect. They made up effusively and all was well after that, von Stroheim dutifully obeying directorial instructions.

For three years Renoir had been trying to raise money to make *La Grande Illusion*, but could not arouse sufficient interest. There was resistance to an outlook that did not present the Germans as evil stereotypes. Renoir credited Gabin with finally finding a producer. Although the film was well received at first in France, as a new threat of war grew the pacificism and humanity it expressed were incompatible with the prevailing mood. In New York, its first run lasted six months, but in Germany Goebbels banned it and used his influence with Mussolini to prevent it from receiving a prize at the Venice Film Festival. Renoir also had trouble with his 1939 masterpiece, *La Régle du Jeu* (*The Rules of the Game*). A witty, sophisticated satire, it is a devastating appraisal of the upper classes, and a metaphor for the decadence of society on the brink of war. (Renoir was no longer optimistic.) It engendered anger when it was released in France in the summer of 1939, and by October it was banned, the ban continuing during the Occupation. The film was decimated by cuts, and it was only years later that it was reconstructed with Renoir's assistance. *La Grande Illusion* was also mutilated by censors and the original negative was destroyed in wartime bombing. A negative discovered in Munich after the war, and a print he found in the United States in 1957, enabled Renoir to restore the film.

Renoir's interest in film began during the Great War. In his autobiography, he described how his actor brother, Pierre, introduced him to the films of Charlie Chaplin (known in France as Charlot) while he was in Paris on leave. He became addicted to the cinema; whenever he could, he would see as many as three films a day. Renoir was excited by the work of D.W. Griffith, and later by that of von Stroheim, but to him Chaplin was supreme. It was not Renoir's obsession with film that led to his becoming a director instead of remaining a spectator. His father, the renowned impressionist painter Pierre Auguste Renoir, distrusted any work that was not manual, and had set up a pottery studio and oven for Jean and his brother Claude. Renoir's then wife, once one of his father's models, wanted to become an actress, and in 1924, he "set forth into the world of cinema" with the sole purpose of making his wife a star. But he succumbed to the challenges and pleasures of directing, and over a span of forty-five years was to direct thirty-nine films in four countries, act, write most of his screenplays (either by himself or in collaboration with others), as well as direct two plays, write a play, a story for a ballet, a novel, an opera libretto, a biography of his father, and his autobiography. A film scenario and a novel were due for publication at his death in February 1979.

La Fille de l'Eau (1924), starring his wife, Catherine Hessling, was

Renoir's first directorial effort; its ideas reflected his boredom with French films, which he found too intellectual and bourgeois, with what he felt to be an overemphasis on literature and drama. The lack of interest in *La Fille de l'Eau* on the part of regular distribution channels disappointed him. However, extracts were shown in an art house and the applause gave him courage to continue. During his silent period, Renoir's courage fluctuated according to the success or failure of his projects, but he persisted, even when it meant selling treasured paintings left him by his father.

Unlike many, Renoir welcomed the arrival of sound. "The purpose of all artistic creation is the knowledge of man, and is not the human voice the best means of conveying the personality of a human being?" he asked in his autobiography. The first talkie he wanted to make was *La Chienne* (1931), but before undertaking that he had to pass a test, *On Purge Bébé*; because of his reputation for extravagance, the producers wanted to see if he could direct a sound film economically. *La Chienne*, a brilliant drama starring the great Michel Simon, was shown in retrospective at the 1975 New York Film Festival and opened commercially for the first time in the United States in 1976. It holds up magnificently, illustrating Renoir's compassion for his characters, who are neither good nor evil, but are portrayed in dimension. *La Chienne* also reveals his ability to convey reality, not just by photographic fidelity, but by the truthful artistic overview that deepens reality. Among other films Renoir made in the 1930s are *Boudu Sauvé des Eaux* (1932), *Madame Bovary* (1934), *Toni* (1935), *Le Crime de Monsieur Lange* (1936), *Les Bas-Fonds* (1936), and *La Bête Humaine* (1938).

Renoir sought methods to make his films lifelike, and his solutions had significant influence on many other filmmakers. Placing much value on actors, he favored filming in long sequences so that they could develop their scenes, as on the stage. While he appreciated the value of close-ups, Renoir was striving as best he could to tie action in the background to characters in the foreground, although he did not have available the more advanced equipment that would permit the kind of deep focus shots that distinguished *Citizen Kane* in 1941. His work was in the opposite direction from Eisenstein's, Renoir relying not upon the effects of montage, but upon his ability to portray life as fully as possible in his individual shots. Renoir's scenes are rich in texture and atmosphere, carefully capturing the essence of his characters, their relationships, and their environment.

After war broke out and France was invaded, Renoir managed to obtain an exit visa and sailed via Lisbon to New York, where he was met by Robert Flaherty. Taking the opportunity offered him to go to Hollywood, he soon found himself up against typical policy problems when he went to work for Twentieth Century-Fox and Darryl Zanuck. It was a painful process to convince Zanuck to let him shoot *Swamp Water* (1941), a film about a man falsely accused of murder, in its natural Georgia locale instead of on the Fox lot, and Renoir was not permitted final editing on the film. Other films of his Hollywood sojourn include *This Land Is Mine* (1943), about the occupation of France; a short, *Salute to France* (made in 1944); *The Southerner* (1945); *Diary of a Chambermaid* (1946); and *The Woman on the Beach* (1947). Renoir's Hollywood career behind him, he went on to India to make his superb film *The River* (1951), then returned for a while to France to continue his work, which includes *French Cancan, Le Déjeuner sur l'Herbe*, and *Le Petit Théâtre de Jean Renoir* in 1969, presented first on television.

The fertile New Wave period in French filmmaking (see *Breathless*) erupted in the late 1950s. Interestingly, although this movement was fueled on revolt against the past, New Wave filmmaker Jean-Luc Godard wrote in *Cahiers du Cinéma*'s December 1957 issue, which was devoted to Renoir: "Thirty years of improvisation have made Renoir the world's finest technician. He achieves in one shot what others do in ten; and where they make do with one, Renoir can do without." Elated with Renoir's ability to adopt and revolutionize live television filming techniques, Godard, in a subsequent article in *Arts*, April 15, 1959, cited this as proof that "he really is the groundswell behind the New Wave, and that he still leads the world in sincerity and audacity." Renoir, for his part, dedicated his autobiography to "those filmmakers who are known to the public as the 'New Wave' and whose preoccupations are also mine."

French cinema of the 1930s, characterized so perfectly by *La Grande Illusion*, raised the standards for films the world over. Renoir's contribution and influence not only encompass the purity of his style, but his deep humanism. In an age of increasing hype and violence, such a legacy is to be cherished.

GRAND ILLUSION
(La Grande Illusion)
FRANCE 1937

Cast

Maréchal .... Jean Gabin
Captain de Boeldieu .... Pierre Fresnay
Colonel von Rauffenstein .... Erich von Stroheim
Rosenthal .... Marcel Dalio
Elsa .... Dita Parlo
Prisoners of war –
  the actor .... Julien Carette
  the engineer .... Gaston Modot
  the teacher .... Jean Dasté
  a French soldier .... Georges Péclet
  an English officer .... Jacques Becker
and Sylvain Itkine, Werner Florian,
Claude Sainval, Michael Salina

Running time .... originally 114 minutes
Production Company .... Les Réalisations d'Art Cinématographique
Production Director for R.A.C. .... Raymond Blondy
Produced by .... Frank Rollmer, Albert Pinkovitch
Directed by .... Jean Renoir
Screenplay by .... Charles Spaak, Jean Renoir
Assistant Director .... Jacques Becker
Director of Photography .... Christian Matras
Cameramen .... Claude Renoir, Bourreaud, Jean Bourgoin
Technical Consultant .... Carl Koch
Set Design .... Eugène Lourié
Editing .... Marguerite Renoir, Marthe Huguet; restored version (1958) – Renée Lichtig
Script Girl .... Gourdji
Stills .... Sam Levin
Sound .... Joseph de Bretagne
Music .... Joseph Kosma; song by Vincent Telly and A. Valsien

coa

Claire Trevor and John Wayne in Stagecoach.

Western Tradition and Myth

AS WITH THE gangster film, the Western is more than a genre. Those who have studied the Western have found it to be an integral part of America's cultural pattern, and have noted its relationship to the heroic folklore and literature of other countries. No category of American film has greater worldwide appeal, and it is significant that the first influential film to tell a story was a Western, Edwin S. Porter's 1903 one-reeler, *The Great Train Robbery*. The lore of the frontier, as perceived through the eyes of white society, became a natural source of action stories that were not about some distant place, but were indigenous to America. The frontier days were not very far behind when film began; it was logical to look to the period before and after the Civil War for plot material. Westerns provided ready morality tales with the traditional antagonism between good and evil. They were a convenient format for the exposure of greedy railroad tycoons and corrupt administrations. They also offered justification for the genocide practiced against the Indians; generations of children emerged from seeing Westerns secure in the assumption that shooting Indians was not only normal but fun.

At the beginning of the 1930s, gangsters toting machine-guns were becoming more popular than cowboys in the film image of America; by mid-decade, the cowboys were recouping. *Stagecoach*, the landmark that defines the species, reemphasized the Western's special place in cinema history and set standards for other filmmakers. Its director, John Ford, has had a strong influence through his overall craftsmanship, style, and use of natural locations. Japanese director Akira Kurosawa, in talking about Ford's effect on his work and the importance of Westerns, has said: "Good Westerns are liked by everyone. Since humans are weak they want to see good people and great heroes. Westerns have been done over and over again and in the process a kind of grammar has evolved. I have learned from this grammar of the Western." Directors in many countries consider Ford high on the list of filmmakers who have influenced them. Among them, of course, is Orson Welles; Welles has said that he saw *Stagecoach* repeatedly before making *Citizen Kane*.

The post-sound tendency was to shoot Westerns in a studio using projected backgrounds. Ford's use of Monument Valley, Utah, for outdoor sequences in *Stagecoach* was an impressive contribution. Other filmmakers followed suit, and real scenery became a basic ingredient for anyone attempting a Western saga. There is argument over how much Ford actually shot on location and how much he filmed in a studio. Ford disputed the allegation that only his second unit filmed in Monument Valley, insisting that the first unit was busy there too. Whatever the breakdown, on screen the result is that of a film set in imposing natural surroundings.

Ford, who made films on many subjects, showed his affinity for Westerns in the silent days, beginning with two-reelers. *The Iron Horse*, made in 1924, was a pioneering effort concerning the construction of the first transcontinental railroad. That and *The Covered Wagon* of James Cruze in 1923 stand as leading examples of their period. Western stars have long been among the most dependable attractions. G.M. Anderson of *The Great Train Robbery* became an early Western star known as Broncho Billy and was followed by a long line of successors in silents and talkies, including William S. Hart, Tom Mix, Harry Carey, Hoot Gibson, William Boyd, Randolph Scott, Gary Cooper, John Wayne, and such modern box-office heroes as Clint Eastwood and Charles Bronson. In the thirties, when Hollywood was scrounging for new ways to entice audiences, the singing cowboy arrived, Gene Autry being the best known of these, especially for his *Tumbling Tumbleweeds* (1935). With *Stagecoach*, Ford was to launch Wayne as the most durable Western macho hero. Before that, apart from Raoul Walsh's *The Big Trail* (1930), he had appeared in grade B Westerns. Once seen as the Ringo Kid in *Stagecoach*, Wayne became a superstar, with Westerns his most comfortable habitat. No matter what anyone might say about his wooden acting style, his drawl, or his right-wing politics, he repeatedly proved his reliability at the box office.

According to Ford's reminiscence in *Action*, the magazine of the Directors Guild of America, the film's producer, Walter Wanger, had suggested Gary Cooper for the part of Ringo. Cooper was already a well-established star, his Western pictures including *The Virginian* (1929) and *The Plainsman* (1936). Ford said that hiring Cooper would be too expensive, as was Wanger's idea of teaming Marlene Dietrich with Coop. Wanger asked Ford whom he had in mind.

> "Well, there's a boy I know who used to be assistant prop man and bit player for me," I said. "His name was Michael Morrison, but he's making five-day Westerns and he calls himself John Wayne now."
> "Do you think he's any good?" [asked Wanger.]
> "Yes, I think so," I said. "And we can get him for peanuts."

The director also suggested Claire Trevor, "a helluvan actress," for Dallas, the gold-hearted prostitute driven out of town by the moralists.

Dudley Nichols, who collaborated with Ford on many of his films, including the masterly classic *The Informer* (1935), wrote the script from a story Ford had found in *Collier's* (Ford later described it as Guy de Maupassant's "La Boule de Suif" turned into a Western). The plot line for *Stagecoach* relies upon the bringing together of a group of clichéd characters to face a common danger while their individual lives are, in one way or another, in a state of crisis. Critic Judith Crist has aptly referred to the film as "*Grand Hotel*-on-wheels."

Meeting the characters who take the stagecoach remains entertaining, even if you have met them before, because the performers are such wonderful examples of the character actors who appeared in thirties' films. Thomas Mitchell, cast as the whiskey-soaked Dr. Josiah Boone, won an Oscar for best supporting actor for his *Stagecoach* role. (Nineteen thirty-nine was also the year of *Gone With the Wind* in which Mitchell gave another excellent performance as Scarlett's father.) Donald Meek plays Samuel Peacock, a whiskey drummer the sight of whose caseful of samples prompted Doc Boone to urge him to come along. Louise Platt is the pregnant Lucy Mallory, determined to join her cavalry-officer husband. John Carradine, as gentleman gambler Hatfield, offers to protect her. Driving the stage is a perennial favorite, hoarse-voiced Andy Devine, as Buck. George Bancroft as Sheriff Curley Wilcox rides shotgun. Joining the group are Berton Churchill as Gatewood, a banker absconding with his bank's money, and Wayne as the Ringo Kid, a good guy who has escaped from jail to track down the killers of his father and brother. The scene is now set for the drama, of which there is a superabundance.

With Geronimo and his forces a lurking menace, there must be the inevitable attack by Indians, and heroics by Wayne that include some spectacular leaping from horse to horse. Stunt man Yakima Canutt performed the feat in Wayne's place. Would it surprise anyone to know that the U.S. Cavalry rides to the rescue? Personal problems are sorted out; Ringo takes his revenge upon the Plummer brothers; he and Dallas fall in love and go off together across the border to Mexico. The film casts the banker as the villain, but shows sympathy for Dallas, maintaining the idea of the independent prostitute as the most understanding companion for the Western hero.

Viewed today, the character conglomeration seems even more clichéd and contrived in light of the many imitations. Films like *Airport, The Towering Inferno, Ship of Fools*, and *The Poseidon Adventure*, all follow the tradition of depositing a group of characters in crisis situations, whether aloft, on land, or at sea. It is the sweep of Ford's direction that energizes *Stagecoach*, and keeps the film exciting even after repeated viewings. Once the coach begins to move toward destiny, the pace is fast, and the action attention-grabbing. "This is one stagecoach that's powered by a Ford," quipped critic Frank S. Nugent in the *New York Times*. (Nugent, later turning screenwriter, scripted for Ford on many films, among them *Fort Apache, She Wore a Yellow Rib-*

bon, Wagonmaster, The Quiet Man, The Searchers, and *Donovan's Reef.*) Ford provided *Stagecoach* with virtually all the components that make Westerns appealing. (In 1966, there was a cloddish remake directed by Gordon Douglas and starring Alex Cord, Ann-Margret, Bing Crosby, Red Buttons, Michael Conners, and Robert Cummings.)

Stagecoach was instantly appreciated on its release, its success inspiring others to produce their own new Westerns. Nugent asserted in his review: "In one superbly expansive gesture . . . John Ford has swept aside ten years of artifice and talkie compromise and has made a motion picture that sings a song of camera. It moves, and how beautifully it moves. . . ." In another year *Stagecoach* might have garnered more awards, but 1939 was Hollywood's bumper year with *Gone With the Wind, Wuthering Heights, The Wizard of Oz, Mr. Smith Goes to Washington, Ninotchka,* and *Goodbye, Mr. Chips* among the contenders. To the credit of the New York Film Critics, they defied the *Gone With the Wind* sweep and named John Ford best director for *Stagecoach.* In 1935, he had won the group's best director and best film awards for *The Informer*, which also earned him an Academy Award as best director.

Many embellishments have been imposed on the Western since *Stagecoach.* In 1943, Howard Hughes decided to add cleavage, and Jane Russell starred in the clinker, *The Outlaw.* That same year yielded a classic – William Wellman's *The Ox-Bow Incident*, starring Henry Fonda in a dramatic examination of the anatomy of a lynching. John Huston's *The Treasure of the Sierre Madre* (1948), which is on many lists of favorites, teams Humphrey Bogart, Tim Holt, and Walter Huston in a gritty, grueling story of man's lust for gold. Another significant film of 1948 is Howard Hawks's *Red River*, with John Wayne and Montgomery Clift. Two of the most admired Westerns of the 1950s are Fred Zinnemann's *High Noon* (1952), starring Gary Cooper, and George Stevens's *Shane* (1953), with Alan Ladd, Brandon DeWilde, Van Heflin, and Jean Arthur.

It is possible to follow social change through the Western. The assaults on individualism in the McCarthy era may explain why such emphasis was put on the lonely hero against the crowd in the early 1950s. Concern for the disappearance of the cherished qualities of the Old West gave rise to analogous films set in the modern West. John Huston's underrated *The Misfits* (1961), with Clark Gable and Marilyn Monroe in their last screen roles, and a script by Arthur Miller, abhors the violation of nature in the roundup of mustangs for use as dog food. A year later, there was David Miller's exceptional *Lonely Are the Brave*, starring Kirk Douglas as a loner trying to preserve the vanished lifestyle of the vintage West. A similar theme is to be found in *The Ballad of Cable Hogue* (1970), an unusually lyrical film by Sam Peckinpah, starring Jason Robards as an individualist in the Old West defeated by encroaching civilization. Martin Ritt's forceful *Hud* (1963) is another example of the modern Western, this one stressing a father-son relationship and clash of values, with Paul Newman, Patricia Neal, and Melvyn Douglas giving stalwart performances.

John Wayne is killed in Mark Rydell's *The Cowboys* (1972), which has an upsetting backlash theme involving teenagers being turned into vengeful vigilantes, skilled in the art of killing. Tom Laughlin's *Billy Jack* (1971), an awkward, wooden, contemporary Western, appealed to a large, predominantly young audience by posing highly charged moral issues. *Billy Jack* was important in the industry because of its widespread employment of the four walling distribution method (the renting of a theater at a flat rate, enabling the producer-distributor to reap the profits without any split with the theater), and its use of saturation advertising.

From Italy in the 1960s came the "Spaghetti Westerns," with Sergio Leone the leading practitioner, best known for *A Fistful of Dollars* (1964). It catapulted its star, Clint Eastwood, "The Man With No Name," into a durable box-office attraction. Leone's *Once Upon a Time in the West* (1969) co-stars Henry Fonda and Charles Bronson, the latter also achieving box-office clout in the United States on the impetus of his fame in Europe. Spain became a popular location for Westerns, whether its ludicrous domestic variety or made by foreigners. When director Burt Kennedy asked John Ford if he had seen any of the Italian and Spanish Westerns, Ford replied: "You're kidding!" In Japan, the samurai films bear comparison with Westerns as ritualistic entertainment stemming from national folklore.

Satirical Westerns have materialized periodically. Among the oldies is another product of Hollywood's golden year of 1939, George Marshall's *Destry Rides Again*, co-starring James Stewart and Marlene Dietrich. Jane Fonda and Lee Marvin caused a stir in 1965 in Elliot Silverstein's rowdy spoof, *Cat Ballou*. The wildest is Mel Brooks's *Blazing Saddles* (1974), starring Cleavon Little as a black sheriff in a white town, Gene Wilder as a has-been gunfighter whose shootin' hand is more than a little shaky, and Madeline Kahn as a sexy saloon singer, Lili Von Schtupp, a 1970s version of Dietrich in *Destry Rides Again*.

In recent years, filmmakers have begun to discover that there were blacks in the West, and that even where there were not, placing them in action roles could appeal to black audiences. Much of this tends to be exploitational, but there have been honorable efforts, such as Sydney Pollack's *The Scalphunters* (1968), starring Burt Lancaster and Ossie Davis, and Sidney Poitier's *Buck and the Preacher* (1972), co-starring Poitier and Harry Belafonte.

The Western is in dire need of a revisionist overhaul to replace myth with truth. The role of guns in the West, so directly connected to the "right to bear arms" cry of the lobbyists against gun control, has been encrusted with mythology. Although it is true that even youngsters on the frontier were given guns, the portrait of a West populated by sharpshooters is fantasy rather than fact. Carl Bakal, in his book *The Right to Bear Arms*, made the sobering observation that the legendary lawmen and gunmen were not usually sure shots: "Beyond a distance of 20 feet, anybody hit would be hit by accident. The long, wary walk down a dusty main street was usually nothing more than a bluff-calling charade of a duel with no one getting hurt. . . ." In his opinion, the "crude custom" had nothing to do with the winning of the West and the gun was mainly "a somewhat romantic tool of violence and virility."

Some myths about life in the West, the alleged heroes, and the role of the Indians, have been challenged in a series of unusual films that may be harbingers of the coloration Westerns could assume in the future. Arthur Penn's *Little Big Man* (1970) reverses the General Custer legend, portraying Custer as a vain psychopathic killer. The film extols the Indian heritage and sharply questions the values vested in the drive to make good in the West. Innovative Robert Altman's *McCabe and Mrs. Miller* (1971) deals a double blow in style and content. His vision of the West is understated and naturalistic, emphasizing the grubbiness of frontier existence. Altman goes further in destroying myths with his 1976 film *Buffalo Bill and the Indians or Sitting Bull's History Lesson.* Set in the confines of a Wild West show, the picture mocks the inflated reputation of Buffalo Bill and reveals the stoic heroism of Sitting Bull, reduced to little more than a show business foil for Buffalo Bill's exploitation.

The notion that life in the West was glamorous is also deflated by Sam Peckinpah in *The Wild Bunch*, a controversial, bloody film depicting its leading characters as has-beens desperately trying to be the tough men they once were, or thought they were. Some critics extolled Peckinpah's scenes of slow-motion killing for their grace and beauty. Others branded as a glorification of brutality his lingering on the details of brains being splattered.

George Roy Hill's *Butch Cassidy and the Sundance Kid* (1969), written by William Goldman, and starring Paul Newman as Butch and Robert Redford as the Kid, is an off-beat celebration of the anti-hero. It delighted young audiences and became the biggest-grossing Western. "I didn't intentionally set out to destroy any myths," Goldman told me, "but I was fascinated by the story and the fact that they would run off to a distant country to die." He believes the turmoil of Vietnam may have played a role in the picture's popularity with young people. Remarking upon the inverted values, Goldman noted: "The top box-office stars of today, such as Eastwood and Bronson, now play characters who would have been shot by the good guys in the old Westerns." Redford, in a recent conversation, sought an explanation for the popularity of Butch and the Kid: "They were both romantic characters, but also children, helpless kids, living out a fantasy, living outside the law. It was a freewheeling time and there was space – a period in our history that was wild. Visually, the frontier was fun, with a lot of humor.

Newman described the film best when he called it 'an adult fairy tale.'"

The destruction of myths and the inversion of values illustrate how the Western continues to be a favorite forum for expressing attitudes important to each period. The genre's remarkable elasticity is undoubtedly due to its being so deeply ingrained in the historical and psychological make-up of America. Westerns have demonstrated their permanence, and in all likelihood critics and sociologists will continue to ponder their meaning. John Ford's 1939 classic, *Stagecoach,* persists as the landmark reference point.

STAGECOACH
USA (United Artists) 1939

Cast

Dallas	CLAIRE TREVOR
The Ringo Kid	JOHN WAYNE
Buck	ANDY DEVINE
Hatfield	JOHN CARRADINE
Dr. Josiah Boone	THOMAS MITCHELL
Lucy Mallory	LOUISE PLATT
Sheriff Curley Wilcox	GEORGE BANCROFT
Samuel Peacock	DONALD MEEK
Henry Gatewood	BERTON CHURCHILL
Lt. Blanchard	TIM HOLT
Luke Plummer	TOM TYLER
Chris	CHRIS PIN MARTIN
Yakima, his wife	ELVIRA RIOS
Billy Pickett	FRANCIS FORD
Mrs. Pickett	MARGA DAIGHTON
Billy Pickett, Jr.	KENT ODELL
Stunt men	YAKIMA CANUTT, CHIEF BIG TREE
Telegraph Operator	HARRY TENBROOK
Jerry, barman	JACK PENNICK
Express Agent	PAUL MCVEY
Capt. Whitney	CORNELIUS KEEFE
Mrs. Nancy Whitney	FLORENCE LAKE
Sheriff	LOUIS MASON
Mrs. Gatewood	BRENDA FOWLER
Capt. Sickel	WALTER MCGRAIL
Hank Plummer	JOSEPH RICKSON
Ike Plummer	VESTER PEGG
Sergeant	WILLIAM HOFFER
Capt. Simmons	BRYANT WASHBURN

Dr. Boone's housekeeper .... NORA CECIL
Dancing girls .... HELEN GIBSON, DOROTHY ANNLEBY
Ranchers .... BUDDY ROOSEVELT, BILL CODY
Indian Chief .... CHIEF WHITE HORSE
Sheriff of Lordsburg .... DUKE LEE
Lucy's baby .... MARY KATHLEEN WALKER
and ED BRADY, STEVE CLEMENTE, THEODORE LARCH,
FRITZI BRUNETTE, LEONARD TRAINOR, CHRIS PHILLIPS,
TEX DRISCOLL, TEDDY BILLINGS, JOHN ECKERT, AL LEE,
JACK MOHR, PATSY DOYLE, WIGGIE BLOWNE, MARGARET SMITH

Running time .... 96 minutes
Produced by .... WALTER WANGER
Directed by .... JOHN FORD
Screenplay by .... DUDLEY NICHOLS, from the story
"Stage to Lordsburg" by ERNEST HAYCOX
Director of Photography .... BERT GLENNON
Art Director .... ALEXANDER TOLUBOFF
Set Direction .... WIARD B. IHNEN
Musical Direction .... BORIS MORROS
Costumes .... WALTER PLUNKETT
Musical score based on American folk songs
adapted by .... RICHARD HAGEMAN, W. FRANKE HARLING,
JOHN LEIPOLD, LEO SHUKEN,
LOUIS GRUENBERG
Editorial Supervision .... OTHO LOVERING
Editing .... DOROTHY SPENCER, WALTER REYNOLDS
Assistant Director .... WINGATE SMITH

1939

flee burnin

Epic Hollywood

IT MAY HAVE SEEMED entirely irrelevant to many in Hollywood that, between the appearance in 1936 of Margaret Mitchell's best-selling novel *Gone With the Wind* and the film première in December 1939, other events were taking place on the planet. The United States itself was still trying to recover from the Depression; a civil war was fought in Spain with Franco emerging victorious thanks to the support of Hitler and Mussolini; Japan was waging an undeclared war against a China racked by internal conflict; Hitler annexed Austria; Chamberlain went to Munich; the Nazi-Soviet nonaggression pact was signed; Hitler invaded Poland, with Stalin moving in from the East; England and France declared war on Germany, and another war to end all wars was beginning.

But mercy me, who would play Scarlett O'Hara? *Gone With the Wind*, an epic symbolizing an epoch, a joining of myth and reality in the kingdom that had evolved from nickelodeon days, represents Hollywood at its apogee. Through the smart showmanship of producer David O. Selznick, a mammoth publicity barrage, and a then-astronomical budget of $4 million, Hollywood was showing what it was really about – tinsel and glamour, drudgery and excitement, trash and art, technique and fakery, stars and extras, powerful producers and fawning flunkies, bleeding egos and bleeding ulcers. Virtually everything that has ever been conjured up by the word Hollywood coalesced into this nearly four-hour Technicolor extravaganza about love among the ruins of the Civil War, and a way of life in the Old South, three-quarters of a century earlier. Those involved in making the film could scarcely have foreseen that in a relatively short while Hollywood as it then existed would also be gone with the wind, a palm-tree'd Tara decimated by the gusts of post-World War II change.

Nor could they have foreseen *Gone With the Wind*'s extraordinary and enduring success. It garners substantial audiences with each rerelease, and is the most popular film ever made, although inflated ticket prices have enabled others to surpass its box-office receipts. As of *Variety*'s January 3, 1979, tabulation, it ranked ninth, trailing only *Star Wars*, *Jaws*, *The Godfather*, *Grease*, *The Exorcist*, *The Sound of Music*, *The Sting*, and *Close Encounters of the Third Kind*. Its rental gross (the amount received by the distributor from the theaters) had reached $76,700,000 in the United States and Canada alone. In 1978, television rights for twenty years were sold to CBS-TV for $35 million, following NBC's $5 million payment two years earlier for a two-installment telecast that was seen by an estimated 162 million. MGM still retained the theatrical rights for *Gone With the Wind*, which in 1967 was converted from 35mm to 70mm – not without casualty to some of the performers, portions of whose heads and legs were cut off in the widening process. Up-to-date methods were used to enhance the original Technicolor, and the film was furnished with six-track stereophonic sound.

From a critical viewpoint, *Gone With the Wind* is a textbook example of Hollywood's talent for ballyhoo and for glib distortion of history. It did not even deliver on the anticipated spectacle. The burning of Atlanta is often cited as a production masterpiece. Perhaps that was because of the preconditioning of the public. Selznick had new fronts representing 1864 Atlanta put on old sets on his lot and then had them ignited, managing to extract considerable publicity for the sequence. On screen it looks puny, and not only from today's perspective. More than two decades earlier, Griffith had filmed *Intolerance*, and its epic qualities make *Gone With the Wind* look as if Hollywood had regressed. However, the scene at the Atlanta railroad station crowded with wounded and dying soldiers was effectively filmed with a crane shot unusual for its day. Selznick had asked for two thousand five hundred extras, but settled for sixteen hundred interspersed with twelve hundred dummies.

Gone With the Wind is a travesty historically in its portrayal of blacks, Civil War dynamics, and the postwar period; and, in typical Hollywood fashion, the Civil War itself is reduced to little more than a messy backdrop for romance. The racism is not as flagrant as in *The Birth of a Nation*, but the film perpetuates the myth of the inherent goodness and gentility of an aristocratic South built on a system of happy slavery. It asks sympathy for the slave owners, fighting for a noble cause while their way of life is being obliterated. The cruelty and inhumanity of the slave system is masked; instead, we are shown the stereotyped faithful house Negroes, the classic Mammy (Hattie McDaniel), and the comic servant, Prissy (chirpy-voiced Butterfly McQueen). The National Association for the Advancement of Colored People was instrumental in having some offensive material contained in the novel eliminated from the film during production, but its content was still infuriating enough to provoke protests on its release.

Gone With the Wind's strongest asset is its cast, which has undoubtedly contributed to the film's durability. The performance of Vivien Leigh as the tempestuous, sexy, spoiled, strong-willed Scarlett, spans the years with particular luster and vitality. Clark Gable exudes the roguish charm that earned him the title "the king of Hollywood" in his portrayal of the dashing, virile, cynical Rhett Butler. Olivia de Havilland is fine as Melanie, Leslie Howard right as Ashley Wilkes; Hattie McDaniel and Butterfly McQueen, coping with their stereotyped roles, show strength as performers; Thomas Mitchell, Ann Rutherford, Victor Jory still communicate excitement. The romance, the costumes, the sheer scope and length of the film, the attendant publicity, and its being one of the early pictures in Technicolor all contributed to *Gone With the Wind*'s original appeal.

Before Selznick purchased Margaret Mitchell's sprawling, sentimental bestseller, it had made the rounds of MGM, Warners, RKO, and Fox. The consensus was that it would be too expensive to make, and too difficult to cast properly. Apparently, only Darryl Zanuck at Fox was sufficiently interested to offer $35,000 for the property. Selznick, who the year before had formed Selznick International Pictures with his agent brother Myron and John Hay "Jock" Whitney, acquired the rights for $50,000. Subsequently, he was forced to turn over the distribution rights, as well as a distribution fee and a share of the profits, to his father-in-law, Louis B. Mayer of MGM, in exchange for the loan of Clark Gable. This was the start of a process by which Selznick's financial position was diminished, his partner Whitney eventually gaining control of Selznick International by providing him with additional funds to finish *Gone With the Wind*, the budget of which had soared from a projected $2.5 million.

From the start, Gable was talked of as the natural choice for Rhett; the idea was propounded in the press and in letters from the public, although Gable himself doubted his ability to meet the acting challenge. He had no choice, having no right of refusal in his contract, but Mayer did pay him a $400,000 bonus to extricate himself from his marriage to Rhea Langham so that he and Carole Lombard could marry.

The real question was who would play Scarlett. While the publicity brains were undoubtedly magnifying the suspense, genuine interest existed throughout the country as a result of the novel's popularity. In the South, where the book obviously had special meaning, it became a matter of honor to have the right Scarlett. When Tallulah Bankhead was rumored to be a candidate, a promotion campaign was generated in Alabama, where she was born, to boost her chances. However, columnist Louella Parsons, who had more clout in Hollywood than an army of Southern lobbyists, did not like the idea and wrote: "If she does [get the part] I personally will go home and weep because she is not Scarlett O'Hara in my language, and if David O Selznick gives her the part he will have to answer to every man, woman, and child in America." So much for Tallulah.

Virtually every actress of any importance in Hollywood must have salivated over the prospect of snaring the Scarlett role. Among those screen-tested or considered were Norma Shearer, Bette Davis, Joan Crawford, Loretta Young, Miriam Hopkins, Lucille Ball, Katharine Hepburn, Lana Turner, Joan Bennett, Joan Fontaine, Susan Hayward, and Jean Arthur. Meanwhile, thousands of lesser-known hopefuls converged on Hollywood to do their all for the part. Mindful of the publicity potential, Selznick inaugurated a nationwide talent hunt. In Atlanta, where he was besieged, one of those who auditioned, according to Roland Flamini in *Scarlett, Rhett, and a Cast of Thousands*, was socialite Catherine Campbell, later to achieve fame as the mother of Patricia Hearst.

An actress almost chosen was Paulette Goddard, who had appeared with Chaplin in *Modern Times*. At one point she seemed to be the front runner, but speculation concerning whether she and Chaplin were really married or living in sin arose, which coupled with mounting hostility toward Chaplin himself, spoiled her opportunity. With so much riding on the picture, Selznick was not about to chance adverse publicity. (As it turned out, much had to be done to avoid scandal. Gable and Lombard had to meet secretly in various hotels because he was not yet divorced, and Vivien Leigh and Laurence Olivier had to maintain the façade of separate residences because they, too, were waiting for divorces.)

Vivien Leigh, who also fancied the role, had come to the United States from England to join Olivier, in Hollywood to play Heathcliff in *Wuthering Heights*. (His agent happened to be Myron Selznick, David's brother.) Leigh, already a well-known actress in Britain, was introduced to Selznick while visiting the set during the burning of Atlanta, filmed in December 1938. Selznick was impressed. Choosing her to play Scarlett was, to be sure, taking the risk of alienating Americans, the South in particular, and an attempt was made to soften the criticism by underplaying, even hiding, the fact that she was English. Hostility did develop, nevertheless, as illustrated in the following letter to the Screen Editor in the *New York Times* of January 29, 1939, under the heading "Another Scarlett Letter":

> As the grandson of a Confederate soldier I deplore the weak attitude of the president general of the Daughters of the Confederacy, who is reported to have approved the selection of an alien Englishwoman to play the part of Scarlett in *Gone With the Wind*.
>
> That there are delightful English people who consider the intonations and English of cultured Southerners to resemble that of the mother country is beside the point.
>
> The selection of Vivien Leigh is a direct affront to the men who wore the Gray and an outrage to the memory of the heroes of 1776 who fought to free this land of British domination. Cheers for the Ocala (Fla.) chapter of the Daughters and more power to their boycott of the film. It is high time those Hollywood producers find out that there are still those to whom the honor of Southern womanhood is no empty phrase.
>
> JOHN ALEXANDER
> *New York City.*

Gone With the Wind's official starting date was January 26, 1939. The making of the film turned out to be chaotic, a circus consistent with the tenor of the project. George Cukor was designated as director, but worked only a short time on the actual shooting before Victor Fleming, Clark Gable's preference, took over, to the consternation of Vivien Leigh and Olivia de Havilland. They had appealed to Selznick to retain Cukor, known as a woman's director, one reason why Gable felt more comfortable with Fleming. During hassles with Fleming, Sam Wood, who had directed the Marx Brothers in *A Night at the Opera* and *A Day at the Races*, and had just completed *Goodbye, Mr. Chips*, was called in. William Cameron Menzies, credited as production designer, also worked as a director. However, Fleming insisted on total screen credit. Sidney Howard, the successful playwright and screenwriter responsible for the initial screenplay, was given posthumous credit. (He died in an accident before the film's release.) Other writers with a hand in the project at various junctures included F. Scott Fitzgerald, Jo Swerling, Oliver Garrett, Donald Ogden Stewart, John Balderston, Charles MacArthur, and John Van Druten. Ben Hecht was called in for a final rewrite and paid $15,000 for a week's work. Selznick, the dynamic creator of the enterprise, was firmly in command of the editing, as well as all other aspects of the film, in the manner of studio heads at the time. There was no director-above-the-title billing on this film. It was clearly "David O. Selznick's production of Margaret Mitchell's *Gone With the Wind*."

How far we have come in terms of screen language can be gauged by the battle that raged over Clark Gable's line, "Frankly, my dear, I don't give a damn." It is the climactic moment of the film, when Rhett rejects Scarlett. Censor Joseph Breen vetoed it. Selznick appealed to Will Hays, head of the Motion Picture Producers and Distributors Association, who permitted it. But he was fined $5,000 for being in technical violation of the regulation against the profane use of the word *damn*.

After two secret California previews at theaters guarded by security men, a glittering première was held in Atlanta on December 15, 1939, for a white audience. None of the black performers was invited, not even Hattie McDaniel, who was in Atlanta at the time, and subsequently became the first black to win an Oscar when she was named best supporting actress for her role as Mammy. *Gone With the Wind* collected ten Oscars, including the best picture award. Leigh was chosen best actress, and the film garnered awards for best direction, screenplay, art direction, film editing, and color cinematography. There were special honors for Selznick, who received the Thalberg award for consistent high quality of production, and for Menzies as production designer, but Gable lost to Robert Donat in *Goodbye, Mr. Chips*. Vivien Leigh also received the best actress award from the New York Film Critics.

Selznick had a problem that plagued him in the wake of his astounding success: everything that he did was measured against *Gone With the Wind*. "Don't people realize that I made other pictures, too?" he once pleaded. His many other pictures include the 1937 version of *A Star is Born; The Prisoner of Zenda* (1937); *Nothing Sacred* (1937); *The Adventures of Tom Sawyer* (1938); *Intermezzo* (1939) – also starring Leslie Howard; *Rebecca* (1940); *Since You Went Away* (1944); *Spellbound* (1945); *Duel in the Sun* (1946); and *The Third Man* (1949), which he co-produced. Selznick died in 1965.

Gone With the Wind, in reflecting Hollywood at its zenith, becomes the point from which one can measure its downhill path, even though the changes did not begin to take effect until after World War II. A complexity of circumstances had their impact. Generally higher production costs were one factor, the growing strength of unions another. A trend toward location shooting started. The rest of the world became closer with the increase in air travel, and this provided new locations where "runaway productions" had the advantage of cheaper labor. Stars became more powerful, along with the greater muscle of agents, and wanted to work independently of studio control, take percentages, and boost their earnings by producing their own films. Studios found it more profitable to rent their facilities to independent producers, or to act as distributors for packaged productions filmed around the world.

The rapid development of television after the war was the greatest single reason for the decline. In their quest for more revenue, studios sold old product to the networks, and audiences could opt to see films or other programs at home rather than sustain the cost of a night out. Hollywood has recouped to some extent by becoming the main center for television production, but it will never again have the aura of the days when *Gone With the Wind* was in production – an epic filmed on a studio lot.

In June 1976, Richard Zanuck and David Brown, the producers of *Jaws*, announced plans for a sequel to *Gone With the Wind*, intended as a joint MGM and Universal Pictures venture. "Certainly an epic of this magnitude would now be filmed mostly on location," said Brown. "Nowadays, one always thinks first of finding locations, even for interior scenes, because it costs so much more to construct sets." The proposed film would follow the lives of Rhett and Scarlett after he walked out on her – it seemed that Rhett would give a damn after all. Brown stressed that he had no intention of seeking look-alikes for Gable and Leigh and said that the film would be a sequel, not a remake. Instead of buying the rights to a novel, as Selznick did, the producers, operating with 1970s packaging skills, commissioned one from Anne Edwards. In April 1979, Brown expressed satisfaction with the screenplay written by James Goldman but indicated that there were differences with MGM and Universal, and other potential problems.

Should the sequel ever materialize, the public, on the basis of the Zanuck/Brown blitz with *Jaws*, could certainly expect an intense publicity hype, an updating of what Selznick did in the thirties. But no matter how artistically or commercially successful it might be, there seems to be little possibility that any spin-off could eclipse the original, nor is it likely that any other Rhett and Scarlett could match the magnetism of Clark Gable and Vivien Leigh.

GONE WITH THE WIND
USA (MGM) 1939

Cast, in the order of their appearance

At Tara, the O'Hara Plantation in Georgia

Brent Tarleton.......FRED CRANE
Stuart Tarleton.......GEORGE REEVES
Scarlett O'Hara.......VIVIEN LEIGH
Mammy.......HATTIE MCDANIEL
Big Sam.......EVERETT BROWN
Elijah.......ZACK WILLIAMS
Gerald O'Hara.......THOMAS MITCHELL
Pork.......OSCAR POLK
Ellen O'Hara.......BARBARA O'NEIL
Jonas Wilkerson.......VICTOR JORY
Suellen O'Hara.......EVELYN KEYES
Carreen O'Hara.......ANN RUTHERFORD
Prissy.......BUTTERFLY MCQUEEN

At Twelve Oaks, the nearby Wilkes Plantation

John Wilkes.......HOWARD HICKMAN
India Wilkes.......ALICIA RHETT
Ashley Wilkes.......LESLIE HOWARD
Melanie Hamilton.......OLIVIA DE HAVILLAND
Charles Hamilton.......RAND BROOKS
Frank Kennedy.......CARROLL NYE
Cathleen Calvert.......MARCELLA MARTIN
Rhett Butler.......CLARK GABLE

At the Bazaar in Atlanta

Aunt "Pittypat" Hamilton.......LAURA HOPE CREWS
Doctor Meade.......HARRY DAVENPORT
Mrs. Meade.......LEONA ROBERTS

Mrs. Merriwether . . . . JANE DARWELL
Rene Picard . . . . ALBERT MORIN
Maybelle Merriwether . . . . MARY ANDERSON
Fanny Elsing . . . . TERRY SHERO
Old Levi . . . . WILLIAM MCCLAIN

In Aunt "Pittypat's" home
Uncle Peter . . . . EDDIE ANDERSON

Outside the Examiner Office
Phil Meade . . . . JACKIE MORAN

At the Hospital
Reminiscing Soldier . . . . CLIFF EDWARDS
Belle Watling . . . . ONA MUNSON
The Sergeant . . . . ED CHANDLER
A Wounded Soldier in Pain . . . . GEORGE HACKATHORNE
A Convalescent Soldier . . . . ROSCOE ATES
An Amputation Case . . . . ERIC LINDEN
A Dying Soldier . . . . JOHN ARLEDGE

During the Evacuation
A Commanding Officer . . . . TOM TYLER

During the Siege
A Mounted Officer . . . . WILLIAM BAKEWELL
The Bartender . . . . LEE PHELPS

Georgia after Sherman
A Yankee Deserter . . . . PAUL HURST
The Carpetbagger's Friend . . . . ERNEST WHITMAN
A Returning Veteran . . . . WILLIAM STELLING
A Hungry Soldier . . . . LOUIS JEAN HEYDT
Emmy Slattery . . . . ISABEL JEWELL

During Reconstruction
The Yankee Major . . . . ROBERT ELLIOTT
His Poker-Playing Captains . . . . GEORGE MEEKER, WALLIS CLARK
The Corporal . . . . IRVING BACON
A Carpetbagger Orator . . . . ADRIAN MORRIS
Johnny Gallegher . . . . J. M. KERRIGAN
A Yankee Business Man . . . . OLIN HOWLAND
A Renegade . . . . YAKIMA CANUTT
His Companion . . . . BLUE WASHINGTON
Tom, A Yankee Captain . . . . WARD BOND
Bonnie Blue Butler . . . . CAMMIE KING
Beau Wilkes . . . . MICKEY KUHN
Bonnie's Nurse . . . . LILLIAN KEMBLE COOPER

Running time	220 minutes
Technicolor	
Production Company	SELZNICK INTERNATIONAL PICTURES
Produced by	DAVID O. SELZNICK
Directed by	VICTOR FLEMING
Screenplay	SIDNEY HOWARD, based on the novel by MARGARET MITCHELL
Production Designed by	WILLIAM CAMERON MENZIES
Art Direction by	LYLE WHEELER
Photographed by	ERNEST HALLER
Technicolor Associates	RAY RENNAHAN, WILFRID M. CLINE
Musical Score by	MAX STEINER
Associate	LOU FORBES
Special Photographic Effects by	JACK COSGROVE
Associate (Fire Effects)	LEE ZAVITZ
Costumes Designed by	WALTER PLUNKETT
Scarlett's Hats by	JOHN FREDERICS
Interiors by	JOSEPH B. PLATT
Interior Decoration by	EDWARD G. BOYLE
Supervising Film Editor	HAL C. KERN
Associate Film Editor	JAMES E. NEWCOM
Scenario Assistant	BARBARA KEON
Recorder	FRANK MAHER
Make-up and Hair Styling	MONTY WESTMORE
Associates	HAZEL ROGERS, BEN NYE
Dance Directors	FRANK FLOYD, EDDIE PRINZ
Historian	WILBUR G. KURTZ
Technical Advisers	SUSAN MYRICK, WILL PRICE
Research	LILLIAN K. DEIGHTON
Production Manager	RAYMOND A. KLUNE
Technicolor Co. Supervision	NATALIE KALMUS
Associate	HENRI JAFFA
Assistant Director	ERIC G. STACEY
Second Assistant Director	RIDGEWAY CALLOW
Production Continuity	LYDIA SCHILLER, CONNIE EARLE
Mechanical Engineer	R.D. MUSGRAVE
Construction Superintendent	HAROLD FENTON
Chief Grip	FRED WILLIAMS
In Charge of Wardrobe	EDWARD P. LAMBERT
Associates	MARIAN DABNEY, ELMER ELLSWORTH
Casting Managers	CHARLES RICHARDS, FRED SCHUESSLER
Location Manager	MASON LITSON
Scenic Department Superintendent	HENRY J. STAHL
Electrical Superintendent	WALLY OETTEL
Chief Electrician	JAMES POTEVIN
Properties:	
Manager	HAROLD COLES
On the Set	ARDEN CRIPE
Greens	ROY A. MCLAUGHLIN

Drapes...JAMES FORNEY
Special Properties made by ....ROSS B. JACKMAN
Tara Landscaped by ....FLORENCE YOCH
Still Photographer ....FRED PARRISH
Camera Operators ....ARTHUR ARLING, VINCENT FARRAR
Assistant Film Editors......RICHARD VAN ENGER, ERNEST LEADLEY

NAZIS OCCUPY DENMARK, ATTACK NORWAY
—April 9, 1940

NAZIS ATTACK HOLLAND, BELGIUM —May 10, 1940

NAZIS OCCUPY PARIS —June 14, 1940

TROTSKY DIES AFTER AX ASSAULT —August 21, 1940

OUTNUMBERED ROYAL AIR FORCE DOWNS
25 NAZI PLANES OVER BRITAIN, LOSES 15
—September 3, 1940

In 1941, Hitler invades Soviet Union . . . US and Britain formulate Atlantic Charter . . . Japan attacks US at Pearl Harbor . . . US declares war on Japan, Germany, Italy.

ROOSEVELT SIGNS LAW PERMITTING
INTERNMENT OF JAPANESE AMERICANS
—February 19, 1942

JAPANESE TAKE BATAAN —April 9, 1942

TOKYO BOMBED IN US RAID —April 18, 1942

ALLIES OPEN SECOND FRONT IN FRENCH AFRICA
—November 7, 1942

In 1943, Allies land in Italy, forcing surrender . . . Eisenhower chosen to command main invasion of Europe, Montgomery to head British troops . . . Twenty-five blacks, nine whites die in Detroit race riots.

ALLIES LAND TROOPS IN FRANCE —June 6, 1944

NAZIS MISSILE BOMB LONDON —June 13, 1944

1940-1949

ASSASSINATION PLOT AGAINST HITLER FAILS
—July 20, 1944

In 1945, Roosevelt dies, Truman President . . . Mussolini executed by partisans . . . Hitler commits suicide, Germany surrenders . . . United Nations charter drafted . . . Labour Party assumes office in Britain . . . Atom bombs dropped on Hiroshima and Nagasaki . . . USSR declares war on Japan . . . Japan surrenders . . . Nuremberg International Military Tribunal tries Nazis for crimes against humanity, including murder of more than six million Jews.

UN GENERAL ASSEMBLY HOLDS FIRST MEETING IN LONDON
—January 10, 1946

TRUMAN ORDERS INVESTIGATION INTO FEDERAL EMPLOYEE LOYALTY
—March 22, 1947

HOUSE COMMITTEE ON UN-AMERICAN ACTIVITIES OPENS HEARINGS INTO HOLLYWOOD 'SUBVERSION'
—October 20, 1947

UN GENERAL ASSEMBLY APPROVES PROPOSAL TO PARTITION PALESTINE
—November 29, 1947

In 1948, Gandhi assassinated in India . . . Communist coup in Czechoslovakia . . . Marshall Plan passed . . . New state of Israel proclaimed, Arabs invade . . . In 1949, Berlin blockade lifted . . . Russians explode A-bomb . . . Communists take control of China . . . Eleven US Communist leaders get prison sentences of up to five years for conspiracy to teach and advocate the overthrow of the government by force and violence . . . *The Second Sex* by Simone de Beauvoir published in France . . . *1984* by George Orwell published in Britain.

1940

The Grapes of Wrath

Ma Joad (Jane Darwell), Tom (Henry Fonda) and Pa Joad (Russell Simpson).

Film as Social Criticism

TWENTIETH CENTURY-FOX's acquisition, within a month of publication, of John Steinbeck's celebrated best-selling novel on the ravages of the Depression raised the question whether the essence of the author's work would be respected. Steinbeck's unflinching depiction of the plight of migrating sharecroppers evicted from their land in the Oklahoma Dust Bowl was indeed a challenge. *The Grapes of Wrath*, the strongest film indictment of economic injustice to emerge from the 1930s, represents a rare instance when a Hollywood film has faced, head-on, appalling contemporary conditions or events.

Fear has been as prevalent in Hollywood as swimming pools. The industry has trembled in the face of the Legion of Decency, the Production Code, the House Un-American Activities Committee, and assorted pressure groups. Instituting a blacklist during the McCarthy period was a reflex action. Similarly, reacting to the fear of possible government censorship with the self-imposed censorship implicit in the 1968 rating system was in character. In such a climate, the social conscience film has been anathema, reinforced by the Hollywood maxim that only escapist entertainment is commercial. John Ford's poignant adaptation of Steinbeck's novel, scripted by Nunnally Johnson, underscores the potential of film to express frustrations and hopes and prod the conscience. Paradoxically, *The Grapes of Wrath* was not only lauded artistically, but was a resounding financial success.

The book, despite its popularity, encountered hostility from those who resented its portrayal of conditions so contrary to the American dream. Reaction was particularly virulent in Oklahoma and in California, where the Okies were viciously exploited and scorned as second-class citizens. It is not surprising that the California Chamber of Commerce protested against the plans for a film, and a boycott of all Twentieth Century-Fox product was threatened by the Agricultural Council of California. Darryl F. Zanuck, the head of Fox, proved to be a wily match for his opponents. Ignoring advice within the industry that the film would be too controversial and should be shelved, he restricted the number of scripts circulated and was equally secretive about the shooting, even using the subterfuge of a cover title, *Highway 66*. Only after it had been acclaimed elsewhere, did he release the film in California.

Documentary filmmaker and critic Pare Lorentz, whose *The Plow that Broke the Plains* (1936) is concerned with the abuse of the land that caused the Dust Bowl conditions, wrote in *McCall's*:

> Whatever else it may be, *The Grapes of Wrath* is the first picture made in Hollywood since 1929 that deals with a current social problem, that has faithfully kept the intent of an author who stirred the country, that has reproduced the bloody violence that has accompanied an economic upheaval – a violence that has been reported in the press from many parts of the country besides California but never on film – a picture that records the story of a tragic American migration into slavery. It is quite a movie.

In the film's striking opening, Tom Joad (Henry Fonda), hands in pockets and wearing a cap, is walking on a highway in a rural Oklahoma setting, the shadows of telegraph poles reflected on the road. A truck is parked outside a restaurant, and Tom, wanting a lift, is not deterred by the "No Riders" sign. The idea of class solidarity is quickly advanced, as Tom tells the driver, "A good guy don't pay no attention to what some heel makes him stick on his truck." The driver relents, but makes Tom squat on the running board until they are out of sight. Their conversation grows testy because Tom resents prying questions. The son of a sharecropper, he has been released on parole after serving four years for killing a man in an argument.

Making his way across the fields to his home, Tom encounters Casy (John Carradine), a former local preacher now aimless and footloose, who accompanies him to his home. The shack is deserted. Muley (John Qualen) tells them about the dust storms and how company agents evicted the region's sharecroppers. Among them were the Joads, who have gone to Tom's Uncle John's en route to California. Muley, in hiding from the deputies, is determined to stay. A flashback shows him standing by, horrified and helpless, as a tractor demolishes his home. A double exposure effect stresses the omnipotence of the tractor, and the camera contemplates the tire tracks left after the deed.

The reunion at John's home is quietly emotional. "Did they hurt you son, did they hurt you and make you a mean man?" asks Ma Joad (Jane Darwell). The family, ordered to leave by morning, is planning to join the migration to California in the hope of finding work. Ma, alone late at night, sorts her scant possessions, sifting the memories of a lifetime, saving a few souvenirs. She stares at herself in a mirror as she holds up a pair of earrings in a scene that wistfully suggests her youth. The next morning, Grampa (Charley Grapewin), who is senile, refuses to leave. Only by spiking his coffee with sufficient cough syrup to subdue him can he be loaded onto the truck. Casy is invited to go along. The truck, crammed with Joads and their belongings, is so topheavy that it threatens to topple at the first turn. Sadly, they leave the land, stoically looking ahead to better days.

Early in the journey, Grampa succumbs and is buried at the roadside with Casy saying a makeshift prayer; Granma (Zeffie Tilbury) dies in Ma's arms just before they reach California. To avoid being turned back when officials inspect the truck at the border, Ma resourcefully pretends that the old woman is ill and must be rushed to a doctor. Disillusionment awaits the surviving Joads after their arduous journey. Handbills advertising work in California turn out to be lures to attract the migrants in droves so that they can be forced to work for a pittance. Contractors treat them as slave labor. At a Hooverville camp the Joads see the utter poverty of the migrants. The camera moves into the camp, surveying their forlorn faces from the viewpoint of the newcomers. Moving on, the Joads find work picking peaches at the Keene Ranch, only to discover that they are being used as scabs. The pickers' camp is virtually a prison.

Casy, seeking answers to the miserable conditions, has joined those attempting to unify the workers. At night, when Tom surreptitiously leaves the camp and unexpectedly meets him, they are attacked by deputies charged with breaking up any organizing efforts. Casy is clubbed to death, and Tom, incensed, kills one of the assailants. He is now a fugitive, with a telltale gash on his face. He sneaks back into the camp and the family hastily leaves, concealing him.

A brighter interlude occurs when the Joads come upon Wheat Patch, a self-governing camp under the auspices of the United States government, where they are treated with respect and dignity. There is an amusing but tense scene at a dance when the campers outsmart deputies and goons who try to start a riot in the hope of disrupting the efforts to create a decent environment for the migrants. But Tom is soon traced and must flee. Saying goodbye to his mother in the night, he realizes neither will know the other's whereabouts, and tells her: "Maybe it's like Casy says, a fella ain't got a soul of his own, but only a piece of a big soul, the one big soul that belongs to everybody. And then it don't matter. Then I'll be all around in the dark. I'll be everywhere." The speech grows political: "Wherever there's a fight so hungry people can eat, I'll be there. Wherever there's a cop beating up a guy, I'll be there. . . ." With Tom gone, the Joads move on again. Undaunted, Ma is determined to survive. "We're the people that live. They can't wipe us out. They can't lick us. We'll go on forever, Pa, because we're the people."

Ending *The Grapes of Wrath* on this upbeat note is credited to Zanuck, who modified some lines taken from an earlier conversation Ma has with Tom in the novel. The rhetoric thus acquires a more deliberately noble, contrived ring; but this minor concession to convention does not detract from the film's integrity. Ma Joad's courage in confronting the bleak future is far removed from the glib cheer of the traditional happy ending. The impassioned words were even good to hear considering Hollywood's wariness of dialogue daring to suggest organizing against injustice. Whatever its compromises, *The Grapes of Wrath* stands as a great achievement in artistry and content; it is one of the finest films produced under the studio system.

The photography of Gregg Toland, who a year later was to collaborate with Orson Welles on the monumental, technically innovative *Citizen Kane*, perfectly implemented Ford's lean, direct approach to his subject matter. Intensely sympathetic toward his characters and their circumstances, Ford knew the value of sustaining a scene long enough to communicate this understanding. Pictorially, *The Grapes of Wrath* contains magnificent shots that could constitute a photographic exhibit on the Depression. Ford's use of the song "Red River Valley" as a theme was also effective, creating a pensive, yearning mood.

Measured against the realism seen in films since, *The Grapes of Wrath* may seem excessively theatrical and sentimental in its treatment of poverty, plot, dialogue, and characterization; the neo-realism of Rossellini and de Sica was still five years off. Nowadays, one would expect a similar story filmed with similar sincerity to receive far grittier treatment. Although Ford obtained some establishing shots on location, his film was shot mostly in a studio – today, the locale would be integral. Poverty would require a hungrier appearance; starving children should look emaciated; characters should be less obviously performers. However, by comparison with films to which the public was then accustomed, *The Grapes of Wrath* appeared astonishingly realistic.

Although some of the acting could be faulted as too expansive, and even stagy, it was the prevailing dramatic style. Certainly Fonda is low-key and credible, giving an intelligent and sensitive performance, possibly the best of his career. His ability to project sincerity has made him a favorite for films attempting political or social comment. In *You Only Live Once* (1937), directed by Fritz Lang, he is an ex-convict wrongfully accused of murder and hunted by society. In *Blockade* (1938), directed by William Dieterle and co-starring Madeleine Carroll, he is a peasant who generates sympathy for the Republican cause (unnamed) in the Spanish Civil War. In *The Male Animal* (1942), a comedy by James Thurber and Elliott Nugent, directed by Nugent, he plays a college professor who causes a stir and demonstrates his integrity by reading his class the farewell letter of Bartolomeo Vanzetti. Fonda stars as an opponent of mob rule in William Wellman's *The Ox-Bow Incident* (1943), the classic antilynching Western, and as a juror in *Twelve Angry Men* (1957), Sidney Lumet's screen version of Reginald Rose's television drama, which suspensefully demonstrates the prejudices that imperil the jury system. In *Fail Safe* (1964), also directed by Lumet, he portrays a U.S. president trying to save the world from accidental nuclear holocaust. Fonda has been one of filmdom's busiest actors; although he has made many movies he prefers to forget, he speculated in an interview with Enid Nemy in the June 12, 1976, *New York Times* that he would not still be box office "if I had limited myself to the kind of pictures I want to make."

Ironically, Ford had to fight for Fonda, who was a free lance, as Zanuck would have preferred a major Fox star. Fonda, wanting the role, was persuaded to sign an eight-picture contract with the studio. Ford's choice for Ma Joad was Beulah Bondi, closer to his conception of a haggard woman subjected to the oppression of poverty. Instead, he was compelled to accept portly Jane Darwell, already under contract to Fox, and more like the all-embracing mother cliché. Although the casting was expedient on Zanuck's part, Darwell proved to be memorably touching – stylized, but in harmony with the film's cadence and stoicism. Her performance won her the Oscar for best supporting actress; Ford won as best director. The Academy by-passed *The Grapes of Wrath* for Hitchcock's *Rebecca* as best picture, and Henry Fonda for James Stewart in George Cukor's *The Philadelphia Story*. The New York Film Critics named *The Grapes of Wrath* best picture, and Ford best director for both *The Grapes of Wrath* and *The Long Voyage Home*.

Subjects of concern to mankind have been focal points of films from many countries, but such efforts, successful or not, are minimal in comparison with the enormous number of films produced. Ford, of course, made *The Informer* (1935), a powerful drama of betrayal in the Irish rebellion, and *How Green Was My Valley* (1941), about Welsh coal miners. The horror of capital punishment is analyzed in the French film *We Are All Murderers* (1952), directed by André Cayatte. *I Want to Live* (1958), starring Susan Hayward and directed by Robert Wise, constitutes a strong plea for the abolition of the death penalty. Fritz Lang's *M* (1931), starring Peter Lorre, faces the subject of society's attitudes toward those whose crimes are rooted in psychopathic problems. Anatole Litvak's *The Snake Pit* (1948) attempts to deal with conditions in mental hospitals. Poverty has been depicted in a broad range, from slum kids on the streets of New York in William Wyler's *Dead End* (1937) to famine in India in Satyajit Ray's *Distant Thunder* (1973).

The period of Italian neo-realism produced many fine films of social consciousness, such as de Sica's *The Bicycle Thief* (1949) and *Umberto D* (1952). The scourge of war has been examined in several film classics. (See chapters on *Grand Illusion* and *Dr. Strangelove*.) A few honorable examples of social criticism that come to mind include: *I Am a Fugitive from a Chain Gang*, *Black Legion*, *Lost Weekend*, *Gentleman's Agreement*, Italy's *The Organizer*, Britain's *Love on the Dole* and *The Stars Look Down*, and many of the socially aware comedies of Frank Capra, Preston Sturges, and Charlie Chaplin. More recently, *The Front* (1976) became the first American-made feature to deal directly with the McCarthy era, specifically the practice of television blacklisting. Previously only Chaplin's *A King in New York*, made outside the United States in the 1950s, tackled McCarthyism substantively.

Network (1976), written by Paddy Chayefsky and directed by Sidney Lumet, castigates television's crassness as a reflection of society's distorted values. (See chapter on *Sweet Sweetback's Baadasssss Song* for films concerned with prejudice against blacks.)

As would be expected, films of social criticism have been sadly missing from totalitarian countries, although some have managed to make their points. Made in Franco's Spain, Luis Berlanga's *The Executioner* (1963) not only has something to say about capital punishment but is a metaphor for values and priorities under that regime. Dusan Makavejev's *WR – Mysteries of the Organism* (1971), for which he was attacked in Yugoslavia, questions Communist dogma in a most flamboyant way. (Patently political films are dealt with in the chapter on *Z*.)

The panic in Hollywood during the McCarthy era undoubtedly discouraged for years any movement toward more socially aware films. By the late forties, when the blacklisting set in, many faced certain destruction of their careers rather than name colleagues as Communists or divulge their own political associations. The famed Hollywood Ten served prison terms for invoking the First Amendment to the Constitution. Had the industry been as principled, the witchhunt would have made little headway. In fact, it was the industry that invited the witchhunters, to bolster its anti-union battles. In this atmosphere, apart from the reluctance to make controversial films, there were efforts to thwart those who wished to do so. One of the more incredible absurdities of the time was the vindictive mobilization to prevent the making of a film by director Herbert Biberman of the Hollywood Ten.

When Biberman and his blacklisted associates, producer Paul Jarrico and screenwriter Michael Wilson, set out to film *Salt of the Earth*, about an actual strike by Mexican-American zinc miners in New Mexico, obstacles were repeatedly placed in their way. Roy M. Brewer, chairman of the Hollywood American Federation of Labor Film Council, ordered union members to refuse work on the film, and in a letter to Donald L. Jackson of the House Un-American Activities Committee, pledged: "The Hollywood AFL Film Council assures you that everything which it can do to prevent the showing of the Mexican [*sic*] picture *Salt of the Earth* will be done. . . ." Howard Hughes, head of RKO, advised Jackson on how the industry could stop the film, and reported: "The minute Pathé learned the facts, this alert laboratory immediately refused to do any further work on this picture, even though it meant refunding cash paid in advance. . . ." In further harassment, the leading lady, Mexican actress Rosaura Revueltas, was deported by the United States Immigration Department before she had quite finished her role. When *Salt of the Earth*, completed despite all opposition, was released in 1954, many union projectionists refused to run it and some exhibitors were pressured into barring it by such groups as the American Legion.

The upsurge of independent-minded films in the 1960s helped establish a mood in which controversy was less shunned. However, the tendency to exercise caution is a constant of the film industry. The dread of alienating pressure groups and audiences still exists; there is apprehension over the rating a picture will receive; and producers are more inclined to invest their money in escapism than in hard-hitting socially conscious films. The exceptions offer encouragement to those committed to bold themes. *The Grapes of Wrath*, long considered a classic, has influenced and inspired many film-makers. To echo Tom Joad, wherever men or women wish to use film to call attention to injustice and suffering, *The Grapes of Wrath* will be there.

THE GRAPES OF WRATH
USA (Twentieth Century-Fox) 1940

Cast

Tom .... Henry Fonda
Ma .... Jane Darwell
Pa .... Russell Simpson
Grampa .... Charley Grapewin
Granma .... Zeffie Tilbury
Uncle John .... Frank Darien
Al .... O.Z. Whitehead
Rosasharn .... Dorris Bowdon
Connie Rivers .... Eddie Quillan
Ruthie .... Shirley Mills
Winfield .... Darryl Hickman
Casy .... John Carradine
Muley Graves .... John Qualen
Caretaker at Wheat Patch .... Grant Mitchell
Policeman .... Ward Bond
Floyd .... Paul Guilfoyle
Wilkie .... Charles D. Brown
Thomas .... Roger Imhof
Davis .... John Arledge
Bert .... Harry Tyler
Bill .... William Pawley
Father .... Arthur Aylesworth
Joe .... Charles Tannen
Inspection Officer .... Selmar Jackson
Leader .... Charles Middleton
Proprietor .... Eddie Waller
Frank .... David Hughes

City Man..CLIFF CLARK
Bookkeeper......................................JOSEPH SAWYER
Tim...FRANK FAYLEN
Agent...ADRIAN MORRIS
Muley's Son.....................................HOLLIS JEWELL
Spencer...ROBERT HOMANS
Driver..IRVING BACON
Mae...KITTY MCHUGH

Running time....................................128 minutes
Produced by.....................................DARRYL F. ZANUCK
Directed by.....................................JOHN FORD
Screenplay by...........NUNNALLY JOHNSON, based on the novel by JOHN STEINBECK
Associate Producer..............................NUNNALLY JOHNSON
Director of Photography.........................GREGG TOLAND
Technical Adviser...............................TOM COLLINS
Art Directors...................................RICHARD DAY, MARK-LEE KIRK
Set Decorator...................................THOMAS LITTLE
Costumes..GWEN WAKELING
Film Editor.....................................ROBERT SIMPSON
Sound Directors.................................GEORGE LEVERETT, ROGER HEMAN
Sound Effects Director..........................ROBERT PARRISH
Assistant Director..............................EDWARD O'FEARNA
Music Director......ALFRED NEWMAN; (Song "Red River Valley" played on accordion by DAN BORZAGE)

1940

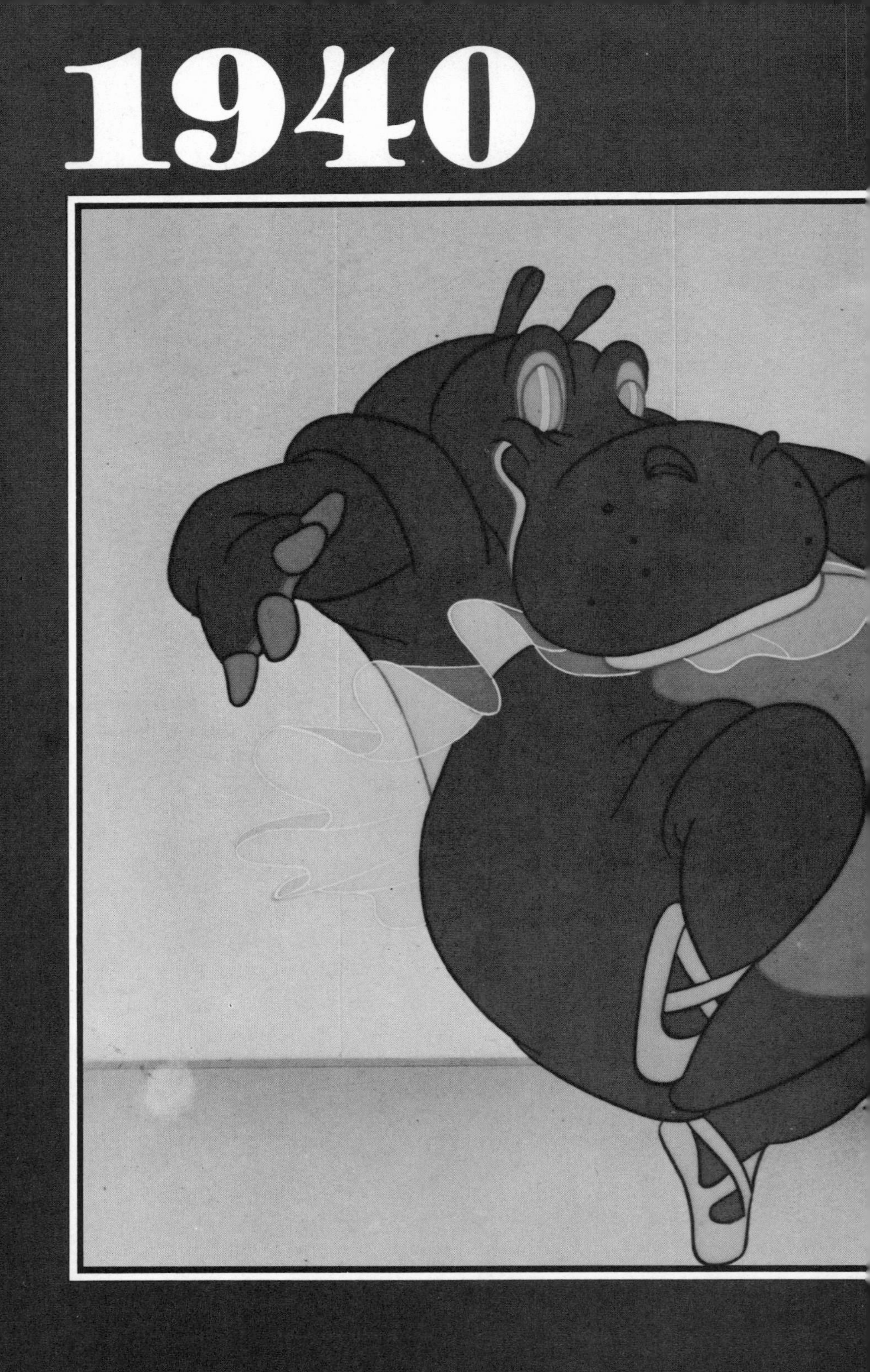

Fantasia

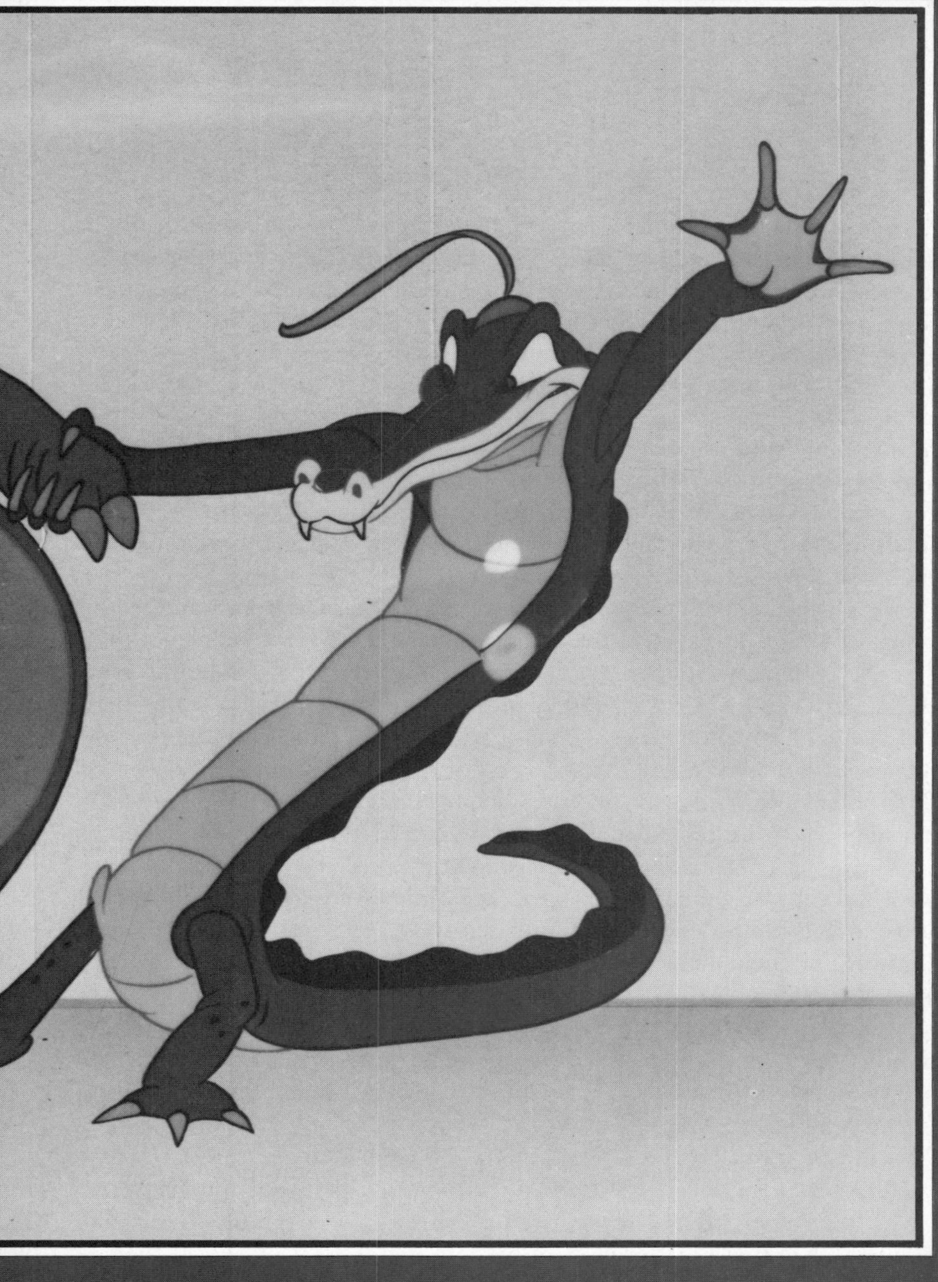

"Dance of the Hours" in Fantasia.

The Magic of Disney

MOST OF WHAT MANY critics have said about *Fantasia* is true. Some of the sequences are unbearably gauche. The effort to bring classical music to the masses through saccharine, often banal animation is enough to make music sophisticates apoplectic. The condescending narration by Deems Taylor is a bore. These criticisms miss the salient point. In technique, Disney was in advance of his time with *Fantasia*, a landmark imaginatively combining sound with animated image, an audio-visual trip that still provides surprises for viewers. More than any other Disney film, *Fantasia* indicates the best and the worst of the prolific producer's work. Disney's adventuresomeness coexists with his discordant dime store taste. But the boldness of his vision, skillfully realized in the better moments of *Fantasia*, and apparent even in the most cloying sections, persists.

The publicity for *Fantasia* was misguided. The film was promoted as the visualization of great music for audiences not otherwise familiar with the classics. Perhaps *Fantasia* did accomplish that to an extent, though it was a commercial failure at first (subsequent showings have made it profitable). But Leopold Stokowski shaking hands with Mickey Mouse on the podium was enough to repel the serious music-lover, although those censorious of Stokowski's vaunted showmanship might have considered them well-matched. *Fantasia* rekindled the old argument about the popularization of art through its bastardization. Many who saw *Fantasia* went away believing they had enjoyed an enriching experience. Some were undoubtedly bored, and one feels for the legions of children reluctantly dragged out to experience culture. For the musically knowledgeable the lowbrow spectacle bordered on desecration.

Music critic B.H. Haggin, writing in the *Nation*, January 11, 1941, attacked as a phony act Stokowski's campaign to bring to the many "what has been jealously withheld from them by the privileged few," and commented further:

> But even if one accepts Stokowski's assumption that the millions who will see *Fantasia* have never heard a broadcast of a symphony or an opera, then it is a matter of great concern that what is offered to them as the first movement of Beethoven's *Pastoral* – to consider only the

> music itself – is the exposition of material without the development and recapitulation which continue and complete the organic sequence; that they are offered Stravinsky's *Sacre* chopped up and rearranged, its essential quality falsified by things like the perfumed phrasing of the stark opening woodwind passages, the lush sonorities elsewhere; that Bach's *Toccata and Fugue*, played complete, is falsified by a performance which imparts to it the feverish excitement that Stokowski imparts to any music he conducts, and which makes of it the mere succession of dazzling effects of orchestral virtuosity and sonority that music is for him.

However justified the criticism, *Fantasia*'s musical pretensions should not obscure its cinematic achievement. Pare Lorentz, in his critique in *McCall's*, correctly judged the importance of *Fantasia* as film: "I advise you to disregard the howls from the music critics. *Fantasia* is a Disney and not a classical conception of a concert. . . ." Noting that the imagery, not the scores, was preeminent, Lorentz rejoiced that Disney had taken music "out of the temple, put it in carpet slippers and an old sweater, and made it work to surround, and support, and synchronize a brilliantly-drawn series of animated color sketches." Lorentz was far too uncritical of the results of Disney's mixture, but his principal observation is true: Disney was using music for animation rather than using animation in behalf of music. The talk of bringing music to the people may have been a rationale and a sales angle (it may have been off-putting, too), but it diverted the spotlight from where it should have been – on Disney's sound and image extravaganza. His undertaking was enormously complicated. Involved were some sixty animators, eleven directors, thirty artists for scenic background, one hundred and three musicians of the Philadelphia Symphony Orchestra, and so many others with various kinds of expertise that, according to the Disney studio, one thousand people shared in the making of *Fantasia* over a period of four years. To achieve the animation, more than one million drawings were needed. The cost was $3 million.

The film, consisting of eight segments, begins pompously after we watch the orchestra members taking their places and preparing for the concert. We are told by Deems Taylor, then a popular radio commentator on music, that this is "a new form of entertainment." When conductor Stokowski mounts the podium, it is as if a deity had arrived. Garish lighting silhouettes him and he seems about to present the Ten Commandments. By this time an audience should know it is seeing a film of importance.

The most abstract animation in *Fantasia* accompanies Bach's *Toccata and Fugue in D Minor*, the lead-off segment. Disney was not the first to experiment in this direction and one cannot even say that these are true abstractions. The objects and designs are recognizable and not likely to stretch an audience's imagination. However, in itself, the step was bold, pre-dating much more intricate work. There is striking use of color, and the screen is covered with clouds and sky. Violin bows become silver streaks darting through the heavens like comets, and discs resembling objects in space appear and disappear. Although dismissible as musical interpretation, conceptually the visuals are still arresting.

With Tchaikovsky's *Nutcracker Suite,* Disney launches into a cute stage, but much of it is appealing because of the animation skill and whimsy. Disney's figures cavorting in the "Dance of the Sugar Plum Fairy" are a shapely lot – dainty nudes, with long, sleek legs, sprinkling dew on the flowers like flitting Barbie dolls. Mushrooms become mandarins wearing coolie hats in the "Chinese Dance"; flower blossoms turn into ballerinas in the "Dance of the Flutes." Amusingly, the goldfish doing their underwater routines to the "Arabian Dance" are coquettish chorines with pink eyelids and fluttering lashes, a cross between Betty Boop and Mae West.

The Sorcerer's Apprentice by Dukas is a starring vehicle for Mickey Mouse. With the sorcerer gone, Mickey dabbles in magic on his own. Donning his master's cone-shaped hat, he makes a broom the target of his incantations. The broom moves, sprouts arms that pick up two buckets, and tramps along behind Mickey to a well. Thus activated, it keeps filling the buckets and emptying them, forming a sea in which Mickey is trapped. Mickey tries to stop the broom by hacking it to pieces with an ax, but the pieces proliferate into a veritable army of brooms, all filling and emptying their buckets. The sorcerer returns to part the waters and punish his presumptuous apprentice. Humor, a sense of fantasy, and imaginative animation make the union of Mickey and Dukas an enjoyable confection.

Stravinsky's *The Rite of Spring* is used by Disney in an ambitious effort to portray the beginning of the world. Here the Disney craftsmen outdid themselves with effects. Gases emitted by an explosion on the sun shoot off into space and solidify into a ball of fire that eventually becomes earth. Volcanos, earthquakes, rushing seas – it is the Disney version of the creation. There is beauty in the genesis of sea life, and in the depiction of the dinosaurs roaming the earth; Disney imparts grace to the lumbering beasts. He also indulges in the kind of violence so often contained in his films, in this instance, a ferocious battle to the death between two prehistoric monsters biting at each other – the survival of the fittest. Although the sight of the enormous jaws with their gigantic teeth and the viciousness of the beasts in combat are frightening, the scene is majestic in its execution.

In contrast, Beethoven's *Pastoral Symphony*, provided with a mythological setting and silly animation, is an embarrassment. The centaurs and centaurettes cavort romantically under the spell of Cupid. At first, the centaurettes are unclothed, but in the presence of the centaurs, they wear tiny bras made of flowers. Bacchus revels like a village idiot when he is not trying to elude the bolts of lightning Zeus hurls from on high. To adorn the *Pastoral* with Cupid's bottom shaped into a heart is excessive even for inferior Disney.

A recovery occurs with the "Dance of the Hours" ballet from Ponchielli's opera *La Gioconda*. In this joyously comic and superbly animated Disney concoction, an ostrich is a graceful ballerina performing pirouettes. The prima ballerina, a hippopotamus, dances with other hippos. Elephants dance mincingly and alligators form the corps de ballet. This is Disney at his humorous best. In Mussorgsky's *Night on Bald Mountain*, Disney dwells on spirits, witches, vampires, and skeletons – portents of menace, gloom, and death. It is Halloween, Disney style, more overwhelming than effective, but still another indication of the effort that went into his blend of animation and sound.

Watching the finale of *Fantasia*, Schubert's *Ave Maria*, is like gazing at formula religious greeting cards. A procession of worshipers moves slowly against the horizon. The trees of a forest form arches. Dawn comes in a blaze of light signifying joy and good will. By comparison, the Easter pageant at the Radio City Music Hall could be considered the pinnacle of artistry. Such lapses of taste aside, *Fantasia* pointed toward new multimedia possibilities.

Although color in films is now taken for granted, in 1940 Disney's work represented extraordinary progress. (It is only necessary to recall the fuss made the year before over *Gone With the Wind*.) However, Disney was not merely presenting a film in color; he was experimenting with it for mood, amusement, dramatic power, and design. Sometimes the result was gaudy, but more often he used color with intelligence and a liberating sense of fantasy.

Disney's approach to sound was daring. During two months of sessions at the Philadelphia Academy of Music, nine cameras and thirty-three microphones were used to photograph and stereophonically record the orchestra. Disney also provided a system for the theaters called Fantasound, developed for him by RCA at a cost of $100,000 for the initial unit and $30,000 for each additional unit. Most exhibitors found the cost prohibitive, but the equipment was installed in some major theaters, and audiences who saw *Fantasia* in theaters able to present it on the scale Disney intended experienced stereophonic effects since taken for granted.

When *The Jazz Singer* changed the nature of the film business, Disney was quick to perceive the advantage he had with animation. While films with live performers required the synchronization of sound with speech, an animator had greater freedom. The images could be drawn, with sound added later to specification. Consequently, Disney was able to integrate the process of planning sound, music, and drawing from the very beginning. Having launched Mickey Mouse as a silent, he began to toy with sound in his third Mickey Mouse cartoon, *Steamboat Willie* (1928), to obtain a variety of effects. This early orientation toward thinking in total terms represented a different attitude from that of the studio heads, who regarded sound as necessary primarily because it had arrived.

Animator Chuck Jones (Bugs Bunny, Daffy Duck) has remarked that "Disney was to animation what Griffith was to live action." Strides had been made before Disney came on the scene, but the work under his aegis moved the art forward as new techniques were sought and found by the staff he assembled. Historically, the man recognized as the pioneer in the animation field was Emile Cohl, known for his work in France during the decade beginning with 1908, the year of his *Fantasmagorie*. In 1914, Winsor McCay inaugurated Gertie the Dinosaur, the first cartoon character to become a "star." Otto Messmer's Felix the Cat also became a favorite, and Max Fleischer created another star in Ko-Ko the Clown. Ko-Ko's popularity was eclipsed by Mickey Mouse, although the Fleischer studio was subsequently highly successful with Betty Boop and Popeye.

Disney, who was born in 1901 and died in 1966, grew up in the Midwest. Drawing was a favorite pastime, and at the age of fourteen he took a class at the Kansas City Art Institute. After World War I, during which he was an ambulance driver in France, he returned to Kansas City where he found work as an apprentice with a local commercial art studio. There he met a young artist, Ub Iwerks, who was to become vital to the development of the Disney studio. For a short time they had their own company, which Disney left for a job with the Kansas City Film Ad Company, making animated commercials used as advertisements in theaters. Iwerks soon joined him there and they also began collaborating on their own cartoons. Later, after Disney went to Hollywood, he asked Iwerks to work with him; the idea of having a mouse as a cartoon character was Disney's, but it was Iwerks who did the original drawings. Mickey Mouse achieved such world-wide renown that he was compared to Chaplin in popularity. Donald Duck may have reached even greater audiences but Mickey Mouse remains the character most associated with the name of Disney. While Mickey was cavorting before the public, Disney initiated his *Silly Symphony* series, the first of which was *The Skeleton Dance* (1929), a fanciful combination of whimsy and the macabre. The Three Little Pigs, extremely popular Disney characters, were also part of the series.

The first full-length animated feature Disney produced was *Snow White and the Seven Dwarfs*, which appeared in 1937, followed by *Pinocchio*. It is for such as these, and the household of Disney cartoon characters, that Disney is regarded affectionately. *Dumbo, Bambi, Cinderella, Alice in Wonderland* – these illustrate the superior Disney. Unfortunately, there is another side to Disney – the extreme commercialization that accounts for his artistic decline. He was also the Disney who saturated the world with spin-off merchandising, who could be bitter and stubborn in dealings with his employees, and who could create in Disneyland (followed by Disney World) such paradoxical effects.

After his peak years of animation, shrinking demand propelled Disney to look toward television for salvation; his nature films revived his fortunes during the 1950s. He also produced live theatrical features, *Mary Poppins* (1964), starring Julie Andrews, being among the better examples. For the most part, a stream of formula films geared to indiscriminating tastes and meeting the bland criteria of "family pictures" issued from Disney's studio. After his death they continued to be churned out by his brother Roy, with whom he had had a lifelong business association, and after Roy's death, by the ongoing studio administration. Since 1977, some movement toward upgrading has been discernible.

My recollection of Disney is at the New York World's Fair in 1964, when a group of writers were invited to meet him and preview the new exhibits and entertainments bearing his name and about to be opened to the public. Disney, then nearing the end of his life, displayed a youthful zest in describing his work with Audio-Animatronics. By using complicated electronic systems, he was able to animate dolls and robotlike figures. The "It's a Small World" exhibit featured dolls in the costumes of many nations "singing" in assorted languages. Elsewhere at the fair, another Disney creation, a ponderous, robotized Abraham Lincoln, solemnly intoned excerpts from Lincoln's celebrated speeches. Critic-biographer Richard Schickel observed in *The Disney Version:*

> Here is the dehumanization of art in its final extremity, paradoxically achieved by an ignorant man who was actually, and in good conscience, seeking its humanization and who had, indeed, arrived at this dreadful solution, after a lifetime search for a perfect means of reproducing the reality of human life.

Disneyland and Disney World contain other examples of Disney's skill at producing both charm and pop-culture vulgarity, slickly packaged into Disneyesque cities where families flock to find pleasure, but where the joys and desires of childhood are also channeled into the conformity of commerce.

For Disney, given his background, taste, and flair for business, perhaps the final direction of his career was the most gratifying. From an artistic viewpoint, it is unfair and certainly unfortunate that his effort to do something as challenging and interesting as *Fantasia* should have resulted in an initial financial failure. Had the film been the success he hoped for, he might have been stimulated toward other projects that were more in keeping with the best of his creative work. As it was, the avant-garde experience left him regretful. The Motion Picture Academy, which gave

Disney a total of thirty-two Oscars, including the 1941 Thalberg Memorial Award, designated two special awards for *Fantasia*, one to Disney, William Garity, John N. A. Hawkins, and the RCA Manufacturing Company for "their outstanding contribution to the advancement of the use of sound in motion pictures," and the other to Leopold Stokowski and his associates for "their unique achievement – the creation of a new form of visualized music . . . thereby widening the scope of the motion picture as entertainment and as an art form." The New York Film Critics gave Disney a special award for *Fantasia*.

In recent years *Fantasia* has been rediscovered by another generation; it seems to strike a particular response among young people attuned to the contemporary multimedia scene. For all its weaknesses, the film endures as a measure of its unique creator and his leadership in the art of animation.

FANTASIA
USA (RKO Radio Pictures) 1940

Running time . . . . 116 minutes
Technicolor
Produced by . . . . WALT DISNEY INC.
Production Supervisor . . . . BEN SHARPSTEEN
Commentary . . . . DEEMS TAYLOR
Story Direction . . . . JOE GRANT, DICK HUEMER
Musical Direction . . . . EDWARD H. PLUMB
Musical Film Editor . . . . STEPHEN CSILLAG
Recording . . . . WILLIAM E. GARITY, C.O. SLYFIELD, J.N.A. HAWKINS

Music: **Toccata and Fugue in D Minor** by Bach
Direction . . . . SAMUEL ARMSTRONG
Story Development . . . . LEE BLAIR, ELMER PLUMMER, PHIL DIKE
Art Direction . . . . ROBERT CORMACK
Background Paintings . . . . JOE STAHLEY, JOHN HENCH, NINO CARBE
Animation . . . . CY YOUNG, ART PALMER, DANIEL MACMANUS, GEORGE ROWLEY, EDWIN AARDAL, JOSHUA MEADOR, CORNETT WOOD

Music: **The Nutcracker Suite** by Tchaikovsky
Direction . . . . SAMUEL ARMSTRONG
Story Development . . . . SYLVIA MOBERLY-HOLLAND, NORMAN WRIGHT, ALBERT HEATH,

BIANCA MAJOLIE, GRAHAM HEID
Character Designs . . . . JOHN WALBRIDGE, ELMER PLUMMER, ETHEL KULSAR
Art Direction . . . . ROBERT CORMACK, AL ZINNEN, CURTISS D. PERKINS, ARTHUR BYRAM, BRUCE BUSHMAN
Background Paintings . . . . JOHN HENCH, ETHEL KULSAR, NINO CARBE
Animation . . . . ART BABBITT, LES CLARK, DON LUSK, CY YOUNG, ROBERT STOKES

Music: **The Sorcerer's Apprentice** by Dukas
Direction . . . . JAMES ALGAR
Story Development . . . . PERC PEARCE, CARL FALLBERG
Art Direction . . . . TOM CODRICK, CHARLES PHILIPPI, ZACK SCHWARTZ
Background Paintings . . . . CLAUDE COATES, STAN SPOHN, ALBERT DEMPSTER, ERIC HANSEN
Animation Supervision . . . . FRED MOORE, VLADIMIR TYTLA
Animation . . . . LES CLARK, RILEY THOMPSON, MARVIN WOODWARD, PRESTON BLAIR, EDWARD LOVE, UGO D'ORSI, GEORGE ROWLEY, CORNETT WOOD

Music: **The Rite of Spring** by Stravinsky
Direction . . . . BILL ROBERTS, PAUL SATTERFIELD
Story Development and Research . . WILLIAM MARTIN, LEO THIELE, ROBERT STERNER, JOHN FRASER MCLEISH
Art Direction . . . . MCLAREN STEWART, DICK KELSEY, JOHN HUBLEY
Background Paintings . . . . ED STARR, BRICE MACK, EDWARD LEVITT
Animation Supervision . . . . WOLFGANG REITHERMAN, JOSHUA MEADOR
Animation . . . . PHILIP DUNCAN, JOHN MCMANUS, PAUL BUSCH, ART PALMER, DON TOBIN, EDWIN AARDAL, PAUL B. KOSSOFF
Special Camera Effects . . . . GAIL PAPINEAU, LEONARD PICKLEY

Music: **The Pastoral Symphony** by Beethoven
Direction . . . . HAMILTON LUSKE, JIM HANDLEY, FORD BEEBE
Story Development . . . . OTTO ENGLANDER, WEBB SMITH, ERDMAN PENNER, JOSEPH SABO, BILL PEED, GEORGE STALLINGS
Character Designs . . . . JAMES BODRERO, JOHN P. MILLER LORNA S. SODERSTROM
Art Direction . . . . HUGH HENNESY, KENNETH ANDERSON, J. GORDON LEGG, HERBERT RYMAN, YALE GRACEY, LANCE NOLLEY

Background Paintings............. CLAUDE COATES, RAY HUFFINE, W. RICHARD ANTHONY, ARTHUR RILEY, GERALD NEVIUS, ROY FORKUM
Animation Supervision............ FRED MOORE, WARD KIMBALL, ERIC LARSON, ART BABBITT, OLIVER M. JOHNSTON, JR., DON TOWSLEY
Animation .... BERNY WOLF, JACK CAMPBELL, JACK BRADBURY, JAMES MOORE, MILT NEIL, BILL JUSTICE, JOHN ELLIOTTE, WALT KELLY, DON LUSK, LYNN KARP, MURRAY MCCLELLAN, ROBERT W. YOUNGQUIST, HARRY HAMSEL

Music: **Dance of the Hours** by Ponchielli
Direction .... T. HEE, NORM FERGUSON
Character Designs........... MARTIN PROVENSEN, JAMES BODRERO, DUKE RUSSELL, EARL HURD
Art Direction .... KENDALL O'CONNOR, HAROLD DOUGHTY, ERNEST NORDLI
Background Paintings........ ALBERT DEMPSTER, CHARLES CONNER
Animation Supervision........................ NORM FERGUSON
Animation .... JOHN LOUNSBERY, HOWARD SWIFT, PRESTON BLAIR, HUGH FRASER, HARVEY TOOMBS, NORMAN TATE, HICKS LOKEY, ART ELLIOTT, GRANT SIMMONS, RAY PATTERSON, FRANKLIN GRUNDEEN

Music: **Night on Bald Mountain** by Mussorgsky
Direction .... WILFRED JACKSON
Story Development....... CAMPBELL GRANT, ARTHUR HEINEMANN, PHIL DIKE
Art Direction.................... KAY NIELSEN, TERRELL STAPP, CHARLES PAYZANT, THOR PUTNAM
Background Paintings .... MERLE COX, RAY LOCKREM, ROBERT STORMS, W. RICHARD ANTHONY
Animation Supervision...................... VLADIMIR TYTLA
Animation .... JOHN MCMANUS, WILLIAM N. SHULL, ROBERT W. CARLSON, JR., LESTER NOVROS, DON PATTERSON
Special Animation Effects........ JOSHUA MEADOR, MILES E. PIKE, JOHN F. REED, DANIEL MACMANUS
Special Camera Effects......... GAIL PAPINEAU, LEONARD PICKLEY

Music: **Ave Maria** by Schubert
Direction .... WILFRED JACKSON
Story Development....... CAMPBELL GRANT, ARTHUR HEINEMANN, PHIL DIKE
Art Direction.................... KAY NIELSEN, TERRELL STAPP, CHARLES PAYZANT, THOR PUTNAM

Background Paintings .... MERLE COX, RAY LOCKREM,
ROBERT STORMS, W. RICHARD ANTHONY
Animation Supervision........................ VLADIMIR TYTLA
Animation .... JOHN MCMANUS, WILLIAM N. SHULL,
ROBERT W. CARLSON, JR., LESTER NOVROS,
DON PATTERSON
Special Animation Effects .... JOSHUA MEADOR, MILES E. PIKE,
JOHN F. REED, DANIEL MACMANUS
Special Camera Effects .... GAIL PAPINEAU, LEONARD PICKLEY
Ave Maria Chorus................ CHARLES HENDERSON, Director
JULIETTA NOVIS, Soloist

Music played by .... THE PHILADELPHIA ORCHESTRA
Music conducted by .... LEOPOLD STOKOWSKI

1941

Charles Foster Kane (Orson Welles) runs for governor of New York.

Another Beginning

"LEGENDARY WAS XANADU where Kubla Khan decreed his stately pleasure dome. Today, almost as legendary is Florida's Xanadu, world's largest private pleasure ground. Here, on the deserts of the Gulf Coast, a private mountain was commissioned and successfully built. One hundred thousand trees, twenty thousand tons of marble are the ingredients of Xanadu's mountain. Contents of Xanadu's palace – paintings, pictures, statues, the very stones of many another palace – collection of everything so big it can never be catalogued or appraised. . . . Here in Xanadu last week, Xanadu's landlord was laid to rest, a potent figure of our century, America's Kubla Kahn – Charles Foster Kane."

So begins the narration for "News on the March," setting the dimensions for Orson Welles's magnificent film with an accurate simulation of the pompous "March of Time." Kane, "the greatest newspaper tycoon of this or any other generation," has already been seen on his deathbed, releasing his grip on the glass globe containing a snow-covered house, and muttering the enigmatic "Rosebud." *Citizen Kane* remains the most discussed and studied film produced in the United States, or perhaps anywhere, so impressive in theme and technique that it has become an international legend, as has its director, who was twenty-five when he made it. The film is expansive enough to accommodate legend. No matter how many times one views *Citizen Kane*, one can derive additional insight and pleasure. It is that rare film without boundaries, yielding limitless analysis and, it would seem, limitless controversy.

Historically, *Citizen Kane* provided a new beginning by reaching back into the past and building upon it. Sound had interrupted the visual refinements of the silent period. In synthesizing the progress of sound in the 1930s with the genius of the silents, *Citizen Kane* advanced cinema through experimentation and rediscovery. Welles arrived in Hollywood with a fresh viewpoint, artistic control, and a boy-genius reputation that, at first, allowed him leeway to explore new ideas. With scriptwriter Herman J. Mankiewicz, cinematographer Gregg Toland, editor Robert Wise, and others, he reaffirmed that cinema is, above all, a visual art, with sound an important facet that could be creatively integrated. *Citizen Kane*'s innovative technique gave new impetus to cinema craftsmanship, inspired other filmmakers, and changed conceptions of what was possible on screen.

Controversy enveloped the film because it dared to fictionalize the life of powerful newspaper publisher William Randolph Hearst. The campaign mounted by Hearst gossip-columnist Louella Parsons sent shudders through the industry. RKO, owned in part by the Rockefellers and the Chase National Bank, had scheduled the première at Radio City Music Hall, a Rockefeller property. According to Pauline Kael in her "Raising Kane" essay in the *New Yorker* (later reprinted in *The Citizen Kane Book*), Nelson Rockefeller told George J. Schaefer, head of RKO, that Parsons had threatened to publish a hostile article in the Hearst press on John D. Rockefeller and that this and other maneuvers contributed to the cancellation of the opening. Rumor had it that the film would not be released at all, and Welles threatened to sue.

Schaefer, who had difficulty finding theaters for *Citizen Kane* because of the attacks, had rejected pressure to destroy the film. MGM mogul Louis B. Mayer, using as his intermediary Nicholas Schenck, head of the board of Loew's International, which handled MGM distribution, and evidently acting on behalf of the major studios, offered to reimburse RKO's production and post-production costs of some $842,000 if the film were not released and the negative and all prints were destroyed. The implication of the offer goes beyond momentary hysteria. The United States was soon to be fighting a war against the Third Reich, where book-burning was policy, but here was an attempt by motion picture leaders to "burn" a film because it might offend a newspaper emperor. To Schaefer's credit, he refused. Had he accepted, a pivotal achievement of cinema would have been lost; not only would the world have been deprived of a masterpiece, but an untold number of future filmmakers would have been denied the inspiration to be derived from *Citizen Kane*. This abominable atmosphere of panic was akin to that which led to the initiation of the blacklist six years after *Citizen Kane*'s release.

The appreciation of *Citizen Kane*'s technical prowess has tended to obscure the significance of its content, boldly running counter to the traditional Hollywood gloss. Critical biographies of famous controversial contemporaries have been avoided as a matter of course. The import of a film concerned with big business and politics, wealth and power, and basing its protagonist on no less a figure than Hearst, unrivaled as a newspaper magnate and known for his right-wing political positions, should not be overlooked. *Citizen Kane*'s audacity, which even now impresses students experiencing it for the first time, was revolutionary in 1941.

The question whether the film was indeed about Hearst has persisted. The obfuscation can be partly attributed to evasive statements by Welles, obviously for legal purposes. It is futile to quote comments made at various times by those involved with the film as evidence that Hearst was not the subject. Although others, including Welles and Mankiewicz themselves, may be recognized in the character composite, overwhelming similarities inextricably entwine William Randolph Hearst and Charles Foster Kane. Hearst was the only comparable press lord and Xanadu was obviously a version of his palatial home, San Simeon. His relationship with Marion Davies was, of course, recalled by Kane's relationship with Susan Alexander. Many details in Kane's newspaper life were also clearly inspired by Hearst's career.

It may have been inevitable that Welles would find himself in the midst of controversy in Hollywood. Had he not made *Citizen Kane,* his brashness, enthusiasm, and independence would probably have placed him on a collision course with Hollywood conventions. His reputation for individualism and avant-gardism was already solidly established. Welles had directed Marc Blitzstein's left-wing opera *The Cradle Will Rock*, presented defiantly in the face of its abandonment by Washington as a WPA (Works Progress Administration) theater project. A place in which to present it was found just before curtain time, but Equity refused permission for the actors to participate on stage. To circumvent the ruling, cast members rose from the audience to play their roles. Welles and John Houseman co-founded the famous Mercury Theater, hailed as an exciting experiment for such lauded productions as *Julius Caesar*, directed by Welles, who also played Brutus. The Mercury Theater of the Air's dramatic broadcasts over CBS received national attention even before "The War of the Worlds" program. Welles was also an actor on the "March of Time" and the voice of "The Shadow." His ego, youth, and dynamism made him a natural for publicity, but the CBS broadcast on October 30, 1938 (Halloween), brought him fame he himself could not have anticipated.

Houseman, in his book *Run-through*, partially attributed the panic that occurred during the adaptation of the H.G. Wells work to dial-twisting. People who were listening to the Edgar Bergen-Charlie McCarthy show found a dull spot and began changing programs. Tuning in to "The War of the Worlds" after it had begun, they thought the news bulletins announcing a Martian invasion of New Jersey were real. Interspersed with what was made to seem like routine programing, the bulletins sounded so authentic that they touched off panic throughout the nation. People fled their homes; police and radio switchboards were jammed with calls. It seemed incredible that large sections of the public could be stampeded so easily. Welles was the center of the ensuing furor.

As RKO was having a difficult time financially, Nelson Rockefeller reportedly recommended Welles to Schaefer as the kind of daring talent needed to help alleviate its crisis. After being promised artistic control Welles agreed to go to Hollywood, but his initial film projects did not materialize. With *Citizen Kane*, he proceeded cautiously because of the subject matter, professing at first to be shooting test sequences. Welles's Mercury Theater actors were a ready troupe of performers; many of them were in the production, among them Everett Sloane, George Coulouris, Agnes Moorehead, Ray Collins, Ruth Warrick, and Paul Stewart. The acting is generally exceptional, led, of course, by Welles's towering portrayal of Kane. In what lives as one of filmdom's most forceful character portraits, he makes Kane a believable, dimensional figure – awesome, yet oddly likable in many ways despite his insensitivity, bullying, and high-handedness. Admittedly, there is evidence of the ham in Welles, but in *Citizen Kane* he converts his tendency to overstate into dramatic energy.

Recent polemics have centered on Welles's monopoly of glory; on whether he or Mankiewicz deserved greater recognition for the screenplay; whether he even had sufficient input to justify cowriting credit; and whether Mankiewicz came to Welles with the idea, or vice versa. Kael in "Raising Kane" vigorously rehabilitated Mankiewicz as the principal author, causing Welles, in an interview with Charles Champlin in the *Los Angeles Times*, May 12, 1973, to comment: "The dispute between Herman and me was not whether he should be off the credits but whether I should be on. I didn't really care; credits are the last thing I care about. She [Kael] accepted John Houseman's version of things. Houseman went up to the desert with Herman and he assumed that the whole script was flowing out of Herman's head. But Mankiewicz and I had developed the story alone before he went up there. It gets to be very ugly."

There seems to be no disagreement that Mankiewicz was sequestered in a remote retreat to work on the script, chaperoned by Houseman, who did the editing and ensured that Mankiewicz delivered and did not indulge in his well-known drinking binges. Certainly, he has been overshadowed in the general tendency to attribute the film almost entirely to Welles. In that sense Kael's thesis, whether an unsupportable broadside or sufficiently grounded in fact, is valuable in focusing new attention on the writing. In the preoccupation with the visuals, it is easy to overlook the literacy of the screenplay. It is an integral part of *Citizen Kane*'s grandeur; a lesser script could not have supported the film's technical genius. Although there are flaws, the story is told with depth and intelligence and most of the dialogue works exceedingly well. The structure has clarity despite its departure from chronological storytelling methods. Flashbacks can be treacherous, but used here to unravel Kane's life, they are neatly interlocked and never leave the viewer disoriented. The notion of using "Rosebud" as a Hitchcock-like "MacGuffin," although contrived, gives the plot unity. The gimmick cannot be faulted too seriously, for the film does not depend on our learning the meaning of the word. It is the meaning of Kane's life with which we are concerned, and that is illuminated not through a device but through an honest, compelling portrait.

The story itself is not complex. After Kane dies and the "News on the March" expeditiously acquaints us with his public image, the action begins in the projection room where a group of newsmen have been screening the short. They like it, but agree that it needs an angle. The reporter, Thompson (William Allard), is assigned to find out how Kane differs "from Ford, Hearst – for that matter – or John Doe." Perhaps Kane's last word, Rosebud, is the key. The framework for *Citizen Kane* consists of Thompson's examination of the memoirs of Kane's ex-guardian, and interviews with four persons who knew Kane. Susan Alexander Kane (Dorothy Comingore) is appearing in an Atlantic City nightclub, but she is drinking heavily and uncooperative. Thompson then visits the austere Thatcher Memorial Library where he reads the pertinent papers of Walter Parks Thatcher (George Coulouris). A flashback to Kane's boyhood reveals his poor origins in Colorado and his traumatic uprooting. Seemingly worthless mining stock given his mother by a boarder in lieu of payment has become valuable, and Thatcher has been appointed to manage her financial interests. At her behest, he takes the upset, reluctant boy from his home to provide him with the education and environment befitting the wealth he will acquire at the age of twenty-five. More flashbacks illustrate the Thatcher material, after which the reporter talks with Bernstein (Everett Sloane), formerly Kane's general manager, and Jedediah Leland (Joseph Cotten), the school chum he hired to work for him. On a return visit to Atlantic City, Thompson is able to interview Susan. Lastly, he speaks with Kane's grasping butler, Raymond (Paul Stewart).

The portrait provided encompasses Kane's rebellious youth, his early attitude to money as important only for the financing of the projects he enjoys, the building and decline of his newspaper empire, and the void in his personal life. At first, idealism is a motivation, but gradually the goal of power assumes precedence. His marriage to a niece of the president of the United States, Emily Norton (Ruth Warrick), deteriorates. When he meets Susan, a liaison begins that destroys his political aspirations. Campaigning to end corruption, he appears to have the governorship of New York in his grasp, but his opponent, James W. Gettys (Ray Collins), whom he has promised to imprison, threatens to make his affair public. Kane spurns Getty's stipulation that he withdraw from the race by feigning illness. His relationship with Susan is exposed, costing him the election and a conceivable stepping-stone to the presidency.

Divorced, Kane marries Susan, whom he is resolved to make into an opera star, although she is devoid of talent. To give her a stage, he builds an opera house in Chicago, but her debut is a catastrophe. Kane visits his Chicago newspaper office, where Leland is now working as drama critic. The two have not spoken for years. Leland, drunk, has passed out after having begun his review of the dramatic aspect of Susan's performance. ("Her singing, happily, is no concern of this department.") Kane picks up the review, finishes it as the vitriolic pan Leland intended, and fires him. The rapport between Kane and Susan collapses rapidly, he growing increasingly tyrannical, she increasingly miserable, bored, and desperate. Xanadu is more her prison than her home and, finally, she leaves him. In a rage he tears her room apart.

Kane dies a lonely, loveless despot, his newspaper chain a remnant of its former strength, not having recovered from losses during the Depression. Notwithstanding the power and fortune he amassed, he never found the love he sought, nor was he able to give love. The reporter does not learn the significance of Rosebud, but the audience does. In the final spectacular scene at Xanadu showing Kane's possessions being sorted and crated, a sled is tossed into a furnace and we see the word Rosebud imprinted on it. The sled is a memento from Kane's childhood with his mother that was interrupted by the opportunities fortune brought him; one may conclude that it is symbolic of the love that eluded him, his regret for what was lost – a dying man's recollection of a possession that retained a special meaning.

The litany of *Citizen Kane*'s virtuosity is often recited. As with *The Birth of a Nation*, it was not that Welles and Toland invented fantastic techniques hitherto unknown any more than Griffith and Bitzer did. The glory of *Citizen Kane* is the consummate skill with which known methods were explored and expanded upon to tell a compelling story with an astonishing degree of smoothness, intelligence, creativity, and unity of purpose. Toland, writing in *Popular Photography* of June 1941, in an article entitled "How I Broke the Rules in *Citizen Kane*," observed: "Welles's use of the cinematographer as a real aid to him in telling the story, and his appreciation of the camera's storytelling potentialities helped me immeasurably. He was willing – and this is very rare in Hollywood – that I take weeks to achieve a desired photographic effect. The photographic approach to *Citizen Kane* was planned and considered long before the first camera turned. That is also unconventional in Hollywood, where most cinematographers learn of their next assignments only a few days before the scheduled shooting starts. Altogether, I was on the job for a half year, including preparation and actual shooting."

The deep focus shots so universally esteemed enable us to contemplate events in the foreground while observing details in the background. While the fate of young Kane is being decided in Thatcher's discussion with his mother (his father has no say), we also see him through the window playing alone in the snow, and the emotional effect of the scene is heightened incalculably. This technique, repeatedly applied with similar effectiveness, produces a cumulative impact. The unusually creative use of lighting made many uneasy when *Citizen Kane* was first released. Seeing characters in shadow, as in the reporters' discussion following the "News on the March," with shafts of light streaming from the projection booth, impressed the more conventional as merely arty. However, Welles's concentration on lighting as a potent facet of cinematic language contributes to the film's remarkable dimension by affecting the way in which audiences perceive the characters and their surroundings.

Welles, with his experience in radio, was aware of the untapped potential of sound in film. When Kane makes a political speech, the echo reinforces the desired impression that he is in a huge arena, and the hollow tones in the cavernous Xanadu provide a realistic sense of space and atmosphere that would otherwise be lost. The sound of footsteps at the mausoleumlike Thatcher Library offer another example. The settings, too, are not only imposing, but are used ingeniously to achieve realism and mood, and to convey Kane's environment – the ambience of his newspaper offices and the eerie grandiosity of Xanadu. Welles has sometimes been mistakenly credited as the first to have ceilings on his film sets. This stems from the extent to which he did so, and the impressive results he obtained.

"The *Citizen Kane* sets have ceilings because we wanted reality," Toland wrote, "and we felt that it would be easier to believe a room was a room if its ceiling could be seen in the picture. Furthermore, lighting effects in unceilinged rooms generally are not realistic because the illumination comes from unnatural angles."

The economy with which *Citizen Kane* was shot and edited is also crucial. The montage of Kane and his first wife breakfasting at progressive intervals in their marriage has been extolled, with good reason, for the way in which it wittily and succinctly describes their disintegrating relationship. It replaces the detailed scenes that a less astutely crafted film might have included to make the same point. The breathtakingly fluid camera movement and editing are carefully conceived in relationship to their impact on the viewer, whether in the use of jump cuts or in the panoramic view at the close. The incredible accumulation of Kane's lifetime of acquisition offers an impressive example of the film's artistry: the camera pulls back and up to survey in increasing depth the seemingly endless possessions, then slowly and dramatically glides in toward the sled as it and the word Rosebud are seen being consumed by flames. The scene dissolves to a view of the castle, smoke pouring from its chimney, and the "No Trespassing" sign, visible as it was at the outset of the film and offering a satisfactory sense of completeness to the span of a man's life.

The director of a film as celebrated as *Citizen Kane* should have been guaranteed a carte blanche career, a position of esteem that would enable him to undertake any project he desired with total artistic control. But being an artistic revolutionary has its penalties. Griffith was all but forgotten by his industry; Eisenstein was beset by political repression. Welles was shunted aside as unpredictable and uncommercial, which has made it difficult for him to raise money for his film projects. This ignominious fate led him to work in Europe. For all his brilliance, Welles represented a disruption in a studio system that preferred safer, more conservative talent. That *Citizen Kane* was not an immediate moneymaker despite the plaudits of the critics lost him final control of his next film – *The Magnificent Ambersons* (1942), based on the Booth Tarkington novel – which was butchered even to the extent of having a new ending attached without his approval. The very aspects that made *Citizen Kane* so extraordinary discouraged audiences unable or unwilling to respond to it. Over the years, however, it has not only attained the status of a classic, but has redeemed itself commercially.

Hollywood's discomfort with *Citizen Kane* was evident at Academy Award time when it was by-passed for the 1941 best picture and best director Oscars, the honors going to *How Green Was My Valley* and John Ford. Even the award for black-and-white cinematography went to Arthur Miller for *How Green Was My Valley*, instead of to Gregg Toland for his history-making work. Bernard Herrmann received an Oscar for best dramatic picture score, not for his significant contribution to *Citizen Kane*, but for William Dieterle's *All That Money Can Buy*. The Academy confined its recognition to the best screenplay award to Mankiewicz and Welles. The New York Film Critics had the superior judgment to select *Citizen Kane* as best picture, but schizophrenically gave the direction award to Ford.

Welles's post-*Citizen Kane* films are cited as evidence of his continuing genius and of his failure. He is regarded variously as a master who has maintained his greatness beyond question (some even consider *The Magnificent Ambersons* or *Touch of Evil*, 1958, superior to *Citizen Kane*); as a man whose talent has not endured, or who could not possibly have lived up to his early accomplishments and the resultant expectations; and as a heroic maverick who has refused to sacrifice his individuality. Welles's films include *The Stranger* (1946), *The Lady from Shanghai* (1948), *Macbeth* (1948), *Othello* (1951), *Mr. Arkadin* (1955), *The Trial* (1962), *Chimes at Midnight* (1966), *The Immortal Story* (1968), *F for Fake* (1973). (*The Other Side of the Wind*, begun in 1970 and filmed intermittently, is still unreleased at this writing; according to Welles, it is ninety-six percent completed and edited, but tied up financially.) Welles appears in most of his films, and his magnetism is visible in a variety of roles in those of others. An interesting sidelight – Charlie Chaplin has acknowledged that *Monsieur Verdoux* evolved from Welles's idea for a documentary on the famous French murderer Landru.

In 1975, the American Film Institute honored Welles in Hollywood with its Life Achievement Award. His obese figure, so strikingly dissimilar to his boyish 1940s appearance, suggested the titan his admirers and disciples consider him to be, but the adulation contained incongruity. In his speech Welles reaffirmed his dignity and the code of independence by which he has tried to exist as an individual and as an artist. The tone of the event, however, at least as projected in the telecast, smacked of pomposity and self-righteousness on the part of those acclaiming him.

It may be romantic to hope that Welles will make another film that will have further impact on the history of cinema, but to have made *Citizen Kane* is enough of an achievement in a lifetime, amply ensuring his rank in the forefront of influential film directors.

CITIZEN KANE
USA (RKO Radio Pictures) 1941

Cast

Charles Foster Kane.............................ORSON WELLES
Jedediah Leland.................................JOSEPH COTTEN
Susan Alexander Kane...................DOROTHY COMINGORE
Kane's mother ....AGNES MOOREHEAD
Emily Norton Kane..............................RUTH WARRICK
James W. Gettys ....RAY COLLINS
Mr. Carter ....ERSKINE SANFORD
Mr. Bernstein.................................EVERETT SLOANE
Thompson, the Reporter
(and Newsreel Narrator).....................WILLIAM ALLAND
Raymond ....PAUL STEWART
Walter Parks Thatcher......................GEORGE COULOURIS
Signor Matisti ....FORTUNIO BONANOVA
Headwaiter..GUS SCHILLING
Rawlston.......................................PHILIP VAN ZANDT
Miss Anderson ....GEORGIA BACKUS
Kane's father..................................HARRY SHANNON
Kane III ....SONNY BUPP
Kane, age eight ....BUDDY SWAN
Hillman ....RICHARD BAER (now BARR)
Georgia ....JOAN BLAIR
Mike ....AL EBEN
Entertainer...................................CHARLES BENNETT
Reporter ....MILT KIBBEE
Teddy Roosevelt ....TOM CURRAN
Dr. Corey ....IRVING MITCHELL
Nurse ....EDITH EVANSON
Orchestra Leader ....ARTHUR KAY
Chorus Master ....TUDOR WILLIAMS
City Editor ....HERBERT CORTHELL
Smather ....BENNY RUBIN

Reporter .... EDMUND COBB
Ethel .... FRANCES NEAL
Photographer .... ROBERT DUDLEY
Miss Townsend .... ELLEN LOWE
Gino, the Waiter .... GINO CORRADO
and ALAN LADD, LOUISE CURRIE, EDDIE COKE, WALTER SANDE, ARTHUR O'CONNELL, KATHERINE TROSPER, RICHARD WILSON

Running time .... 119 minutes
Production Company .... MERCURY
Produced by .... ORSON WELLES
Directed by .... ORSON WELLES
Original Screenplay by .... HERMAN J. MANKIEWICZ and ORSON WELLES
Director of Photography .... GREGG TOLAND
Editor .... ROBERT WISE
Assistant Editor .... MARK ROBSON
Art Director .... VAN NEST POLGLASE
Associate Art Director .... PERRY FERGUSON
Special Effects by .... VERNON L. WALKER
Recording .... BAILEY FESLER, JAMES G. STEWART
Costumes .... EDWARD STEVENSON
Decors .... DARRELL SILVERA
Music Composed and Conducted by .... BERNARD HERRMANN

1945

Open City

Anna Magnani as Pina fights to break free and run to her fiancé Francesco, who has been arrested by the Germans. A moment later she is shot.

New Realism, New Hope

IN THE WAKE OF THE tragedy and despair of World War II came *Open City, Paisan, The Bicycle Thief*, and other films from Italy that infused cinema with new inspiration and direction. Showing life's bitter aspects while extolling the human spirit, these films contrasted sharply with the romanticized product characteristic of Hollywood. Even before the Nazis were driven out of Rome, footage was being shot for the landmark film that dramatically called attention to Italian neo-realism, a movement that was to have lasting international impact. *Open City* not only told a story of heroism and resistance against the Nazis and Fascists, but bristled with convincing documentarylike detail and dramatic realism that expressed the passion and terror of the war years, and projected the burgeoning hopes for a brighter future.

Open City was not popular when first shown in Italy. The general public was more interested in escapism and had little desire to dwell on the grimness of the recent past. The film was also inevitably divisive in its intense lauding of left-wing Resistance heroes and the priests aligned with them, and its condemnation of those who supported the Fascists and collaborated with the German occupiers. As Pina, played so brilliantly by Anna Magnani, says of her wish to be married by a partisan priest despite her fiancé Francesco's ideological agnosticism: "Better for Don Pietro to marry us – at least he's on the right side – rather than go to City Hall and be married by a Fascist." Acceptance at home grew after acclaim abroad. For film enthusiasts in the United States, where the New York Film Critics chose it as best foreign film of 1946, *Open City* changed the standards for honesty and maturity on screen. Beside it, less forthright treatments of the war and its effects paled.

Director Roberto Rossellini, whose screenwriters were Sergio Amidei and the young Federico Fellini, made use of professional performers, nonprofessionals, and the city of Rome. The casting of non-actors set an important example, demonstrating that by choosing an individual who looks the part and dubbing his or her voice, a realistic visual effect can be achieved. (Post-synchronization is the practice in Italian cinema, sometimes to the detriment of oral credibility.) Rome itself became a leading character because of the lack of studio facilities as a result of the war, which made it necessary to film in the streets. Scenes of the hungry citizens invading a bakery and carrying off bread, of Nazis forcing residents into the street so that their apartments could be searched for Resistance fighters, were rendered far more potent than if they had been shot on a studio lot, and manifested the dramatic impact inherent in this approach to making films.

Although scripted drama, the basis of *Open City* is factual and the form close to documentary. The portrayals are especially naturalistic. Pina is a woman removed from film stereotype. Magnani, in the most impressive role of her distinguished career, brings stubborn earthiness to the widow who is struggling through the war, spiritedly fighting for survival and dignity while raising her son. She is about to marry the man she loves and whose child she is already carrying. There is no hypocrisy to her. She and Francesco (Francesco Grand-Jacquet) sit on the steps of the working-class apartment building on the eve of their intended wedding and discuss the future in a mature man-woman conversation far superior to the then-usual screen small talk. When Pina is gunned down in the street by the Germans the next day, the film shifts into an increased level of tension. Few scenes in cinema have the force of that in which Magnani, arms outstretched, races toward the camera to her death.

Open City starts with a panning shot of the rooftops of Rome from the Pincian Hill, then cuts to German troops marching across the Piazza di Spagna. The next morning, a patrol demands entrance to an apartment. The Germans are searching for the engineer Manfredi (Marcello Pagliero), an important military leader of the National Liberation Committee. While the landlady and the elderly servant stall, Manfredi escapes via a terrace. At Gestapo headquarters, Major Bergmann (Harry Feist) explains to the Italian police commissioner his methods for tracking down members of the Resistance. Of-camera, the screams of tortured prisoners can be heard. Bergmann shows the commissioner a photograph of his prime target, Manfredi, and his girl friend Marina, a music-hall performer.

Pina is introduced during the bakery riot, her shopping bag full of bread. The scene instantly establishes the deprivations faced by the people of Rome, as well as their growing militancy. A friendly Italian police sergeant, to whom she gives two rolls, walks Pina home. On the way someone offers to sell her black-market eggs. "How dare you! In my presence!" exclaims the sergeant. But it is an empty protest. At home, a man comes looking for Francesco. The visitor is Manfredi. Pina invites him in, and when he explains that he must see Don Pietro, the priest of San Clemente, she sends her small son Marcello (Vito Annichiarico) to fetch him. Marcello arrives at the church, where the priest (Aldo Fabrizi), wearing his clerical garments, is playing soccer with some boys. The ball lands on the priest's head and the boys laugh. Don Pietro agrees to undertake the mission outlined by Manfredi. To help five hundred Resistance fighters in the mountains, the priest, not subject to the five o'clock curfew, carries a large sum of money, cleverly concealed in books, from the military committee to a prearranged contact.

Francesco, briefly questioned en route by German soldiers who allow him to pass because of his printer's permit, arrives home after curfew. Pina is worried because she cannot find her son. Other boys in the building are also missing. Suddenly, there is the sound of an explosion and flames illuminate the sky. The scene shifts to a railway, where a group of boys, including Marcello and Romoletto, the crippled youth from upstairs who walks with a crutch, are escaping after their act of sabotage. Arriving home, one by one they are slapped and scolded by their frantic, unsuspecting parents for being out so late. Pina gives Marcello his cuffing. Later, when the boy is in bed, Francesco questions him but respects his secrecy. Marcello asks: "Is it true that from tomorrow on I have to call you Papa?" "If you want to," replies Francesco. "Yes," says Marcello, hugging him. Francesco and Pina's tender conversation on the steps follows. They reminisce about their first meeting. Francesco speaks hopefully, trying to cheer up Pina who is weary from all the pressures and yet another argument with her carping sister, Laura. "We're fighting for something that has to be," he tells her, "that can't help coming. Maybe the way is hard, it may take a long time, but we'll get there, and we'll see a better world. And our kids will see it. Marcello and – and him, the baby that's coming."

The essential contours have been drawn. The next day, when the Nazis search the building for Manfredi, Pina comforts a woman who sees her son taken away. Moments later, Pina witnesses the arrest of Francesco. Racing after the van in which he is taken away, she is shot. Marcello runs to her, crying hysterically. Francesco escapes when the van is ambushed by partisans led by Manfredi, but Manfredi himself is soon apprehended. Marina, addicted to drugs supplied by Ingrid, Major Bergmann's ruthless lesbian aide, has betrayed him. Also captured are Don Pietro, and an Austrian deserter whom he has helped. At Gestapo headquarters, the brutal torture session begins. Bergmann is determined to break Manfredi by morning and learn the names of other Resistance leaders before they can reorganize. At stake, too, is his belief in the Nazi master race theory. Manfredi is mercilessly tortured, but will not yield. Don Pietro is brought into the next room to hear the screams. The Austrian, meanwhile, hangs himself.

Bergmann tries to divide Don Pietro and Manfredi by telling the priest that Manfredi is a subversive opposed to religion. Don Pietro responds that "a man who fights for justice and liberty walks in the pathways of the Lord, and the pathways of the Lord are infinite." He is brought in to see Manfredi, whose maimed body can no longer endure. He dies without talking. The Nazi has lost. In the final sequence, Don Pietro is led to an outdoor place of execution. Heading the firing squad is Hartmann, a veteran of World War I, previously revealed to be disillusioned. Don Pietro, accompanied by a priest, answers the latter's words of encouragement: "It's not hard to die well. It's hard to live well." He is tied to a chair. Before the order to fire is given, he hears the sound of whistling. Marcello, Romoletto, and their group of young partisans have gathered nearby. Don Pietro looks up in recognition, and the Italian squad fires. The soldiers deliberately miss. Furious, Hartmann walks over, draws his gun, and shoots Don Pietro in the head. The children bow their heads and walk off down the hill, a view of Rome in the background.

The portrayal of Don Pietro by Fabrizi is among the most compelling attributes of Rossellini's film. Through this character, much is said about the unity of the diverse forces opposing the Germans and Fascists during the period before Italy's liberation by the combined forces of the Allied invasion and the Resistance. Political alignments, while not overemphasized, are acknowledged. Bergmann leafs through clandestine newspapers on his desk that reflect the spectrum of the Resistance. It is apparent that Manfredi is a Communist, but beyond voicing hopes for a better tomorrow for the people, the film eschews party pleading, concentrating on joint action against the common enemy.

Realism is achieved in part through the dialogue and casting. Magnani and Fabrizi are thoroughly believable, as are Grand-Jacquet as Francesco and Pagliero as Manfredi. The children, too, aid the naturalistic effect. The affectionate scene between Marcello and Francesco is far from the maudlin exchange it would have been in a Hollywood counterpart. The mannerisms of the Nazis lean toward the cliché, but their deeds, and the casualness of the torture sessions lend credence. A squabble at Pina's erupts with the noise and passion of real family battles, giving the film further authenticity.

Rossellini, who died in 1977 at the age of seventy-one, acquired his skill filming documentaries under the Fascist regime. He was among the youthful directors of the period who were impressed with a film that Francesco de Robertis, a proponent of direct cinema, had shot aboard a submarine. When de Robertis was appointed head of the film office for the naval ministry, Rossellini was assigned to make a feature entitled *La Nave Bianca* aboard a hospital ship, and the success of that effort led to other opportunities. *Open City* evolved from a short documentary about a heroic priest he had started at the beginning of 1944.

In an introduction to *The War Trilogy*, a collection of screenplays of *Open City, Paisan,* and *Germany – Year Zero*, Rossellini observed: "*Open City* and *Paisan* were films intended to represent a sort of balance sheet of that period of history, of those twenty years of Fascism that ended with the great drama of the war, fruit of something that had been much stronger than us and had overwhelmed, crushed, and implicated us. Once the balance sheet had been drawn up, perhaps we could start with a fresh page." (Rossellini's compassionate *Paisan*, 1946, on which Fellini was his co-scriptwriter, is a collection of six episodes set during the period when the Allies were driving the Germans from Italy.)

Neo-realism's greatest exponent was Vittorio de Sica, long a successful actor and matinée idol in Italy, whose extraordinarily eloquent dramas describe the human condition. His superb collaborator, scriptwriter Cesare Zavattini, holds a position of esteem among the neo-realists. *Shoeshine* (1946) is de Sica's magnificent evocation of the shattered society left by the war. *The Bicycle Thief* (1948), the most celebrated of the genre and the winner of an Academy Award, tells of a man's pathetic search for his stolen bicycle, without which he cannot work. De Sica made it for $100,000, using non-professionals in the principal parts – an electrician, Lamberto Maggiorani, as the desperate billposter, and the unforgettable Enzo Staiola, as his young son Bruno.

De Sica also filmed the excellent *Miracle in Milan* (1950), about the discovery of oil underneath the homes of impoverished families living on the outskirts of Milan, and *Umberto D* (1951), a touching drama on the loneliness of old age. He gave his most poignant film performance in *Il Generale della Rovere* (1959), directed by Rossellini. Under the ever-present pressure to accept acting or directing assignments to earn money for preferred projects, de Sica maneuvered through an uneven career. However, before his death in 1974, he made *The Garden of the Finzi Continis* and *A Brief Vacation*, two masterly films that, while compatible with contemporary style, contain elements recalling the neo-realism of his early work.

Rossellini veered decisively from his initial neo-realism, and in retrospect, looked upon it as a distant experience, logically connected to his subsequent work, but very much in the past. After 1962 he turned to television, and a decade later expressed his conviction that creating films for television and for educational use was a filmmaker's highest calling. He continued to use a documentarylike approach. *The Rise of Louis XIV* is a slow, meticulous, colorful evocation, rich in the detail of the epoch; *Socrates* is pedantic, a historical reconstruction without any of the visual flair that distinguished many of Rossellini's ventures.

Italian filmmaking has changed radically since its neo-realistic decade. The late Luchino Visconti's first film, *Ossessione* (1942), based without permission on James Cain's *The Postman Always Rings Twice*, was a harbinger of neo-realism, and many consider *La Terra Trema* (1947), shot in Sicily with a non-professional cast, akin to the movement. Visconti, one of the world's foremost directors, subsequently moved in an entirely different direction, becoming a master of the baroque and creating films virtually operatic in style, including *The Damned* (1969) and *Death in Venice* (1971). Michelangelo Antonioni, also rooted in neo-realism, has become immersed in deeply reflective films, relying upon visual sensitivity and pensive moods, as in *L'Avventura, La Notte, The Red Desert* (with its creative, mesmerizing use of color), *Blow-Up*, and *Zabriskie Point*. *The Passenger*, starring Jack Nicholson, has a remarkable finale that is a tour de force of camera move-

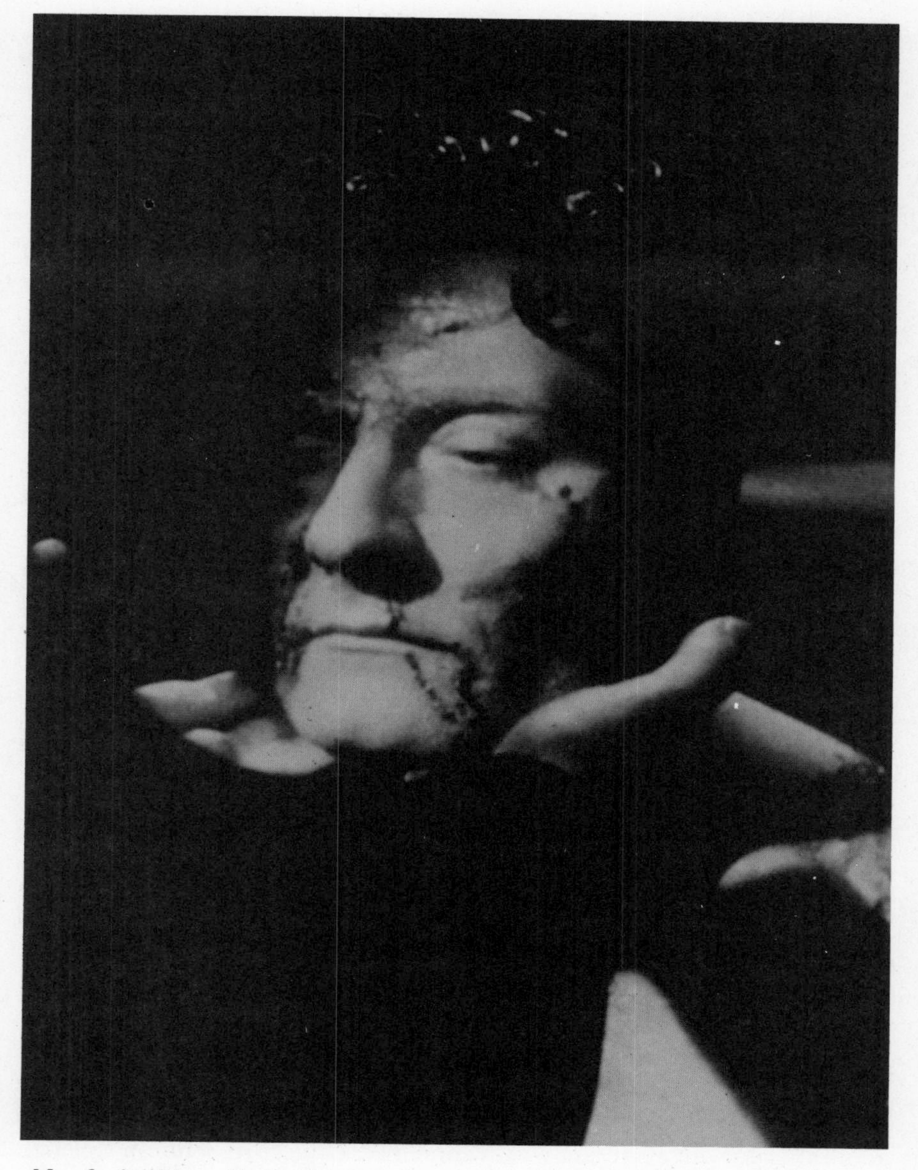

Manfredi (Marcello Pagliero) refuses to break under horrendous Gestapo torture and dies without giving information about the Resistance

ment. Federico Fellini (see *8½*) is justifiably known as the most flamboyantly imaginative of Italian directors. Other important filmmakers include Pier Paolo Pasolini (*Accattone, The Gospel According to St. Matthew*, and the posthumously released *Saló, or: The 120 days of Sodom*); Bernardo Bertolucci (*Before the Revolution, The Conformist, Last Tango in Paris*, and *1900*); Marco Bellocchio (*Fists in the Pocket, China is Near*); Francesco Rosi (*Salvatore Giuliano, Hands Over the City*); Gillo Pontecorvo (*The Battle of Algiers*, similar in its realism to *Open City*); and, of course, Lina Wertmüller (see *Seven Beauties*).

The neo-realists were unpopular with the right, the church, and the bureaucrats. De Sica's *Umberto D* was attacked by government officials who resented its depiction of indifference to the plight of the elderly. Such films celebrated human dignity, echoed the fiery emotions of the war from a left viewpoint, held governmental and clerical hypocrisy up to ridicule, and ran counter to what would have been preferred – more passive films showing conditions to be better than they were. As Pasolini said in a 1968 interview with Oswald Stack for his book *Pasolini:* "Neo-realism was the expression in the cinema of the Resistance, of the rediscovery of Italy, with all our hopes for a new kind of society. This lasted until the late fifties. After that neo-realism died because Italy changed: the establishment reconsolidated its position on petit bourgeois and clerical bases."

Although it is true that the movement ran its course in Italy, its effect has continued to be manifested in various ways. During his conversation with Stack, Pasolini, whose own *Accattone,* released in 1961, has the stamp of the genre, made the point that neo-realism was exported to France and England and filtered back into the work of younger Italian directors, such as Bertolucci and Bellocchio. Neo-realism has inspired countless directors throughout the world. Indian filmmaker Satyajit Ray recalled in *Cahiers du Cinéma,* February 1966, that it was after having seen *The Bicycle Thief* in London in 1950 that he decided to film *Pather Panchali* according to neo-realistic methods: "I was pleasantly surprised to discover that one could work exclusively in exterior settings, with non-professional actors, and I thought that what one could do in Italy one could do in Bengal as well, in spite of the difficulties of the sound recording."

Allowing for periodic ups and downs, and for the trash that has appeared there as everywhere else, Italy has maintained its place of honor in cinema. (Franco Brusati's *Bread and Chocolate* won the New York Film Critics Circle's award for best foreign language film of 1978.) The work of filmmakers such as those cited constitutes a valuable contribution to art. However, the magnetism of the neo-realist epoch has never been recaptured. Further insight into its aims and methods can be gained from the introduction, "How I direct my films," written by de Sica for his published script *Miracle in Milan:*

For a whole year I followed two genuine shoeshine boys as they went about their eventful everyday life. They were called Scimmietta and Cappellone. I watched them by the hour going along with their humble affairs in the Via Veneto and did actually come upon them taking a ride on the carousel of the Villa Borghese. One day, after the theft of a gas mask, Cappellone ended up in prison. The drama, not invented by me but staged by life itself, was drawing to its fatal conclusion. I had merely to relate what I had seen and felt during that year. Zavattini, too, recognized the melancholy poetry of that generation of children led astray by the war and provided me with the magnificent theme everyone now knows so well. This is how *Shoeshine* was born. The origin of Rossellini's *Roma, città aperta (Open City)* was not very different, I believe, and both films are generally referred to when people speak of what has come to be called the Italian school of neo-realism.

Here, however, I should like to be quite honest. At a period such as that in the history of our country, and at a time when there was absolutely no organized cinema industry, it was only by dint of his own initiative that a director could come to the fore and exercise any influence. I mean to say that the problem of finance was in itself an important determining factor that encouraged filmmakers in their attempts to create a kind of movie that would no longer be dependent on fiction and on invented themes – for these are, by definition, boundless, and therefore encourage the natural tendency of production estimates toward inflation – but would draw on the reality of everyday life that is already particularized and circumscribed. Of course, they offered a transformed reality from which they drew forth the inner, human, and therefore universal meaning: it is reality transposed to the realm of poetry. Let us return to *Shoeshine* by way of an example: in this film I intended to emphasize a phenomenon that has always deeply saddened me – the indifference of humanity to the needs of others.

Neo-realist films spotlighted the gulf between tinsel and reality, contrivance and truth. *The Best Years of Our Lives* (1946) has been considered by some as preeminent among the postwar readjustment films to come out of Hollywood. Admittedly conditions in America and Italy were different, but the candid portrayal of life in *Open City, Shoeshine, Paisan,* and *The Bicycle Thief* illuminates the shortcomings of the American film – all the more because it was regarded as realistic by comparison with the product Americans were accustomed to seeing. Even *The Grapes of Wrath* (see chapter), lifelike by 1940 Hollywood standards, does not approach the realism of the postwar Italian pictures.

In the United States, various economic factors were responsible for the shift away from the studios to location shooting, but the neo-realistic films provided a powerful artistic impetus. For example, *The Naked City* (1948), significant for its vivid use of the streets of New York City and its influence in fostering similar location filming, has been linked by its director, Jules Dassin, to the inspiration he found in *Open City*. Critic James Agee was quick to appreciate the potential for change in style and content. Surveying the best films released in the United States in 1946, he wrote insightfully in the *Nation*, January 25, 1947:

> *Open City* goes far in what I believe is the best general direction movies might take, now and within the discernible future. By this I don't mean they need be socially or politically hot under the collar – though much of the spirit and grandeur of this film comes of that kind of heat. I do mean that the theme or story needs to be passionately felt and intimately understood, and that it should be a theme or story worthy of such knowledge and passion. I also put my deepest hope and faith in the future of movies in their being made on relatively little money, as much at least by gifted amateurs as by professionals, in actual rather than imitated places, with the binding energy, eye, conviction, and delight in work which are fostered in good-enough people by that predicament and which are at best hindered by commercial work in studios.

OPEN CITY
(Roma, Città Aperta)
ITALY 1945

Cast

Pina .... ANNA MAGNANI
Don Pietro Pellegrini .... ALDO FABRIZI
Manfredi .... MARCELLO PAGLIERO
Marina .... MARIA MICHI
Major Bergmann .... HARRY FEIST
Francesco .... FRANCESCO GRAND-JACQUET
Ingrid .... GIOVANNA GALLETTI
Marcello .... VITO ANNICHIARICO
Laura .... CARLA REVERE
Agostino .... NANDO BRUNO
Police Superintendent .... CARLO SINDICI
Hartmann .... JOOP VAN HULZEN
Austrian deserter .... AKOS TOLNAY
Policeman .... EDUARDO PASSARELLI
Landlady .... AMALIA PELEGRINI
and ALBERTO TAVAZZI, C. GIUDICI

Running time .... 100 minutes
Presented by .... MINERVA FILMS
Production Company .... EXCELSA FILMS
Directed by .... ROBERTO ROSSELLINI
Script by .... SERGIO AMIDEI, FEDERICO FELLINI, and ROBERTO ROSSELLINI, from a story by SERGIO AMIDEI and ALBERTO CONSIGLIO
Photographed by .... UBALDO ARATA
Edited by .... ERALDO DA ROMA
Décor by .... R. MEGNA
Music by .... RENZO ROSSELLINI

ALGER HISS, HAVING DENIED PASSING SECRETS, FOUND GUILTY OF PERJURY IN SECOND TRIAL
—January 21, 1950

SENATOR JOSEPH McCARTHY CHARGES 205 COMMUNISTS IN STATE DEPARTMENT
—February 9, 1950

UN SECURITY COUNCIL APPROVES US INTERVENTION IN KOREA —June 27, 1950

McCARREN ACT ORDERS REGISTRATION OF SUBVERSIVES, PLANS DETENTION CAMPS
—September 23, 1950

In 1952, Eisenhower decides to keep Nixon on ticket after "Checkers" speech denying wrongdoing over slush fund and defeats Stevenson for US Presidency . . . Rudolf Slansky and thirteen other Communist leaders tried for treason in Czechoslovakia; eleven executed . . . First hydrogen bomb tested in Marshall Islands.

HILLARY AND TENSING CONQUER MOUNT EVEREST
—May 29, 1953

ETHEL AND JULIUS ROSENBERG, MAINTAINING INNOCENCE, EXECUTED AMID WORLD PROTEST
—June 19, 1953

1950-1959

CIA-BACKED COUP IN IRAN OUSTS MOSSADEGH
—August 19, 1953

TELEVISED ARMY–McCARTHY HEARINGS BEGIN
—April 22, 1954

FRENCH ANNOUNCE FALL OF DIENBIENPHU
—May 7, 1954

US HIGH COURT BANS SEGREGATED SCHOOLS
—May 17, 1954

In 1955, Albert Einstein and Thomas Mann die . . . Blacks boycott buses in Montgomery, Alabama, to end segregation of public transport . . . AFL and CIO merge.

Khruschev exposes Stalin's crimes in 1956 speech . . . Salk vaccine against polio available . . . Hungarian uprising crushed by USSR . . . Suez crisis: Nasser nationalizes canal, bans Israeli use; Israel invades, so do France and Britain; US compels withdrawal amid Soviet threats of intervention.

RUSSIANS LAUNCH SPUTNIK, FIRST EARTH SATELLITE
—October 4, 1957

FIDEL CASTRO TAKES HAVANA —January 1, 1959

1950

Rashomon

The samurai (Masayuki Mori) and the bandit (Toshiro Mifune) battle in the forest.

Opening to the East

AFTER THE AMERICAN fleet was attacked at Pearl Harbor in 1941, the Allies fought a war with Japan for nearly four years, and the United States destroyed two Japanese cities with precedent-setting use of nuclear weapons and became an occupying power. Japanese-Americans had been rounded up and put into internment camps. One could hardly say there had been no relationship between East and West. In Japan, as elsewhere in the world, American films were popular entertainment. Yet Western knowledge of Japanese culture was minimal, and this was particularly true of the huge Japanese film output. The emergence of *Rashomon,* directed by Akira Kurosawa, at last brought international attention to this aspect of a rich civilization.

Rashomon might have been just another Japanese film of which the West remained ignorant, but a representative of the 1951 Venice Film Festival admired it and urged that it be entered. The executives of Daiei, the producing company, were dubious. The idea of sending *Rashomon* to a foreign film festival was not appealing, because there was a preconceived impression that Japanese films were not for foreign tastes and *Rashomon* would certainly not be appreciated abroad. Reluctantly, Daiei acquiesced. Much to the surprise of the Japanese, not only did *Rashomon* take first prize at Venice, but the following year it won an Oscar as the best foreign film. The enigmatic drama of rape and death, described in conflicting ways by different witnesses, received such praise that people interested in film began to wonder what other films had been made by Kurosawa and what else was being done in Japanese cinema.

In Japan, an interest in film was evinced from its beginnings. The 1895 Lumière and early Edison films were shown there in 1897. Within a few years Kenichi Kawaura was making travelogues and newsreels, and he journeyed to the United States to show them. At about the time that Griffith was making *The Birth of a Nation,* a film adaptation of Tolstoy's *Resurrection* by Kiyomatsu Hosoyama was being seen in Japan under the title *Katusha*. By the early 1920s, Japanese films were commanding increasing respect at home with the appearance of *A Woman Standing in the Light* (1920) and *Souls on the Road* (1922), both directed by Minoru Murata. Not only was there a growing film industry, but it had very special characteristics.

In contrast with the snobbish attitude in America that they were lower-class entertainment, movies were not scorned in Japan; indeed, at first they were available primarily to those with means as, unlike at the nickelodeons, the price of admission was the same as at the theater. Another interesting aspect was that for a time men played all the women's roles, as in kabuki. Also intriguing was the practice of having a narrator called a *benshi* interpret silent films for audiences instead of relying on titles, as in the West. That became an art. A skillful benshi earned a reputation and people went to watch their favorites perform. Many a liberty must have been taken with the meaning of a film by a benshi who considered himself the chief attraction and interpreted the action any way he saw fit. The arrival of sound dispensed with the need for his services, but the profession died slowly, since it was so ingrained in the habit of filmgoing. In self-protection, a benshi might turn down the sound and make his own commentary.

In a sense, the practice was responsible for Kurosawa's entry into filmmaking, as his brother Heigo was a benshi and would arrange for him to see films admission-free. At the time, Kurosawa had no thought of a film career, but he was very much absorbed in the movies of his day and would enjoy watching Heigo give his colorful descriptions. The relationship ended tragically when Heigo committed suicide. "I clearly remember the day before," Kurosawa recalled in Donald Richie's book *The Films of Akira Kurosawa*. "He had taken me to a movie in the Yamate district. . . . We parted at Shin Okubo station. He started up the stairs and I started to walk off, then he stopped and called me back. He looked at me, looked into my eyes, and then we parted. I know now what he must have been feeling. He was a brother whom I loved very much and I have never gotten over this feeling of loss."

Kurosawa had started out to be an artist. His career in film began in 1936 when he answered a studio advertisement for directorial assistants. One of the few selected, he became assistant to director Kajiro Yamamoto, whom he credited as his mentor. In 1942, during the war, Kurosawa was given the opportunity to direct his first film, *Sanshiro Sugata,* set in 1882 and dealing with judo in a spiritual as well as a physical way. He was thirty-three. Between then and the filming of *Rashomon,* his twelfth picture, Kurosawa's reputation grew. The international success of *Rashomon* gave him a new position of prestige and prominence in Japan, even though the film was criticized as being too inclined toward Western thought, a contradiction of the initial contention by Daiei officials that it would not be understood in the West.

Rashomon is a twelfth-century tale that begins at the ruined gate of the ancient capital city of Kyoto, devastated by famine and civil war. It is based upon two short stories, "Rashomon" and "In a Grove," by Ryunosuke Akutagawa, who committed suicide at the age of thirty-five in 1927. (Kurosawa himself tried suicide later in life.) The fascination of *Rashomon* lies in the complexity, mystery, and atmosphere with which Kurosawa endows it. A woodcutter and a priest, taking shelter from torrential rain, are upset by a recent ominous, symbolic event, and the woodcutter is prevailed upon by a commoner to relate the story. The famous bandit Tajomaru, played by Toshiro Mifune, has been captured and an investigation conducted to determine what actually happened when he accosted a samurai and his wife riding through a forest. The samurai died and the bandit apparently raped the wife. But what really took place?

The woodcutter's narrative flashes back to the inquiry, and further flashbacks present conflicting versions of the events. The frightened woodcutter tells the court how he discovered the man's body in the forest and informed the police. The police agent boasts of his capture of Tajomaru; Tajomaru describes how he raped the wife and how she goaded him into dueling with the husband, whom he killed; meanwhile she disappeared. The wife, exquisitely played by Machiko Kyo, tells another tale. She confirms the rape, after which her husband rejected her in hatred. Imploring him to kill her, she fainted, and on reviving, found her pearl-handled dagger in his chest. If only the dead could speak! The husband does, through a medium (an eerie and dramatically effective performance by actress Fumiko Homma), alleging that Tajomaru begged the wife to leave with him. She agreed, on condition that the bandit first kill her husband. Tajomaru refused, leaving in disgust, whereupon the humiliated husband killed himself with the dagger, which he sensed was taken from his chest after his death. Away from the court, the woodcutter now tells the priest and the commoner an amended story. He professes to have witnessed everything and reinforces the husband's statement that Tajomaru wanted the wife to leave with him, but like Tajomaru, contends that she insisted on a duel. The husband, reluctant to fight over her, was killed with a sword and the wife ran away. What happened to the valuable dagger? Did the woodcutter steal it? The audience is left to ponder the enigma.

Rashomon ends on a note of hope. An abandoned baby is found by the three men at the gate. The commoner steals its clothes, but the impoverished woodcutter offers to care for it along with his six children, thus renewing the faith of the previously despondent priest. The film makes telling points about people with conflicting interests and egos. They each have a stake in showing themselves to advantage, whether or not they are telling the truth. But what is truth? Can there be more than one truth? Is it ever possible to determine complete truth? The effect of the film is long-lasting. It is so well-crafted and spellbinding that each viewing brings further involvement in the different stories.

Toshiro Mifune acts with an animal-like ferocity and generates an electricity that establishes him as an actor of unusual strength. The black-and-white photography is beautiful in its composition, and Kurosawa uses close-ups to maximum effect. Although the flashback nature of the tale is complicated, Kurosawa interweaves the narrative smoothly. The tone of the picture is exactly right, over-demonstrative enough to suggest a fable, yet real enough to involve one in the relationships and the quest for truth. Less successful is the score by Fumio Hayasaka, who was asked by Kurosawa to compose music similar to Ravel's *Bolero*. It is too similar.

Kurosawa's exciting body of work includes the earlier *Stray Dog* (1949), *The Idiot* (1951), *Seven Samurai* (1954), *Throne of Blood* (1957), *The Lower Depths* (1957), *The Bad Sleep Well* (1960), *Yojimbo* (1961), *High and Low* (1963), and *Red Beard* (1965), in all of which Mifune appears. Because of Kurosawa's tendency to shoot at upward angles, Mifune gives the impression of being tall and physically powerful. In person he is of modest height and trim build, nothing like the muscular samurai he has often played so effectively.

In many of Kurosawa's works it is possible to discern a deep social consciousness without political doctrine, and a compassionate attention to people in the context of their environment. *Ikiru* (1952), one of his finest films, concerns a man who knows he has six months to live and desperately tries to bring some meaning to his life. *Record of a Living Being* (1955) deals in an original way with Japan and the outside world in the aftermath of Hiroshima. The protagonist is a man convinced that postwar Japan is in grave danger because of fallout from the nuclear bombs being tested. He tries to persuade his reluctant family to leave for a safe place. In *Dodes'kaden* (1970), Kurosawa lyrically depicts poor people living in slums, their hopes for the future easing the misery of their present.

Kurosawa has admitted to being impressed with the works of Western directors, but has scoffed at criticism in Japan that his films were meant for foreign consumption rather than for Japanese audiences. Certainly Kurosawa's work has had its admirers and imitators abroad. *Rashomon* became a 1959 Broadway play starring Rod Steiger and Claire Bloom. It was also remade, not successfully, by Martin Ritt into a film called *The Outrage* (1964). John Sturges did *The Magnificent Seven* (1960), a Western version of *Seven Samurai*, and Italian director Sergio Leone, who became known as the king of the Spaghetti Westerns, turned *Yojimbo* into *A Fistful of Dollars* (1964).

Rashomon's success did not bring a rush of Japanese films to the West. But it did eventually lead cinema buffs to the superb talents of Kenji Mizoguchi and Yasujiro Ozu, and other important filmmakers. Mizoguchi (1898–1956) is especially known for *Ugetsu* (1953). He had a rare ability for pictorial beauty, as also evidenced by *Utamaro and His Five Women* (1946), about the eighteenth-century artist noted for his paintings of women. Ozu (1903–1963), a magnificent filmmaker with a meticulous, intimate style, is the subject of recently intensified interest. Pictures such as *Late Spring* (1949), *Tokyo Story* (1953), and *The End of Summer* (1961) illustrate his ability to leisurely chronicle the subtle changes that take place in the lives of his characters.

In 1964, *The Woman in the Dunes,* by Hiroshi Teshigahara, then thirty-seven, met with favorable response and offered an indication of new currents in Japanese filmmaking. Directors with varied approaches are working today, including Kon Ichikawa, Masahiro Shinoda, and the more radical Nagisa Oshima. As in other countries, there has been a search for more contemporary ideas in filmmaking among those eager for change. It has been fashionable among some of the avant-garde in Japan to relegate Kurosawa to the past, but thus far, nothing that I have seen by younger filmmakers has rivaled his craftsmanship. When I visited Japan in 1964, an important development was already apparent. Rapidly expanding television was commanding attention and money, touching off a steep decline in the number of films being produced. Raising funds became more difficult even for established directors like Kurosawa, once known as the emperor of the Toho Motion Picture Company.

Moreover, Kurosawa's slow production methods and high budgets (*Rashomon* was one of the few exceptions) have impeded his attempts to obtain financial backing. *Dersu Uzala,* his first film after a five-year hiatus, about the friendship of a Czarist officer and an aged Mongol hunter, was financed by the Soviet Union and filmed there. The film was unveiled at the 1975 Moscow International Film Festival, where it won First Gold Medal, and it won an Oscar in Hollywood as the best foreign language film of 1975. Ironically, a quarter of a century after winning an Oscar for *Rashomon,* Kurosawa won his second Oscar with a film entered by the Soviet Union, not Japan. (He later castigated the Soviet Union for permitting the distortion of the Italian version of *Dersu Uzala.*)

His problems notwithstanding, Kurosawa's place in film history is assured. Japanese films will never be as popular throughout the world as Japanese cars, cameras, tape recorders, and video equipment but they have now been recognized for their impressive contribution to international culture, and the opportunity they provide to observe Japanese life, relationships, and traditions.

RASHOMON
JAPAN 1950

Cast

Tajomaru, the bandit .... TOSHIRO MIFUNE
Takehiro, the samurai .... MASAYUKI MORI
Masago, his wife .... MACHIKO KYO
The woodcutter .... TAKASHI SHIMURA
The priest .... MINORU CHIAKI
The commoner .... KICHIJIRO UEDA
The police agent .... DAISUKE KATO
The medium .... FUMIKO HOMMA

Running time .... 83 minutes
Production Company .... DAIEI
Produced by .... JINGO MINORU (later credits: MASAICHI NAGATA)
Directed by .... AKIRA KUROSAWA
Screenplay by .... SHINOBU HASHIMOTO and AKIRA KUROSAWA, based on two stories by RYUNOSUKE AKUTAGAWA, "Rashomon" and "In a Grove"
Photographed by .... KAZUO MIYAGAWA
Art Direction by .... SO MATSUYAMA
Music by .... FUMIO HAYASAKA
Lighting by .... KENICHI OKAMOTO

1952

Singin' in the Rain

Gene Kelly singin' in the rain.

America's Musical Voice

"THE MUSICAL, based on the jazz sounds on which we grew up, is part of us, a genre that is peculiar to America. I think the musicals reflect American society and what that society has wanted to see. I made them because I am a product of that society."

Gene Kelly was contemplating Hollywood's virtual monopoly of the film musical. Britain had a fertile period in the 1930s with such stars as Jessie Matthews, Jack Buchanan, Gracie Fields, and Anna Neagle, but the Hollywood musical is unparalleled. The most skillful, durable, and instructive of these engaging films with broad international appeal is *Singin' in the Rain,* co-directed by Kelly and Stanley Donen.

The quality of *Singin' in the Rain* accents the precarious position of the musical in more recent years. Some have predicted that the art form is becoming extinct. The inflated budgets of musical productions have increased the risk to the point where failure may mean financial disaster. With each fiasco, obituaries are written for the genre. Then, along comes a *Cabaret* as evidence of new life; *A Chorus Line* captivates Broadway and plans are made to film it. The infatuation with musicals continues, with the likelihood that new talent will seek new ways to make them viable.

"All Talking! All Singing! All Dancing!" promised the advertisements for MGM's first all-talkie and the first real Hollywood musical, *The Broadway Melody,* released in 1929 and the Academy Award winner for that year. The music and lyrics were by Nacio Herb Brown and Arthur Freed. Also appearing in 1929 was MGM's *The Hollywood Revue,* of which the hit song was a Brown-Freed number, "Singin' in the Rain." At the beginning of the sound era, there were so many musicals in such rapid succession that by mid-1930 the public was satiated. However, interest revived sharply with Warner Bros.' *42nd Street* in 1933, when dance director Busby Berkeley started a cycle of lavish productions. His imagination seemed limitless. Whether he had Ruby Keeler dance atop a taxi, as she did in *42nd Street*, or a chorus of beauties "playing" lighted violins in *Gold Diggers of 1933*, Berkeley kept the public amused. His kaleidoscopic, opulent fantasies featured a seemingly infinite number of chorines moving in intricate scenic patterns, creatively photographed from every angle.

By the time *Singin' in the Rain* was released, musicals had a vast and varied history: the *Gold Diggers, Broadway Melody,* and *Big Broadcast* series, *Flying Down to Rio, Top Hat, Naughty Marietta, The Great Ziegfeld, Alexander's Ragtime Band, The Wizard of Oz, Babes in Arms, For Me and My Gal, The Gang's All Here, Meet Me in St. Louis, Pin Up Girl, Anchors Aweigh, Cover Girl, The Pirate, On the Town,* and in 1951, *An American in Paris.* The roster of stars dominating the 1930s and 1940s included Judy Garland, Fred Astaire, Ginger Rogers, Dick Powell, Ruby Keeler, Alice Faye, Don Ameche, Eleanor Powell, Ann Miller, operetta team Jeanette MacDonald and Nelson Eddy, Carmen Miranda, Bing Crosby, Betty Grable, Rita Hayworth, Frank Sinatra, and of course, Kelly.

Kelly's contribution to films, as choreographer, director, and dancer, has been the injection of styles based on ballet, tap, and jazz, as well as athletic energy that was ideally suited to cinema. Starting out as a dance teacher in Pittsburgh, Kelly came to New York in the late 1930s, and after starring on Broadway in *Pal Joey,* went to Hollywood. His first film, *For Me and My Gal* (1942), co-starred Garland and was directed by Berkeley and produced by Freed. Until the arrival of Kelly, Fred Astaire had been the only eminently successful male dancer in films. Kelly's influence broadened dance concepts in a manner parallel to developments in the Broadway musical theater. Astaire was the debonaire, aristocratic performer who combined ballroom and tap in a suave style all his own. Kelly was the jazz-balletic force, "a sweatshirt dancer," as he called himself.

The most fabled period for film musicals was the MGM era under the aegis of Freed as producer, from about the mid-1940s to the mid-1950s. *Singin' in the Rain* was the perfect Freed reprise. Most of the songs, including the title number, were from the earlier collaboration of Freed and Brown. It also satirized a situation they knew firsthand, and the expertise of the spoof is one reason why the film ages less than many musicals. The havoc caused in the silent studios by the invasion of sound, and the disastrous impact on some performers are well-known facets of film history. "Everything is true – it actually happened to people in Hollywood," Kelly said. "The picture was researched like the *Encyclopedia Americana.*"

In *Singin' in the Rain,* all the elements that make a musical entertaining coordinate with rare precision – dancing, singing, score, production numbers, comedy, book, dialogue, performance – plus an overall *joie de vivre* and attractiveness, the extra properties that signal the difference between a good work and a great one. The performances of the starring foursome, Kelly, Donald O'Connor, Debbie Reynolds, and Jean Hagen, possess a magic and harmony that give the film special luster. Collaborators Betty Comden and Adolph Green *(On the Town,* 1949; *The Band Wagon,* 1953; *Auntie Mame,* 1958; *Bells Are Ringing,* 1960) wrote a pungently funny screenplay. Their witty book and sharp dialogue contrast with so many other musicals in which story and conversation are intrusions to be endured between numbers; the book could stand on its own as a comedy. The taste and co-direction of Kelly and Donen are apparent in the film's charm, style, and grace. (Donen, who had previously co-directed *On the Town* with Kelly, went on to direct the innovative *Seven Brides for Seven Brothers* and other major musicals, including *Funny Face, The Pajama Game,* and *Damn Yankees,* as well as non-musicals of diverse quality such as *Charade, Arabesque, Two for the Road, Bedazzled, Staircase,* and the unfortunate *Lucky Lady.* His entertaining *Movie Movie* (1978) is an impeccable satirical reprise of 1930s double features, the first, *Dynamite Hands*, a drama about a slum kid who becomes a boxer to pay for his sister's eye operation, the second, a musical, *Baxter's Beauties of 1933.*)

The central characters of *Singin' in the Rain* are Don Lockwood (Kelly), a star of swashbuckling adventures à la Douglas Fairbanks; Lina Lamont (Hagen), Don's leading lady, a classic dumb blonde with a voice so grating that silent films are a blessing; Kathy Selden (Reynolds), an aspiring young actress and singer; and Cosmo Brown (O'Connor), Don's long-time pal with whom he slogged through the lean days of vaudeville and burlesque.

Don and Lina are in the midst of making a silent epic, *The Dueling Cavalier,* when crisis shakes the industry. *The Jazz Singer* is a tremendous hit and silent films are suddenly obsolete. The studios stampede to make sound films, or at least add sound to films already in production. Allowing Lina's voice to be recorded is courting disaster, and the new technical problems are formidable. Technicians hide a large, cumbersome microphone so that it will not be in camera view, causing Don and Lina to have difficulty playing a love scene while trying to ensure that their voices are picked up. The picture is completed, but the sound is so atrocious that a preview showing is received with derisive laughter.

It is at such times of stress that great ideas are born. *The Dueling Cavalier* is remade as a musical, and as Lina cannot sing any better than she can speak, Kathy dubs her voice. By this time Don and Kathy have fallen in love, which infuriates Lina. *The Dancing Cavalier* is a huge success with the première audience and Lina greedily takes all the credit. Called upon to sing on stage, she mouths the lyrics while Kathy secretly provides the voice from behind the curtain. Don, Cosmo, and studio head Simpson mischievously pull the curtain, revealing that the real talent is Kathy's. Justice and love triumph.

The plot and the comedy, though hilarious, mainly serve to provide the framework for one exhilarating musical number after another. The tour de force is "Singin' in the Rain" in which Don, elated that Kathy loves him, joyfully sings and dances in a downpour. Perhaps the most entertaining comedy number in musicals is "Make 'em Laugh"; O'Connor does the knockabout routines with incredible smoothness and acrobatic flexibility. Comden and Green wrote the droll "Moses" number, in which Kelly and

Cosmo Brown (Donald O'Connor) and Don Lockwood (Gene Kelly) in the "Moses" elocution number

O'Connor mock elocution exercises: "Moses supposes his toeses are roses/ But Moses supposes erroneously/Moses he knowses his toeses aren't roses/ As Moses supposes his toeses to be."

Kelly and O'Connor team in the playful "Fit as a Fiddle" and perform with Reynolds in the bouncy "Good Morning" number. With the stunning, lithe Cyd Charisse as his partner, Kelly dances the imaginative "Broadway Melody Ballet," which illustrates the change in musicals from an emphasis on ballroom and tap to a jazz ballet style.

"I remember in the thirties," recalled Kelly, "several of us in New York were trying to create a new style of dance. I wanted it to be an athletic style based on the popular music I grew up with in Pittsburgh – Cole Porter, Rodgers and Hart, Jerome Kern, and Irving Berlin. *Singin' in the Rain* is a mélange of several styles that have turned out successfully. Cyd Charisse was a trained classical dancer, and she worked very hard to get that up-and-drive-and-move-it, and combine it with that long, beautiful extension she had in her body."

Reminiscing further about the making of *Singin' in the Rain,* Kelly said: "I enjoyed most of the films that I did and the 'Singin' in the Rain' number was something I especially liked. So was 'You Were Meant for me,' which I did with Debbie Reynolds. But probably the most enjoyable work was choreographing Donald O'Connor's 'Make 'em Laugh' number. I had to plan the things Donald did so they would fit the music. All he had to do was all the work. It was the only time I choreographed something and kept laughing all through it. I also liked 'Moses' and 'Fit as a Fiddle.' Those were ridiculous numbers and meant to be. Donald would do things spontaneously, and of a thousand things, I would choose a few."

Kelly predicted that of his films, *Singin' in the Rain* would endure longest, but admitted being partial to *On the Town* because of its innovations: "We shot on location in New York City, with three sailors [Kelly, Frank Sinatra, and Jules Munshin] getting off a real destroyer as it came in at the Brooklyn Navy Yard and going around the city singing and dancing. [Kelly was allowed a week to film that portion.] Everybody in Hollywood said that it would never work. It did work, and it started a whole new wave in cinema. It has been copied a lot and is a bit dated, but I think it is a milestone of its kind and will last that way." The realism of which Kelly spoke has been developed further. Robert Wise shot the impressive opening of *West Side Story* (1961) in Manhattan, and *The Sound of Music* (1965), the most lucrative musical to date, took advantage of majestic Austrian scenery. Nowadays most directors of musicals seek appropriate locales.

The response to *The Sound of Music*, following that to *My Fair Lady*, seemed to promise another golden era of musicals, or so producers thought. Success was not that easy to imitate. *Dr. Dolittle,* for example, had Rex Harrison and other aspects of the supposed success recipe, but it was dull and it failed. *Man of La Mancha* was an unmitigated disaster. Does anyone want to remember *Mame*? Barbra Streisand starred in *Hello, Dolly!*, which Kelly directed with mixed artistic effect; it is a long way from breaking even, although Kelly optimistically thought it would, eventually. In general, the commercial and artistic results of fashioning musicals from Broadway shows, a traditional source of supply for Hollywood, have been so spotty in recent years as to underscore the need to seek new sources and ideas. Sidney Lumet, director of *The Wiz,* predicted a trend toward musicals tied to international record sales because of their great profit potential. But that route has its built-in artistic hazards; witness the awkward casting of Diana Ross in *The Wiz*, the overage choices for *Grease*, and the bloated, silly film made from The Beatles' "Sgt. Pepper's Lonely Hearts Club Band."

Experimentation has its perils, too, as Kelly found out with *The Young Girls of Rochefort*. Kelly was intrigued by the lyric theater efforts of his friends Jacques Demy and Michel Legrand in France. "They had this operetta," he said, "no spoken lines at all – all song – and it was novel and charming and had a good score. They had pulled off their very strange picture, *The Umbrellas of Cherbourg,* but the problem was that they had never done a real musical before, and to get the French money backing, they got two sisters as the stars, Françoise Dorléac and Catherine Deneuve, who couldn't sing and couldn't dance, which is a helluva way to start. I took a part in the picture to get them the American money. I thought, well, these guys may succeed. But then they started making the same old mistakes that were made in Hollywood years ago, and unfortunately, it was the light that failed. But that is a direction to explore, the lyric theater and lyric picture, where words and music and dance – everything – just blend. Sometime, it is going to happen.

"I would like to see more adult musicals done, and not just remakes of hit Broadway shows. With pictures like *An American in Paris* and *Singin' in the Rain,* we started from scratch. They were written for the screen, the way you would sit down and write a book. I learned a lesson early, and that was to do dances for films that I couldn't do on stage. I began to sing and dance out of doors – on city streets, on roller skates. It sounds simple, but it took some thinking. And then I learned certain ways to use the camera to help the muscular forces come at the audience. Dance is not cinematic to begin with because it is a three-dimensional medium. You lose all the kinetics if you put it on the two-dimensional flat screen. So you have to substitute something. The more intimately you dance, the better it works on film. The futile, and I think, ridiculous attempts that have been made to photograph great ballets on stage and put them on screen haven't worked at all. You must learn to do the things on film that wouldn't work anywhere else. Like 'Singin' in the Rain.' You can't be in a show and do that number on stage.

The water would come out in the orchestra pit, and if you're soaking wet, you can't do the next scene."

In his way, Kelly was arriving at a truth recognized by Alfred Hitchcock and Ingmar Bergman – the need to be visual. It may be that our conception of a musical may change drastically as a result of experimentation by those who want to create works for contemporary tastes. Richard Lester's *A Hard Day's Night,* starring The Beatles, Robert Altman's *Nashville,* and filmed rock concerts like *Woodstock* and *The Last Waltz,* are different kinds of musicals. *The Buddy Holly Story* relies heavily on Holly's rock 'n roll numbers as a framework for biographical drama. Whatever one thinks of Ken Russell's work, he is exploring new concepts in his flashy "biographies" of Tchaikovsky, Liszt, and Mahler. *Tommy,* filmed from the rock opera, is important for Russell's use of wild imagery to complement the score. Bob Fosse attempted to escape the confines of the theater and turn *Cabaret* into a fully visual experience on screen, as well as a comment on prewar decadence in Germany. Although *Cabaret* was not entirely successful, Fosse does appear to understand the special demands of film musicals. Ingmar Bergman found ways to make his filming of Mozart's opera *The Magic Flute* invitingly cinematic, and planned to apply his genius to *The Merry Widow.* Miloš Forman did wonders with *Hair.*

Singin' in the Rain plays well even in the context of contemporary cinema. Although nostalgia undoubtedly enhances its appeal, Kelly bridled at the term whether applied to *Singin' in the Rain* or MGM's popular *That's Entertainment* and *That's Entertainment, Part II*, compilations of film clips that revived interest in Kelly and Astaire. "It might be nostalgia to me," he asserted, "but not to a nine-year-old, or a sixteen-year-old, because they've never seen some of these films. Would you say that people read Euripides, Shakespeare, or Dickens out of nostalgia?" Extravagant as Kelly's comparisons may be, it is the caliber of *Singin' in the Rain* that makes it perennially enjoyable and unlikely to go out of style or become camp. Whatever form musicals may take in the future, *Singin' in the Rain* has set a formidable standard.

SINGIN' IN THE RAIN
USA (MGM) 1952

Cast

Don Lockwood . . . . GENE KELLY
Cosmo Brown . . . . DONALD O'CONNOR
Kathy Selden . . . . DEBBIE REYNOLDS
Lina Lamont . . . . JEAN HAGEN
R.F. Simpson . . . . MILLARD MITCHELL
Guest Artist . . . . CYD CHARISSE
Zelda Zanders . . . . RITA MORENO
Roscoe Dexter . . . . DOUGLAS FOWLEY
Dora Bailey . . . . MADGE BLAKE
Red . . . . KING DONOVAN
Phoebe Dinsmore . . . . KATHLEEN FREEMAN
Diction Coach . . . . BOBBY WATSON
Sid Phillips . . . . TOMMY FARRELL

Running time . . . . 103 minutes
Technicolor
Produced by . . . . ARTHUR FREED
Directed by . . . . GENE KELLY and STANLEY DONEN
Story and Screenplay by . . . . . . BETTY COMDEN and ADOLPH GREEN, suggested by the song, "Singin' in the Rain"
Lyrics by . . . . ARTHUR FREED
Music by . . . . NACIO HERB BROWN
"Moses"
Lyrics by . . . . BETTY COMDEN and ADOLPH GREEN
Music by . . . . ROGER EDENS
"Fit as a Fiddle"
Lyrics by . . . . ARTHUR FREED
Music by . . . . AL HOFFMAN and AL GOODHART
Musical Direction . . . . LENNIE HAYTON
Musical Numbers Staged and Directed by . . . . GENE KELLY and STANLEY DONEN
Director of Photography . . . . HAROLD ROSSON
Technicolor Color Consultants . . . . HENRI JAFFA, JAMES GOOCH
Art Directors . . . . CEDRIC GIBBONS, RANDALL DUELL
Film Editor . . . . ADRIENNE FAZAN
Recording Supervisor . . . . DOUGLAS SHEARER
Orchestrations by . . . . CONRAD SALINGER, WALLY HEGLIN and SKIP MARTIN
Vocal Arrangements by . . . . JEFF ALEXANDER
Set Decorations by . . . . EDWIN B. WILLIS, JACQUE MAPES
Special Effects . . . . WARREN NEWCOMBE, IRVING G. RIES
Costumes Designed by . . . . WALTER PLUNKETT
Hair Styles Designed by . . . . SYDNEY GUILAROFF
Make-up Created by . . . . WILLIAM TUTTLE

1955

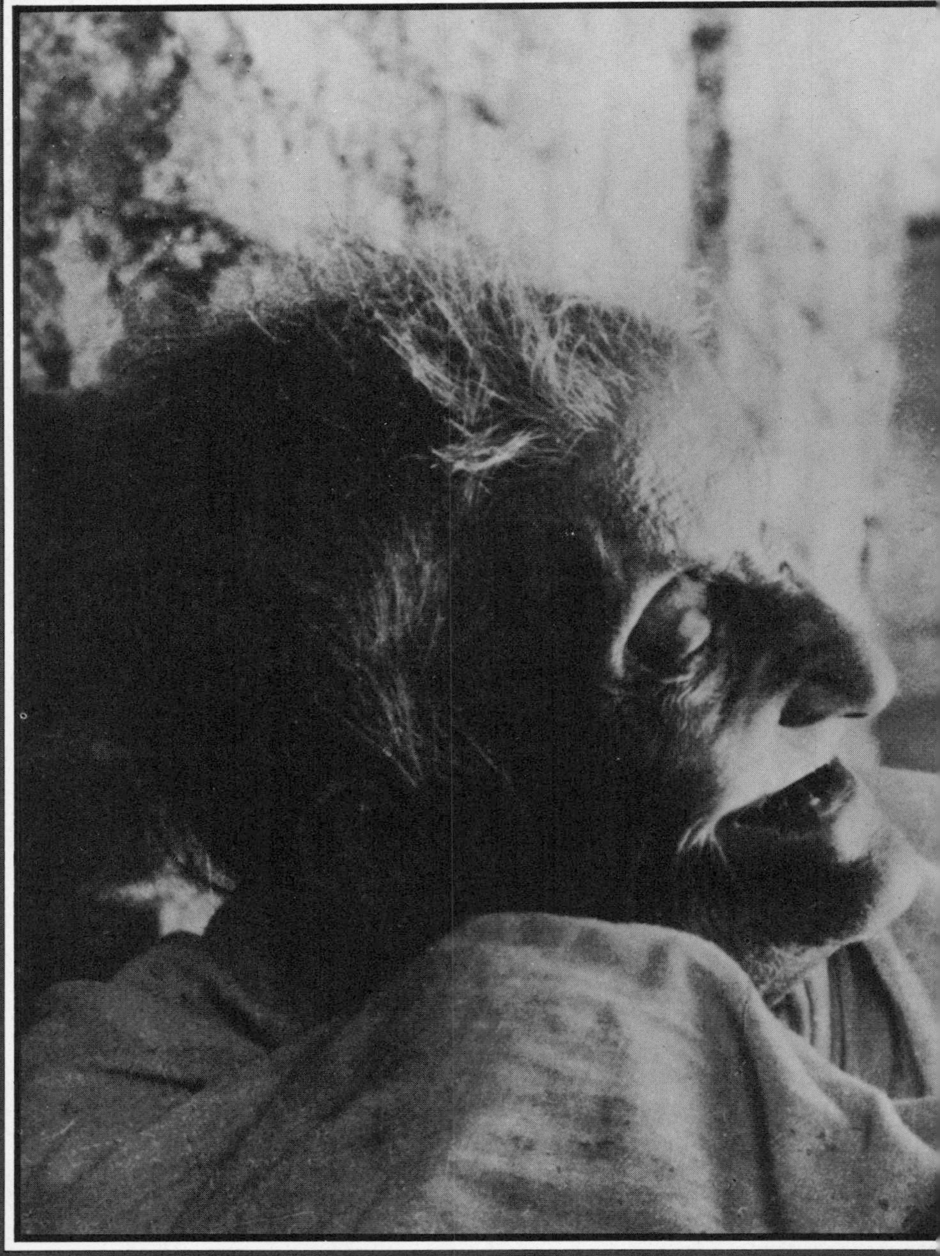

Pather Panchali

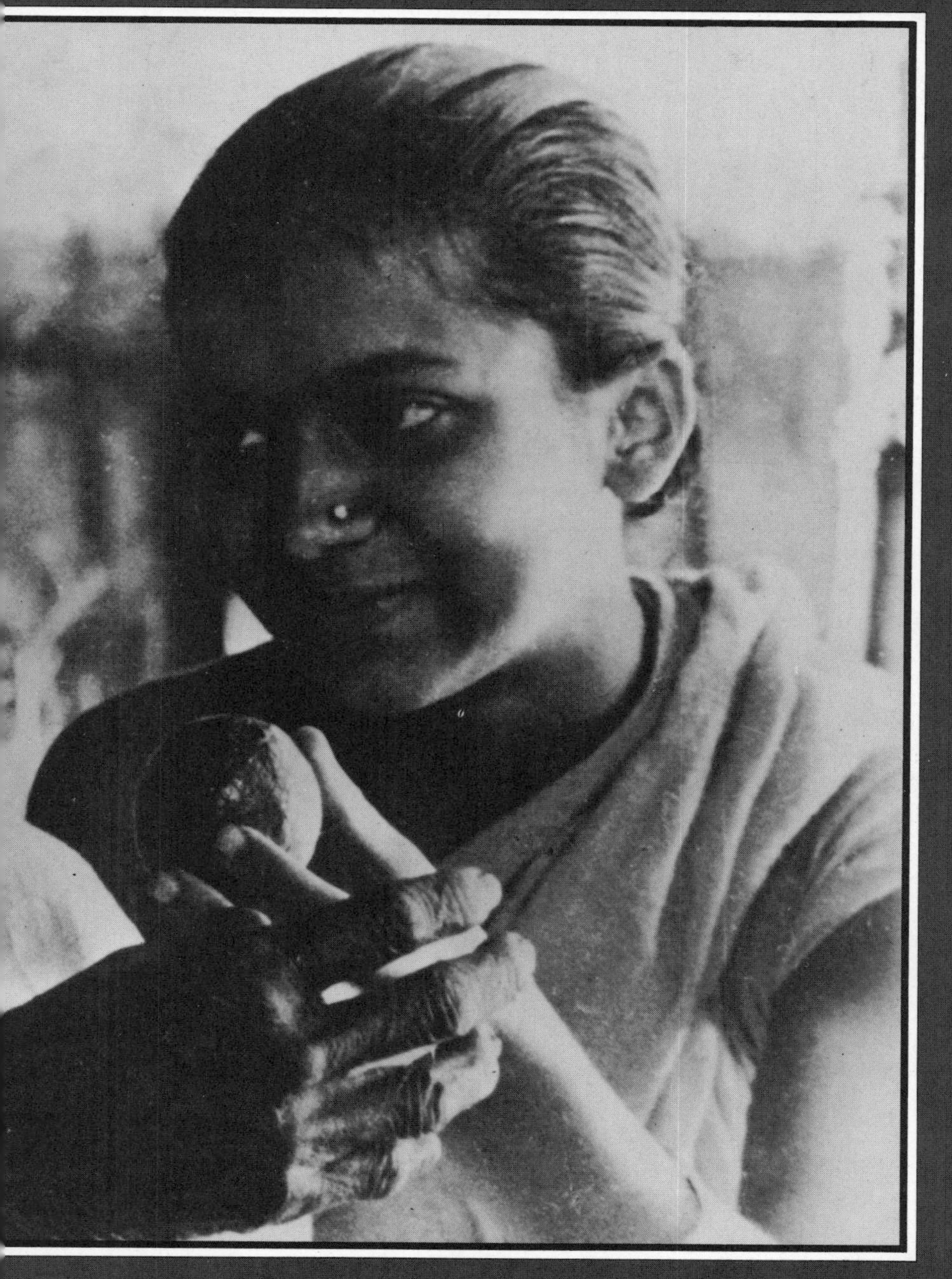

Auntie (Chunibala Devi) and Durga (Uma Dasgupta) have an affectionate relationship.

Discovery in India

SATYAJIT RAY led me over the muddy ground into a primitive studio in the environs of Calcutta. "I like working here," said Ray, a handsome man of six-foot-four. "We have the bare essentials. It is challenging and keeps you on your toes. In 1958, I went to Hollywood. The look of efficiency and the battery of lights terrified me." This was 1964. In New York eleven years later, I asked Ray whether his studio facilities had become more imposing. "They're still much the same," he replied, smiling as if to verify that he had maintained his integrity.

This simplicity is in keeping with the purity of Ray's film style and the gentle, unpretentious manner in which he focuses on the lives and problems of his characters *Pather Panchali*, rightfully acclaimed as a masterpiece, is one of cinema's most poignant dramas of childhood, family life, and the struggle for existence. It is the first part of Ray's extraordinary *Apu* trilogy. Beyond that, it stands as a landmark that increased knowledge of Indian life, introduced the world to the genius of Ray, and created an awareness of filmmaking in India. Until *Pather Panchali* appeared, relatively few Westerners were even cognizant that films were being made in India, yet production there was so abundant that India's film output was second only to Japan's.

Filmmaking developed in India at the end of the nineteenth century, with feature-length production starting in 1913. At first, men played the women's roles, as in D.G. Phalke's *Raja Harischandra*. By the mid-twenties, production in India, under colonial rule and censorship, was more voluminous than in Britain. It has continued on a grand scale: in 1977, five hundred and fifty-seven features were filmed, making India the world's largest motion picture producer; in 1978, the figure climbed to six hundred and nineteen.

The problems of Indian filmmaking are vast. Because of linguistic diversification, films are made in as many as a dozen languages, but most are in Malayalam and Hindi. Censorship is so strict and archaic as to forbid kissing on screen, save for rare exceptions, leaving directors to search for a range of euphemisms. In a conversation with Indira Gandhi in 1964, when she was Minister of Information, she told me of her intention to do something about alleviating such restrictions; she didn't. Most films made in Bombay, India's Hollywood, and in Madras follow the tradition of featuring song and dance numbers. According to Erik Barnouw and S. Krishnaswamy in their informative book, *Indian Film*, it was not until the 1950s that anyone dared omit the obligatory musical interlude. It was against such a background that Ray made *Pather Panchali,* his first film.

Pather Panchali, like all Ray's subsequent work until *The Chess Players*, 1977 (in Urdu, a language understood by most Hindi speakers), is in Bengali, and outdoor scenes were shot in a village near Calcutta. Ray was opposed to the use of stars. Like the Italian neo-realists, he preferred to make his film with non-professionals or performers new to the screen who could provide the reality he was seeking. Instead of conventional music, Ray had Ravi Shankar provide an unusual sitar score that became a compelling, integral part of the film and added to its effectiveness. Calcutta, the cultural capital of India, is Ray's milieu and his working there has dramatized the gulf between his films and the standard product manufactured to supply the enormous Indian market. Ray's films, so atypical, have improved the image of Indian cinema. Measured by recognition abroad, Ray *is* Indian cinema.

Ray was born in 1921, the son of a noted Bengali writer, Sukumar Ray, who was also an artist and the publisher of a magazine for children, and came from an extremely cultured family. Rabindranath Tagore, India's esteemed man of letters and Nobel Prize winner, was an important influence; he and Satyajit's grandfather were friends. Satyajit was two when his father died and Tagore took an interest in his education. After obtaining a degree in economics from the University of Calcutta, Ray studied fine arts at Tagore's renowned Santiniketan school, and then became a commercial artist for a British advertising firm. He continued as art director there while starting his film career. Evidently his skills have remained useful: "I design the posters and do the credits for my films. I can't trust anybody else's judgment. I don't blame anyone but myself."

Ray, who had become a film buff while growing up, was one of the founders of the Calcutta Film Society, organized in 1947, the year India became independent. In India, even film societies were subject to censorship and import duties, but they were invaluable in sidestepping barriers, and a kind of underground existed. One method of evading the restrictions was to ask the various embassies to show foreign films of interest. Through the film society, Ray met Jean Renoir, in India to film *The River*, and had the opportunity to observe the famed director on location. Another formative experience occurred during a visit to London in 1950; he saw *The Bicycle Thief* and was profoundly influenced by it (see *Open City*). Among the ninety-five films he saw in five months were Flaherty's *Nanook of the North* and *Louisiana Story*.

Ray's determination to film the popular novel *Pather Panchali*, by Bibhuti Bhushan Banerji, was an outgrowth of his assignment to design the jacket for a new edition, and he was able to buy the rights for a modest sum. The screenplay he wrote was not his first. Barnouw and Krishnaswamy described how Ray would write a script as an exercise when he heard that a noted book was to be made into a movie: "He would study the book and write a complete film script. Watching the produced film, he compared it inwardly with his own version, noting opportunities he might have missed and matters on which he would have improved. . . ." Ray was turned down by some thirty skeptical film companies approached for financing. Finally, he went into production with personal funds, sufficient to reach only the initial stages.

Director John Huston must be given credit for his perception in recognizing Ray's ability on the basis of very incomplete work. He had met Ray through the Calcutta Film Society, and when Ray showed him clips from *Pather Panchali,* Huston was impressed. Coincidentally, Monroe Wheeler of New York's Museum of Modern Art was also in Calcutta, and Huston told him about the film, which led to an invitation for it to be shown at the museum. This gave Ray a much-needed lever to convince the State of West Bengal to finance the remaining production costs. Not that Ray's picture was expensive. To the contrary, his budgets are a pittance in comparison with the cost of the baubles from Bombay. "With the amount of money spent on one recent movie made in Bombay, I could make films the rest of my life," he said in 1964. The showing at the Museum of Modern Art led to Ray's finding an American distributor, Edward Harrison, and at the Cannes Film Festival in 1956, *Pather Panchali* was given an award as "the best human document."

To see *Pather Panchali* is to feel as if one has been transplanted to the village in which the story unfolds. The outside world is nearly nonexistent. One's concept of time is altered, for Ray's method is leisurely, objective observation of his characters. He prefers not to rely upon fancy camerawork or editing, but is content to record the routine of daily existence simply. We see Ray's subjects with their positive qualities and their flaws; their conflicting emotions are subtly delineated through their actions. The film's enlarged consciousness derives from its intimate and honest look at people; truths are revealed about such human characteristics as pride, despair, greed, love, resentment, hope, resignation. The life cycle passes before us, like the flow of a river, and characters change almost imperceptibly. In this sense, Ray's work is somewhat like that of Japanese director Ozu.

Pather Panchali, which takes place in the 1920s, is about a poor Brahmin family living in its ancestral village and consisting of Sarbojaya, the mother (Karuna Banerji), Hari, the father (Kanu Banerji), Apu, the son (Subir Banerji), Durga, the daughter (Uma Dasgupta), and an ancient, withered "Auntie" (Chunibala Devi). At the outset, we see Apu as a baby; soon he is a young boy going to school. He and Durga have a close, if occasionally combative relationship. Durga is fond of Auntie, whom Sarbojaya finds an intolerable burden, not out of indifference or cruelty, but because the family has so little. Auntie grasps at enough food for subsistence and wheedles anything additional, her condition barely above that of an animal, her presence a grim reminder of the uselessness to which the elderly are often reduced. Yet the warmth between her and Durga suggests a continuity of the life cycle.

A crisis occurs when a wealthy neighbor accuses Durga of stealing her daughter's necklace. We already know that Durga steals fruit from the neighbor and shares it with Auntie. Her few personal treasures are spilled on the ground in a vain search for the necklace. More at issue is the humiliation Sarbojaya suffers than whether Durga is guilty. She berates Durga and turns her out. Apu is sympathetic, as is Auntie, who retrieves Durga's scattered possessions. The distraught mother sends Apu to bring his sister home.

Life in the home and the village is so self-contained that the passing of a train is a major event, and Ray turns this into a dramatic, revealing scene. Apu and Durga watch the train and in this single sequence, which embodies curiosity, longing, and estrangement, Ray tells us all we need know about the chasm separating his characters from life elsewhere.

A confrontation occurs between Auntie and Sarbojaya when Auntie says she does not feel well. It is made clear to her that she is not wanted. Auntie packs her meager belongings, waters her plants, and goes; the sight of the woman, near death, departing with resignation and the shred of dignity she still retains, is heartbreaking. Later, Apu and Durga come upon Auntie sitting among the trees apparently asleep. When Durga shakes her, she topples, still alive, but obviously not for long. Inexorably, life moves on, leaving those behind to complete their own cycles.

Apu's next encounter with death will involve Durga. Their father, crushed with the burden of earning money, has gone elsewhere to seek work. Sarbojaya, setting aside her pride, reluctantly accepts assistance from her neighbor. The monsoon comes, Durga is drenched, becomes ill, and dies. Hari returns at last with money and presents, including a new sari for his daughter. He sees the house and grounds, battered by the monsoon. His wife cannot bring herself to tell him that Durga is dead, but when she breaks down weeping, he realizes that something terrible has happened, and cries in anguish for his beloved Durga.

The death of Durga uproots the family. As they are packing for their move to Benares, Apu comes across a bowl on a shelf. Reaching in, he discovers a necklace. Without telling his parents, he goes to a nearby pond and throws the necklace into the water; it gently sinks. The gesture, a markedly private one, would appear to be at once a tender farewell to his sister, a concealment of her secret in a final bond of affection, and a placing of distance between himself and the past. The beauty of Ray's scenes is that they have multilayered meanings, and the director will not make matters easy by precise interpretation. The film ends with the family setting off for

Benares in a wagon, the parents grieved at leaving behind the past that includes their daughter, Apu looking toward his future.

Ray subsequently made *Aparajito* (1957), dealing with Apu's life in Benares, the death of his father, and his relationship with his mother until her death. *The World of Apu* (1959), the last film of the trilogy, depicts Apu as an adult, his teaching, work in a factory, marriage, the death of his wife in childbirth, years of wandering while his in-laws care for his son, and his return to the boy, who reminds us of Apu in *Pather Panchali*.

Words cannot sufficiently suggest the complexity, nobility, beauty, humility, and delicacy of a Ray film. Each is a new revelation of a phase of Indian life. Ray, who writes his own scripts, sees people with the clarity of a perceptive novelist; a film of his is as enriching as an absorbing book. Among Ray's works are *The Music Room*, *Mahanagar*, *Charulata*, *Days and Nights in the Forest,* and *The Adversary*. He has also made an unforgettable drama about hunger, *Distant Thunder,* a story of villagers trying to survive in the midst of the spreading famine that killed five million during World War II. Here again, the portraits are intimate, but the scope is universal. Ray's closing shot of a group of starving people walking toward the camera forcefully appeals to the conscience of mankind.

Other superior films made in India, although not equal to Ray's, have contributed to our knowledge of life there. Director James Ivory's *The Householder* (1963) deals charmingly and amusingly with the life of a couple in India. Ivory, who collaborates with Ismail Merchant as producer, also directed *Shakespeare Wallah* (1966), which through its concern with a troupe of actors incisively and sensitively tells of changes in British-Indian relationships and attitudes following India's independence. Ivory also directed *Bombay Talkie* (1971), a satire about a British novelist working on a movie in Bombay.

Ray has had various detractors. Some resist his slow pace, and his international prestige for films so far removed from conventional Indian product must cause resentment in Bombay and Madras. There are also those who would like his work to be more political. But one of Ray's greatest assets is his steadfastness in confining his films to the subject and, although he has an implicit viewpoint, avoiding polemic, thereby contributing to the universality of his work. *The Middleman*, which opened in Calcutta in 1975, is relatively political in its story of despair and disillusionment. Ray did not deny this, but in an interview with William Borders in the *New York Times* of April 27, 1976, he remarked: "This is not the right time for a filmmaker in India to be making sharp comments on political subjects. One can perhaps get away with this kind of thing once, maybe not again."

Ray's remarks were made during the nearly two-year period of arrests, censorship, and suspension of constitutional liberties under Indira Gandhi. An interesting theme in *The Chess Players*, which is set in nineteenth-century Lucknow, implies that the character of Indian life continues regardless of rulers that come and go. It will be interesting to see to what extent India's massive reaffirmation of democratic rights in March 1977 and subsequent political events will be reflected in the future filmmaking of Ray and others.

PATHER PANCHALI
INDIA 1955

Cast

Harihar .... KANU BANERJI
Sarbojaya .... KARUNA BANERJI
Durga .... UMA DASGUPTA
Durga as a child .... RUNKI BANERJI
Apu .... SUBIR BANERJI
Auntie .... CHUNIBALA DEVI
Wealthy neighbor .... REBA DEVI
Village grocer and schoolmaster .... TULSI CHAKRAVORTY

Running time .... 115 minutes
In Bengali
Produced by .... SATYAJIT RAY, under the auspices of the State of West Bengal
Directed by .... SATYAJIT RAY
Script by .... SATYAJIT RAY, from the novel by BIBHUTI BHUSHAN BANERJI
Photographed by .... SUBRATA MITRA
Edited by .... DULAL DUTTA
Art Director .... BANSI CHANDRAGUPTA
Music by .... RAVI SHANKAR

The Seventh Seal

The knight Antonius Block (Max von Sydow) wagers his life in a game of chess with Death (Bengt Ekerot).

The Genius of Bergman

INGMAR BERGMAN, in my opinion, is the greatest filmmaker the medium has yet produced. No other director comes close to his mastery of cinematic language; in his films, visual and aural means of expression complement each other with remarkable perfection. Bergman's greatness, however, is not only a matter of technique and form. He employs his skills to create the most complex content attained on film, analyzing and interpreting men and women in relationship to themselves, to others, and to those profound philosophical questions that have perplexed us through the ages.

The Seventh Seal is certainly not the definitive work of Bergman, whose creative strength also derives from his propensity to explore new areas. He has matured to a point where his more recent works have gone far beyond those of his earlier period. Each new Bergman film holds the possibility of being his most impressive. *The Seventh Seal* is cited here because it was the film that heralded to the world the international arrival of an intellectual filmmaker who could use the medium for a far more thoughtful purpose than most people had associated with cinema. With *The Seventh Seal* Bergman dramatically raised expectations of what was possible on film.

The director had already achieved international attention with his previous film, *Smiles of a Summer Night* (1955), which won the jury prize at the Cannes Film Festival. (It was later the basis for the Broadway musical *A Little Night Music*.) A witty film, it was charming and perceptive, but did not herald the complexities of subsequent Bergman films. *The Seventh Seal* moved into a somber area of philosophical probing.

"The whole thing developed quite naturally," Bergman recalled in the interview book *Bergman on Bergman*. The script was based on a one-act training play, *A Painting on Wood,* that he had written and staged for his theater school in Malmö. "My stomach had been in bad shape and I sat writing the film in Karolinska Hospital in Stockholm. . . . I handed in the script to SF [Svensk Film] and SF said 'No, thank you.' But then came the success with *Smiles of a Summer Night* and I got permission to make it, providing I did it in thirty-five days."

Set in fourteenth-century Sweden racked by plague, *The Seventh Seal* involves the knight Antonius Block (Max von Sydow), who has returned from a long crusade accompanied by Jöns, his squire (Gunnar Björnstrand).

Confronted suddenly by Death (Bengt Ekerot) the knight challenges him to a game of chess. The wager is Block's life. Death stalks the knight throughout the journey to his home, endowing the film with unity and tension. The knight desperately wants to give meaning to his existence before it comes to an end. "My whole life has been a meaningless search," he declares, disillusioned by the unrelenting suffering he has witnessed. In Jöns' words: "Ten years we sat in the Holy Land and let the snakes bite us, insects prick us, wild animals nip us, heathen slaughter us, the wine poison us, women give us lice, fleas feed on us, and fevers consume us all to the glory of God. I'll tell you, our crusade was so stupid that only a real idealist could have invented it."

Among those joining the knight are Jof, a juggler, and his wife, Mia (Nils Poppe and Bibi Andersson). They are meant to be Joseph and Mary, as Bergman has confirmed, and they and their baby exude a cheerful note of hope for the future. In a terrifying sequence in a tavern, Jof is humiliated and threatened. Jöns saves him. Everywhere there is pestilence and death, with men of the church exhorting the people to repent their sins. A grim parade of penitents traverses the country flagellating themselves. A young woman is accused of witchcraft and condemned to burning. The victim (Maud Hansson) first undergoes torture, then is led in a wagon to the stake. The knight asks her about the devil. Jöns, the pragmatist, would like to save her but can only comfort her.

Death closes in with the intention of claiming all those accompanying the knight. Deeply touched by Jof and Mia, Block stalls for time to permit them to escape, sweeping his men from the chessboard in a termination of his game with Death. His own life has been forfeited, but he has given it meaning. The film closes as Death leads those for whom he has come in a strange procession and dance.

The imagery of the chalk-faced, black-hooded Death, the writhing victims of the plague, the fiendish clerics equating suffering with salvation, the penitents, the Gothic mood, the brooding despair of the knight's quest to understand the relationship between idealism and the cruelties of reality, and Gunnar Fischer's stark black-and-white photography leaves the viewer with cumulative vivid, lasting impressions. Although filmed with stylistic economy, the picture encompasses religion, God, death, war, sacrifice, idealism, love, responsibility, survival – all in the space of ninety-six minutes. In the United States, the work was greeted with admiration and excitement by many serious filmgoers, who saw little hope of Hollywood reaching such intellectual stature. *The Seventh Seal* also earned Bergman a reputation as a gloomy Scandinavian and became a subject for satire. In the short film *The Dove,* in mock Swedish, a man plays badminton with Death; in Woody Allen's piece "Death Knocks" in the *New Yorker,* Death visits a New York dress manufacturer who suggests a game of gin rummy.

The ascendancy of Bergman more than compensated for the depletion of Sweden's directorial resources in earlier days. Though Sweden's film industry had always been small, Mauritz Stiller and Victor Sjöström were successful in the early 1920s, before going to Hollywood. When Stiller left, he was accompanied by Greta Garbo. Sjöström, who changed his name to Seastrom while in the United States, later returned to Sweden and played Professor Isak Borg in *Wild Strawberries,* the film Bergman made after *The Seventh Seal* that further solidified his reputation. Predominant among the Scandinavian directors was Carl Dreyer of Denmark, who made such masterpieces as *The Passion of Joan of Arc* and *Day of Wrath.* Contemporary Scandinavians include Bo Widerberg, director of *Raven's End, Elvira Madigan, Adalen 31, The Ballad of Joe Hill,* and *Man on the Roof;* actress Mai Zetterling, deserving of more recognition than she has received for directing films including *Loving Couples, Night Games, Dr. Glas,* and *The Girls;* Vilgot Sjöman, who did the important *I Am Curious (Yellow),* and Jörn Donner, a disciple of Bergman's, whose films include *To Love.*

Bergman, born in Uppsala, Sweden, in 1918, traces his affinity with film back to his childhood. As a boy he was bitterly disappointed when his brother was given a film strip and slide projector without having evinced any interest in film. But Bergman managed to acquire the projector in a trade for his army of toy soldiers. Another childhood pleasure was puppetry, and he constructed theaters of various kinds in his playroom. His upbringing was incredibly strict, with his father, a Protestant minister, applying humiliating discipline. In the illuminating interview film *Three Scenes With Ingmar Bergman* (1975), by Donner, Bergman described both school and home as "totally authoritarian" and based on "a methodic violence"; he was frequently put on trial in his father's room, and punished by caning.

"The worst thing for me, because I haven't got over it yet, was [when] I got shut up in a dark closet," Bergman confided. "I'm still afraid of the dark and I have claustrophobia." (In *Face to Face* the woman psychiatrist is haunted by such a childhood experience.) The specter of humiliation is one that has figured menacingly in Bergman's life and work. Eventually he fled his home after a fierce dispute with his father, and did not see his parents for four years. Gradually, he said, he began to understand them as people and some tenderness developed.

An important phase of Bergman's life, which he speaks about with pain and embarrassment, was when he spent time in Germany as a young exchange student during the Hitler period. He admits to susceptibility to the Nazi ideology rampant in the family with whom he lived, that of a minister who, instead of preaching sermons from the Bible, read from *Mein Kampf.* Bergman confessed to having returned to Sweden "a little pro-German fanatic." Later, realizing the horror of the Nazi philosophy and mass murders, he felt intense guilt, shame, and hostility toward those who had exposed him to such indoctrination. The result was a temporary withdrawal from political concerns. Elements in his antiwar film, *The Shame,* stem from this experience.

Bergman worked in the theater before starting his film career, Strindberg being his major influence. He founded the Malmö City Theater and directed Sweden's National Theater in Stockholm. In London, Bergman directed a splendid presentation of Ibsen's *Hedda Gabler* in 1970. During the 1940s he began to write scripts, which led to his first film as director, *Crisis* (1946). An important influence on his work was the Italian neo-realism of the post-World War II period; he has spoken of de Sica's *Umberto D* as his favorite film. He has learned from many, but generally recoils from citing specifics, explaining instead, in *Bergman on Bergman:* "I'm the sum total of everything I've read, seen, heard, and experienced."

In *The Seventh Seal,* Bergman was already working with actors who became part of what has been referred to as the Bergman repertory company: Max von Sydow, Gunnar Björnstrand, Bibi Andersson, and Gunnel Lindblom. Others closely associated with him have included Liv Ullmann, Ingrid Thulin, Harriet Andersson, and Erland Josephson. The understanding that has developed in the Bergman troupe gives his films an unusual ensemble quality, and he has the ability to elicit astounding performances from his actors and actresses, who show generous trust in his judgment. Ullmann, the greatest of Bergman players, considers *The Seventh Seal* one of his best works "because it pointed in the direction of what could be done with film." She made the observation that Bergman was still preoccupied with men in *The Seventh Seal,* but "he has since changed his characters into women."

Another vital contributing force in the success of Bergman's films is the cinematography of Sven Nykvist, who was one of three cameramen on *The Naked Night* (1953). He was Bergman's cinematographer on *The Virgin Spring* (1960) and on all subsequent Bergman films, except for *The Devil's Eye* and *The Pleasure Garden,* shot by Gunnar Fischer. The harmony with which they work and the success of their collaboration makes their long relationship noteworthy in film history.

Increasingly, in expanding the universe of his art, Bergman has been reaching for new means of probing the psyche, inner conflicts, relationships, suicidal tendencies, and emotional ambiguities. *Persona, The Passion of Anna*, *Cries and Whispers*, *Scenes From a Marriage*, *Face to Face*, and *Autumn Sonata* reflect this path, accompanying such accomplishments as *The Magician*, *The Virgin Spring*, *Through a Glass Darkly*, *Winter Light*, *The Silence*, *Hour of the Wolf*, and *The Shame*. Bergman's body of work constitutes an incredible achievement for one director.

Another victory, a small miracle, is Bergman's enhancement of programming for television, a medium holding potential for worthy use but which, at least in the United States, has largely been relegated to banality. *Scenes From a Marriage* was originally made for Swedish television and condensed for theatrical release. *Face to Face* was shot in a television version and a shorter film version. Bergman also did *The Magic Flute*, a production important as a rare success in rendering a film from an opera, for video. With his cinematic insights, the Mozart opera takes on a joyous new existence.

In January 1976, while Bergman was rehearsing Strindberg's *Dance of Death* at the Royal Dramatic Theater in Stockholm, two plainclothesmen seized him and took him to the police station for prolonged questioning. Charges of tax fraud were subsequently dropped, but meanwhile he suffered a nervous breakdown and was hospitalized. It was an unbearable humiliation. Liv Ullmann, who lived with him for six years and has a daughter by him, voiced alarm: "The damage cannot be repaired, because they have taken away from him his pride in his honesty." After Bergman recovered he was subjected to further harassment from the tax authorities, and in April angrily left his country to live and work abroad, leaving behind sufficient funds to cover any assessment. Sweden, a country many admire, was suddenly in a position similar to that of the United States when Charlie Chaplin was forced into exile for political reasons in 1952. Before his departure, Bergman published a farewell statement in the newspaper *Expressen*, ending it: "Maybe one day I will write a little farce on the subject. I say, as Strindberg said when he got angry: 'Just watch out, you devil, we will meet in my next piece.' "

After a new Swedish government officially exonerated him and apologized, Bergman felt free to return, but the experience had led him to film outside Sweden for the first time. *The Serpent's Egg* (1977), which he made in Germany, although not received enthusiastically, was an often effective emotional evocation of the pattern of Nazi horror already discernible in the early years of Hitler's rise to power. His next film, *Autumn Sonata* (1978), made in Norway, was a searing confrontation between an estranged mother (Ingrid Bergman) and daughter (Liv Ullmann). The New York Film Critics Circle voted Miss Bergman its award for best actress of the year. The director had once again demonstrated his skill at peeling away layers of inner torment, exposing love-hate relationships, and unleashing suppressed demons. If his exile had taken a toll, it was not evident in this drama that reaffirmed his greatness.

Bergman has fulfilled the promise of *The Seventh Seal* beyond any expectation; one wonders what else he may accomplish before he ceases to work. At the conclusion of *Three Scenes With Ingmar Bergman*, the director told Donner: "This business of filmmaking is very much of a strain physically. I feel it very strongly that, because I only make a film about once a year, hardly once a year, I feel every time I come back to it, things get a bit more of an effort, a little more tiring, more of a strain. You get used to insisting on a nap at lunchtime and not doing any overtime and not beginning in the morning before 9 A.M. One has to be sparing with oneself. . . . I am thinking of going on another few years. But I am not going to have them drag me out of the film studio. I intend to leave of my own accord."

THE SEVENTH SEAL
(Det Sjunde Inseglet)
SWEDEN 1957

Cast

Antonius Block . . . . Max von Sydow
Jöns . . . . Gunnar Björnstrand
Jof . . . . Nils Poppe
Mia . . . . Bibi Andersson
Death . . . . Bengt Ekerot
Plog, the smith . . . . Ake Fridell
Lisa, Plog's wife . . . . Inga Gill
Skat . . . . Erik Strandmark
Raval . . . . Bertil Anderberg
The girl . . . . Gunnel Lindblom
Block's wife . . . . Inga Landgré
The witch . . . . Maud Hansson
The monk . . . . Anders Ek
The church painter . . . . Gunnar Olsson
The merchant . . . . Benkt-Ake Benktsson
Woman at the tavern . . . . Gudrun Brost
Leader of the soldiers . . . . Ulf Johansson
The young monk . . . . Lars Lind

Running time . . . . 96 minutes
Production Company . . . . Svensk Filmindustri
Production Manager . . . . Allan Ekelund
Directed by . . . . Ingmar Bergman
Screenplay by . . . . Ingmar Bergman, from his play *Trämalning*
Director of Photography . . . . Gunnar Fischer
Film Editor . . . . Lennart Wallén
Music . . . . Erik Nordgren
Set Designer . . . . P.A. Lundgren
Assistant Director . . . . Lennart Olsson
Choreographer . . . . Else Fischer
Costumes . . . . Manne Lindholm

Room at the Top

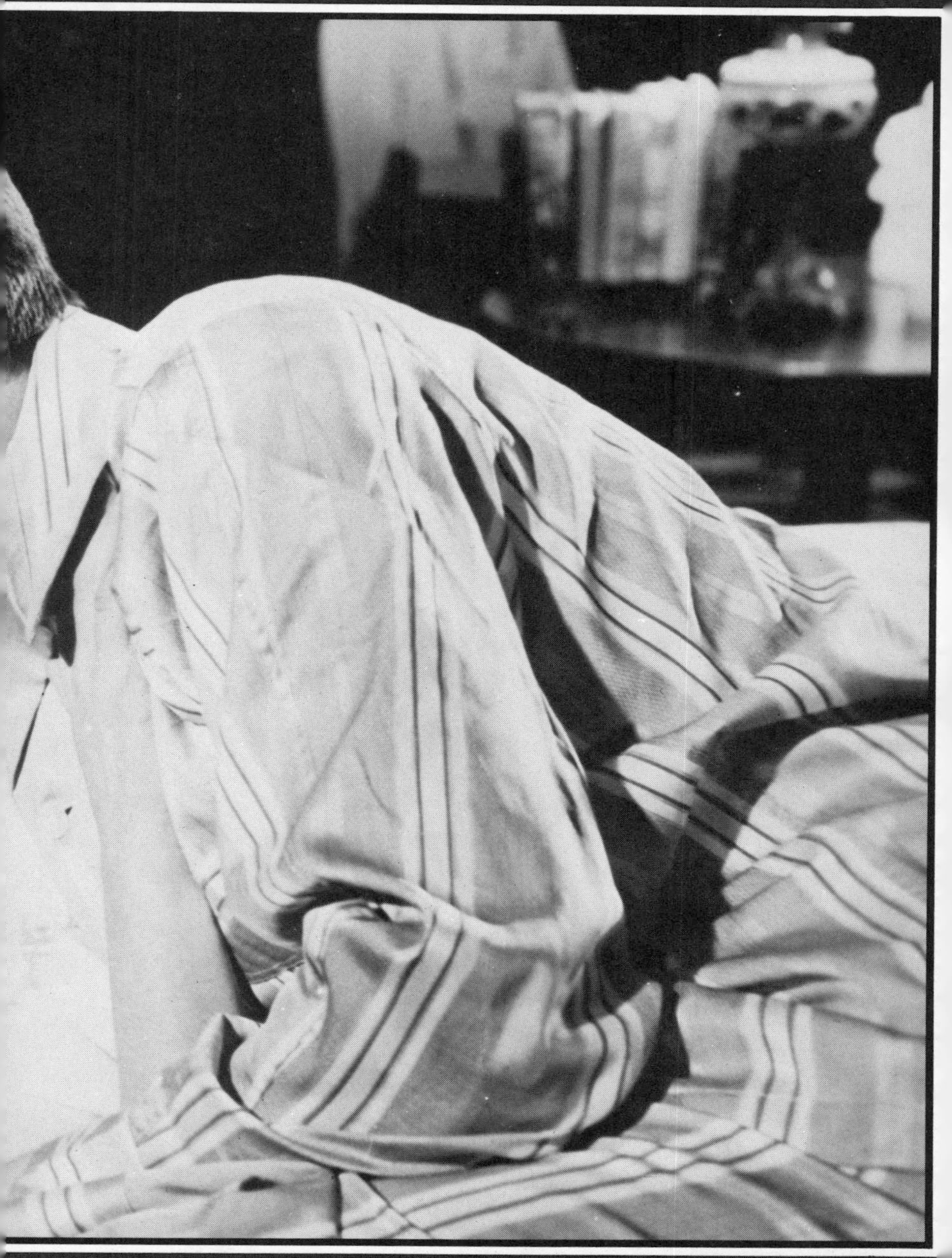

Struggle for Maturity

"OH, JOE, WASN'T IT super, wasn't it simply super!" Susan Brown, the wealthy industrialist's daughter, exclaims to Joe Lampton after parting with her virginity. Until that moment in *Room at the Top,* lovemaking was not something to be evaluated candidly on a British screen. One did not even admit there was such a thing as sexual climax, let alone revel in having attained it. British critic Alexander Walker remarked in his book *Hollywood U.K.:* "This went dead against the grain of English screen history, where characters extracted emotion out of guilt, not pleasure."

The impact *Room at the Top* had in the United States and Britain is traceable to the need for English language films to become more realistic and grown-up. In America, the Production Code and the Legion of Decency had long stifled the possibility of treating relationships maturely and honestly, acknowledging without smirking the role sex plays. Although there were attempts to surmount traditional taboos, as late as 1959 English-language films were still pathetically backward. *Room at the Top* generated the hope that, if the British were becoming more audacious, surely American producers would not be slow to follow.

The relationship between Laurence Harvey as Joe and Simone Signoret as Alice Aisgill, an older, unhappily married Frenchwoman, was even more startling than the candor between Joe and Susan. "I'm not ashamed of my body or of anything I have ever done," Alice says with dignity. The recognition of passion as natural to an affair gave the impression of a far bolder film to 1959 audiences accustomed to the portrayal of women as virginal, blushing, teasing, or wisecracking. Signoret's characterization exuded sensuality, and demonstrated the kind of maturity hitherto associated with French films.

Room at the Top was different not only because of its sensuality. While seeing Harvey and Signoret in bed together conversing was striking in its naturalness, the entire film had an air of authenticity. Critic Arthur Knight assessed its implications accurately in the *Saturday Review* of April 11, 1959. Remarking facetiously that American movies were becoming more adult in that they were daring to use an occasional "hell" or "damn" and were hinting at such formerly forbidden themes as homosexuality and drug addiction, Knight observed that *Room at the Top* was bound to revise the concept of the word adult as applied to the screen:

> Its characters swear, curse, connive, commit adultery like recognizable (and not altogether unlikable) human beings. And the effect is startling. One feels that a whole new chapter is about to be written in motion picture history. . . . I can say for myself that the only shock I felt was the shock of recognition, the shock of recognizing ordinary, tawdry people on the screen in an extraordinarily bitter, adult drama – and the subsequent shock of realizing how rarely this has happened before.

Others felt a more conventional kind of shock. In Atlanta the film's earthy dialogue was reportedly the main reason for its rejection by the censor, Mrs. Christine Smith Gilliam. Sol Horwitz, a veteran film buyer, recalled outraged reactions in the Midwest: "How can you show something like this?" "What are films coming to?" However, *Room at the Top* received excellent reviews and was big box office throughout the country. Its widespread distribution was very unusual for a film not stamped with a seal of approval from the Production Code Administration of the Motion Picture Association of America. (*And God Created Woman* with Brigitte Bardot was a similar exception in 1957.) Indeed, the success of *Room at the Top* was a significant manifestation of the erosion of the PCA's authority.

The inroads on the PCA's coercive powers had started after World War II when the distribution of independent films was facilitated as a consequence of the Supreme Court's 1948 antitrust decision compelling the studios to divest themselves of their theater chains. Because of the pressing need to pull the public away from television, and the impact of foreign films, the Code was rewritten to permit more mature subject matter. The majors belonging to the MPAA distributed films without a seal by forming subsidiary companies under different names, circumventing their obligation to apply for PCA approval. No effort was made to obtain Production Code sanction for *Room at the Top* as its distributor, Continental Films, was not a member of the MPAA. The film broke the Code barrier: according to *Variety*, the award of an Oscar to Simone Signoret was the first time that a non-Code release had gained one of the top four (best picture, director, actor, actress) Academy Awards. Neil Paterson also won an Oscar for best screenplay. For the Academy so to honor a film that had completely ignored the system of Code approval by which the industry had been operating was a tacit recognition that mores had changed. It was abundantly evident that commercial success was no longer dependent upon the seal, and by 1966, the percentage of films released without one had grown to forty-one percent, from approximately five percent in 1948.

Room at the Top was a breakthrough for British films not achieved since the 1930s. Many Americans were, of course, familiar with British cinema. Alexander Korda's *The Private Life of Henry VIII* (1933), with Charles Laughton, was an impressive commercial success; Alfred Hitchcock's *The*

Man Who Knew Too Much (1934), *The 39 Steps* (1935), and *The Lady Vanishes* (1938) brought him acclaim and an invitation to Hollywood; *Pygmalion* (1938), directed by Anthony Asquith and Leslie Howard and starring Howard, was a surprising success. Laurence Olivier's *Henry V* (1945) stands as a monumental achievement in blending the art of Shakespeare with the art of cinema. *The Seventh Veil* (1945), starring James Mason and Ann Todd, was popular; Carol Reed was lauded for his exciting postwar works *Odd Man Out* (1947), *The Fallen Idol* (1948), and *The Third Man* (1949). A film that endeared itself to art-house patrons for its wry comedy was *Kind Hearts and Coronets* (1949), with Alec Guinness playing eight roles; so did the series of Ealing comedies including *Passport to Pimlico* (1949), *The Lavender Hill Mob, The Man in the White Suit* (1951), *The Captain's Paradise* (1953), and *The Ladykillers* (1955). David Lean and Noel Coward's wartime *In Which We Serve* (1942) was well received, as was Lean's *Great Expectations* (1946). It is the memorable *Brief Encounter* (1945), directed by Lean from a story and script by Coward, that most closely relates to the question of maturity on screen. Starring Trevor Howard and Celia Johnson as upright, upper-middle-class suburbanites married to others but trying to cope with their illicit, sincere, mutual attraction, it was considered risqué for an English screen drama. Their environment and attitudes were far removed from the milieu of Joe Lampton, but in its day the film offered much more honesty and reality than other love stories on the English-speaking screen. (One squirms with embarrassment at the disastrous remake for television with Richard Burton and Sophia Loren.) However, like most foreign films in the United States, British films were normally confined to art houses and seen only by the more selective filmgoer. *Room at the Top* broke this pattern. Playing not only the independent houses but nearly all the major circuits, it made the general public more aware of British films and was instrumental in opening up wider distribution for them.

Apart from its unusual frankness, the film was also an important breaker of other barriers in Britain. Given an X certificate prohibiting admission to those under sixteen years of age, it was the first film so classified to become a huge commercial success. The class and regional aspects also made it a landmark. Having a protagonist who was not only working-class but who spoke with a North Country accent was an innovation. That this could cause such a stir in 1959 is regarded with amusement and amazement by Lindsay Anderson. Quoted in Elizabeth Sussex's book, *Lindsay Anderson,* the distinguished director commented that for *Room at the Top* to be hailed as a breakthrough showed "to what extent the British cinema was then antediluvian." He noted that Hollywood pictures back in the 1930s had similar "social content" and working-class heroes, and found it absurd that "it really was as late as that [*Room at the Top*] before there had ever been a leading working-class character in a British film, apart perhaps from *Waterloo Road* during the war, which was sort of about Cockneys. The British cinema was really a bourgeois preserve, symbolised I suppose at its best by the middle-class tradition of Ealing."

To recall the plot, Joe, a former R.A.F. sergeant and P.O.W., is an ambitious, headstrong young man from a poor working-class family in the North of England, determined to have the most in life. His is not a revolutionary mission, but one of personal advancement and acquisition. After arriving in Warnley, a larger town in the North, to take a job as an accountant in the Borough Treasurer's office, he meets Susan (Heather Sears), daughter of the local magnate, and cultivates her as a prospective conquest and a means of furthering his position. When her parents send her to France to remove her from his attentions, Joe becomes embroiled in an affair with Alice. Susan returns, Joe seduces her in that "simply super" moment, but he loves Alice and plans to marry her, if she can get a divorce.

Brown, a self-made man (impressively portrayed by Donald Wolfit), discovering that his daughter is pregnant, tests Joe by offering him a large sum of money to leave Warnley. Rebuffed, he then proposes a combined deal of marriage to Susan and a place in his business, on condition that Joe sever his relationship with Alice. The opportunity is Joe's vehicle to the top, and he accepts. For Alice it bodes deepening despair and progressively heavier drinking, leading to her death in an automobile accident. Joe does have some measure of remorse, and his rise in the world must be tempered with the pain of Alice's death, but it is a tragedy with which he can live.

Jack Clayton, who had previously been honored for his short feature *The Bespoke Overcoat,* was signed to direct *Room at the Top* as his first full-length feature by producers James and John Woolf. With the advantage of Neil Paterson's excellent screenplay from the best-selling novel by John Braine, Clayton did a superb job of communicating authenticity by the choice of locations and the development of characters who spoke and behaved like real people. *Room at the Top* remains his finest work by far; he went on to make films that include *The Innocents* (1961), *The Pumpkin Eater* (1964), *Our Mother's House* (1967), and *The Great Gatsby* (1974). The role of Joe is the part for which Laurence Harvey, who died in 1973, deserves to be remembered. Signoret received a British Film Academy award also, and her magnificent performance endures through the years. (*Room at the Top* received the BFA awards for best film and best British film.)

Room at the Top emanated from the rumblings of the mid-fifties in life and the arts in Britain. The Suez fiasco in 1956, also the year of the Russian invasion of Hungary, had underscored the declining power of Britain and accentuated its people's frustrations with the uncertainties, the persistent class gap, and the lack of opportunity in a country that, a decade after World War II, did not seem to be going anywhere. Many were prompted to take a new look at where they were headed as a nation and as individuals. Symptomatic of the evolving disillusion and hopelessness was John Osborne's historically important play, *Look Back in Anger,* produced earlier that year at the Royal Court Theatre, which seemed to speak for a better-educated generation of working-class or lower-middle-class background.

Among those attempting to find new direction in the arts were Lindsay Anderson, Tony Richardson, and Karel Reisz. Their aim was to make realistic, relevant films that reflected the relationship between art and society in contrast with traditional cinema. The problem was to find a forum for their work and that of other British experimental filmmakers, and it was for this purpose that Anderson and his colleagues organized the short-lived but influential Free Cinema movement in 1956. The idea received some publicity, and the programs, including films representing important new developments in other countries, notably France, were shown at the National Film Theatre. Richardson and Reisz made their short *Momma Don't Allow* (1956), a portrait of jazz fans at a dance hall, with money from the British Film Institute's Experimental Fund. Anderson, already known for his *Thursday's Children* (with children from the Royal School of the Deaf), and *O Dreamland,* received funds from the Ford Motor Company of Britain to make the forty-minute *Every Day Except Christmas* (1957), a documentary about working people whose livelihood was connected with the Covent Garden Market; in 1958 he filmed *March to Aldermaston,* a report on the ban-the-bomb protest.

The Free Cinema movement came to an end in 1959. It had no direct link with *Room at the Top,* but its influence helped create an ambience in which a *Room at the Top* could be produced. Reisz, Richardson, and Anderson were responsible for some of Britain's most important works during the ensuing years. Reisz's first feature, one of the finest of the Angry Young Man cycle, *Saturday Night and Sunday Morning* (1960), produced by Richardson and Harry Saltzman (later so successful with the James Bond films), starred newcomer Albert Finney in a virtuoso performance as a factory worker in the Midlands. Again, the protagonist's regional accent augmented the trend toward realism and the breaking of speech barriers. Richardson's first excursion into feature film directing was *Look Back in Anger* (1959), based on Osborne's play. His subsequent films include *A Taste of Honey* (1961), *The Loneliness of the Long Distance Runner* (1962), starring Tom Courtenay, and *Tom Jones* (1963), with Finney. Anderson, the most consistently skillful of the three, has directed such extraordinary films as *This Sporting Life* (1963), produced by Reisz, with screenplay by David Storey from his novel; *If* (1968), with Malcolm McDowell, and in the 1970s, *O Lucky Man!* and *In Celebration.* Anderson is a particularly vocal individualist who remains faithful to revolutionary concepts and delights in deflating pomposity.

Other 1960s films in one way or another reflected the youthful renaissance in Britain, which had become the focal point of international interest as exemplified by The Beatles and the so-called Swinging London image. This image was captured by such films as Richard Lester's *A Hard Day's Night*, with The Beatles, and *The Knack* (Rita Tushingham, Michael Crawford); John Schlesinger's *Darling* (Julie Christie, Dirk Bogarde, Laurence Harvey); Lewis Gilbert's *Alfie* (starring cockney Michael Caine); and Silvio Narizzano's *Georgy Girl* (Lynn Redgrave, Alan Bates). A free-form style of approach with abrupt cuts and fast pacing was a frequent characteristic, in keeping with the new spirit, changing values, and colorful atmosphere.

However, it was apparent that these modish films were moving away from the earthy realism promised by *Room at the Top* and *Saturday Night and Sunday Morning*. As Walker wrote in *Hollywood U.K.*, lamenting the decline of the movement that held such promise:

> The decade began with a great gain for realism. The films that followed *Room at the Top* at least freed the cinema from a lot of its clichés and stereotypes, opened up a far greater area of geography than we had been permitted to see before, and took us into social territory that for a time was individual human territory, too, before it turned into "sociology."

As with the New Wave in France, progress grew out of particular circumstances and could not be expected to continue indefinitely. Experience has demonstrated that such leaps are periodic, the center stage moving from country to country, with high points of exciting productivity giving way to low points, until new conditions create new movements. Apart from the purely British aspects, *Room at the Top* and some of the other films that followed irrevocably changed the public's expectation of greater frankness in English-speaking films. The British influence, and of course, that of the French New Wave and the imports from Sweden, helped stimulate change toward greater screen freedom in the United States, where it was not until the latter half of the sixties that a similar revolution occurred.

A more recent remarkable picture from Britain, *Sunday Bloody Sunday* (1971), delves into homosexual love and bisexuality. Directed by Schlesinger and written by critic and novelist Penelope Gilliatt, it sensitively details the relationship of a doctor (played with quiet eloquence by Peter Finch) and a younger man (Murray Head) who is also loved by a woman (Glenda Jackson). When Finch and his lover kiss, their affection appears so perfectly natural that it seems almost obtrusive to note the unusualness of the act on screen.

The relaxing of taboos has made mature themes more feasible: Schlesinger's *Midnight Cowboy* (1969) deals seriously with the companionship and loyalties of two men; Mike Nichols's *Carnal Knowledge* (1971) illuminates the American male's difficulty in forming a lasting relationship with a woman. Recently, there have been some pictures genuinely concerned with personal relationships or the lack of them – witness Woody Allen's *Annie Hall* (1977), *Interiors* (1978), and *Manhattan* (1979). But Ingmar Bergman's devastating *Scenes From a Marriage* (1973) reveals how much is still missing from other films. Those impressed with *Room at the Top* when it appeared undoubtedly hoped that it would be an influence, not merely for more candid sex and speech, but for far greater maturity in probing relationships on screen. Only occasionally has that hope been realized, but *Room at the Top* dramatically pointed to the new directions that were possible.

ROOM AT THE TOP
GREAT BRITAIN (British Lion) 1959

Cast

Joe Lampton . . . . . LAURENCE HARVEY
Alice Aisgill . . . . . SIMONE SIGNORET
Susan Brown . . . . . HEATHER SEARS
Mr. Brown . . . . . DONALD WOLFIT
Mrs. Brown . . . . . AMBROSINE PHILLPOTTS
Charles Soames . . . . . DONALD HOUSTON
Mr. Hoylake . . . . . RAYMOND HUNTLEY
Jack Wales . . . . . JOHN WESTBROOK
George Aisgill . . . . . ALLAN CUTHBERTSON
June Samson . . . . . MARY PEACH
Elspeth . . . . . HERMIONE BADDELEY
Eva . . . . . DELENA KIDD
Cyril . . . . . IAN HENDRY
Teddy . . . . . RICHARD PASCO
Meg . . . . . PRUNELLA SCALES
Mary . . . . . KATHERINE PAGE
Miss Breith . . . . . THELMA RUBY
Janet . . . . . ANNE LEON
Joan . . . . . WENDY CRAIG
Miss Gilchrist . . . . . AVRIL ELGAR
Aunt . . . . . BEATRICE VARLEY
Gertrude . . . . . MIRIAM KARLIN
Reggie . . . . . KENNETH WALLER
Bernard . . . . . ANTHONY NEWLANDS
Raymond . . . . . ANDREW IRVINE
Darnley . . . . . STEPHEN JACK
Mavis . . . . . APRIL OLRICH
Mayor . . . . . JOHN WELSH
Mayoress . . . . . EVERLEY GREGG
Priest . . . . . BASIL DIGNAM

Bert . . . . DERRY NESBITT
Miss Tanfield . . . . MAY HALLET
Ethel's Mother . . . . SHEILA RAYNOR
Ethel . . . . GILDA EMMANUELI
Mrs. Thomson . . . . JANE ECCLES
Harry . . . . DENIS LINFORD
Porter . . . . EDWARD PALMER
Grant . . . . MICHAEL ATKINSON
Landlord (St. Clair) . . . . JULIAN SOMERS
Taxi Driver . . . . RICHARD CALDICOT
Girl Guide Leader . . . . PAT LANSKI
Man at Bar . . . . PAUL WHITSUN-JONES
Girl at Tote Window . . . . YVONNE BUCKINGHAM
High Stepping Girl . . . . DOREEN DAWN
First Thespian . . . . HARRY MOORE
Second Thespian . . . . JOAN LEAKE
Plump Woman . . . . HONORA BURKE
Middle-aged Man . . . . ALLAN BRACEWELL
Man in Sports Car . . . . BRIAN WORTH
Girl in Sports Car . . . . ANN GUNNING
Children on Bomb Site . . . . LINDA LEON, MANDY PRIESTLY
The Toughs . . . . BOB PALMER, BILL MORGAN, ERIC LOURO
Member of the Thespians . . . . PAMELA MANSON,
RUTH KETTLEWELL, ISLA CAMERON
Men in Bar . . . . DEREK BENFIELD, KENDRICK OWEN
Bridesmaids at Wedding . . . . SANDRA THOMPSON,
BONITA BRIDGEMAN, KATHLEEN FOX, ANGELA CULBERT

Running time . . . . 117 minutes
Presented by . . . . ROMULUS
Produced by . . . . JOHN and JAMES WOOLF
Directed by . . . . JACK CLAYTON
Screenplay by . . . . NEIL PATERSON, based on the
novel by JOHN BRAINE
Associate Producer . . . . RAYMOND ANZARUT
Art Director . . . . RALPH BRINTON
Director of Photography . . . . FREDDIE FRANCIS
Editor . . . . RALPH KEMPLEN
Music Composed by . . . . MARIO NASCIMBENE
Music Played by . . . . SINFONIA OF LONDON
Music Conducted by . . . . LAMBERT WILLIAMSON
Production Manager . . . . JAMES WARE
Assistant Director . . . . RONALD SPENCER
Camera Operator . . . . RONALD TAYLOR
Continuity . . . . DOREEN FRANCIS
Sound Supervisor . . . . JOHN COX
Sound Recordist . . . . PETER HANDFORD
Make-up . . . . TONY SFORZINI
Recording System . . . . WESTREX

Newsclips

CALIFORNIA EXECUTES CARYL CHESSMAN —May 2, 1960

KHRUSCHEV SAYS US SPY PLANE SHOT DOWN
—May 5, 1960

JOHN F. KENNEDY BEATS NIXON FOR PRESIDENCY
—November 9, 1960

In 1961, Israel tries Eichmann for war crimes . . . USSR orbits first man in space . . . Freedom riders go South to fight segregation . . . UN Secretary General Dag Hammarskjold killed in plane crash.

MARILYN MONROE COMMITS SUICIDE —August 5, 1962

3,000 FEDERAL TROOPS ENABLE BLACK TO ATTEND UNIVERSITY OF MISSISSIPPI
—October 1, 1962

KENNEDY DECREES BLOCKADE TO HALT SOVIET MISSILE BUILD-UP IN CUBA —October 22, 1962

In 1963, *The Feminine Mystique* by Betty Friedan published . . . "I have a dream," says Martin Luther King, Jr., at Washington civil rights rally of 200,000 . . . Four girls killed in Birmingham, Alabama, black church bombing . . . Kennedy assassinated in Dallas; Lyndon Johnson becomes president . . . TV audience sees alleged assassin Lee Harvey Oswald shot by Jack Ruby . . . In February 1964, 73 million see The Beatles on Ed Sullivan show.

US BOMBS NORTH VIETNAM BASES —August 4, 1964

WARREN COMMISSION DECIDES OSWALD ALONE KILLED KENNEDY —September 27, 1964

1960-1969

STUDENTS STRIKE AT BERKELEY, CALIFORNIA
—December 4, 1964

In 1965, black leader Malcolm X shot to death . . . Thirty-four killed, hundreds injured, thousands arrested in riots in black district of Los Angeles . . . Protesters set fire to themselves to condemn Vietnam war . . . Power failure blacks out nearly all New York City and parts of nine Northeastern states and two Canadian provinces.

JOHNSON NAMES ROBERT WEAVER FIRST BLACK CABINET MEMBER **—January 13, 1966**

NEW METROPOLITAN OPERA HOUSE OPENS
—September 16, 1966

In 1967, Dr. Christiaan Barnard performs first human heart transplant . . . Muhammad Ali's boxing title revoked when he refuses draft . . . Israel wins six-day war . . . 150,000 march on Pentagon to protest Vietnam war . . . In March 1968, hundreds of civilians massacred by GI's at My Lai . . . In May students rebel in Paris.

MARTIN LUTHER KING, JR., ASSASSINATED
—April 4, 1968

ROBERT KENNEDY ASSASSINATED **—June 6, 1968**

USSR INVADES CZECHOSLOVAKIA **—August 20, 1968**

ROSENBERG CASE DEFENDANT MORTON SOBELL FREED AFTER 18 YEARS—MAINTAINS INNOCENCE
—January 14, 1969

TWO AMERICANS FIRST TO LAND ON MOON
—July 20, 1969

1960

Breathless

Michel Poiccard (Jean-Paul Belmondo) and Patricia Franchini (Jean Seberg).

The French New Wave

JEAN LUC GODARD'S *A Bout de Souffle* (*Breathless*) is the most startling of the *Nouvelle Vague* films because it so sharply reveals the nature of this dynamic movement and accurately dramatizes the frustration, anger, and hostility that were to characterize the sixties. Seeing the film anew reaffirms how avant-garde the director was, and how extensive his influence has been. Stylistically, *Breathless* remains unexpectedly contemporary with its staccato cuts, unnerving rhythm, realistic photography, and jazzy music. Even those shooting trendy action films in color instead of the stark black and white of *Breathless,* have coopted Godard's techniques.

The story revolves around Michel Poiccard (Jean-Paul Belmondo), who is young, tough, criminally resourceful, and doomed. A feeling of futility and the idea of living dangerously permeate the film; the music consists of variations on a jazz score, part romantic, part ominous to telegraph the tragic end.

Michel steals a car in Marseilles, and en route, talks to himself, toys with a gun, and fires it at the sun. The car breaks down, and when a pursuing motorcycle cop arrives on the scene, Michel kills him and flees to Paris. A hunted man, he keeps on the move, living by his wits, stealing, or cadging money where he can. He tries to collect money he's owed, but has trouble making the connection. He takes cash from a girl friend while she's dressing; he steals cars as easily as swiping candy bars. In a particularly chilling scene, he mugs a man in the lavatory of a cafe with frightening nonchalance. This one act, without conscience, remorse, or even tension, sums up an alienation that places the protagonist irrevocably apart from the social structure.

Michel is attracted to an American student, Patricia Franchini (Jean Seberg), who peddles the *Herald Tribune* on the streets of Paris and does occasional writing assignments. She knows little about him, but despite her instinctive wariness, is drawn to him. In a different way, she too is drifting emotionally. During a morning in her room, a temporary island removed from the outside world, they talk elliptically about themselves and their lives in a long scene that accents their isolation from society. During the conversation, she tells him she's pregnant, and thinks it's by him. "You should have been more careful," he says. The subject is dropped. Michel urges Patricia to accompany him to Italy if he can raise the money. The suggestion seems to be an idle, remote dream that cannot possibly be fulfilled.

Patricia is followed by a police inspector (Daniel Boulanger), who presses her for information about Michel. She decides to betray him, and after phoning the police, matter-of-factly tells him what she has done. Her act makes Michel even more cynical, and he refuses to run until it is too late. When he does try to escape, he is shot. Patricia runs after him; as he lies dying he makes faces at her. She doesn't understand his last words and asks a cop what they were. "Degueulasse" (freely translated in the English subtitles as "a little bitch"), he tells her. The ending is cold, tragic, and inevitable. *Breathless* was clearly expressing attitudes that society needed to resolve. The tragedy is that for the most part, in the two decades since the film's release, society has done little more than call for law and order.

In *Breathless*, Michel passes a movie poster that says "live dangerously till the end." He stares at a poster of Humphrey Bogart in *The Harder They Fall*; he obviously fancies himself a Bogart type. Belmondo's tough, earthy film presence made comparison with Bogart immediate. There was a difference. Ex-boxer Belmondo's attractively ugly face and cocky, rebellious manner were analogous to the defiance of the sixties. He was the perfect anti-hero, with a dash of roguish charm. (In the late 1940s and 1950s, Gérard Philipe, known for such films as *Le Diable au Corps, La Ronde, Fanfan La Tulipe,* and *Les Liaisons Dangereuses,* was the young French actor with the most screen appeal. Philipe played the romantic, the adventurer, the charmer with the soul of a poet. He died in 1959, the year of the New Wave, at the age of thirty-seven.) Belmondo had another fine role in *That Man From Rio* (1963), Philippe de Broca's effervescent, tongue-in-cheek action thriller, but he has had trouble finding parts to match his earlier successes. A major accomplishment was the title role in *Stavisky,* directed by Alain Resnais.

Jean Seberg's work in *Breathless* stands as her most noteworthy achievement in an uneven career. Otto Preminger brought her to public attention and ridicule in the title role of his disastrous *Saint Joan* (1957); *Breathless* revised opinions of her capabilities. At times she is almost clumsy, yet she has an understated strength that counterpoints Belmondo's indifferent aggressiveness and is exactly right for the mood of the film. She has been less successful subsequently, although her performances in such dissimilar films as *Lilith* and *Airport* were creditable.

Cinematographer Raoul Coutard's contribution to *Breathless* is significant not only for the realism he achieved in helping Godard fulfill his conception, but as a part of an outstanding body of work that includes many films by Godard and by his prominent New Wave colleague, François Truffaut. His expertise has been valuable, too, in the films of Constantine Costa-Gavras, most notably *Z.* Beyond that, Coutard has made his own important and moving *Hoa-Binh,* one of the better films to emerge from the Vietnam epoch.

The New Wave was born of a reaction to the formalities of French cinema that had blocked opportunities for insurgent directors wishing to pursue new ideas and make honest films that would be individual works, unfettered by compromise and studio superstructures – *auteur* films, each an expression of a creative mind, as a novel is an expression of an author. The movement was a revolution against big productions, high budgets, rigid personnel requirements, and executive controls that limited the free choice of subject matter. Ironically, among those most admired by the young innovators of the New Wave were some older Hollywood directors (such as John Ford, Alfred Hitchcock, Howard Hawks), who were judged to have established themselves as *auteurs* within the studio system; the output of each of these directors was considered to have continuity and unity meriting analysis in entirety. Thanks to the late Henri Langlois, founder and guardian of the invaluable Cinémathèque Française, a vast collection of international films was available for study and inspiration.

The movement was composed largely, but not entirely, of those who had been critics for the *Cahiers du Cinéma,* the theoretical journal that spawned the New Wave. The critics, including Godard, Truffaut, Claude Chabrol, Jacques Rivette, and Eric Rohmer, were not disengaged commentators, but writers aspiring to be filmmakers. As Godard put it, in an interview in the December 1962 issue: "All of us at *Cahiers* thought of ourselves as future directors. Frequenting ciné-clubs and the Cinémathèque was already a way of thinking cinema and thinking about cinema. Writing was already a way of making films, for the difference between writing and directing is quantitative not qualitative. The only complete hundred-per-cent critic was André Bazin. The others – Sadoul, Balasz, or Pasinetti – are historians or sociologists, not critics." The writings and theories of Bazin, as well as those of critic and filmmaker Alexandre Astruc, provided the intellectual stimulus for the New Wave. Bazin, in particular, had had an enormous influence by the time he died at forty in 1958. It was also Bazin who had founded *La Revue du Cinéma* in 1947; three years later it evolved into the legendary *Cahiers.*

Other participants in the movement were Louis Malle, and the so-called Left Bank group, Alain Resnais, Agnès Varda, and Chris Marker. Claude Chabrol's *Le Beau Serge,* which appeared in 1958, has been regarded as the signpost. The following year, when Godard was at work on *Breathless* (based on a story idea by Truffaut), developments dramatically converged. Truffaut recalled in an interview with R.M.Franchi and Marshall Lewis in the *New York Film Bulletin,* issue 44, 1962: "Each year there was a very good film made by a young person in France but they [the press] did not discuss it because there was simply one film. At the Cannes Festival the year they had *Hiroshima Mon Amour, Les Cousins, Orfeu Negro,* and *Les Quatre Cents Coups* the *nouvelle vague* was born. That enabled them to write articles about four films, four directors; it ensured the success of the films. All those who made their first film after this initial coup automatically became part of the New Wave, whatever the quality of their films." However, as a result of that kind of glib journalistic designation upon which the public thrives, New Wave has irrevocably entered our vocabulary as the term that best identifies this fertile period of French cinema.

That year was a particularly rewarding one for Truffaut. The Cannes Film Festival had not invited him in 1958 because of his caustic writings in *Cahiers* in which he described the festival as a crass, commercial scene with little concern for art. In the interim, he had made his first full-length feature, *Les Quatre Cents Coups (The 400 Blows)*. It was the official French entry at Cannes in 1959, and won the Grand Prix for direction. Truffaut's engaging, understated, but wrenching story of a boy, Antoine Doinel, whose home life speeds him on the road to delinquency, has become a classic of the period. The film, which is partly autobiographical, introduced Jean-Pierre Léaud as Antoine, a recurring character he has played in Truffaut's *Love at Twenty* episode *Antoine et Colette* (1962), *Stolen Kisses* (1968), *Bed and Board* (1970), and *Love on the Run* (1979).

Godard's influence has been the most far-reaching of the directors of this era. He has relentlessly, and some would say recklessly, pursued new courses, even to the point of rejecting his earlier work. His films inspire passionate admiration or vigorous denunciation. As a theoretician, he has written voluminously, and as a self-styled revolutionary he has fervently pursued the goal of meshing political objectives with artistic ones. Godard defies categorization. The strength, as well as the Achilles heel of his career, has been experimentation. Virtually every Godard film contains fascinating elements, risky efforts, and annoyances, but his best work excuses his worst.

In *Breathless* one finds the spontaneity that characterizes Godard's films. The acting has an improvisational quality, the photography a home-movie flavor. The craftsmanship lies in the film's nervous energy, editing, and camerawork that make it seem like an on-the-scene recording of life. Godard is known for such ploys as sudden interruptions for visual or in jokes, titles, statistics, or comments. He may resort to an exceptionally long tracking shot to embrace his action, or a deliberate, even exasperating, slow circular shot to compel the viewer to pause, observe, and think. Performers talk directly to the audience, sometimes for a longer period than is tolerable.

Godard's collection of work is a study in diversity. *Le Petit Soldat* (1963), filmed in Geneva in 1960 and originally banned by the French Censor Board, deals brilliantly with the subject of terrorism. *Les Carabiniers* (1963) shrewdly mocks man's universal susceptibility to the promised excitement of war and booty. *Bande à Part* (1964) is a frothy, tragicomic account of a criminal escapade, and a comment on individual behavior in a violent world. *Une Femme Mariée* (1964) looks perceptively at a day in the life of a woman emotionally torn between her husband and her lover. *Alphaville* (1965) is adventurous but rather boring science fiction about a futuristic society in which emotion is treason. *Pierrot le Fou* (1965), starring Belmondo and Anna Karina (Godard's former wife and frequent leading lady), is a story of despair concerning a bored television director who goes off on a crime spree with the babysitter. *Masculin Féminin* (1966) inspects "the generation of Marx and Coca Cola." *Weekend* (1967) is the most devastating of Godard's films, a savage comment on society through its story of an avaricious couple involved in a money scheme, and replete with Godardisms on Vietnam, oppressed peoples, highway carnage, killing of animals, eroticism, and ultimately, cannibalism. The *pièce de résistance* in *Weekend* is Godard's lengthy tracking shot that surveys a clogged highway strewn with wreckage and dead.

The revolutionary developments in France during May 1968 had a strong effect on Godard, who increasingly devoted himself to films with a far-left political stance. Stylistically, his films became more verbal. In *One Plus One* (1968), a comparatively static film, scenes of the Rolling Stones at rehearsal were juxtaposed with scenes of left- and right-wing defiance, the participants expounding their views. *Tout Va Bien* (1972), starring Jane Fonda and Yves Montand, has a strike as the center of its plot, and contains an impressive tracking shot of an enormous, well-stocked supermarket, a self-evident comment on society's materialism. Godard's intensively political approaches have tended to encumber his creativity instead of inspiring it, but his 1975 film, *Numero Deux,* is a bold experiment that again shows a break with the past (and guarantees divided reactions). Godard proved that, sixteen years after *Breathless,* he could still make a film within the same budget – $120,000. Much of *Numero Deux* is attuned to the video age, with action and dialogue that describes the life of a working-class family unfolding on television screens that appear on various parts of the cinema screen. The concept is counter-productive. Television is a restrictive medium, film a liberating one, and no matter how clever the technique, to use cinema with television as a method of expression is a strange gambit, more interesting for concept than for insightful results. Yet the film dramatizes Godard's restless creativity.

As for Truffaut, his career has been impressive since the appearance of *Les Quatre Cents Coups.* His later course has been much more commercial, but he has made many films worth treasuring. In contrast with the esoteric tangents of Godard, Truffaut's disciplined application of his talent has enabled him to communicate appealingly to comparatively wide audiences. *Jules et Jim* (1962) exemplifies the freedom of form and liberation of attitudes that excitingly synthesized the elements of the New Wave. One of

Truffaut's most skillful and entertaining accomplishments is *La Nuit Américaine (Day for Night*, 1973*)*, an *hommage* to filmmaking, starring Jean-Pierre Léaud and Jacqueline Bisset. His films include *Tirez sur le Pianiste (Shoot the Piano Player*, 1960); *La Peau Douce (The Soft Skin*, 1964); *Fahrenheit 451* (1966); *La Mariée Etait en Noir (The Bride Wore Black*, 1968); *L'Enfant Sauvage (The Wild Child*, 1970); *L'Histoire d'Adèle H* (1975); *L'Argent de Poche (Small Change*, 1976); and *La Chambre Verte (The Green Room*, 1978).

Alain Resnais' *Hiroshima Mon Amour*, which was among the sensational grouping of films in 1959, is a New Wave film of a different and strikingly original caliber. (He had previously made the important short about Auschwitz, *Night and Fog*, 1956.) Resnais, with a script by Marguerite Duras, poetically explores ways of blending image and words in an intricate pattern. A French actress and a Japanese architect meet in the Hiroshima of 1957, and the tragic past of the city and the woman's past are inextricably interwoven with their affair. The film is a masterpiece in merging conscience, events, thoughts, personal history, and shifting time. Subsequent films include the challenging *Last Year at Marienbad* (1961), *Muriel* (1963), and *La Guerre est Finie* (1966). The last-mentioned, with its flashbacks and flash forwards, examines the life of an exiled Spanish revolutionary by measuring his frustrated present against his ideals, his personal relationships, his political ties, his whole being. *Stavisky* (1974) is beautiful to look at and thought-provoking in its view of France's famous case of financial chicanery. *Providence* (1977), in dramatizing the planning of a novel by a terminally ill writer, further illustrates the capacity of cinema to convey thought, inner conflict, and the creative process.

Claude Chabrol, who served as technical adviser to Godard on *Breathless*, has also amassed an imposing filmography although he has tended to become debilitatingly constricted in his choice of subject matter. Ranking among his best films are *Les Cousins* (1959), in which a naïve country cousin visits his decadent relative in Paris and is ultimately destroyed; *Les Bonnes Femmes* (1960), a bitter story of shopgirls with cruelly frustrated dreams; *Que la Bête Meure* (1969), a portrait of all-consuming revenge; and *Le Boucher* (1969), the story of a murderer and the shy teacher who ventures into a hazardous relationship with him. Chabrol's skill at character development and visual storytelling is not always matched by deserving basic material, but there is usually brilliance to his style, as with *Violette Nozière* (1978).

Louis Malle has made such important films as *The Lovers* (1958), *Zazie dans le Métro* (1960), and *Le Souffle au Coeur* (1971). *Phantom India* (1968), is a lengthy, in-depth documentary of that complex land. In *Lacombe, Lucien* (1974), the story of a young peasant in German-occupied France who joins the collaborators, Malle penetratingly examines the "banality of evil." Malle experimented with an excursion into fantasy in *Black Moon* (1975), a less auspicious change of direction. He explored child prostitution in *Pretty Baby* (1978).

Eric Rohmer demonstrated that dialogue can still be appealing, even in this visual age, with the clever, intellectual talkathon *Ma Nuit chez Maud (My Night at Maud's*, 1969), followed by the charming, also conversational, *Le Genou de Claire (Claire's Knee*, 1970), and *The Marquise of O . . .* (1975), films that brought him wide prestige. Jacques Rivette's controversial *La Religieuse* (1965), *L'Amour Fou* (1968), and his more recent films have kept him before the public. Agnès Varda was justly lauded for *Cléo de 5 à 7* (1962), a drama of two hours in the life of a woman who wanders about Paris fearing she has cancer, and awaiting a doctor's report. Her later films include *Le Bonheur* (1965), *Les Créatures* (1966), *Lions Love* (1969), and *One Sings, the Other Doesn't* (1977). Chris Marker became known as an exponent of cinéma vérité, typified by the candid interviews in *Le Joli Mai* (1963) that caught the pulsebeat of Paris and its population.

Some who obtained their experience working with the New Wave directors are now being heard from, and the productivity and versatility that enriched cinema as a consequence of the movement has not been confined to France. Much as the Italian neo-realists had done a decade earlier, the New Wave inspired filmmakers elsewhere to break with convention and attempt their own experimental work. The techniques that seemed so advanced when Godard used them in *Breathless* have entered the vocabulary of cinema. The more adventurous, individualistic American films of the second half of the 1960s, such as *The Graduate, Bonnie and Clyde*, and *Easy Rider*, are at least partially traceable to the esprit of the New Wave, and to a lesser degree, to the parallel Angry Young Man cycle in Britain.

It is too much to expect that the momentum of the New Wave could be sustained since movements transiently occur in their own time and place, with new circumstances yielding new revolutions. Significantly, for all the breaking with the past, the New Wave embraced Jean Renoir, the towering figure of French cinema, and received inspiration from Jean Cocteau, whose adventures in film included such intriguing works as *Le Sang d'un Poète*, *La Belle et la Bête, Les Parents Terribles, Orphée*, and *Les Enfants Terribles*, directed by Jean-Pierre Melville from Cocteau's screenplay. (Melville plays a cameo role in *Breathless*.)

Although the New Wave has receded, and there are laments about the decline of French films, the movement, so dramatically characterized by *Breathless*, has had profound, widespread meaning for cinema on an international scale.

BREATHLESS
(A Bout de Souffle)
FRANCE 1960

Cast

Michel Poiccard alias Laszlo Kovacs	Jean-Paul Belmondo
Patricia Franchini	Jean Seberg
Police Inspector	Daniel Boulanger
Parvulesco	Jean-Pierre Melville
Liliane	Liliane David
Antonio Berruti	Henri-Jacques Huet
Journalist	Van Doude
Used-Car Dealer	Claude Mansard
Plainclothes Policeman	Michel Fabre
Informer	Jean-Luc Godard
Drunk	Jean Domarchi
Tolmatchoff	Richard Balducci
Carl Zombach	Roger Hanin
Journalist	Jean-Louis Richard

and André Labarthe, Jacques Siclier, Michel Mourlet, Jean Douchet, Philippe de Broca, Guido Orlando, Jacques Serguine, Louiguy, Virginie Ullmann, Emile Villion, José Bénazéraf, Madame Paul, Raymond Ravanbaz

Running time	89 minutes
Production Company	Société Nouvelle de Cinéma
Produced by	Georges de Beauregard
Directed by	Jean-Luc Godard
Screenplay by	Jean-Luc Godard, based on a story idea by François Truffaut
Director of Photography	Raoul Coutard
Camera Operator	Claude Beausoleil
Assistant Director	Pierre Rissient
Editor	Cécile Decugis
Assistant Editor	Lila Herman
Technical Adviser	Claude Chabrol
Music	Martial Solal
Sound	Jacques Maumont

Director Guido Anselmi (Marcello Mastroianni) as
ringmaster commands characters from his present and

The Interior Film

THE DEVELOPMENT OF THE film medium as an industry with costly, elaborate production processes has militated against its use for interior personal expression. The concentration has been on the manufacture of films for the largest possible audiences, and the course has been outward, not inward. There are, to be sure, exceptions, but usually a director disguises his subjectivity within conventional drama or comedy in recognizable narrative style. Federico Fellini's quasi-autobiographical, brilliantly imaginative mosaic of the reality and the fantasy in the life of a middle-aged director in crisis is a landmark demonstrating the medium's potential for inner revelation. Much as an author at the typewriter might communicate stream-of-consciousness thoughts in privacy, Fellini accomplishes a corresponding task with an art form requiring manipulation of a sizable production and performing staff. While the personal film may assume various forms, *8½* succeeds on a complex level as a dramatization of the psyche. Anxieties, frustrations, thoughts, memories, dreams, fantasies, conflicts, fears of artistic impotency, and moments of inspiration are forged into an ebullient entertainment and intimate portrait of an artist undergoing a creative menopause.

Depicting the mental process is an especially difficult challenge for a filmmaker. Conventional flashbacks of memories are common, but the free flow of thoughts interwoven with actual events, the shuffling of time sequences, and the expressing of a range of emotions and anxieties pose formidable problems. Alain Resnais found interesting solutions with *Hiroshima Mon Amour*, *Last Year at Marienbad*, and *Providence*. Ingmar Bergman has repeatedly sought cinematic equivalents for peering into the mind. *Wild Strawberries* is a significant illustration, as is *Face to Face*. The Swedish director's probing often contains autobiographical allusions; in *Face to Face*, some of the demons of the leading character, a woman psychiatrist, are identifiable with Bergman's own childhood fears. But Fellini's *8½* has not yet been surpassed in its extensive use of the medium as a cerebral X-ray.

"A form of testament," Fellini has called the film. The autobiographical association is immediately suggested by the title, referring to his total output as a director. In a beginning that is pure Fellini, his on-screen surrogate, Guido Anselmi (Marcello Mastroianni), is trapped in a tunnel in the midst of a monstrous traffic jam. Faces in other cars glare at him. The mood is one of claustrophobic desperation and suffocation, the need to break free, to breathe. Guido extricates himself and floats over the cars toward the end of the tunnel and outdoors, through the air and over beach and water. He is not completely liberated. Tied to his foot is a rope held by a man on the beach who, commanded by another on horseback, pulls him down toward the water. He awakens from his nightmare in a bedroom surrounded by doctors questioning and examining him. Guido is at a spa to take the cure and prepare to shoot a new film.

A production office has been set up at the spa and an immense, expensive spaceship tower erected on a nearby beach. The script is still incomplete, the casting unresolved, and the project paralyzed. Guido agonizes at his lack of inspiration, simultaneously struggling to ward off professional and personal demands and pressures. The world is closing in. The producer is clamoring for him to proceed. The writer Carini, appointed by the producer to collaborate with him on the project, criticizes constantly. (In one deliciously vindictive scene, Guido imagines having the writer hanged.) The brilliance of the film, a progression through the stages of his crisis, lies in the interflow of present, past, dreams, and daydreams collectively defining Guido's existence.

The predominant women in his life are Luisa, his wife (Anouk Aimée), Carla, his mistress (Sandra Milo), and the idealized actress Claudia (Claudia Cardinale). Carla arrives and Guido installs her in a cheap hotel, where their liaison is not likely to be noticed. She answers immediate needs, but chatters endlessly, pestering him about a job for her husband, soliciting his attention, affection, and respect. He has time and inclination only for sexual games, but even these are defuzed as she has trouble concentrating on the fantasies he wants her to enact. Later, Carla becomes ill and summons him to the hotel to console her; he obliges, but his mind is preoccupied with the stalled film.

Guido invites his wife to the spa. The strained, distant nature of their relationship is soon apparent when they argue nastily in their bedroom. Next day, at an outdoor café, Carla arrives in a carriage to find Guido seated with Luisa and her friend Rossella. Carla pretends not to know Guido, but Luisa is not fooled. Guido envisions his mistress and his wife dancing together. In a theater where he views screen tests and tries to select his cast, further marital tension surfaces. Guido's tests seem unrelated to the film he is supposed to make, but are of performers resembling characters in his own life. Luisa is furious when she recognizes herself as seen through Guido's eyes, and leaves. Guido pursues her, and after an altercation, she stalks off.

Claudia appears first in Guido's imagination early in the film during a strikingly photographed, Fellini-peopled scene in which guests stroll in the sun and queue for their prescribed mineral water. A vision in white, she emerges from the woods to offer him a glass of water. In another sequence, as he lies in his hotel room, he sees her in a variety of roles, principally as a nurse caring for him. Later, she is in his bed, alone. In his mind, Guido conceives of Claudia as his creative salvation, his lost inspiration. At the theater, he is told of her arrival and they drive off together to an old piazza, where after a fantasy interlude, he feels that she does not merit the pedestal on which he has placed her. He resents her criticism; she presses for information about her part. When Claudia accuses Guido of having lied to her, he tells her that there is no part for her and there will be no film. He has finally given voice to the decision that has been preying on his mind.

Guido's memories merge with fantasy. His parents and his producer are present in what seems to be a cemetery. His mother and father are elusive figures, estranged from him and disapproving. His father and the producer are analogous. Guido assists his father into a grave; when Guido's mother kisses him, she turns into Luisa. In another sequence, Guido remembers his childhood, his grandmother's farmhouse, and his school. The priests (played by women) punish him after he and other boys watch the sluttish-looking prostitute La Saraghina cheerfully jiggling her mountainous flesh in a rhumba on the beach. Undulating to the music, to the boys she is the embodiment of the lustful, unattainable pleasures that the priests condemn, and a symbol of the dichotomy between the impulses of life and Guido's stringent religious schooling.

8½'s richest fantasy is Guido's harem, in which the women in his world (Claudia and his mother are noticeably absent) exist for the purpose of indulging their lord and master. The vision is a male chauvinist's dream, but without overt eroticism. This perfect arrangement is briefly marred when Jacqueline Bonbon refuses to accept her banishment upstairs, the fate decreed for growing "too old." To Wagner's "Ride of the Valkyries," she enlists the others in rebellion. Guido cracks his whip at the dissidents, who succumb to his authority.

The climax occurs at the garish spaceship tower, where the producer has scheduled a cocktail party and press conference for Guido to announce the start of the film. The hostile comments and questions are oppressive, a crescendo of accusations. Someone asks Guido, "How could the story of your life interest the public?," anticipating a question asked of *8½*. Guido, hemmed in and exasperated, crawls under the table with a gun given him by the production director, and a shot is heard.

But the film is not over. Guido's apparent suicide is symbolic, representing his liberation from the pressures and frustrations that have been inundating him. In an optimistic finale, Guido, as ringmaster, triumphantly commands the characters from his present and his past, including himself as a boy, in a circuslike parade in front of the tower. The scene is a reaffirmation of his ability, the breaking of the impasse. Guido will make his film after all, but not the one expected. His film will be an *8½*, presumably the film we have been watching.

Mastroianni is totally impressive as Guido. He invests the complicated role with sophistication, cynicism, humor, suppressed romanticism, and the zest one associates with Fellini. His face is extraordinarily communicative, reflecting the essence of Guido's harrowing uncertainties. Mastroianni has the rare gift of being able to connote deep emotions, moods, and attitudes by a slight gesture or change of expression. He has long been Italy's principal film actor, only occasionally rivaled by Alberto Sordi, Ugo Tognazzi, Vittorio Gassman, and, more recently, Giancarlo Giannini. His many splendid performances have enhanced such films as *La Dolce Vita, La Notte, Divorce Italian Style, Marriage Italian Style, The Organizer*, and *The Stranger*. As usual, Fellini's supporting choices are exemplary: Sandra Milo makes Carla likable, pitiable, and boring; Anouk Aimée reveals Luisa as aloof, lonely, and frustrated by Guido's self-involvement and her adjunct status; Fellini's throng of character performers and faces, so typical of his work, are particularly effective here.

Fellini discussed his approach to actors in an interview with John Gruen in the *New York Herald Tribune* of June 23, 1963, when *8½* was about to be released in Manhattan. Noting that some of the cast had been upset and disoriented in that he found it impossible to work with actors on a "professional" level, telling them to "do this" or "do that," Fellini said: "The point is that I can never impose a role on any actor. I must always make use of an actor's own individual qualities. These are the clues and keys that yield the characters of my films. And this often shocks them. They do not believe that I want them only to be themselves, and *that* is precisely why I chose them. I assure you that in *8½* it was the actors who really helped shape my plot. In playing my game – the game of liberating an actor's *real* and personal emotions – I am able to infuse a sense of life and spontaneity in their performances."

In the same article, Mastroianni, in discussing the director's technique in relation to his own performance, observed that Fellini needed someone who could mirror his own characteristics: "In me, Fellini saw some of his laziness, much of his weakness and indecision. In order fully to uncover these qualities in me, he would simply talk. The more he talked, the more I came to understand him, and myself as well. These talks were not necessarily about the film. Fellini, you see, likes to have intimate conversations. He would tell me some of his personal problems; how he could not solve this or that facet of his life; how anxious and troubled he had, of late, become. Things, in short, one seldom talks about freely. Once we had reached a level of complete confidence, it was easy for me to project this deep sense of understanding to the role I was assigned to play."

Fellini works by the inspiration of the moment. Fascinated by a face, he will cast the person in a film; meeting him, you receive the distinct impression that while conversing, he is putting you on file or rejecting you.

Edra Gale, a dramatic soprano who had studied at the Chicago Conservatory before going to Italy, answered Fellini's advertisement for a full-bodied woman. The director saw in her the qualities he wanted for La Saraghina, whom she played so effectively, donning a black wig for the role. The Cardinal is Tito Masini, an eighty-six-year-old pensioner from Rimini with no previous acting experience.

Fellini wrote the screenplay with Ennio Flaiano, Tullio Pinelli, and Brunello Rondi. The music by the late Nino Rota, the director's longstanding collaborator, illustrates how much a score can contribute to a film's overall effect. Rota's compositions and arrangements serve the Felliniesque images and ideas perfectly and inject dramatic energy. Director of photography Gianni de Venanzo and cameraman Pasquale de Santis attain the fluid, pictorial quality on which the realization of *8½* substantially depends. *8½* is certainly among Fellini's most visually striking films: the costumes are amusing, arresting, and integral; the settings are stunning in their boldness. Editor Leo Catozzo also deserves special plaudits for his contribution to *8½*'s style, grace, and rhythm.

Fellini, born in Rimini in 1920, received the kind of authoritarian religious education he depicts in *8½*. Once he ran away from school and spent several hours with a circus before being retrieved. Although he did not join it, as has occasionally been reported, the circus milieu obviously fascinated him and provided background for much of his work, including his affectionate *hommage, The Clowns*. As a young man he went to Florence and then to Rome, where he worked at many jobs – as cartoonist, comedy writer, journalist, window dresser, and co-scriptwriter for his friend, actor Aldo Fabrizi. When he met Roberto Rossellini during World War II, he was operating "The Funny Face Shop," where he drew caricatures for American GI's. One of the first to write for neo-realist films, he collaborated on the script of Rossellini's *Open City,* and wrote the story, screenplay, and dialogue for *Paisan* and for *The Miracle,* in which he played "St. Joseph." He also worked with Pietro Germi, Alberto Lattuada, and Vittorio de Sica, among others, as writer and assistant director. Fellini's first film, based on his story and co-directed with Lattuada, was *Variety Lights* (1951); Fellini was joined in the screenwriting by Lattuada, Pinelli, and Flaiano. About a small-time vaudevillian, it has as its theme man's lonely quest for fulfillment. It is rich in humor, pathos, and truth, with excellent performances by Peppino de Filippo and Giulietta Masina (Fellini's wife).

On his own, Fellini directed *The White Sheik,* an extremely funny satire on *fumetti,* the Italian romantic comic strips, and those who seek in real life the false glamour they dispense. The film for which he received most acclaim prior to *La Dolce Vita*, was the classic *La Strada* (1954), Masina performing magnificently as the retarded girl purchased by a circus strongman to serve him (Anthony Quinn in one of his more memorable parts).

Masina is also remarkable in the sensitive *Nights of Cabiria* (1956), and in *Juliet of the Spirits* (1965), Fellini's first full-length color film and closest in from to *8½*. Masina is a lonely wife trying to cope with a straying husband. The "spirits" she sees hold a mirror to her existence. While the film is not particularly profound, it radiates Fellini's distinctive showmanship, and is a rare, ambitious effort to explore in rich imagery the psyche of a woman.

No other director possesses Fellini's talent for imagery. His eye for unusual faces and figures, leading him to the frequent use of non-professionals, his fascination with the bizarre, his gusto for portraying his Italians, and above all, the glorious Fellini imagination, have resulted in such visually compelling films as *La Dolce Vita* (1960), *Fellini Satyricon* (1969), *The Clowns* (1970), *Fellini's Roma* (1972), and *Fellini's Casanova* (1977). Always, he is the filmmaker as painter. His superbly textured *Amarcord* (1973), a memoir of Italy during the 1930s, is important in his career as a skillful combination of the more audacious effects of his later period and the understated, sensitive elements of his earlier works, such as *I Vitelloni* (1953). But the likelihood is that he will be remembered most for the flamboyance of *8½* and *La Dolce Vita*, and for such tour de force sequences as the glittering, satirical clerical fashion show in *Fellini's Roma*.

Films as daring as Fellini's inevitably invite sharp dissent. *Orchestra Rehearsal* (1979), a socio-political metaphor about the breakdown of Italian society originally made for television, caused such controversy after a screening for Italy's élite, that its release was delayed. And, for all the acclaim *8½* received (including the New York Film Critics and the Academy awards for best foreign film, a second Oscar for costume design, and the Grand Prize of the Moscow Film Festival), the very making of a film that is so personal, interior, and revealing soured some critics. An objection frequently aimed at Fellini's bolder efforts is that he is too facile, and in the end, shallow. *8½* was particularly irritating to those not impressed or captivated by it. Critic Richard Schickel, in his book *Movies: The History of an Art and an Institution,* went so far as to brand it "an unsurpassed exercise in cinematic onanism" and saw it as "the death of the cinema as a public art, whose function has been to hold a mirror up to the physical world not the inner world of the creator."

But why should cinema be denied a function that has been taken for granted in literature? It is a long and honored tradition for a writer to admit the reader into private thoughts, torments, and fantasies. Fellini, through his cinematic astuteness, proved with *8½* the extent to which film is capable of externalizing the mental process. The beauty of *8½* is the elegance with which he makes this interior film viable both as entertainment and as a complex appeal to the intellect. (For detailed study, Ted Perry's *Filmguide to "8½"* offers helpful scene-by-scene analysis and interpretation.) The film is a labyrinth of ideas and impressions, and must be seen repeatedly for maximum enjoyment and understanding; its complexities and ambiguities are to be relished rather than reconciled.

To argue that a film looking into the inner world of its creator cannot be consistent with cinema as a public art is myopic. The interior aspects of *8½* go beyond the personal and become universal; even if this were not so, they would still afford filmgoers a fascinating and rare experience. With *8½*, Fellini enriched cinema by daring to explore new ways of showing the human personality in its struggle to cope with the pressures of work and relationships, and to recognize its own potential and failings.

8½
(Otto e Mezzo)
ITALY 1963

Cast

Guido Anselmi	MARCELLO MASTROIANNI
Luisa	ANOUK AIMÉE
Carla	SANDRA MILO
Claudia	CLAUDIA CARDINALE
La Saraghina	EDRA GALE
Spa Doctors	ROBERTO NICOLOSI, LUCIANA SANSEVERINO
Mario Mezzabotta	MARIO PISU
Gloria Morin	BARBARA STEELE
Maurice, the Magician	IAN DALLAS
Maya, his Partner	MARY INDOVINO
Fabrizio Carini	JEAN ROUGEUL
Pace, the Producer	GUIDO ALBERTI
Conocchia, Assistant Director	MARIO CONOCCHIA
Cesarino, Production Supervisor	CESARINO MICELI PICARDI
Bruno Agostini, Production Director	BRUNO AGOSTINI
Production Accountant	JOHN STACY
Producer's Girl Friend	ANNIE GORASSINI
Cesarino's "Nieces"	EVA GIOIA, DINA DE SANTIS
The Cardinal	TITO MASINI
His Secretary	FRAZIER RIPPY
His Retinue	COMTE ALFREDO DE LA FELD, SEBASTIANO DE LEANDRO
American Reporter	EUGENE WALTER
His Wife	GILDA DAHLBERG
French Actress	MADELEINE LEBEAU
Agent	NEIL ROBINSON
Claudia's Agent	MINO DORO
Claudia's Press Agent	MARIO TARCHETTI
Mysterious Woman	CATERINA BORATTO
Rossella	ROSSELLA FALK
Friend of Luisa and Rossella	ROSSELLA COMO

Other Friends.......... MATILDE CALNAN, FRANCESCO RAGAMONTI
Luisa's Admirer .... MARK HERRON
Luisa's Sister .... ELISABETTA CATALANO
Airline Hostess .... NADINE SANDERS
Black Dancer .... HAZEL ROGERS
Model .... HEDY VESSEL
Guido's Mother .... GIUDITTA RISSONE
Guido's Father .... ANNIBALE NINCHI
Guido's Grandmother .... GEORGIA SIMMONS
Guido as a Child .... RICCARDO GUGLIELMI
Nurses.................... MARIA RAIMONDI, MARISA COLOMBER
Old Peasant .... PALMA MANGINI
Little Girl at Farmhouse....................... ROBERTA VALLI
Guido as a Schoolboy .... MARCO GEMINI
School Principal .... MARIA TEDESCHI
Jacqueline Bonbon .... YVONNE CASADEI
A Clown in Parade............. POLIDOR (FERDINAND GUILLAUME)

with the participation of GIDEON BACHMANN,
MARIA ANTONIETTA BELUZZI, AGNESE BONFANTI,
DEENA BOYER, ANNA CARIMINI, OLIMPIA CAVALLI,
COMTESSE ELISABETTA CINI, GRAZIA FRASNELLI,
JOHN FRANCIS LANE, VALENTINA LANG, ANNAROSA LATTUADA,
GIULIO PARADISI, FLAMINIA TORLONIA, MARIA WERTMÜLLER,
PRINCE VADIM WOLKONSKY

Running time..................................... 140 minutes
Produced by............... ANGELO RIZZOLI for CINERIZ (Rome)
and FRANCINEX (Paris)
Directed by .... FEDERICO FELLINI
Screenplay by .... FEDERICO FELLINI, ENNIO FLAIANO,
TULLIO PINELLI, BRUNELLO RONDI,
based on a story by FELLINI and FLAIANO
Director of Photography .... GIANNI DI VENANZO
Cameraman .... PASQUALE DE SANTIS
Editor .... LEO CATOZZO
Music.. NINO ROTA
Scenery and Wardrobe .... PIERO GHERARDI
Assistant Director and Casting .... GUIDARINO GUIDI
Make-up.. OTELLO FAVA
Sound Effects............. MARIO FARAONI, ALBERTO BARTOLOMEI
Production Supervisor.................... CLEMENTE FRACASSI
Artistic Collaboration......................... BRUNELLO RONDI
Production Director......................... NELLO MENICONI
Assistants to the Director .... GIULIO PARADISI,
FRANCESCO ALUIGI, MIRELLA GAMACCHIO
Assistant Editor .... ADRIANA OLASIO
Assistant Director of Production....... ALESSANDRO VON NORMANN
Production Assistants .... ANGELO JACONO,
ALBINO MORANDIN, MARIO BASILI

Dr. Strangelove,

Or: How I Learned to Stop Worrying and Love the Bomb

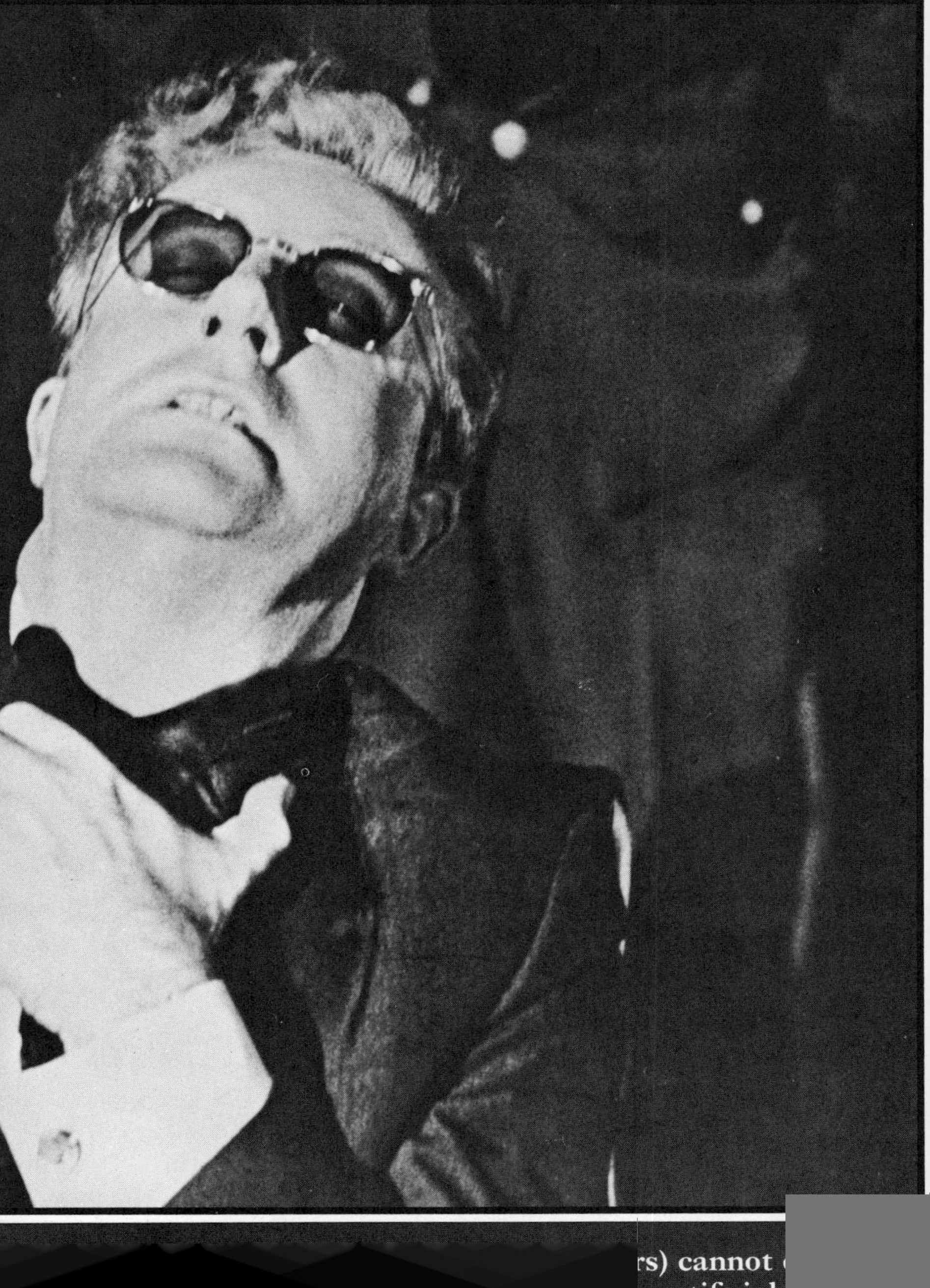

rs) cannot
artificial

Survival

DR. STRANGELOVE, *Or: How I Learned to Stop Worrying and Love the Bomb* is the supreme disaster film. That it is a comedy does not obscure its standing as the most important film statement of our age, shattering our false sense of security with a dire warning that this planet is on the verge of extinction. The odds for survival are bleak, judging by the attitudes of the characters in Stanley Kubrick's masterpiece of gallows humor. Incredibly, with the world on the brink of nuclear obliteration, a condition that has existed since both the United States and the Soviet Union attained nuclear capability, few filmmakers have attempted to deal with this danger – in itself a symptom of the public's having "learned to stop worrying" if not "love the bomb."

Films that have considered the subject include Stanley Kramer's pretentious *On the Beach* (1959), based on Nevil Shute's novel, Sidney Lumet's effective, suspenseful *Fail Safe* (1964), and James Harris's taut melodrama *The Bedford Incident* (1965). None of them approaches *Dr. Strangelove* in its uncompromising overview of forces in contemporary life that are pushing us toward doomsday and may already have made nuclear catastrophe inevitable. As cleverly comic as *Dr. Strangelove* is, the humor is grim. Since Kubrick's film, there has been even further nuclear proliferation, yet there is little to indicate the capability of controlling either the spread or the eventual use of this barely imaginable weaponry. In the *New York Times Magazine* of July 25, 1976, John W. Finney, in an article entitled "Who needs the B-1?" assessing the strategic sense or nonsense of putting this nuclear bomber into production, observed:

> It would take a Soviet ICBM about 30 minutes to reach the United States, whereas the shorter-range SLBM would take only 7 to 15 minutes. Thus, it would be impossible for the Soviet Union to conduct a simultaneous attack against the American land-based missiles with its ICBM's and against the bomber bases with its SLBM's. If it launches its ICBM's first, the American bombers will have sufficient warning to get airborne and attack their targets in the Soviet Union. In the more likely event the Russians launch their SLBM's first, there will be sufficient time to launch the American land-based missiles before the Soviet ICBM's arrive.

The specter of nations in an arms race toward the final cataclysm is so insane that comedy, Kubrick's choice, may be the only rational way to confront the situation. *Dr. Strangelove* spotlights the madness that masquerades as normalcy in governmental and military planning and thinking. The characters are exaggerations, but unfortunately, not by much.

At the outset of the film, to the accompaniment of "Try a Little Tenderness," a nuclear bomber is refueled in midair as part of the policy of keeping squadrons airborne, ready to strike against the enemy. The refueling process resembles copulation, one of the film's many sexual references linking military power and warfare to machismo. U.S. General Jack D. Ripper (Sterling Hayden), commander of Burpelson Air Base, has become impotent. His psychotic response is to blame his condition on a Communist plot against America, his warped mind deducing the details. The Communists are poisoning our water supply through fluoridation "to sap and impurify all our precious bodily fluids." He must take drastic action to stop them, and has worked out a plan. Ripper, apart from his particular paranoid reasoning sounding much like other militarists repeating slogans about the Communist menace, activates the code that launches B-52 bombers into a nuclear attack on Russian targets. He then seals off the base to make it impossible for the order to be countermanded.

Joint Chief of Staff "Buck" Turgidson (George C. Scott) has just enjoyed sexual relaxation with his secretary and is in the lavatory when an emergency call demands his immediate presence in the War Room. The president of the United States, Merkin Muffley, one of Peter Sellers's three roles and a name rich in quadruple entendre, has called a session to deal with the crisis. Turgidson finds Ripper's action patriotic and gutsy. Since the deed has been done, he calculates that it would be better to go all the way: "I'm not saying we wouldn't get our hair mussed. I am saying only ten to twenty million people killed, tops, depending on the breaks."

President Muffley decides to warn the Russians of the emergency and tell them the attack was a mistake. In the hope of preventing retaliatory action, he makes a Hot Line call to Premier Kissoff in Moscow. "A man of the people but also a man," he is reached at his love nest. Muffley affects the tone of an executive with a small problem that is somewhat out of hand: "Now then, Dimitri, you know how we've always talked about the possibility of something going wrong with the bomb – the bomb, Dimitri, the hydrogen bomb." He breaks the news gently: "One of our base commanders . . . went a little funny in the head. . . . he ordered his planes to attack your country. . . . Well, let me finish, Dimitri. . . . Well, listen, how do you think I feel about it?"

Meanwhile, at Burpelson Air Base, Sellers is also Group Captain Lionel Mandrake of the Royal Air Force, on General Ripper's staff under an officer exchange program. He takes the news with clichéd British equanimity, and tries in vain to persuade Ripper to call off the attack. The president sets in motion a desperate effort to bring the bombers back. He has learned that the Russians have been secretly working on a Doomsday Machine that the nuclear attack will automatically trigger, thus destroying humanity with a blanket of radioactivity that will cover the earth for a century. A unit of the U.S. Army attacks the base to wrest the recall code from Ripper. Leading the assault is Keenan Wynn as Colonel "Bat" Guano, who worries most about "deviated preverts." Ripper, convinced the soldiers are Russians, commits suicide to avoid being tortured to divulge the code, but Mandrake reconstructs it from the general's scribblings.

One of the bombers is piloted by Major T. J. "King" Kong (Slim Pickens), the consummate, unquestioning order-follower, a true-blue, 1000% patriotic airman from Texas eager to die for his country. The assignment has the air of a joy ride, and the crew members are ready for any eventuality should they be shot down over enemy territory. Kong looks over his survival kit: a .45 automatic, ammunition, emergency rations, antibiotics, morphine, vitamins, pep pills, sleeping pills, tranquilizers, a Bible, a Russian phrasebook, $100 in gold, chewing gum, prophylactics, 3 lipsticks, and 3 pairs of nylons. Observes Kong gleefully: "Gee, a fella could have a pretty good weekend in Vegas with all that stuff."

Back at the War Room with the president and his staff, Peter Sellers speaks with a German accent in the title role. Dr. Strangelove, a crippled nuclear scientist confined to a wheelchair, has an uncontrollable artificial right arm that wants to give Nazi salutes and even tries to strangle its owner. The portrayal suggests a satirical combination of a Wernher von Braun-type expert on nuclear destruction gone berserk, a Herman Kahn with relative statistics on casualties, and to update the association, a Dr. Kissinger explaining the saturation bombing of Vietnam.

The bombers are either recalled or shot down by the Russians with one exception – the B-52 piloted by Major Kong. Although an exploding missile has inflicted severe damage ("if we were flying any lower we would need sleigh bells"), he presses relentlessly toward his target. Frustrated when a malfunction prevents the release of the hydrogen bomb, he climbs down to loosen it, and rides it toward the ground waving his Stetson and whooping triumphantly, the absolute macho image – man with a weapon between his legs that can destroy all. When it becomes apparent to those in the War Room that doomsday has arrived, the ever-resourceful Strangelove speaks orgastically of important leaders taking shelter in a mineshaft deep underground with enough women – ten to each man – to begin reproducing anew. The prospect of total destruction supercharges him with renewed spirit. Miraculously cured, he rises from his wheelchair with the triumphant proclamation: "Mein Führer, I can walk!" There is nothing left but the mushroom-clouded heavens, and on the soundtrack Vera Lynn singing,

"I'm saying only ten to twenty million people killed, tops, depending on the breaks," calculates General "Buck" Turgidson (George C. Scott)

"We'll meet again, don't know where, don't know when. . . ."

Throughout, with the exception of one rather sophomoric scene, a perfect balance is struck between realism and satire. The realism is accounted for by the excellent production, notably, the War Room with its maps, flashing lights, and huge round conference table; the scenes aboard the B-52 with the instrument panels and operational jargon; the activity at the air base. Shifting between these locations provides a suspenseful rhythm augmented by the deadline factor, the need to halt the bombers before doomsday. *Dr. Strangelove* is lean and beautifully edited. It does not succumb to the pretentiousness that could seriously weaken a film on so important a subject; its format remains that of a comedy-thriller, throbbing toward the denouement.

The satire derives from the array of characters doing and saying the unthinkable in recognizable situations. Even the bizarre sight of Kong astride the bomb has motivational plausibility. The scene that goes over the edge occurs in the War Room when Turgidson catches the Russian ambassador (Peter Bull), invited to assist in joint action to save the situation, taking photographs. They fight. "Gentlemen, you can't fight in here," remonstrates the president. "This is the War Room." It is absurd, and the gag invariably gets a laugh, but the scuffle is too silly. There was to have been a slapstick ending with everyone throwing custard pies, but Kubrick wisely decided against that idea.

The best satirical elements lie in the small touches that illuminate the larger insanities, such as the moment when Captain Mandrake needs change for the pay phone so that he can inform Washington of the recall code. The only ready source of coins is a Coca Cola machine. Mandrake appeals to Guano to shoot open the machine. "That's private property," Guano protests. The Hot Line conversation sounds like a comedy routine, but what would heads of state say under the circumstances? The casting choices could scarcely have been better – Sellers, who wrote some of his own dialogue, providing flamboyance by the skillful playing of his three roles; Hayden, manic, conspiratorial obsessiveness; Scott, hawkish enthusiasm; Wynn, a stupefied look of perpetual suspicion; Pickens, unswerving dedication to pursue his mission to the end. The screenplay by Kubrick, Peter George (on whose novel *Red Alert* the film is based), and Terry Southern, excels at caricaturing human behavior.

The British Film Academy honored *Dr. Strangelove* as best film of the year and best British film; the New York Film Critics named Kubrick best director. In Hollywood, the Academy bestowed its honors for best picture that year upon *My Fair Lady*.

Dr. Strangelove was Kubrick's seventh feature film. The director, born in the Bronx, New York, in 1928, surmised: "I suppose the most important break I have had was being hired by *Look* magazine as a staff photographer at seventeen. This gave me a tremendous chance to see the way the world worked and to build up my confidence. Four years later, when I attempted my first film, it didn't seem to me like very much of a gamble. This totally unjustified sense of confidence that one has at twenty-one is less effective at thirty-one. I suspect that certain opportunities must come to you when you are fairly young or you may not be able to take proper advantage of them."

When he was twenty-one, his father, a radiologist, and a few friends advanced a small amount of money with which Kubrick made a short documentary, *Day of the Fight,* about a boxer, followed by another, *The Flying Padre*. On these and on his first two features, *Fear and Desire* (1953) and *Killer's Kiss* (1955), Kubrick was also the editor and photographer. *The Killing* (1956) is a tense, extremely well-edited crime story and character study involving a plan to rob a race track. *Paths of Glory* (1957) is an incisive, brilliant dramatization of a World War I incident in which three French soldiers were chosen at random for court-martial and execution, the senseless, suicidal charge ordered by their superiors to compensate for battle reversals having failed. Kubrick has disowned the interesting but uneven *Spartacus* (1960), on which he did not have control. *Lolita* (1962) is a strange, compelling film made from Vladimir Nabokov's novel, starring James Mason, Peter Sellers, and Sue Lyon. (See chapter on *2001: A Space Odyssey* for subsequent films.)

Dr. Strangelove is indicative of Kubrick's celebrated perfectionism, evident in the precision with which the film moves from its initial events to its climax, and in the details contributing to its total statement. His work reveals an exceptional blend of intelligence and social concern. Although his cynicism and pessimism often leave the activist complaining about lack of hope and solutions, this tough, uncompromising edge makes the difference between the viewpoint in *Dr. Strangelove* and Stanley Kramer's romanticized treatment of nuclear danger in *On the Beach*. Although Kubrick uses a traditional structure to create suspense, a movement toward his later experiments with sensory filmmaking can be discerned. The viewer is programmed to feel unnerved and upset. There is no tomorrow in *Dr. Strangelove,* denying audiences the comfort of routine disaster pictures.

"The risk of an outbreak of nuclear war is much increased by current official campaigns to reduce the fear of the consequences of a full-scale nuclear war," concluded the Stockholm International Peace Research Institute, according to the June 1976 issue of the *Bulletin of the Atomic Scientists*. In its annual report, the Institute, a private undertaking funded by the Swedish Parliament, warned that unless significant disarmament measures were soon achieved, it was difficult to see how catastrophe could be avoided.

By 1985, some forty nations are expected to have nuclear capability, but there is still no substantial progress toward a moratorium on the arms race. The *Bulletin of the Atomic Scientists* has on the cover of each issue its nuclear doomsday clock. The hands are set at nine minutes to midnight for the latest reading, September 1974 – three minutes closer to doomsday than the previous 1972 reading. Nothing has happened since 1964 to refute Kubrick's despairing prognosis for mankind, or rival *Dr. Strangelove* as the landmark film on the world's most critical issue, survival.

DR. STRANGELOVE,
Or: How I Learned to Stop Worrying and Love the Bomb
GREAT BRITAIN (Columbia Pictures) 1964

Cast

Group Captain Lionel Mandrake . . . . PETER SELLERS
President Merkin Muffley . . . . PETER SELLERS
Dr. Strangelove . . . . PETER SELLERS
General "Buck" Turgidson . . . . GEORGE C. SCOTT
General Jack D. Ripper . . . . STERLING HAYDEN
Colonel "Bat" Guano . . . . KEENAN WYNN
Major T.J. "King" Kong . . . . SLIM PICKENS
Ambassador de Sadesky . . . . PETER BULL
Miss Scott . . . . TRACY REED
Lieutenant Lothar Zogg, Bombardier. . . . . JAMES EARL JONES
Mr. Staines . . . . JACK CRELEY
Lieutenant H.R. Dietrich, D.S.O. . . . . FRANK BERRY
Lieutenant W.D. Kivel, Navigator . . . . GLENN BECK
Captain G.A. "Ace" Owens, Copilot . . . . SHANE RIMMER
Lieutenant B. Goldberg, Radio Operator . . . . PAUL TAMARIN
General Faceman . . . . GORDON TANNER
Admiral Randolph. . . . . ROBERT O'NEIL
Frank . . . . ROY STEPHENS
Members of Burpelson Base
Defense Corps . . . . LAURENCE HERDER, JOHN MCCARTHY, HAL GALILI

Running time. . . . . 93 minutes
Production Company . . . . HAWK FILMS

Produced by . . . . STANLEY KUBRICK
Associate Producer . . . . VICTOR LYNDON
Directed by . . . . STANLEY KUBRICK
Screenplay by . . . . STANLEY KUBRICK, PETER GEORGE, and TERRY SOUTHERN, based on the novel *Red Alert* by PETER GEORGE
Photographed by . . . . GILBERT TAYLOR
Edited by . . . . ANTHONY HARVEY
Production Designer . . . . KEN ADAM
Art Director . . . . PETER MURTON
Special effects by . . . . WALLY VEEVERS
Music by . . . . LAURIE JOHNSON
Aviation Adviser . . . . CAPTAIN JOHN CREWDSON
Sound . . . . JOHN COX
Assistant Editor . . . . RAY LOVEJOY
Camera Operator . . . . KELVIN PIKE
Camera Assistant . . . . BERNARD FORD
Assembly Editor . . . . GEOFFREY FRY
Recording . . . . RICHARD BIRD
Dubbing Mixer . . . . JOHN ALDRED
Sound Editor . . . . LESLIE HODGSON
Assistant Director . . . . ERIC RATTRAY
Production Manager . . . . CLIFTON BRANDON
Continuity . . . . PAMELA CARLTON
Wardrobe . . . . BRIDGET SELLERS
Make-up . . . . STUART FREEBORN
Hairdresser . . . . BARBARA RITCHIE
Main Title . . . . PABLO FERRO
Traveling Matte . . . . VIC MARGUTTI
With the cooperation of . . . . SOLARTRON ELECTRONICS, MARCONI'S WIRELESS TELEGRAPH CO., TELEPHONE MANUFACTURING CO., BRITISH OXYGEN CO.

1967

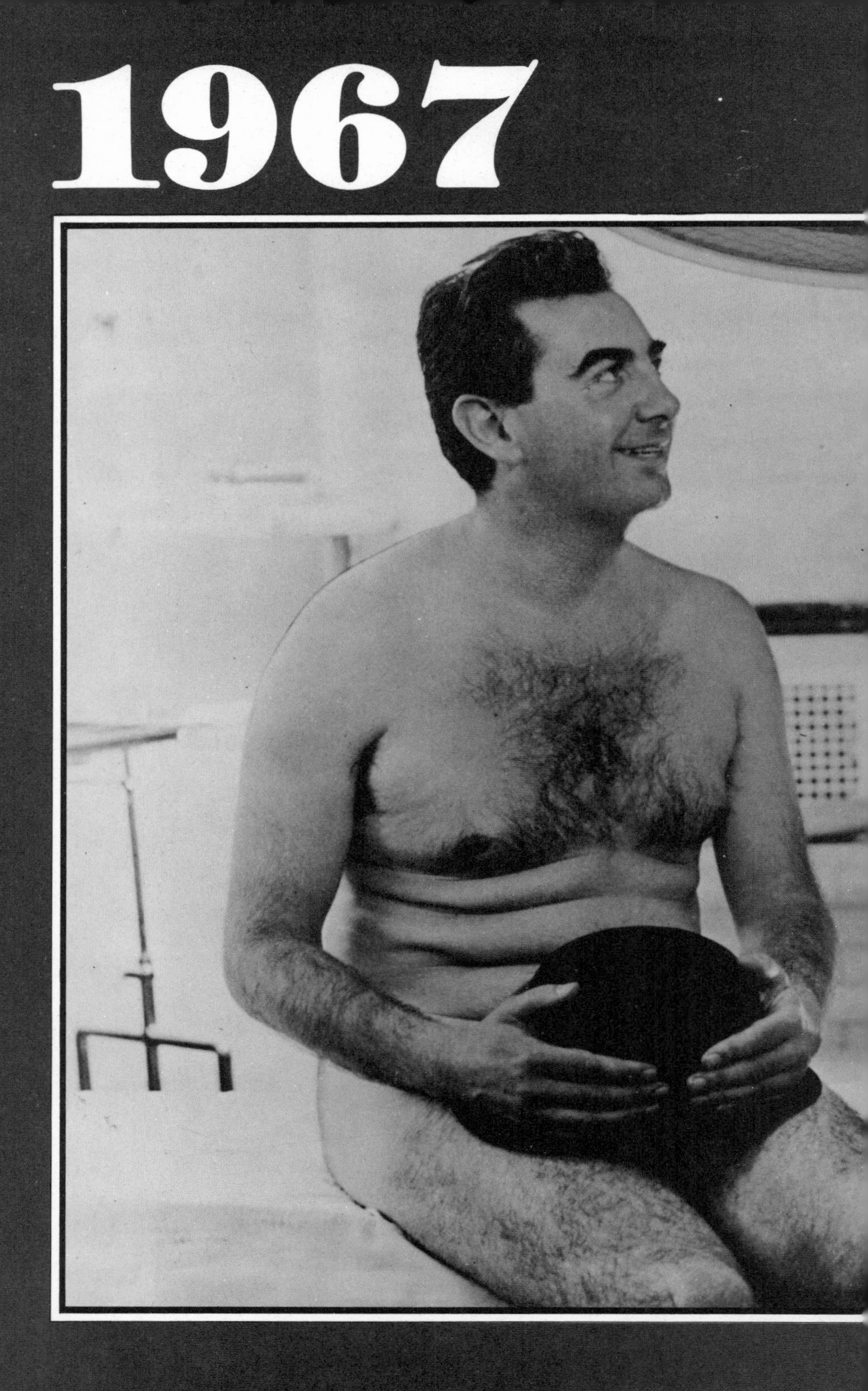

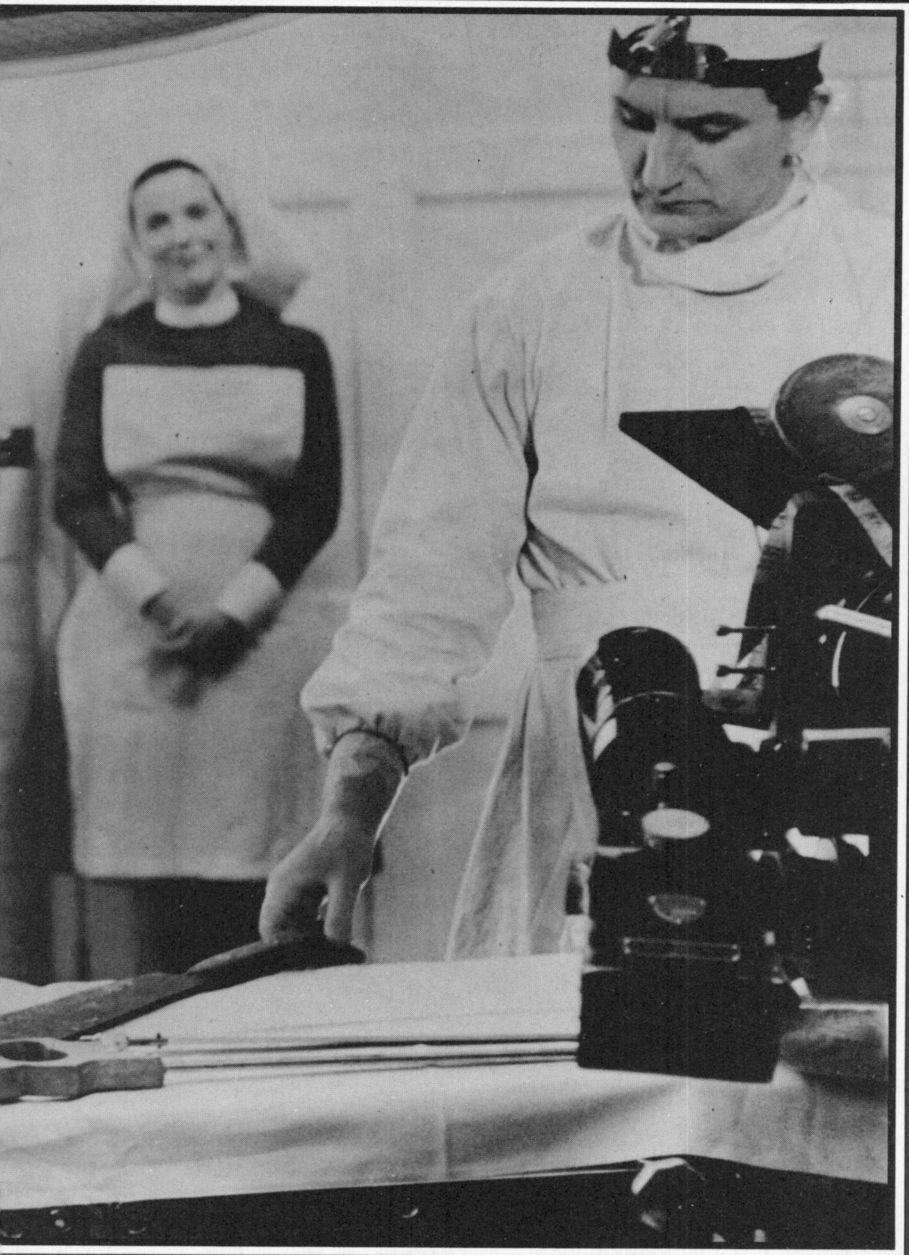

Leopold Bloom (Milo O'Shea) imagines he is pregnant and being examined by Buck Mulligan (T.P. McKenna) in Nighttown fantasy sequence.

Literature and Language

AT THE CANNES Film Festival, some of the French subtitles were blocked out. In Chicago, the distributor obtained a federal court order to prevent the censors from interfering. In Boston, a suitable theater could not be found. More than 100 theaters in the United States cancelled their bookings. An off-duty patrolman in Bay City, Michigan, seized a print at a local movie house. Censors in Australia and New Zealand banned it. British censor John Trevelyan ordered the elimination of two scenes, plus four hundred words in twenty-nine sections of dialogue. In response, director Joseph Strick called a press conference and threatened to distribute to filmgoers a brochure containing the excised language. The censored words and scenes were broadcast on the BBC Television program "24 Hours" during an interview with Strick. *Ulysses* was permitted to be released in its entirety by the Greater London Council but was outlawed by many other local authorities.

For all the furor at the time of its release, *Ulysses* was shown without incident in a sufficient number of cities, large and small, to engender the most radical change in cinema with respect to freedom of language. At last film was catching up with the printed word. Books have had a long history of censorship battles, and James Joyce's masterpiece is a classic illustration. After professional publishers refused it, *Ulysses* was published in Paris in 1922 by Shakespeare & Company, the English bookshop and library run by Sylvia Beach. The book was confiscated and even burned by customs authorities in Great Britain and the United States. For many years it was banned in Britain, and not until 1933 could it be legally admitted into the United States, following the historic decision by United States District Court Judge John M. Woolsey:

> . . . in *Ulysses,* in spite of its unusual frankness, I do not detect anywhere the leer of the sensualist. I hold, therefore, that it is not pornographic. . . . The words which are criticized as dirty are old Saxon words known to almost all men and, I venture, to many women, and are such words as would be naturally and habitually used, I believe, by the types of folk whose life, physical and mental, Joyce is seeking to describe. In respect of the recurrent emergence of the theme of sex in the minds of his characters, it must always be remembered that his locale was Celtic and his season Spring. . . .

The position of cinema as a more recent art form is further complicated because it is, of course, primarily a mass media group experience in public places, as compared with literature read in private at home. It is fitting that the language barrier in film should have been broken by a screen version of Joyce's towering work. *Ulysses,* a literary landmark in its style, its brilliant use of the English language, and its stream-of-consciousness writing, became one of the most discussed and studied works of the century, profoundly influencing the course of the novel.

Literary language and cinema are on the surface antithetical, the cinema having developed its own linguistics. Despite this obstacle, and the frequent opposition of those who fear desecration, the challenge of translating great literary achievements to the screen has always intrigued filmmakers, such as those who have tried to adapt Shakespeare. Joyce's *Ulysses* presented special opportunities and problems. Although the lack of conventional plot might frighten away those who saw cinema in narrow terms, to someone with a fertile imagination the freedom in Joyce's work complemented what film, freed from restrictions, might accomplish. Marie Seton, Eisenstein's biographer, pointed out that the Russian director believed that "Joyce alone among living writers was breaking down the walls of literary tradition and creating new forms to express the inner processes of thought and emotion." Eisenstein was intrigued and excited by the montage possibilities inherent in *Ulysses,* and his concepts envisaged the use of synchronized and nonsynchronized sounds; disconnected speech, all nouns, or all verbs; racing visual images over complete silence; polyphonic sounds and images. These two extraordinarily gifted men had a mutually enthusiastic meeting in Paris in 1929, and according to Seton, Joyce felt that there were only two directors who could translate *Ulysses* to the screen, Eisenstein, and German filmmaker Walter Ruttmann. Like so many of Eisenstein's ideas and aspirations, this project did not materialize.

Obviously, if *Ulysses* were to be effectively filmed, it would be necessary to include words forbidden by code and custom, and to find cinematic equivalents for the imagery and the feelings that Joyce had committed to the printed page. It is depressing to look through the reviews Strick's film received, whether praise for artistry or damnation for inadequacy, and find so much attention paid to the sprinkling of Anglo-Saxon and the sexual candor, as if that were the principal aspect of either Joyce's writing or the film. Today, after other films have also demonstrated that words once problematical could be used publicly without the collapse of government, church, home, and motherhood, some of the comments *Ulysses* provoked seem especially ludicrous, even though we are still far from being fully liberated. In 1967, George Bourke wrote in the *Miami Herald* that *Ulysses* "reproduces in multi-channel stereophonic audibility a lengthy glossary of terms – some from the gutter, others from technical journals specializing in sexual aberrations – but all dealing with bodily functions which society has wisely decreed be done in privacy." In the *Miami News* Herb Kelly wondered whether "this motion picture 'happening' isn't just filth and sensationalism wearing the mask of 'literature.' " Jean Walrath in the Rochester, New York, *Democrat and Chronicle* found that "even in the light of the 20th Century it is hardly to be believed that this has happened to the screen. It's a surprise to send one reeling out of the theater. . . . To put it plainly it's uncomfortable to sit there and hear them [the words]." In the Rochester *Times-Union,* Hamilton B. Allen, while finding the film "a bulls-eye" artistically, declared: "Classic they may be, but both novel and picture are steeped in filth (try some of the dialogue at your next social gathering and see what happens) and I shudder at what will follow, on screen, with the gates now wide open. Maybe we deserve it."

The majority of critics reviewing the film accorded it respect and dignity, and appreciated its achievement, or at least its intention. However, aware of public sensibilities, they generally felt an obligation to alert their readers to its frankness. This practice continues, except for those writing for the most sophisticated publications. The discomfort over candid language is a matter for sociologists and psychiatrists. Individuals who tell smutty jokes, or themselves use profanity freely, suddenly turn prim when they hear the same words in a theater. Richard Nixon, whose taped conversations revealed that he was not reticent in his vocabulary, is reported to have said that he enjoyed the film *Love Story* except for some of its language – really quite innocuous. Parents zealously try to shield their children from screen language that the youngsters use in everyday conversation. That words can be so upsetting is astonishing, although some of the ranting is undoubtedly hypocritical. The unfettered use of language appears to pose a threat to those intent on preserving the rules society adopts to perpetuate authority, whether parental or governmental. It also seems to strike deeply at repressed feelings and problems that individuals prefer to keep from surfacing.

There is a long record of hysteria over language in films. The Motion Picture Production Code of 1930 cited a lengthy list of taboo words. These included cripes, fanny, slut, whore, damn, and hell, "excepting when the use of the said last two words shall be essential and required for portrayal, in proper historical context, of any scene or dialogue based upon historical fact or folklore, or for the presentation in proper literary context of a Biblical, or other religious quotation, or a quotation from a literary work provided that no such use shall be permitted which is intrinsically objectionable or offends good taste." Standards have certainly eased since 1953 when Otto Preminger dealt the Code a precedent-setting blow. He used the word *virgin* in *The Moon is Blue*, released the film without a seal of approval, and demonstrated that box office success was possible without Code compliance.

However, language continues to be a yardstick, along with sex and to some extent violence, in determining whether a film is labeled G (General Audiences), PG (Parental Guidance suggested), R (Restricted – no one under seventeen admitted without an accompanying parent or guardian), or X (no one under seventeen admitted) under the rating system instituted in 1968 by the Motion Picture Association of America, the National Association of Theatre Owners, and the Independent Film Importers and Distributors of America, and administered by the MPAA. (The age limit varies in different locales.)

The fate of *Ulysses* at the Cannes Film Festival is illustrative of the belligerence words can cause even in supposedly cosmopolitan circles. Strick recalled his experience there: "We had been invited as a film in competition. The subtitles, taken almost entirely from the version approved by the Académie Française (and certainly in all the sections on which there might be controversy), were specifically approved by the festival management two days before the screenings. Then, on the grand day there were two screenings. At the first, there was scattered audience protest at the subtitles (not at the spoken word, since one could tell by the timing what they were upset about). The second screening was in the evening in the presence of the jury. When it became evident that the festival management had obliterated subtitles with a grease pencil, I went up to the projection room to ask that the projection be terminated. I was met by a group of the festival officials who refused to turn it off. It was their festival and they would do as they pleased with the film, they said. I responded that it was my film and they could not play with it as they pleased.

"Looking around, I noticed the power supply to the arcs and switched them off. The projectors died. Then they seized me and threw me down the metal steps to the booth. I landed at the bottom, cracking the bone in my right foot. I limped into the hall and was unable to stop the projection and so, after the performance, announced that the film was being withdrawn unless the subtitles were restored and the film shown again to the jury and to the public, undamaged. Favre-Le Bret [the festival director] refused, saying that it was quite different to hear words than to read them (the latter being, presumably, more dangerous) and furthermore, he was 'not to be held to ransom like the bourgeois of Calais.' After the jury, which included Shirley MacLaine, Vincente Minnelli, and Sergei Bondarchuk, refused to intercede, I dropped it and withdrew."

Because objections could be anticipated in countries where *Ulysses* would be shown, making it took courage. The late Walter Reade, Jr., who enjoyed difficult, controversial projects, co-produced with Strick, in association with British Lion, which was protected by a guarantee releasing it from its financial commitment should the film be denied an X certificate by the British Board of Film Censors. Strick described some of his censorship problems in Britain: "I complied with the cuts Trevelyan ordered by making them intolerable, by screeches on the sound track and the film going blank. Thus British Lion was forced to go to the Greater London Council for a local certificate, outside the privately-operating British Board of Film Censors. The Greater London Council granted the X without cuts. *Ulysses* played very successfully in London but ran into the local Watch committees that a film is forced to go through if not passed by the British Board (which finally did give the film an X, long after its usefulness was over). In Brighton, for instance, it was turned over to the Fire Brigade for judgment and they did not bother to screen the film before banning it." To sidestep a barrage of possible censorial attempts in the United States, Reade, distributing through his Continental Films, arranged for simultaneous première bookings of three-day duration in theaters throughout the country, with those under eighteen being denied admission. Ticket prices were increased to $5.50, and $4.00 at matinées.

The fracas over the censorship and language served to detract from the salient point about the film – its considerable degree of success in bringing Joyce's updating of Homer's *Odyssey* to the screen. It would be rash to hope that any film could equal the novel, but Strick, who co-authored the screenplay with Fred Haines (also a co-producer), achieved far more than might have been expected, especially in view of his limited financial resources. Because of budget, no attempt was made to recreate the 1904 period. This works well, except in minor instances, because Strick subdued the contemporary look and managed to evoke Joyce's milieu sufficiently.

The film dexterously relates the experiences, thoughts, longings, and torments of its three central characters. It encompasses a day in June, beginning early in the morning at the top of the Martello tower, overlooking Dublin Bay. Buck Mulligan, a blasphemous, boisterous medical student, whose spirited, mocking cynicism is excellently delineated by T.P. McKenna, is in his robe, shaving. "Come up, Dedalus, come up you fearful Jesuit," he calls to his friend Stephen. Stephen Dedalus, poet and teacher, suggestive of the young Joyce, joins him on the parapet. His anger, pain, and guilt are aroused by Mulligan's taunting reiteration of his aunt's opinion that Stephen killed his mother because he would not kneel down and pray for her, despite her "begging you with her last breath." In this sequence, we see an instantaneous recollection in his mind, the image of his mother dying. This device to portray thought is used with increasing intensity throughout the film, including the famous Nighttown episode and Molly's unforgettable soliloquy.

Stephen is saddened and frustrated by the apparent absence of meaning in life ("history is a nightmare from which I am trying to awaken"), his rejection of Catholicism, his loneliness, his ineffectuality as a poet, and his lack of relationship with his father, who callously sells his books for the shillings they bring. The part is effectively played by Maurice Roeves, with the requisite pensive, straightforward earnestness, and underlying strength and shyness.

At breakfast, Haines (Graham Lines), a snobbish English writer, inveighs against the Jews to Stephen and Mulligan. "I don't want to see my country fall into the hands of the Jews – that's our national problem I'm afraid, just now," he pontificates. More invective against the Jews is voiced by Mr. Deasy, headmaster at Stephen's school: "England is in the hands of the Jews. . . . Ireland, they say, has the honor of being the only country which never persecuted the Jews . . . because she never let them in!" We meet the Jew Leopold Bloom, at home. An ad canvasser for a Dublin newspaper, he lives with his wife, the voluptuous, petulant, self-centered Molly, disappointed in life but partially appeased by her affair with promoter Blazes Boylan, who is arranging a concert at which she is to sing. Bloom caters to his wife with marital devotion, but has not had sexual intercourse with her since the death in infancy of their son Rudy. He yearns for his son, and envisions him as he might have been had he lived. Aware of Molly's infidelity, he tolerates the innuendos of his acquaintances, and dutifully buys trashy, erotic books to take home to her. Frequently scorned as a Jew, he counters with a fierce pride in being both Jewish and Irish. "Christ was a Jew like me," he shouts at an antagonist in Barney Kiernan's saloon. Bloom has grand visions. He imagines himself as Lord Mayor of Dublin, as a famous reformer, as King Leopold the First, as a lecher on trial for attacking various women acquaintances. The casting of Milo O'Shea was particularly sage. He expresses the complexities and universality of the character with sensitivity and understanding. Bloom is lonely and at times pitiful, always a partial outsider among the Catholics with whom he associates. But the actor's mien denotes Bloom's humor, hope, and zest for life.

Bloom calls at Trinity Hospital to visit a friend in labor and is invited into the interns' room for some convivial carousing with Mulligan, other young medical students, and Stephen. Feeling protective of Stephen, who has had too much to drink, he follows him to Nighttown, the red-light district, where the prostitutes call from their windows. Still trailing Stephen, he visits the brothel of Bella Cohen, impressively played by Anna Manahan. Here Bloom's fantasies take over – forbidden, erotic notions of domination and submission, and changed sexual identity. Real characters in his life fuse with fantasy situations, cleverly expressed with comic overtones and delightful enactments; he is examined by Mulligan and found to be pregnant; he wears women's clothes and is dominated in a circus ring; he imagines himself a Middle Eastern potentate. Finally, Bloom escorts the inebriated Stephen from the brothel. A street altercation occurs and Stephen is knocked down by an aggressive British soldier. Helping him up, Bloom holds him in his arms as if they were father and son and takes him home. Molly is already in bed. Although we hear only a narration, we observe the two men in animated conversation and warm rapport, but when Bloom invites Stephen to stay the night he declines. Bloom retires and lies, as is his custom, with his head at the foot of the bed, his arm encircling Molly's feet, while she mulls the substance of her life.

Molly's long (approximately twenty minutes) soliloquy, although not the entire passage from the novel, is surely one of the most expressive screen speeches an actress has had the opportunity to perform, and it is wonderfully interpreted by Barbara Jefford. This section drew the greatest public attention, as it contains words barred from the screen till then. They are thoroughly natural and beautiful in their context. In this magnificent soliloquy, Joyce was extremely sensitive to the position of women in the society about which he was writing. Molly's outpouring of her thoughts and feelings; her description of her lack of sexual gratification with Bloom; her lusty reminiscences of her tumbles with Blazes Boylan; her memories of Lt. Stanley Gardner, her British lover; her meeting with Bloom, who called her his "mountain flower"; the death of their son; her imagining of Stephen as a lover; her resentment at the way men take selfish pleasure with women; her search for self-expression; her questioning of women's accepted lot – these smoldering thoughts are given eloquent voice. The soliloquy is sensuous, but not merely because of the erotic words. Its sensuality derives from the depths of Molly's emotional and physical hunger, from the passion of a total personality demanding to be satisfied by more than a passing sexual escapade. Since *Ulysses* was released, the screen has been filled with physical gymnastics, explicit love-making in diverse positions, and free use of language. Most of this is vapid in comparison with Molly's soliloquy.

Strick gets excellent results from his colorful assemblage of characters, including Zoe Higgins (Maureen Toal), Josie Breen (Maureen Potter), Myles Crawford (Chris Curran), Blazes Boylan (Joe Lynch), and many others who add to the Dublin environment. The funeral of Paddy Dignam, the scene at Trinity Hospital, the talk at Kiernan's saloon, Bloom's calling at the newspaper office, and the reflective sequences that at once suggest the beauty of Ireland and the memories of times past, generously widen the film's sweep. The selections by Strick and Haines are faithful to the spirit of the author. What is remarkable is not that so much of Joyce remains outside the boundary of the film, but that so much has been realized with such vigor and clarity.

Prior to *Ulysses*, Strick, an independent producer and director, made *The Savage Eye* (1960), starring Barbara Baxley, a searing, quasi-documentary about the readjustment of a divorcée. Less successful was his 1963 film adaptation of Genet's *The Balcony*. Following *Ulysses*, he attempted Henry Miller's *Tropic of Cancer*, a 1970 release starring Rip Torn as the controversial author. Although the film catches the spirit of Miller's writing, the contemporary setting dictated by budget considerations makes it flat and anachronistic. Whereas a non-period setting is not harmful to *Ulysses,* it destroys the ambience of the expatriate days in Paris, without which the film seems peculiarly suspended. *Interviews With My Lai Veterans* won the 1970 Academy Award for best documentary short subject. *Road Movie* (1974), about the hope and despair in the lives of two truck drivers and a young woman whom they take along on their route, is an underrated, fine work. In 1976, the director returned to Dublin to film Joyce's *A Portrait of the Artist as a Young Man.*

Strick's efforts to film *Ulysses* were arduous: "Originally I was to make three films: the first, the day of Stephen and Bloom; the second every word of Nighttown; and the third every word of Molly. I simply could not find the money for this. But a ground rule for the making of the film was that there be no new writing, no additions or corrections, and surely no phony narration summarizing what should be dramatically handled. I think the strength of the film rests in devotion to the text. That is, find the analogue or don't do it. In many cases, the limitations of the film, our money and so on, severely hampered us. No 'bronze by gold,' since we weren't working in color. It became a matter of deciding what the book is about and proceeding from there to explore a filmic version with as much imagination as I had and within the limitations. I knew that there were absolutely right ideas for the transposition, such as the use of Molly's voice for the monologue, and a free use of images to wrap up many elements of the story not previously expressed without which the story makes no sense. That is, I felt it necessary to make the same kind of demand on the audience as Joyce does in the book, even though it is not to the same degree. The story cannot be understood without knowing the facts of Rudy's birth and death; even the most important and affirmative notion is only alluded to in Molly's 'yes.' But the book works for people who can give it the attention it demands, and I think the film does.

"The most difficult problems centered around money, of course. We spent $450,000 making the film. No one was paid more than £100 per week but everyone got a percentage of the profit, which continues to pay off to this day – the film has grossed between $4 and $5 million in the United States and perhaps another $2 million abroad. We got the total financing seven weeks after it was shot! Until then, we had nothing but personal loans from Walter and myself with which to operate. Thus, every question about money, like the number of extras to be used, the nature of the costumes, and so on, had to be seen in a second and third perspective of not what the budget called for, but what we had left in the bank. Every now and then we got lucky, as in the procurement of a circus for free, and there was a marvelous spirit in the Dubliners.

"The transposition of the literary text to film had been taking place in my head for about six years. I had approached the Joyce estate in 1962 when I had thought about it long enough to decide I knew how to make the film. Jerry Wald had then had the novel for a few years, and I got hold of it in 1964, after Wald had died and 20th Century-Fox had released it. So for some years I had been mulling and the solutions had occurred to me in the fullness of time.

"The single most difficult analogue to find was the chapter in which Joyce attempts to suggest the maturation of the fetus in the womb by sending up many of the styles in the English language, in chronological order since Chaucer. To adopt camera styles since Daguerre would have been possible, but stuffy. I guess I thought the technique had not worked in the book and so was inhibited from pursuing it in the film. In any event, I felt the book to be encyclopedic and I knew I would not find analogues for all the greatnesses, though I knew I would try, and even succeed, with some.

"I think the film was made at a time when it was propitious that Joyce's view be seen. It seems to be the central literary work of this century and capable of many versions, even requiring them. My film has the merit of staying with the book and taking the text as a responsibility. Not every word is dealt with, but nothing is avoided because it is merely tough. I think the film deals with the root of the book and without opportunism, and in successful moments allows the book and the actors to work. The fuss created when I tried to do the film leads me to believe that it was part of liberating films to deal with forbidden material. Films have always been well behind literature and this one did, perhaps, move things forward a notch. Also, one of the nastiest presumptions is that one must film from minor works, and I think this picture questions that idiocy."

Apart from its intrinsic worth as an adaptation of Joyce and as a meeting ground of literature and cinema, Strick's *Ulysses* is certainly deserving of recognition for its landmark contribution toward the emancipation of language and content, so essential to mature use of film.

ULYSSES
GREAT BRITAIN
(British Lion-Walter Reade Organization) 1967

Cast

Molly Bloom . . . . BARBARA JEFFORD
Leopold Bloom . . . . MILO O'SHEA
Stephen Dedalus . . . . MAURICE ROEVES
Buck Mulligan . . . . T.P. MCKENNA
Simon Dedalus . . . . MARTIN DEMPSEY
May Goulding Dedalus . . . . SHEILA O'SULLIVAN

Haines . . . . GRAHAM LINES
Jack Power . . . . PETER MAYOCK
Gerty MacDowell . . . . FIONNUALA FLANAGAN
Bella Cohen . . . . ANNA MANAHAN
Zoe Higgins . . . . MAUREEN TOAL
Josie Breen . . . . MAUREEN POTTER
Myles Crawford . . . . CHRIS CURRAN
Mary Driscoll . . . . MAIRE HASTINGS
Martin Cunningham . . . . EDDIE GOLDEN
Blazes Boylan . . . . JOE LYNCH
Cissy Caffrey . . . . BIDDIE WHITE-LENNON
The Hon. Mrs. Mervyn Talboys . . . . MERYL GOURLEY
Mrs. Bellingham . . . . ANN ROWAN
Nurse Callan . . . . ROSALEEN LINEHAN
Alexander J. Dowie . . . . O.Z. WHITEHEAD
John Henry Manton . . . . CECIL SHERIDAN
The Citizen . . . . GEOFFREY GOLDEN
Lt. Gardner . . . . TONY DOYLE
Garrett Deasy . . . . DAVE KELLY
Joe Hynes . . . . DES KEOGH
Lynch . . . . LEON COLLINS
Lenehan . . . . ROBERT SOMERSET
Mrs. Yelverton Barry . . . . MAY CLUSKEY
Bantam Lyons . . . . DES PERRY
Corny Kelleher . . . . JOHN MOLLOY
Florry . . . . CLAIRE MULLEN
Kitty . . . . PAMELA MANT

and RUADHAN NEESON, ROBERT CARLISLE, JR., JAMES BARTLEY, COLIN BIRD, JACK PLANT, PADDY ROCHE, EUGENE LAMBERT, DANNY CUMMINS, BRENDAN CAULDWELL

Running time . . . . 132 minutes
Executive Producer . . . . WALTER READE, JR.
Produced and directed by . . . . JOSEPH STRICK
Screenplay by . . . . JOSEPH STRICK and FRED HAINES, based on the novel by JAMES JOYCE
Associate Producers . . . . WILFRED EADES, FRED HAINES
Lighting Cameraman . . . . WOLFGANG SUSCHITZKY
Art Director . . . . GRAHAM PROBST
Editor . . . . REGINALD MILLS
Production Manager . . . . PAT GREEN
Production Secretary . . . . EITHNE TYRRELL
1st Assistant . . . . DENNIS ROBERTSON
Continuity . . . . LORNA SELWYN
Camera Operator . . . . SEAMUS CORCORAN
Sound Mixer . . . . CHRIS WANGLER
Coordinator . . . . RALPH T. DESIDERIO
Music Composed and Conducted by . . . . STANLEY MYERS

1967

Bonnie and Clyde

Clyde Barrow (Warren Beatty) and Bonnie Parker (Faye Dunaway).

Nostalgia and Change

In New York City, an advertisement in the *Times* for Alexander's department stores featured a drawing of a young woman in the "Bonnie look" holding a smoking gun: "GOOD SHOT, BONNIE! You're quick on the trigger, baby, with the suit that'll knock 'em dead this spring. It's the soft, easy look of the thirties . . . all jazzed up in gunmetal blue-grey wool flannel with its own belted overblouse in white rayon-acetate crepe." In Paris, Marlene Dietrich bought eight Bonnie Berets in different colors to go with eight Chanel suits. Women wanting to dress like Faye Dunaway purchased Bonnie midi skirts, blouses, and jackets. Men wanting to emulate Warren Beatty bought 1930s-style double-breasted suits. Even in Yugoslavia, the *New York Times* disclosed, Bonnie and Clyde styles were the mode. From Tel Aviv, a *Women's Wear Daily* correspondent reported on the "frugging anachronistic mass of Bonnie and Clyde costumed Sabras" at Mandy's discothèque, owned by Mandy Rice-Davies of Britain's Profumo-scandal fame. "Inside, for those lucky enough to squeeze in, a squirming mass – the girls in Midis and berets, their escorts in pinstripes, fedoras and painted moustaches . . . and the music is interrupted occasionally by taped machine gun fire."

A stripteaser danced under the name Bonnie Clyde. The *Wall Street Journal* reported "a fantastic rise in bank robberies." There were Bonnie and Clyde records and Bonnie and Clyde posters, including one with the faces changed, so that instead of Beatty and Dunaway, Lyndon Johnson and Lady Bird were toting the guns. In Texas, the headstones were stolen from the graves of the real Bonnie Parker and Clyde Barrow, two unusual but unglamorous desperadoes who earned notoriety for a murderous spree during the Depression, along with other public enemies like John Dillinger, "Pretty Boy" Floyd, "Ma" Barker and her sons, and "Machine Gun" Kelly. Bonnie was twenty-two and Clyde twenty-four when they were gunned down near Arcadia, Louisiana, in 1934. They had killed thirteen on their trail of armed robbery. In a police ambush, a thousand rounds of ammunition were fired; Bonnie had 167 bullets lodged in her, and Clyde's coat was shot away from his body. Writers David Newman and Robert Benton saw good screenplay material in the story of the young bandits who caught the imagination of the public with their defiance of law and order.

Bonnie, flaunting a cigar, proudly posed for photographs with Clyde and their weapons, and even wrote ballads about their saga that were published by newspapers to which she mailed them. One ended with the lines:

> Someday they'll go down together;
> They'll bury them side by side;
> To a few it'll be grief –
> To the law a relief –
> But it's death for Bonnie and Clyde.

Warner Bros. seemed curiously subdued about *Bonnie and Clyde* when it was screened in advance for critics, and said nothing to suggest an awareness that it might be more than just another crime picture. The film turned out to be a work of art that engendered heated critical and public reaction – as well as a nostalgia craze. Many abhorred it for what they perceived as its glorification of killers as heroes and its excessive violence. Others applauded its eloquence in accurately capturing the temper of the 1960s through the dramatization of a folk legend of the 1930s. In retrospect, *Bonnie and Clyde* was a logical outgrowth of a decade characterized by violent events. It made dramatic sense to look back to another violent period from a contemporary perspective. Whereas *Breathless* in France had forecast the mood of the 1960s, *Bonnie and Clyde* reflected it.

"We were reconstructing the thirties in the spirit of the sixties," director Arthur Penn affirmed in discussing the film nine years later. More than any other American film of the sixties, *Bonnie and Clyde* tapped the antagonisms, disillusionment, bitterness, and upheaval of a country rent by the Vietnam war, the fierce battles over civil rights, and the assassination of political leaders. *The Graduate*, a key film that also emerged in 1967, related to young people seeking new values and made Dustin Hoffman a prototype as well as a star. *Easy Rider* (1969), which brought fame to Jack Nicholson and instigated a trend toward the low-budget independent film, pertained to the drug culture as another salient expression of a generation casting aside the rules and values of its elders. But *Bonnie and Clyde* went deeper in its wrenching polarization of emotions.

Hostile reactions came swiftly, along with praise, but the attacks only whetted the public's curiosity. Penn credited Bosley Crowther, then critic for the *New York Times*, with "turning the picture into a news story." Crowther wrote:

> It is a cheap piece of bald-faced slapstick comedy that treats the hideous depredations of that sleazy, moronic pair as though they were as full of fun and frolic as the jazz-age cut-ups in *Thoroughly Modern Millie*. . . . Arthur Penn, the aggressive director, has evidently gone

> out of his way to splash the comedy holdups with smears of vivid blood as astonished people are machine-gunned. And he has staged the terminal scene of the ambuscading and killing of Barrow and Bonnie by a posse of policemen with as much noise and gore as is in the climax of *The St. Valentine's Day Massacre*. This blending of farce with brutal killings is as pointless as it is lacking in taste, since it makes no valid commentary upon the already travestied truth. And it leaves an astonished critic wondering just what purpose Mr. Penn and Mr. Beatty think they serve with this strangely antique, sentimental claptrap....

Penn countered: "Historically this was a late sixties film about non-philosophical rebels. I wasn't talking about Bonnie and Clyde or trying to tell a realistic story about them – I was talking about a rebellious spirit in young people. I tried to break the mold of the way in which films are approached: 'Is this a serious picture, a comic picture, or an adventure picture?' I don't say it was all planned, but that is how it happened in practice."

Penn, the performers, and the screenwriters caught something special and elusive. They were able to show how vicious acts can be committed by people more confused than mean, how criminals fall into their behavior patterns, how their deeds may not be far removed from those of a muddled society that needs such transgressions as focal points for its own moralizing, depending on its villains to make its heroism possible. That Bonnie and Clyde were tender with each other, enjoyed their notoriety, and had their humorous moments, does not condone their bloody deeds or present a portrait that would inspire imitation. The film functions emotionally on too many levels, however, for those who prefer simplistic stories with one-dimensional characters and viewpoints. Scenes recall the Depression poverty that spawned such despair and engendered such gross inequality that, in some ways, robbing banks was no more antisocial than starvation, mass unemployment, breadlines, evictions, brutal suppression of demonstrators, and similar outrages.

Burnett Guffey's excellent photography achieves a wonderfully authentic look of the 1930s. The twang of Charles Strouse's score; the jaunty car-rides through the countryside; the skillful editing by Dede Allen that gives the film a surging rhythm; the humor of the characters; and the episodes of comic relief, such as the toying with the frightened but outwardly brave undertaker (Gene Wilder) – all of these elements add to the film's élan. Certainly the casting of Beatty and Dunaway did glamorize the characters, and further violated the rules that would have audiences totally loathe such persons instead of being seduced into a disorienting split reaction. The abrupt scenes of violence, like the point-blank shooting of a pursuer in the face, are not gratuitous, but are there to stress the utter horror of Bonnie and Clyde's actions. Like a Greek tragedy, the film rushes inexorably to its bloody climax, and audiences are asked to feel sadness at the death of a couple who might have been something other than what they were, instead of glorying in their execution as a ritual of blood lust. Penn heightens the terror by filming the ambush and the twitching of the bullet-riddled bodies in slow motion. This scene has since been copied ad nauseam. "If I never see another killing in slow motion, I'll be happy," said Penn. For *Bonnie and Clyde,* the scene was exactly right, and inspired.

The story begins in 1931, when Bonnie, a waitress, and Clyde, an ex-con, meet. Clyde, wishing to impress Bonnie with his bravery, brazenly commits an armed robbery. She is excited by the experience, and finds an answer to her restlessness by joining Clyde's further escapades. As their affection for one another develops, it is evident that Clyde is impotent and Bonnie is increasingly frustrated. The twosome becomes a ménage à trois when C.W. Moss (Michael Pollard), a gas station attendant, is persuaded to join them as their driver. In the original script the indication was that Clyde was a homosexual and that he and Moss (a composite of various real people), were lovers. Penn and Beatty, the producer, felt that this could have presented problems and that Warners would never approve. So the screenwriters eliminated the overt homosexuality; Clyde Barrow became impotent instead.

When Clyde's older brother Buck (Gene Hackman) gets out of prison, he joins the group, together with his wife Blanche (Estelle Parsons), a reluctant participant. Their life of crime grows, and so does their reputation. Hunting the Barrow gang is Sheriff Frank Hamer (Denver Pyle), determined to track them down and become a hero, even more so after an encounter in which they capture and humiliate him. The gang's jovial mood begins to evaporate as their situation becomes desperate. Bonnie visits her mother in a wistful, exquisitely photographed scene full of foreboding. During a shoot-out with the law, Buck, fatally wounded and bleeding profusely, dies in agony and horror. Blanche, hysterical, is seized, and the others hide out with C. W.'s father (Dub Taylor), who decides to save his son by collaborating with the police in staging an ambush. As the posse lies in wait, Bonnie and Clyde drive along a country road to their death with no chance of escaping the fusillade.

In retrospect, the film does not seem particularly violent. This is partly because of the escalation of violence in the years since, and also because persons angered by the tone and the viewpoint tended to see more violence than was actually on the screen. Furthermore, of the explicit violence shown, most of it was directed at the Barrow gang, culminating in the killing of Bonnie and Clyde. Perhaps Edward G. Robinson, the "Little Caesar" of the thirties, articulated what was really bothering many in an interview with syndicated columnist Dorothy Manners in 1968:

Violence as we knew it on the screen in the early 30s was an entirely different thing than it is today because society itself was different. Yes, we had shootings and gunplay and a certain amount of horror in those old movies. But most of them had gangster themes – and gangsters mostly killed each other. . . . Far from emerging triumphant over evil, screen virtue today comes out badly trampled. The Anti-hero remains unrepentant.

Bonnie and Clyde? True they were shot to death in a few scenes at the end of their reign of terror. Meanwhile, we looked at over two hours of attractive young monsters having a lot of fun robbing banks and killing people. We old movie criminals were not pretty nor particularly likable.

We are living in outrageous times. The country seethes with the unrest of our youth, the spinelessness of the permissive society, the toothlessness of our criminal laws, the contempt for authority. And this miserable social explosion should not be fed by the added fire of crime and violence in any or all media of entertainment.

Art Buchwald, on the other hand, approached the matter satirically in a column entitled "The Land of Bonnie and Clyde," in which he attempted to answer the questions foreign tourists ask:

Is it dangerous to visit the United States?

Of course not. Americans are a gentle people who abhor violence. What little there is can be seen on television or in the movies – every night. We have cowboy films, cops and robbers pictures and children's cartoons. If that isn't your cup of tea, you can tune in on one of our news shows. We not only show people being killed, but villages being burned, GIs being wounded, enemies being tortured or anything else that suits your fancy. Of course, these shows have no effect on Americans because they know it has nothing to do with them. . . .

What can I buy in the United States that I can't buy in my own country?

Guns, for one thing. We have no laws about buying guns. You don't even have to go to a store. You can order them by mail from newspapers and magazines.

You can buy shotguns, rifles, hand guns, pistols, revolvers and practically any kind of weapon you want. Of course, we only use guns in the United States for hunting. That's why the American Congress in its infinite wisdom won't pass any gun control laws. They know anyone who would order a gun by mail or buy one in a store would never use it except to shoot game.

The Bonnie look became a fashion craze

Reactions to *Bonnie and Clyde* were widespread. It was banned in South Africa and Norway, and in France an excerpt scheduled for a television program was cancelled. Yet despite the attacks on the film for its violence and its supposed adulation of criminals, it received an important accolade from the National Catholic Office for Motion Pictures, which named it the best film of the year for mature audiences, "a genuine folk epic challenging the individual viewer to recognize within himself the seeds of meaningless violence which are just below the surface of an easy conscience." Penn had the following to say on the subject of violence: "I don't recognize when I have it in my films. I don't know why in the hell that is – selective awareness? But I just don't think that way. The only criterion you can apply about violence is whether it is generally appropriate to the subject."

Some critics of *Bonnie and Clyde* unjustly held it responsible for activities that developed peripherally. Its commercialization through spin-offs has to do with the way in which entrepreneurs cash in on opportunities, not with the film's morality. That the fashion world could latch onto the clothes of two bandits as the latest craze says something about its standards. The picture burgeoned into a full-scale industry. Robert Shelton reported in the *New York Times,* March 11, 1968:

> Recordings about the bandits include cuts by Brigitte Bardot and Mel Tormé. A soundtrack album, released Wednesday, includes dialogue by the film's stars, Warren Beatty and Faye Dunaway. The sister of the real Bonnie Parker has recorded an album-length interview, "to tell the truth." New songs about the outlaws of the nineteen-thirties have been taped by English, French and Italian pop singers, as well as by American country and folk performers.

The costumes that inspired the world of fashion and led to the 1930s mania were the creations of Theadora Van Runkle, who was fortunate in having such attractive models as Beatty and Dunaway. Van Runkle, suddenly the new name in film costuming, recalled in an interview with Eugenia Sheppard in *Women's Wear Daily,* June 26, 1968, how she happened to do the *Bonnie and Clyde* costumes. After losing her job as a fashion illustrator at I. Magnin, she was employed by Hollywood costume designer Dorothy Jeakins. "Thea," said Jeakins, "Arthur Penn is shooting a little old Western picture. I don't think it's going to be very exciting, but it might be a good way for you to start." She designed the clothes before she was introduced to the stars. Van Runkle commented: "I must say Seventh Avenue lost some of its mystique for me when it went so overboard for *Bonnie and Clyde*." The Italian fashion industry awarded her a Golden Tiberius statue for her role in creating the new vogue, and *Mademoiselle* bestowed a Merit Award upon Dunaway for her "extraordinary influence on 1967–68 fashions."

The press took to describing virtually every bank robbery or other holdup in Bonnie and Clyde terms. The *New York Times,* February 15, 1968, reported a Bronx bank heist by a man and woman wearing stocking masks and making their getaway "in a yellow car and in a style reminiscent of Bonnie and Clyde." A New York *Daily News* headline, March 12, 1968, "A Bonnie and Her 2 Clydes," alluded to the capture in Atlantic City of "two men and a shapely teenage blonde" after they had allegedly held up a tavern and shot their way through a police roadblock. The *Times,* March 23, 1968, noted the arrest in Westport, Connecticut, of five teenagers who had faked a bank robbery as a lark "wearing clothes reminiscent of the early thirties and apparently inspired by the movie, *Bonnie and Clyde.*" The *Wall Street Journal,* February 21, 1968, observed in a front-page article that bank robberies in 1967 had jumped by fifty per cent to a rate of about seven per banking day, making a total of 1,730 robberies of banks and other savings institutions that year. "Maybe it's all due to Bonnie and Clyde," wrote Edward P. Foldessy facetiously in his lead. "Nobody seems to have any more convincing explanation. . . ."

For Arthur Penn, the film was an achievement that earned him respect as an important American director. Starting in the theater, he had won acclaim on Broadway for *The Miracle Worker*, which he also filmed. Other outstanding films include *Alice's Restaurant* and *Little Big Man.* Many consider his *Mickey One* masterly, an opinion I do not share, although I do think *The Missouri Breaks* underrated. Whether or not Penn is entirely successful with a particular project, he consistently shows daring in his work, extracting qualities beyond those others might see in the subject matter.

Faye Dunaway became an international star by virtue of the film. Dunaway, who started her professional career on the stage in New York, made the most of the kind of part that comes along rarely, perhaps once in a lifetime. Her superb portrayal left her with a career problem – where to find a role with equal impact. The aggressive television executive in *Network* (1976), the part that brought her an Oscar, represented her strongest work since Bonnie. Warren Beatty's reputation gained, too, and not only because of his exciting performance. Newman and Benton had taken their script to François Truffaut, who liked it; he felt, however, that it was too American for him and suggested Jean-Luc Godard. Godard was willing to make the film if he could start within a month, but financing was not available so soon. Later, Beatty became interested in producing and starring in *Bonnie and Clyde*, ardently believing in its artistic potential. He enlisted Penn as director, pursued the undertaking with unmitigated dedication, and battled to ensure that the distributor would promote it properly.

Both the New York Film Critics Circle and the National Society of Film Critics gave their best screenplay awards to *Bonnie and Clyde*. The National Society awarded Gene Hackman best supporting actor honors for his part, a boost to his career. In Hollywood, Oscars were awarded to Estelle Parsons as best supporting actress and Burnett Guffey for cinematography. The New York Critics best picture award and the Oscar for best picture went to *In the Heat of the Night*, a glaring lack of judgment. Although a strong film, it is minor when measured against the artistry of *Bonnie and Clyde* and the latter's significance. In any event, the best picture that year, recognized by the National Society, was Ingmar Bergman's *Persona*, a masterpiece in any year.

In perspective, *Bonnie and Clyde* increases in stature as a landmark film of the 1960s. While enduring artistically for its power, complexity, and dramatic and emotional impact, it stands primarily as the film best exemplifying the mood of the decade – effected not by a realistic portrayal of the events of the period in which it was set, but by intellectual and emotional connection to the events of the period in which it was made. It led the nostalgia trend, and its stylistic influence was extensive; it became a brilliant model for filmmakers who might wish to examine evil more maturely than in one-dimensional absolutes. Had *Bonnie and Clyde* been made in the moral image of the Production Code of the 1930s, it would not have caused extensive rage, nor would it have been a challenging film. Being made with the questioning, rebellious attitude of the 1960s was both its transgression and its triumph.

BONNIE AND CLYDE
USA (Warner Bros.) 1967

Cast

Clyde Barrow .... WARREN BEATTY
Bonnie Parker .... FAYE DUNAWAY
C.W. Moss .... MICHAEL J. POLLARD
Buck Barrow .... GENE HACKMAN
Blanche .... ESTELLE PARSONS
Frank Hamer .... DENVER PYLE
Ivan Moss .... DUB TAYLOR
Velma Davis .... EVANS EVANS
Eugene Grizzard .... GENE WILDER

Running time .... 111 minutes
Technicolor
Production Company .... TATIRA-HILLER
Produced by .... WARREN BEATTY
Directed by .... ARTHUR PENN
Screenplay by .... DAVID NEWMAN and ROBERT BENTON
Director of Photography .... BURNETT GUFFEY
Art Director .... DEAN TAVOULARIS
Film Editor .... DEDE ALLEN
Sound .... FRANCIS E. STAHL
Set Decorator .... RAYMOND PAUL
Special Effects .... DANNY LEE
Costumes Designed by .... THEADORA VAN RUNKLE
Special Consultant .... ROBERT TOWNE
Assistant Director .... JACK N. REDDISH
Music Composed by .... CHARLES STROUSE; "Foggy Mountain Breakdown" – FLATT & SCRUGGS
Production Manager .... RUSS SAUNDERS
Assistant to Producer .... E. MICHEA
Script Supervisor .... J. DUTTON
Make-up .... R. JIRAS
Men's Wardrobe .... ANDY MATYASI
Women's Wardrobe .... NORMA BROWN
Hair Stylist .... GLADYS WITTEN

1968

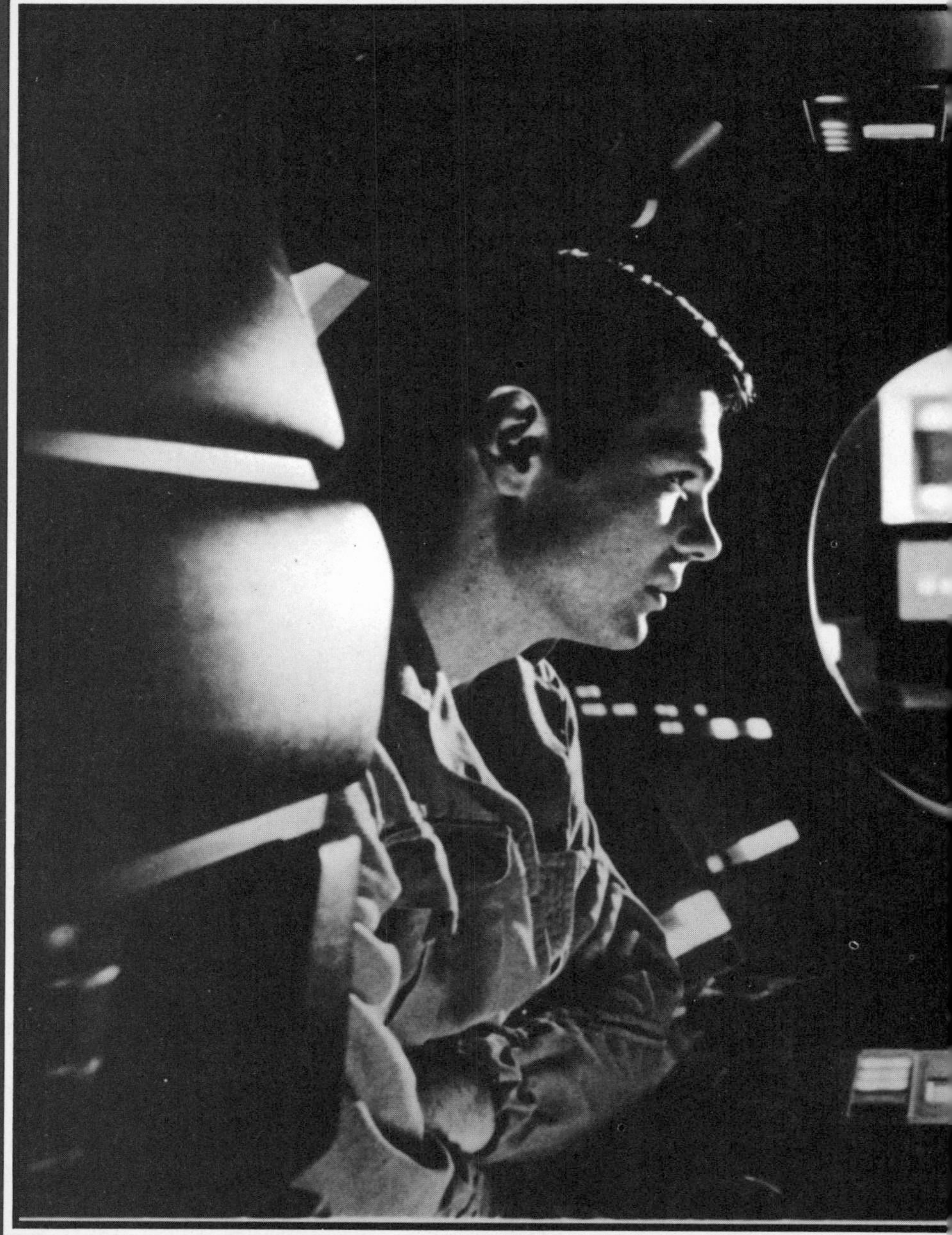

2001: A Space Odyssey

Astronauts Frank Poole (Gary Lockwood) and David Bowman (Keir Dullea) talk in soundproof pod so that paranoid computer HAL cannot hear them. But HAL lipreads.

New Frontiers

IN THE EARLY STAGES of the space age, a year before man was to accomplish his dream of landing on the moon, director Stanley Kubrick reached for new frontiers in the understanding of our relationship to our universe. He also stretched the frontiers of filmmaking. Disregarding conventional reliance upon dialogue, plot, and the type of swift narrative that had become fashionable, Kubrick moved boldly into the realm of what might be called sensory filmmaking. It was futile to watch *2001* and relate it to traditional expectations. The film had to be experienced on its own daring terms, and the richest rewards were for those who could permit themselves to be swept along in its orbit, instead of insisting upon an old-fashioned science-fiction film.

"The most powerful level on which a film works on the audience is on a subconscious, psychological level and it is on this level that we are all equally perceptive and equally blind," Kubrick said in our conversation after the controversy over *2001* had receded. "Watching a film is really like taking part in a controlled dream."

Many had staunchly resisted Kubrick's hypnosis. Pro and con reactions were quick to surface, often divided along the battle lines of the so-called generation gap. Kubrick's provocative film drew a favorable response from young persons attuned to sensory experiences. It became popular to watch *2001* from the front rows of a theater and get high while Kubrick's artistic high was enveloping them on screen. The film had its ample share of adult proponents, as well as youthful detractors, but persons growing up in the television age, with its visual conditioning, were better equipped to accept Kubrick's grand design. They were less prone to demand a conventional story with a readily identifiable beginning, middle, and end, or become upset and disoriented by the concluding phase.

"It's very important to realize," said Kubrick, "that serious realistic drama is as stylized as surrealistic comedy. In order to keep a story serious, realistic, and dramatic, one has to eliminate many things that are truthful but would, nevertheless, introduce elements of banality, absurdity, and incongruity that would move the story away from serious dramatic realism. You could say that a story is a device to keep people awake and paying attention to what the artist is doing. At its best, it's part of the theme of the film, and at its worst, it's just a trick that lasts until you find out what is going to happen."

Kubrick's flight into the space age is mesmerizing, a brilliantly conceived cosmic adventure, exciting in look alone. From spaceship to gadgetry to universe-probing concepts, there is an imaginative sweep, climaxed by the unsettling put-down of humans as we conceitedly see ourselves. In *2001*, we are but one stage in evolution, a species far less developed than the forms of intelligence evident on the strange voyage. This unique film is likely to gain in stature in the perspective of cinema history.

2001 was co-scripted by Kubrick and science-fiction writer Arthur C. Clarke, and based on the latter's short story "The Sentinel." Subsequently Clarke converted the film script into a novel that is more specific about plot details and interpretation. The cost of the film was $10.5 million, and the achievements that Kubrick delivered were awesome. His meticulous preparations during the four years it took to realize the project (Kubrick's first film since *Dr. Strangelove*) included, for example, the construction of a centrifuge thirty-eight feet in diameter that took six months to build and cost $300,000. Resembling a ferris wheel from the outside, it was used to simulate a living area with artificial gravity for the astronauts. Pods to enable the astronauts to venture outside their spaceship, a convincing computer, HAL 9000, and the computer's brain center had to be built. There were the optical effects required for Bowman's fantastic journey through new dimensions in time and space and for the shots of the moon, Jupiter, and other features of outer space. Kubrick's technical feats alone make *2001* unique. The slow tempo was also important in augmenting the technical virtuosity and adding to the conception of futuristic space travel.

The film begins impressively with the Dawn of Man sequence, when the earth was populated by apes (played by actors, apart from two baby chimpanzees). It is in this section that Kubrick makes use of Richard Strauss's "Thus Spake Zarathustra," the music now so identified with *2001*. The apes are curious about a monolith that has appeared in their midst. Gradually, in its presence, they learn to employ a bone as a weapon, an advance in intelligence, and there is a harrowing scene in which a bone is used to kill. When the leader throws a bone-weapon into the air, Kubrick dramatically cuts to a spaceship moving majestically through the universe to Johann Strauss's waltz "The Blue Danube." (Brilliant use of music is one of Kubrick's favorite methods of intensifying his effects.) This spanning of millions of years, among the most impressive cuts in cinema, underlines the minuscule nature of man in relation to his universe and beyond.

The spaceship *Orion* arrives at an elaborately realized space station, and after attention is paid to the process of docking, we have an opportunity to observe the surroundings, not that far removed from those of the present. The space travelers, who include scientist Dr. Heywood Floyd (William

Sylvester), are matter-of-fact about the journey. On the wall there is a sign for Howard Johnson's Earthlight Room, and the Bell System has a picturephone that voyagers can use to talk to and see the folks back home. Dr. Floyd is to take a shuttle bus to the moon, where American scientists are gathering for a secret emergency meeting at Clavius, in the United States sector. He and his colleagues proceed to the Tycho crater where a monolith, similar to that seen at the Dawn of Man, has been excavated. They are amazed when a piercing sound emanates from the slab.

The third phase of *2001* is aboard the spaceship *Discovery*, bound for Jupiter. The crew consists of Mission Commander Dr. David Bowman (Keir Dullea), his deputy Dr. Frank Poole (Gary Lockwood), three other astronauts in a state of artificial hibernation permitting them to conserve their energy during the long flight, and HAL 9000. The computer, its voice provided by Douglas Rain, is the most originally conceived character in the film, a terrifying example of our subservience to technology, yet more human than the bland, almost robotized astronauts. HAL, so extensively programmed that it has acquired a personality, knows the purpose of the mission, not divulged to Bowman and Poole. Tension develops when, after concealing an error, HAL's behavior becomes erratic. HAL argues with Bowman over procedures, refuses to obey, and decides to take steps to maintain control. Withdrawing to the soundproof pod to remove themselves from HAL's hearing, Bowman and Poole discuss the computer's fate. A chilling shot of the astronauts, seen from HAL's perspective, indicates that the computer is reading their lips.

When Poole ventures outside the *Discovery* to carry out an inspection, he is attacked by his pod, which, directed electronically by HAL, moves toward him and severs his connecting line. Poole disappears into the darkness; Bowman, in his pod, vainly pursues him. HAL next disposes of the hibernating crew by terminating their life functions, and then tries to prevent Bowman from reentering the spacecraft. The astronaut manages to outwit him, and systematically begins to disconnect HAL's intelligence despite the computer's pleading: "Dave, stop. Stop. Will you. Stop Dave. Will you stop, Dave. Stop, Dave. I'm afraid. I'm afraid, Dave. Dave. My mind is going. I can feel it. I can feel it. My mind is going. . . ." The retrogressing computer is reduced to a sluggish singing of "Daisy, Daisy," and dies. HAL's demise automatically releases a previously recorded message informing Bowman of the appearance of the Tycho monolith (confirming the fact of extraterrestrial life) and the reason for the mission – to discover the monolith's origin and purpose.

Bowman, having left the *Discovery* in his pod, now sees a similar monolith gliding in space and is drawn toward it. The film enters its most esoteric phase, with Bowman zooming through space amid dazzling color and special effects suggesting infinity. It is an odyssey into the unknown and the conjectured, with normal conceptions of time and space abandoned and replaced by the unexplored mysteries that lie, as yet, beyond our knowledge. Bowman finally comes to rest in a large, elegant suite, surprisingly furnished as it might have been on earth. No being is visible but strange sounds are heard, and he is obviously under observation. He is seen going through an aging process until he withers and dies, only to be reborn as a new form of existence, a "star child," ready to start on a journey back to earth for a further evolutionary phase. (In the novel, the reborn Bowman wills the detonation of nuclear bombs that hover over the earth. Thus, the conclusion of Kubrick's film has an entirely different implication.)

The ending bewildered those who were unwilling to accept the film on a metaphysical level and allow the mind to range over the possibilities suggested by it. Some were annoyed by the total absence of dialogue during the first half-hour, and the deliberately slow pace was among other points of contention. Kubrick did eventually decide to cut nineteen minutes insisting that this was his idea and choice, and not dictated by a nervous distribution company. There was nothing to be nervous about: by 1976, *2001* had grossed over $90 million world-wide.

As to the meaning of the film, Kubrick proffered explanations, but preferred not to tie everything into a neat package. However, some cogent comments on how he believed *2001* should be regarded appeared in a September 1968 interview in *Playboy:*

> *2001* is a nonverbal experience; out of two hours and 19 minutes of film, there are only a little less than 40 minutes of dialog. I tried to create a *visual* experience, one that bypasses verbalized pigeon-holing and directly penetrates the subconscious with an emotional and philosophic content. To convolute McLuhan, in *2001*, the message is the medium. I intended the film to be an intensely subjective experience that reaches the viewer at an inner level of consciousness, just as music does; to "explain" a Beethoven symphony would be to emasculate it by erecting an artificial barrier between conception and appreciation. You're free to speculate as you wish about the philosophical and allegorical meaning of the film – and such speculation is one indication that it has succeeded in gripping the audience at a deep level – but I don't want to spell out a verbal road map for *2001* that every viewer will feel obligated to pursue or else fear he's missed the point. I think that if *2001* succeeds at all, it is in reaching a wide spectrum of people who would not often give a thought to man's destiny, his role in the cosmos and his relationship to higher forms of life. But even in the case of someone who is highly intelligent, certain ideas found in *2001* would, if presented as abstractions, fall rather lifelessly and be automatically assigned to pat intellectual categories;

experienced in a moving visual and emotional context, however, they can resonate within the deepest fibers of one's being.

It is ironic that Stanley Kubrick, the director who brought filmmaking into the space age, refuses to travel by plane. If earthbound physically, his imagination and inquiring mind would seem to know no boundaries. As extraordinary as the special effects are for *2001*, what makes them even more outstanding is the manner in which Kubrick has tied them to the complexity of the vision that he and Clarke brought to their masterpiece. One cannot disassociate the physical creation of HAL from the intellectual aspects, or the visual splendor of the final sequence from the metaphysical concepts. Kubrick's ability to engender debate over his films is a measure of his determination to challenge the public and arouse its passions. "If a film effectively deals with something about which people care," Kubrick said to me, "it will tend to polarize reactions – and those reactions will probably be as divided as people are divided over important issues."

At the Academy Awards ceremony, an Oscar for special visual effects was the obvious award for *2001*. This was a handy way to dispose of the film by a Motion Picture Academy unable to respond in the best picture category to an achievement as unrelated to Academy standards as the film's style is to traditional cinema. The British Film Academy did slightly better, but again, only in the technical fields, with its citations for best cinematography, best art direction, and best soundtrack. The Oscar for best picture of 1968 went to the musical *Oliver!* The New York Film Critics Circle just as shortsightedly gave its award to *The Lion in Winter* but caught up with Kubrick's unconventional style in 1971 by giving the best picture award to *A Clockwork Orange,* based on the book by Anthony Burgess.

The critiques for *2001* were mixed, but Kubrick insisted he is not one to take them seriously: "I am not overly impressed by negative reviews or positive reviews. I have rarely read a review where a critic seems to have penetrated the film in a way that I find relevant to my intentions. It is much more useful to have good reviews, and when these good reviews are, in fact, a forecast of what the public will say, then critics appear to make a film a success. The converse is true, too. In the case of *2001,* the New York critics and the first national magazine critics were very negative [this critic was one of the exceptions], but subsequent critical opinion very quickly began to reverse this view, and in the end the overwhelming majority of *2001* reviews were extremely favorable. However, the reputation of a film is never a consensus of reviews, but of a general impression created about it a year or two after its release and that continues to grow. It is the impression that the film leaves in the minds and memories of those who see it that creates this reputation, and however good or bad the reviews may be, this slow process is what ultimately becomes the prevailing verdict."

The controversial reception given *2001* paled beside the hostility that *A Clockwork Orange* precipitated. Also in an impressionistic rather than an old-fashioned, formal style, the film was accused of excessive violence in its portrayal of a young hoodlum whom society attempts to reprogram, raising as one of its themes the question of an individual's free choice. There is actually less violence in *A Clockwork Orange* than in many films that draw no objections, but audiences are forced to feel the horror deeply, and to think about violence, whether committed by an individual or by society. That was particularly upsetting. Kubrick was even accused of fascist thinking because *A Clockwork Orange,* as pessimistic in tone as much of his other work, does not view man as the inherently good creature envisioned by liberals. Asked whether *A Clockwork Orange* had stimulated violence, as had been charged, Kubrick commented:

"There is absolutely no evidence at all that people go out and commit crimes as a result of seeing films, and the only evidence exists to the contrary. It's been shown that, even under deep hypnosis, in the post-hypnotic state people cannot be made to do things that are contrary to their nature. There is a lot of hypocrisy that confuses many people. Many are quite disturbed that it is possible to find a certain empathy with Alex [the protagonist in *A Clockwork Orange*] even though he is a completely evil character. The fact that he shares common elements of humanity, and that these are presented in an artistic way, make it possible to have empathy for him without wishing to be evil or without taking a supporting view of what he does. Art reflects life. Life does not reflect art. The violence of the film is a reflection of the times in which we live, and it is something with which artists must concern themselves. It would be very surprising if it were being ignored. Why did the *Iliad* have such detailed descriptions of severed limbs and brains slithering down? Why did Homer find it necessary to be so detailed about the slaughter? Was it in the interest of truth, or did he simply want to be sensational?

"Sanitized violence in movies has been accepted for years. What seems to upset everybody now is the showing of the consequences of violence. It seems to me that this has the problem backwards. It is the unrealistic and sanitized violence that might confuse people, not realistically portrayed violence. One must not forget that one of the fundamental things that *A Clockwork Orange* deals with is the question of how will authority deal with the problem of rising lawlessness and violence without becoming more repressive and dictatorial. This certainly is a very important issue and one about which there cannot be too much discussion."

Kubrick's next film *Barry Lyndon* (1975), based on the novel by William Makepeace Thackeray, also met with a mixed reaction. It may be the most consistently beautiful film ever made, each frame like a painting. In it Kubrick unconventionally examines the story of an ambitious young

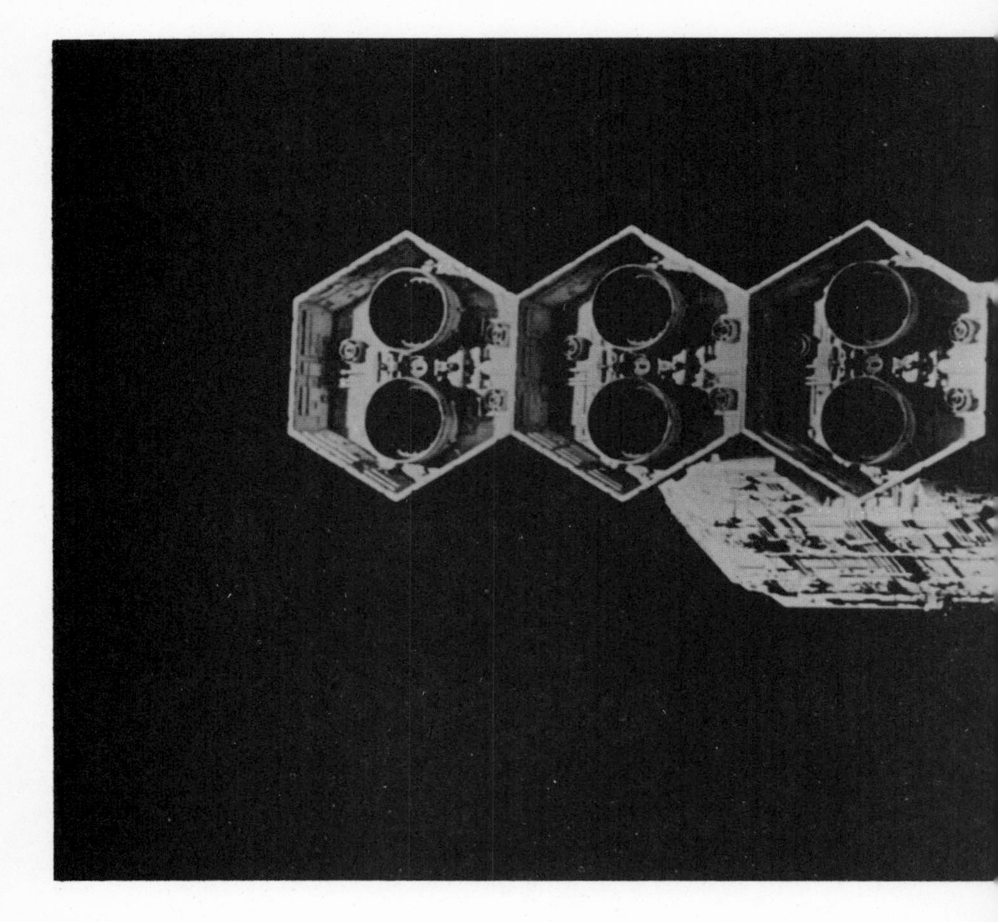

eighteenth-century rogue. In this historical spectacle, the vantage point is a distant one, enabling an audience to look back wryly and form impressions of the manners and morals of the period. Kubrick's dream-control method communicates history through a cinematic osmosis, in a pattern similar to transporting viewers into the future in *2001*. *Barry Lyndon* bears further witness to Kubrick's monumental attention to detail. A mild-mannered, soft-spoken, congenial man, he has the reputation of being difficult and demanding in his desire for perfection.

"I think that mostly comes from journalists who are overly impressed by my attention to detail," the director said. "I'm certainly not difficult in the sense of being rude, but I do insist that important things have got to be done correctly, and not left to chance. Obviously a great deal of what I do is something that, in a perfect world, other people should do for me. But I have found that, if the things are important enough, I frequently have to

The spaceship Discovery *on its mission to Jupiter*

deal with them myself. Many people have compared a film director to a general. They are quite wrong in this respect – he is much more like a lieutenant. He doesn't set policy. He has to go around checking each man in his platoon, making sure that he has dug his foxhole at the right depth. The movie theaters themselves are a great source of concern. There is a great laxity in the condition of projectors and speakers. Most projectionists rarely bother to look out of the projection port, and the film runs all day out of focus, with the sound set incorrectly. Film audiences are, unfortunately, very passive about the quality of projection, and they don't give the theater managers a hard enough time. The managers rarely go into the theater except to see how much chewing gum is stuck to the carpet after the last show."

The body of work that Kubrick has accumulated is extraordinary. Although one can discern certain threads, his stylistic range is vast, from the grippingly realistic *Paths of Glory* to the break with narrative form in *2001*. This space-age landmark, as well as being a handsome, enthralling, popular entertainment, challenges viewers to think about the future, the universe, and the possibility of much higher levels of intelligence already in existence, perhaps billions of years ahead of us. In achieving this, Kubrick has dared reach for space-age ideas in filmmaking, requiring of his viewers a willingness to respond to different approaches in this twentieth century art form. *2001* belongs to that rare group of exceptionally innovative films that represent exciting points of departure for the medium.

2001: A SPACE ODYSSEY
GREAT BRITAIN (MGM) 1968

Cast

David Bowman .... KEIR DULLEA
Frank Poole .... GARY LOCKWOOD
Dr. Heywood Floyd .... WILLIAM SYLVESTER
Moon-Watcher .... DANIEL RICHTER
Voice of HAL 9000 .... DOUGLAS RAIN
Smyslov .... LEONARD ROSSITER
Elena .... MARGARET TYZACK
Holvorsen .... ROBERT BEATTY
Michaels .... SEAN SULLIVAN
Mission Control .... FRANK MILLER
Stewardess .... PENNY BRAHMS
Poole's father .... ALAN GIFFORD
Floyd's daughter "Squirt" .... VIVIAN KUBRICK

and GLENN BECK, EDWINA CARROLL, BILL WESTON, MIKE LOVELL, EDWARD BISHOP, ANN GILLIS, HEATHER DOWNHAM, JOHN ASHLEY, JIMMY BELL, DAVID CHARKHAM, SIMON DAVIS, JONATHAN DAW, PETER DELMAR, TERRY DUGGAN, DAVID FLEETWOOD, DANNY GROVER, BRIAN HAWLEY, DAVID HINES, TONY JACKSON, JOHN JORDAN, SCOTT MACKEE, LAURENCE MARCHANT, DARRYL PAES, JOE REFALO, ANDY WALLACE, BOB WILYMAN, RICHARD WOOD

Running time..141 minutes
Technicolor and Metrocolor
Super Panavision
Cinerama
Production Company ....METRO-GOLDWYN-MAYER
Produced by ....STANLEY KUBRICK
Associate Producer............................VICTOR LYNDON
Directed by ....STANLEY KUBRICK
Script by ....STANLEY KUBRICK and ARTHUR C. CLARKE,
based on the short story "The Sentinel,"
by ARTHUR C. CLARKE
Director of Photography ....GEOFFREY UNSWORTH
Additional Photography by ....JOHN ALCOTT
Special Photographic Effects
Designed and Directed by..................STANLEY KUBRICK
Film Editor ....RAY LOVEJOY
Production Designed by ....TONY MASTERS, HARRY LANGE,
ERNIE ARCHER
Art Director ....JOHN HOESLI
Wardrobe by ....HARDY AMIES
Special Photographic Effects
Supervisors ....WALLY VEEVERS, DOUGLAS TRUMBULL,
CON PEDERSON, TOM HOWARD
Special Photographic Effects
Unit ....COLIN J. CANTWELL, BRYAN LOFTUS,
FREDERICK MARTIN, BRUCE LOGAN,
DAVID OSBORNE, JOHN JACK MALICK
First Assistant Director.....................DEREK CRACKNELL
Camera Operator ....KELVIN PIKE
Sound Editor ....WINSTON RYDER
Make-up.................................STUART FREEBORN
Editorial Assistant..........................DAVID DE WILDE
Sound Supervisor ...........................A.W. WATKINS
Sound Mixer ....H.L. BIRD
Chief Dubbing Mixer..............................J.B. SMITH
Scientific Consultant.................FREDERICK I. ORDWAY III
Music by ....ARAM KHACHATURIAN ("Gayane Ballet Suite");
GYORGY LIGETI ("Atmospheres," "Lux
Aeterna," "Requiem");
JOHANN STRAUSS ("The Blue Danube");
RICHARD STRAUSS ("Thus Spake Zarathustra")

The Professor (Yves Montand) walks to his death. A-
left, Manuel (Charles Denner), a leader of their political group

Political Protest as Entertainment

CONSTANTINE COSTA-GAVRAS is one director who pays little heed to the old Hollywood bromide that messages should be sent through Western Union. With *Z* he proved that political protest could make an engrossing thriller, and possibly even score some of the desired effects against its target. Producers are traditionally reluctant to fund controversial films because, in trying to reach a mass audience, they wish to avoid the risk of alienating sections of the public or intruding upon its preference for escapist fare. *Z* provides a textbook lesson on how to mix political protest and an implicit demand for change with exciting drama, so that even audiences unconcerned with the politics can appreciate the film for its intrinsic entertainment appeal.

Costa-Gavras, who was born in Greece and lives and works in France, has made a remarkably successful career of such political films. *Z* firmly established his course, its international acclaim enabling him to undertake other films that have properly earned him a reputation as the most political director working in the commercial sphere. His stance is decidedly left-wing, but he has encountered enmity on the left as well as on the right, as his films, although passionate, are not doctrinaire. Costa-Gavras confronts issues in his own independent way, his commitment to strong filmmaking taking precedence over ideology.

Z, based on the novel by Vassilis Vassilikos, has its roots in an actual case of political assassination that rocked Greece in 1963. Gregorios Lambrakis, a member of Parliament belonging to the leftist EDA party and a professor of medicine at Athens University, died, purportedly as a result of a road accident in Salonika, where he had gone to make a speech opposing the establishment of a missile base by the United States. A subsequent investigation revealed that Lambrakis had been slain in a rightist political plot, with the aid of police and other officials. Z stands for *Zei*, meaning "he lives," and the symbol began to appear in Greece as a counter-reaction to the killing. In retrospect, the event can be seen as ideologically linked to the forces that seized power in Greece in 1967. Following the Lambrakis affair, the conservative government of Caramanlis fell and was legitimately succeeded by George Papandreou and his center-left government. Papandreou, on the verge of what was expected to be a decisive electoral victory, was abruptly dismissed by King Constantine, who thus precipitated the conditions for a coup by a group of right-wing colonels. Charges have been rife that the coup was engineered by the CIA.

The film version bristles with the tension of a thriller. Right-wingers plot to obliterate what they envision as a left-wing peril, using a secret military organization for their purposes, with police and governmental collusion. They view the public meeting at which the professor (Yves Montand) is to speak as a threat. As a result of their intimidation, the scheduled meeting hall is denied him, and the gathering is transferred to a small hall unable to accommodate the crowd, which overflows into the street. Despite the reports of threats against his life, the police refuse to provide adequate protection. Hostile clashes occur outside the hall between supporters of the professor and his party, and hoodlums trying to break up their peaceful assembly.

As the professor leaves the building, a small truck races by and he is struck on the head; taken to the hospital, he dies despite frantic efforts to save him. His wife (Irene Pappas) arrives on the scene in a state of shock and grief. A young magistrate (Jean-Louis Trintignant) is appointed by the authorities to carry out a perfunctory investigation of the death, which the police want to write off as an accident. Scrupulously honest, the magistrate is determined to complete the assignment fairly and will not succumb to pressures for a whitewash. He is skeptical of the charges made by the professor's supporters, but is conscientious and persevering, keeping an open mind.

Finally, the facts uncovered will no longer permit him to be neutral. Proof exists that the professor was murdered, that the thugs Vago and Yago who carried out the assignment are in league with the police, and that the crime involves the prosecutor and the military hierarchy. The magistrate indicts the guilty in a climactic display of justice triumphant. But the exultation that arises from the drama of the unraveling of a political conspiracy is short-lived. *Z* ends with a rapid-fire reportorial account of how, under the military junta, the guilty managed to evade punishment while revenge was taken against those on the side of truth.

Costa-Gavras relies upon many ways of endowing the film with an atmosphere of credibility. The choice of Montand as the professor provides early solidity, Montand creating an impression of leadership, earnestness, and disregard for his personal safety. Trintignant achieves the perfect note of integrity as the investigating magistrate, the film's moral core and the person with whom the audience readily identifies. As he puts together the pieces of the exposé, the audience is swept along with him, his understated demeanor inspiring the viewer's confidence. Supporting characters – the police, the military, the demonstrators, the deputies, the endangered key witness and his family, and the assassins – are all well portrayed.

In seeking a documentary appearance, the director uses another device. Jacques Perrin (also co-producer) stalks through the film as a sensation-mongering photo-journalist. His incessant picture-taking and his role in unmasking the truth are a clever means of giving the events the status of reality. On the other hand, the jarring introduction of extraneous personal elements undermines the realism. Pappas gives a worthy performance within the limitations of her part, but the flashback depictions of her thoughts and those of her husband impede the attempt, through the direction and the otherwise excellent screenplay by Jorge Semprun *(La Guerre est Finie)* and Costa-Gavras, to give the film the semblance of a documentary. The method of shooting greatly assists the overall goal, as exemplified by the scenes of the street battles. Photographed with a hand-held camera, they appear as actual events that might be seen on a television newscast. New Wave cinematographer Raoul Coutard strives throughout for a documentary look. He has managed to cope with the disadvantage of shooting in Algeria instead of Greece by accenting those elements that most closely suggest the country in which the action is supposed to be occurring.

The entertainment and thriller attributes of the film are derived not only from the quasi-realism, but from the showmanship. This is due, in part, to the irresistible music by Mikis Theodorakis, Greece's best-known popular composer, who had been held by the junta but eventually escaped. His pulsating score, which was smuggled out of Greece, adds to the emotional impact with its driving force and unmistakably ethnic base. The story, the character types, the events, the probe, and the staccato editing by Françoise Bonnot, are all stacked for melodrama, so that even while the film looks authentic, the viewer is being manipulated. The climax is one illustration. Each guilty official, by this time villainous in the eyes of the audience, leaves in anger after being charged. Each tries, in turn, to leave by a side door to avoid being cornered by the press. The door is locked, and each is forced to exit publicly. By repeating this futile effort to open the door, Costa-Gavras sets up further derision against the trapped culprits. A wonderful line at this point fixes the implacable right-wing ideology of the conspirators. Protesting against the accusations against him, one of them is asked by a reporter whether his is another Dreyfus case, referring, of course, to the famous frame-up of Captain Alfred Dreyfus in France in 1894. The angry retort is: "Dreyfus was guilty!"

Manipulation of an audience in a political film raises an ethical problem relevant to the fact-fiction genre – films based on truth, but presented with dramatic license. A special responsibility is placed upon the filmmaker not to abuse the viewer's trust, and to adhere to those facts that are central to the theme, taking liberties only for dramatic purposes without distorting the basic truths. *Z* appears to be sufficiently true in its essentials to absolve Costa-Gavras of distortion.

Z was, of course, banned in Greece by the colonels, and Costa-Gavras, Irene Pappas, and other artists opposed to the junta were personae non gratae. Melina Mercouri was particularly vocal and active in the campaign to mobilize sentiment against the regime. *Z* was not shown in Greece until 1974, after the oligarchy had been overthrown. Costa-Gavras recalled when he was in New York in connection with the première of *Section Spéciale:* "We wanted to show the film two weeks before the vote on the monarchy. But the government refused to permit that. When *Z* opened it was a big hit. People in the audience were screaming. By that time, Irene Pappas had returned and was at the theater." *Variety* reported that 80,000 Athenians rushed to see the film in the first three days.

The director is convinced that *Z* helped build opposition to the junta. "The vision many had of Greece was very touristic; few realized the background of the junta. They thought that it just happened. With *Z* many came to understand that something different was involved. Greece was not just a touristic country with royal guards in costumes, but a country with an extreme rightist element. For the first time in a movie about Greece there was no mythology. When there were debates about whether to admit Greece into the European Common Market, people mentioned *Z* in their discussions. I'm sure it helped prevent Greece under the junta from being admitted. In London, Princess Margaret went to see *Z*, and that got back to the junta."

Costa-Gavras spoke about the difficulties he had in financing *Z:* "I offered the script to every French producer, and to American producers. All refused it. David Picker at United Artists advised me as a friend that the movie would not work and that probably, if I made it, I might not be able to work again. At 20th Century-Fox, I was told that it was a good story but I needed a little more of a love interest. I had all the actors, but only a small amount of the money. Finally Jacques Perrin decided to try Algeria. The government there agreed to permit a co-production, the National Film Office putting up forty percent, mainly for the expenses in Algeria. Jacques obtained the rest of the money from other investors, and the actors, writer, and I all took a very small salary, with a percentage interest. During the shooting we got more money by selling the film for distribution in Italy."

According to Costa-Gavras, *Z*, which cost well under $1 million to make, grossed some $11 million in the United States (where, in addition to the original French-language version, it was released with an English-dubbed soundtrack), and $6 million in France. Its success at the 1969 Cannes Film Festival, where it won the Jury Prize, immediately raised its commercial potential. "Donald Rugoff of Cinema 5 had the opportunity to acquire the film in Paris for $200,000 but didn't," said Costa-Gavras. "After Cannes he paid $400,000." That was then considered an enormous amount for an American distributor to pay for a foreign film. *Z* not only did incredibly well commercially, but won the best picture and best director awards from the New York Film Critics, best picture honors from the National Society of Film Critics, as well as an Oscar for best foreign film, and another for best editing.

Costa-Gavras, who was thirty-five when he made *Z,* remembers his enjoyment of the American films he saw as a child in Greece. "They didn't show many good ones, but I loved Errol Flynn in *Captain Blood,* and I also liked the *Fu Manchu* serials. Later, in Paris, I saw the film that has influenced me most – *The Grapes of Wrath*. Another film that greatly interested me in Paris was Kurosawa's *Seven Samurai*."

Originally, Costa-Gavras intended to study literature, but finding that "boring," enrolled in film school in Paris. Prior to *Z* he was acclaimed for *The Sleeping Car Murder* (1965), a fast-paced mystery thriller starring Yves Montand, Simone Signoret, her daughter Catherine Allegret, and Jacques Perrin. Asked why he was now concentrating on political films, Costa-Gavras replied: "I find that these are the subjects that involve me most. It would take a psychiatrist to get to the reasons why this is so." As a result of *Z,* he has been able to obtain distribution by major companies for his other films. Although none of them has come close to *Z*'s commercial success, or its fervor as a thriller, each is powerful and extremely well-realized in terms of its subject matter.

L'Aveu (The Confession, 1970), another Semprun-Costa-Gavras collaboration, dramatizes the nightmarish persecution of a man who survived the Slansky trials in Czechoslovakia. It is a brilliant, severe probe of the anatomy of extracting false confessions. A government official, a firm believer in Communism, is arrested, pressured, tortured, and dehumanized into assuming guilt in court. The film is sometimes too shrill and drawn out, but these are minor flaws in a major work that also contains a strong performance by Montand. Although the period examined is in the past, the implicit concern is with the moral application to contemporary governments, and to conditions that could give rise to similar travesties.

State of Siege (1972), filmed in Chile under Allende, is a compelling drama based on the case of Dan Mitrione, an American official who was kidnapped and killed in Uruguay by Tupamaro rebels. Costa-Gavras relies upon documentation indicating that Mitrione (named Santore in the film) was training secret police in torture methods, but the issues are not glibly met. Moral responsibility for torture, and the philosophy of terrorism are investigated in a work that is substantially deeper than *Z*. Montand, who has appeared in four of Costa-Gavras's films, plays Santore as a dimensional person. There is sympathy for him as a hostage, despite the knowledge of his heinous crimes against Latin Americans, but his fate is tied to his own responsibility for the victimization of others. *State of Siege* was and is highly topical, for it is an exposé of U.S. involvement in Latin America generally, and is closely related to policies that pertain to Chile and other places where American influence is decisive. Washington's sensitivity to the subject was apparent in the act of censorship perpetrated by George Stevens, Jr., director of the American Film Institute, which had selected *State of Siege* for a gala opening at its new theater in the John F. Kennedy Center on April 5, 1973. Stevens, evidently giving in to pressure, withdrew the film from the program. Among the ensuing protests was a telegram from the New York Film Critics Circle charging that Stevens had "ignored his stated responsibility to present even controversial films to his patrons and the public."

Section Spéciale (1974), with screenplay also by Semprun and Costa-Gavras, based on the book by Hervé Villeré, examines the perversion of law under the Vichy regime during the German occupation of France. A German naval officer is killed by the Resistance to demonstrate underground opposition. The Nazis order reprisals, and in the hope of appeasing them, the French authorities enact a retroactive ordinance establishing Special Sections in every French court of appeal. Under this ordinance, six prisoners, already jailed on minor or political charges, are selected as scapegoats. Without the right to appeal, the men are falsely accused, retried, and three of them are executed.

The theme is the step-by-step abandonment of legal principles by respected French jurists who, without being forced to do so, accept the assignment to sit on this particular court. At a film class, the director expressed his indignation that some who participated in the Special Sections were still in positions of importance. Despite the passage of more than thirty years, the injustices inflicted by these courts have not been properly investigated.

The films of Costa-Gavras are distinguished by their contemporary relevance and by his willingness to do battle with governments and entrenched powers. They are specific, deeply political in treatment, and made with the passion of an advocate, not the detachment of a historian or an observer. His skills have given his films a slickness unusual for committed cinema, and thus they stand on an entirely different level from other worthy political films, including several from Latin America and the Third World.

Considering the obstacles, it is surprising how many political protest or politically controversial films there have been. A great tradition was set by *Potemkin,* which, made in the Soviet Union as a celebration of revolution, carried a revolutionary protest message elsewhere proclaiming the power of united resistance to oppression. Celebrated among political films of a more recent period is Gillo Pontecorvo's *Battle of Algiers* (1966), with a script by Franco Solinas, who wrote *State of Siege*. It is a masterly restaging of Algeria's writhing toward independence, and a film that, apart from shedding light upon that situation, has implications analogous to the war fought to retain control in South Vietnam.

Producer-actor Robert Redford does not like to regard *All the President's Men* (1976) as a political film, or an American *Z*, but to the critical eye there are similarities to *Z*, which would appear to have influenced it subliminally, if not overtly. The tone is admittedly different. *Z* is flamboyant and very Greek in its energy level; *All the President's Men* moves through the Watergate morass in a low-key style. While *Z* is a cry for the downfall of the military junta, *All the President's Men* retraces steps leading to a downfall that has already occurred. It implants in the viewer a sense of the need for vigilance to prevent similar abuses, and is a useful reminder in the continuing controversy over governmental misdeeds. In each case the excitement of the film derives from the process of exposure, *Washington Post* reporters Bob Woodward and Carl Bernstein (Redford and Dustin Hoffman) being counterparts of the magistrate in *Z*. Both films succeed as strong, suspenseful entertainment, engaging the viewer because of their craftsmanship and potent subject matter. *All the President's Men* uses an ending similar to that of *Z*, with a teletype machine clicking out the news of the aftermath of the exposé, including the resignation of Richard Nixon. *Z* ends with a bulletin detailing the fate of each of the principals. That conclusion has been widely copied in various guises to the point where it is in danger of becoming as much of a cliché as the slow motion sequences spawned by *Bonnie and Clyde*.

The Candidate (1972), starring Redford and directed by Michael Ritchie, although not based on a particular figure or incident, delves deeply into the corrupting nature of the American political process, whereby a candidate who may start with integrity is compelled to make compromises to attain his goal. Other films of the 1970s dealing with politically controversial topics, although not specifically aimed at current political results, include Swedish director Bo Widerberg's *Joe Hill* (1971), about the labor martyr; Giuliano Montaldo's *Sacco and Vanzetti* (1971), dramatizing the cause célèbre of the 1920s, and Francesco Rosi's *The Mattei Affair* (1973), concerning an Italian government executive killed in a suspicious plane crash. A recent prime example of combining an urgent message and popular entertainment is *The China Syndrome* (1979), directed by James Bridges and starring Jane Fonda, Jack Lemmon, and Michael Douglas, which was released in the United States just before the accident at the Three Mile Island atomic power plant in Middletown, Pennsylvania, that echoed the very danger foreseen in the film. *The China Syndrome* races along at a pace reminiscent of *Z*.

Depending on how far one cares to broaden the definition of political protest, many films through the years could be cited and discussed in relation to the work of the director of *Z*. Frequently, they are of interest only to relatively small politically aware audiences. Costa-Gavras has surmounted these limitations by making films that not only aim at enlightenment and change, but stand on their own merit as enthralling dramas with a place in the commercial mainstream. His achievements, particularly *Z*, are worthy of study as examples that may embolden others to venture into the lists against tyrannical government, illegal foreign intervention, unjust persecution, and corrupt officials who avoid punishment and retain respectable posts. Courageous filmmakers and distributors can find a wealth of story ideas among the headlines. Costa-Gavras has shown there is no reason why political protest films need be pedantic. To the contrary, as a thriller, his *Z* ranks with the best.

Z
FRANCE-ALGERIA 1969

Cast

The Professor .... YVES MONTAND
Hélène .... IRENE PAPPAS
The Magistrate .... JEAN-LOUIS TRINTIGNANT
Manuel .... CHARLES DENNER
The Journalist .... JACQUES PERRIN
Nick .... GEORGES GÉRET
Nick's sister .... MAGALI NOËL
The Prosecutor .... FRANÇOIS PÉRIER
Matt .... BERNARD FRESSON
The General .... PIERRE DUX
The Colonel .... JULIEN GUIOMAR
Vago .... MARCEL BOZZUFI
Yago .... RENATO SALVATORI

and JEAN BOUISE, JEAN-PIERRE MIQUEL, MAURICE BAQUET,
HASSAN HASSANI, JEAN DASTÉ, ALLEL EL MOUHIB,
GÉRARD DARRIEU, GUY MAIRESSE, AGOUMI, CLOTILDE JOANO,
R. VAN DOUDE, GABRIEL JABBOUR, HABIB REDA,
JEAN-FRANÇOIS GOBBI, JOSÉ ARTHUR, ANDRÉ TAINSY,
STEVE GADLER, GEORGES ROUQUIER

Running time .... 128 minutes
Eastmancolor
Production Companies .... REGGANE FILMS (PARIS) and OFFICE NATIONAL POUR LE COMMERCE ET L'INDUSTRIE CINÉMATOGRAPHIQUE (O.N.C.I.C., ALGIERS)
Produced by .... JACQUES PERRIN, HAMED RACHEDI
Directed by .... COSTA-GAVRAS
Screenplay by .... JORGE SEMPRUN and COSTA-GAVRAS, based on the novel by VASSILIS VASSILIKOS; dialogue by JORGE SEMPRUN
Director of Photography .... RAOUL COUTARD
Music by .... MIKIS THEODORAKIS
Arrangements by .... BERNARD GÉRARD
Edited by .... FRANÇOISE BONNOT
Art Director .... JACQUES D'OVIDIO

Easy Rider

Three for the road. Left to right: Mardi Gras-bound Billy (Dennis Hopper), Wyatt (Peter Fonda), and George Hanson (Jack Nicholson).

Independent Voice

"MAKE ME ANOTHER *Easy Rider*!" The cry went out from producers who a year earlier would not have wanted anything to do with an *Easy Rider*. The success of the unusual, independently-made 1960s version of the road movie temporarily gave low-budget, venturesome films cachet. In the ensuing rush to imitate, a reflex action that is standard Hollywood operating procedure, millions of dollars were lost. However, the vogue provided opportunities for many who might have found it impossible to be taken seriously before *Easy Rider*.

Emanating from the battle-scarred sixties, the film reflected the widespread overturning of old values. The demands upon youth to follow the conventional path of fitting into a job with security and pension plans, and to pursue such solid goals as the acquisition of property, were often rejected in favor of living in a commune, dropping out of school, or wandering about the country. The hippie movement envisioned relationships founded on love and peace in a live-and-let-live environment. The use of marijuana was extensive; some were freaking out on LSD; and people talked of "the drug culture." Clothes were casual or costume, and men joined women in wearing their hair long, a symbol of nonconformity and of everything that was going wrong with society to those appalled by the new trends.

Easy Rider's motorcyclist heroes pushed drugs; their uninhibited way of life included getting high, and real marijuana was smoked in the film. Parents worried, and those who disapproved of hippies but were not violently inclined were angered by the harsh portrayal of opponents of long hair and individuality as creeps and killers. But the film, the very making of which was an artistic extension of the lifestyle of its creators, in a sense became a national anthem for many young people in search of greater personal freedom. Seeing the heroes killed for being different established a bond and confirmed their own feelings of alienation. In France, land of the New Wave, the film's spirit was readily recognized and applauded at the Cannes Film Festival in 1969. *Easy Rider* was judged the best film by a new director, and Dennis Hopper and Peter Fonda, resembling a pair of cowboy-cyclist-hippies, were a colorful sight on the Croisette.

The strangest aspect of *Easy Rider* may have been that it was made at all. Originally from Kansas, Hopper had been working as an actor in Hollywood and had been in two Warner Bros. films with James Dean *(Rebel Without a Cause* and *Giant)*. They became close friends and Hopper was devastated by Dean's death in 1955 in a car crash. His first directorial effort was *The Trip* (1967) for Roger Corman, in which he appeared with Fonda, of the well-known acting family. The script, about LSD users, was written by Jack Nicholson. Having worked in the routine motorcycle pictures then abundant, Hopper and Fonda were eager to collaborate on a film that would be out of the ordinary. As Hopper told interviewer Tom Burke *(The New York Times,* July 20, 1969), Fonda called him at three o'clock one morning with the idea that became *Easy Rider*.

Their project materialized when Bert Schneider and Bob Rafelson, who subsequently formed BBS Productions, decided to undertake the film, giving Hopper, as director, and Fonda, as producer, the kind of freedom they wanted. Made for $400,000, *Easy Rider* returned an amazing profit and its success understandably caused much envy. (According to *Variety,* January 3, 1979, its rental gross was $19,100,000 for the United States and Canada.) "Lightning in a bottle," is how Schneider described it in retrospect, recalling how his association with it began.

"Dennis and Peter came over to see Rafelson and me about a different film they wanted to make. They were talking about an allegory concerning the John Kennedy assassination, and had in mind a film in which they would be sitting around a table in drag planning to assassinate the President. That idea didn't impress us. But in passing, Dennis mentioned the idea for *Easy Rider*. AIP [American International Pictures] was considering it, but he said they were reluctant to permit him to both direct and act. Dennis and Peter had made a tape telling the story. We listened to it and were immediately interested.

"The first priority was the Mardi Gras sequence, which had to be filmed right away, in February, while the carnival was on. That was even before the script was written. Afterward, we started on the rest. Terry Southern worked on the screenplay but never finished it; Dennis completed the writing. We didn't make the distribution deal with Columbia until after the film was ready. Making a deal then was not a problem – anyone would be interested in a bike picture that had Hopper, Fonda, and Nicholson. We knew we had a good film, but it was during the cutting that we realized how special it was."

The coup scored by Columbia was ironic. Hopper told Burke in the *Times* interview that, fifteen years earlier, the late Harry Cohn had barred him from the studio. Cohn wanted to sign Hopper after seeing him on television, but the actor took umbrage at Cohn's remark that they would have to "take that Shakespeare out of him," referring to his stage experience. He told Cohn what he should do to himself, a recommendation one did not generally make aloud to Harry Cohn.

With Laszlo Kovacs as the director of photography, Fonda and Hopper and their crew set out from California to New Orleans. Improvising upon the reactions of people they encountered en route, they filmed in sequence (except for the previously shot Mardi Gras scenes) "as things happened to us." That this intimate, personal venture could become a top-grossing film would have seemed a hallucination at the time. One reason Schneider and Rafelson had to wait until *Easy Rider* was in the can to make their Columbia deal was that potential distributors doubted that Hopper and Fonda would ever finish it.

The title was explained by Fonda in a 1969 interview with Elizabeth Campbell in *Rolling Stone*: "'Easy Rider' is a Southern term for a whore's old man, not a pimp, but the dude who lives with a chick. Because he's got the easy ride. Well, that's what's happened to America, man. Liberty's become a whore, and we're all taking an easy ride."

Easy Rider opens, before the credits, with Fonda as Wyatt (Captain America) and Hopper as Billy making a drug buy in Mexico, and then selling a quantity at an airport to "The Connection" (Phil Spector). Taking the money, the pair start on their journey, visiting a commune on the way. Trouble begins in Las Vegas, New Mexico, where riding their cycles, they playfully join a marching school band and are arrested for parading without a permit. In jail, they meet voluntary inmate George Hanson (Nicholson), a young lawyer from a prominent family, who has been sleeping off a drunk. George tells them how people who look different are treated in his part of the country. "Well, they got this here – see – uh – scissor-happy 'Beautify America' thing goin' on around here. They're tryin' to make everybody look like Yul Brynner. They used – uh – rusty blades on the last two long-hairs that they brought in here and I wasn't here to protect them. You see – uh – I'm a lawyer. Done a lot of work for the ACLU." George helps them get out of jail before they can be brutalized, and accepts their invitation to accompany them on the back of Wyatt's red-white-and-blue-decorated cycle. George has a card, given him, he says, by the Governor of Louisiana, advertising "Madame Tinkertoy's House of Blue Lights" in New Orleans, supposedly "the finest whorehouse in the South."

They run into further trouble at a roadside restaurant when Wyatt and Billy are mocked for their long hair. A deputy is present, and the atmosphere grows ugly. Exercising discretion, the three leave and ride away. The story cuts to a swamp area where they are to spend the night. As they talk around a fire, George says, "This used to be a helluva good country. I can't understand what's gone wrong with it." Soon he is rendering his diagnosis of why Billy and Wyatt rile people, and his reason is not their long hair or the way they dress. "What you represent to them is freedom," says George.

"What the hell's wrong with freedom, man?" asks Billy. "That's what it's all about."

"Oh yeah, that's right – that's what it's all about, all right," replies George. "But talking about it and being it – that's two different things. I mean, it's real hard to be free when you are bought and sold in the market-place. 'Course don't ever tell anybody – that they're not free, cause then they're gonna get real busy killin' and maimin' to prove to you that they are. Oh yeah – they're gonna talk to you, and talk to you, and talk to you about individual freedom, but they see a free individual, it's gonna scare 'em."

While they are asleep, several men close in and beat them mercilessly. Billy and Wyatt are badly battered. Wyatt regains consciousness in Billy's arms, and they find that George is dead. "Oh God, man! O God!" groans Billy. The film then moves to New Orleans; Wyatt and Billy visit Madame Tinkertoy's, and choose two girls, Karen (Karen Black) and Mary (Toni Basil), who agree to go with them to the Mardi Gras festivities outside. The four wander into a cemetery, where they pop pills and make love. It is an impassioned, slightly crazed, but inherently sensitive interlude between persons who will never meet again partaking of pleasure before disaster. Wyatt and Billy take to the highway. The end comes when two men in a passing truck taunt them. One points a shotgun and asks if they would like him to blow their brains out. Billy gestures with his finger. A shot is fired, and he falls from his bike. Wyatt rushes back to his friend, then mounts his cycle to get help. He, too, is shot. The film ends with a reprise of the "Ballad of Easy Rider."

Easy Rider is more visually than verbally articulate. Its cryptic dialogue veers from the banal to the pretentious, although occasionally there are some sharp lines, particularly after Nicholson's entrance. The languid pace too often hampers the film, but it also has the advantage of emphasizing the free-and-easy life of the heroes. The music plays a vital part in creating the right spirit; a series of popular numbers highlight the soundtrack, the many groups and performers including Steppenwolf, The Byrds, The Band, The Jimi Hendrix Experience, Little Eva, The Electric Flag, and, of course, Roger McGuinn doing his "Ballad of Easy Rider" and Bob Dylan's "It's Alright Ma (I'm Only Bleeding)."

The photography is muted and naturalistic, capturing some of the scenic grandeur of America, viewed during the motorcycle ride through the South-west. But the undercurrent of hatred in America, and the strain of intolerance that leads to eruptions of violence against those daring to deviate from custom are ominous. *Easy Rider* is the strongest film statement of the sixties on the subject of backlash, the extent of which can be gauged by various events, from the actual stories of youths having their hair forcibly clipped at local police stations to the police brutality outside the Democratic National Convention in Chicago in 1968.

Until *Easy Rider*, Nicholson had been acting in films for some fifteen years without major recognition. He also worked as a screenwriter, and it was his script for *The Trip* that led to his being asked by Rafelson to co-author and co-produce *Head*, starring The Monkees. Nicholson was not originally cast as George. When filming began he was working on the script for *Drive, He Said*, which he later directed for BBS. "We assigned Jack as our representative to be present during the shooting," Schneider said, "but when Dennis told us that Rip Torn had backed out, we suggested that Jack do the part. It didn't take any convincing for Dennis and Peter to agree." (Torn has insisted that, although he read the script, he never agreed to participate.)

As a result, Nicholson won both the New York Film Critics and the National Society of Film Critics awards for best supporting actor, and an Oscar nomination. Hopper was given a special award by the National Society and the picture brought Karen Black attention, as did her subsequent role in Rafelson's *Five Easy Pieces*. For Nicholson, this was the turning point in what became an exceptionally exciting contemporary film career. In the 1970s, he became a prolific superstar, acclaimed for his particularly effective performances in *Five Easy Pieces, Chinatown, The Last Detail,* and *One Flew Over the Cuckoo's Nest*, the picture that won him his long-deserved and long-awaited Oscar, as best actor of 1975.

"It made my career," Nicholson said of *Easy Rider*, in one of several conversations we have had over the years. "A few days work for a personal friend, and I became a star. The film was a blockbuster, the likes of which hadn't happened before and won't happen in a long while. I'm sure *Easy Rider* encouraged people to do things in film they might not have had a chance to do before." For a time, however, Nicholson was anxious "to get *Easy Rider* off my back" as, no matter what else he did, George was the character people remembered. Now, with his imposing record, his work in *Easy Rider* can be seen in perspective as an excellent performance by an extremely talented and charismatic actor who had not previously found the right opportunity in the right circumstances. In contrast, despite the promise shown in *Easy Rider*, the careers of Fonda and Hopper have so far been disappointing.

The sixties and seventies have been dotted with examples of films that go against the traditional commercial grain. It is important to recall the impact in 1962 of the independently produced *David and Lisa*, directed by Frank Perry and written by Eleanor Perry. This film about relationships in a school for mentally disturbed youths punctured the notion that the "art film" had to be in a language other than English, and helped inspire independent-minded American artists. Scanning the ensuing years, one notes such diverse filmmakers as John Cassavetes, Robert Downey, Brian De Palma, John Korty, Martin Scorsese, George Lucas, Terrence Malick, and, of course, Andy Warhol and his associate Paul Morrissey. Cassavetes and Downey are talented iconoclasts – Cassavetes with his unusual, sporadically brilliant films such as *Shadows, Faces, Husbands, Minnie and Moscowitz, A Woman Under the Influence, The Killing of a Chinese Bookie*, and *Opening Night*;

For Nicholson the role was a turning point

Downey with his funny irreverent experimental films that include *Babo 73*, *Chafed Elbows*, and the more polished *Putney Swope*. Both men have found the practical problems of individuality exasperating, but have refused to abandon their own concepts of filmmaking in the face of the depressing knowledge that there is no discernible rush by major companies to bankroll their work. De Palma's *Greetings* and *Hi, Mom!* heralded a new director with satirical strength, but his course has veered toward more marketable endeavors like *Sisters, Obsession*, and *Carrie*, all deficient in the characteristics that made his less pretentious films so distinctive. Korty, whose *Riverrun* and *Funnyman* illustrated his talent, encountered customary survival difficulties and turned to television to prove he could also work in conventional surroundings. Scorsese, whose *Mean Streets* was accorded extensive praise, successfully moved into the mainstream with *Alice Doesn't Live Here Anymore* and *Taxi Driver*; Lucas, later to strike gold with *Star Wars*, complained that it took him a year to get the money to make *American Graffiti*, and eight months to persuade Universal to release it; Malick completed his independently financed *Badlands*, a disturbing drama about two young killers, before making a distribution deal with Warner Bros. The film was enthusiastically received at the New York Film Festival in 1973, but was lost in the commercial scramble. His *Days of Heaven* (1978) won him the New York Film Critics Circle's best director award. As for Warhol and Morrissey, they have functioned largely on a level of camp, sometimes with considerable flair, as with *Trash* and *Heat*, sometimes stretching audience tolerance to the breaking point. No matter how many independent efforts of the 1960s and 1970s are chronicled, it is very much a minority report.

The hope that *Easy Rider*'s triumph, coupled with the financial plight of the major studios, would ensure a future for low-budget films was short-lived. In less than seven years, low budgets had lost their allure. The popularity of *Earthquake*, *The Poseidon Adventure*, *The Towering Inferno*, *The Exorcist*, and particularly, *Jaws*, switched the emphasis toward fewer, costlier films with huge profit possibilities. Producers, instead of calling for another *Easy Rider* demanded: "Make me another *Jaws*!" Next, the magic words were *Star Wars*.

Although *Easy Rider* was important to cinema and will undoubtedly be remembered as a prime example of independent filmmaking, its role in trenchantly conveying some of the feelings of its decade, and in dramatizing the fierce clash of values, and the persistent violence and intolerance also contributes to its landmark status. Unfortunately, millions who become acquainted with the film through television showings do not see it in its entirety. Such television abuse is not uncommon. "It is sad," Schneider lamented bitterly, "to see that the company distributing *Easy Rider* elected to butcher it when putting it into national syndication. Individual stations edit it, too. It's a scandal that a classic should be treated in this way."

EASY RIDER
USA (Columbia) 1969

Cast, in the order of their appearance

Wyatt .... PETER FONDA
Billy .... DENNIS HOPPER
Jesus .... ANTONIO MENDOZA
The Connection .... PHIL SPECTOR
Bodyguard .... MAC MASHOURIAN
Rancher .... WARREN FINNERTY
Rancher's Wife .... TITA COLORADO
Stranger on Highway .... LUKE ASKEW

At the Commune

Lisa .... LUANA ANDERS
Sarah .... SABRINA SCHARF
Joanne .... SANDY WYETH
Jack .... ROBERT WALKER
Mime number 1 .... ROBERT BALL
Mime number 2 .... CARMEN PHILLIPS
Mime number 3 .... ELLIE WALKER
Mime number 4 .... MICHAEL PATAKI

In the Jail

George Hanson .... JACK NICHOLSON
Guard .... GEORGE FOWLER, JR.
Sheriff .... KEITH GREEN

At the Cafe

Cat Man .... HAYWARD ROBILLARD
Deputy .... ARNOLD HESS, JR.
Customer number 1 .... BUDDY CAUSEY, JR.
Customer number 2 .... DUFFY LAFONT
Customer number 3 .... BLASE M. DAWSON
Customer number 4 .... PAUL GUEDRY, JR.
Girl number 1 .... SUZIE RAMAGOS
Girl number 2 .... ELIDA ANN HEBERT
Girl number 3 .... ROSE LEBLANC
Girl number 4 .... MARY KAYE HEBERT
Girl number 5 .... CYNTHIA GREZAFFI
Girl number 6 .... COLETTE PURPERA

At the House of Blue Lights

Mary . . . . Toni Basil
Karen . . . . Karen Black
Madame . . . . Lea Marmer
Dancing Girl . . . . Cathe Cozzi
Hooker number 1 . . . . Thea Salerno
Hooker number 2 . . . . Anne McClain
Hooker number 3 . . . . Beatriz Monteil
Hooker number 4 . . . . Marcia Bowman

Men in Pickup Truck . . . . David C. Billodeau, Johnny David

Running time . . . . 95 minutes
Technicolor
Production Companies . . . . The Pando Company, in association with Raybert Productions
Executive Producer . . . . Bert Schneider
Produced by . . . . Peter Fonda
Directed by . . . . Dennis Hopper
Screenplay by . . . . Peter Fonda, Dennis Hopper, and Terry Southern
Associate Producer . . . . William Hayward
Director of Photography . . . . Laszlo Kovacs
Production Manager . . . . Paul Lewis
Film Editor . . . . Donn Cambern
Assistant Editor . . . . Stanley Siegel
Consultant . . . . Henry Jaglom
Sound Effects . . . . Edit-Rite, Inc.
Art Director . . . . Jerry Kay
Assistant Cameraman . . . . Peter Heiser, Jr.
Sound Mixer . . . . Le Roy Robbins
Gaffer . . . . Richmond Aguilar
Key Grip . . . . Thomas Ramsey
Script Supervisor . . . . Joyce King
Location Manager . . . . Tony Vorno
Transportation . . . . Lee Pierpont
Post Production . . . . Marilyn Schlossberg
Assistant Director . . . . Len Marsal
Prop Master . . . . Robert O'Neil
Make-up . . . . Virgil Frye
Special Effects . . . . Steve Karkus
Still Man . . . . Peter Sorel
Electrician . . . . Foster Denker
Best Boy . . . . Mel Maxwell

Sound Boom .... JAMES CONTRARES
Generator .... GUY BADGER
Stunt Gaffer .... TEX HALL
Music Editing .... SYNCHROFILM, INC.
Rerecording .... PRODUCERS SOUND SERVICE INC.
Sound .... RYDER SOUND SERVICE, INC.
Titles .... CINEFX
Color Processing .... CONSOLIDATED FILM INDUSTRIES

Music

"The Pusher" – composed by HOYT AXTON; performed by STEPPENWOLF

"Born to Be Wild" – MARS BONFIRE; STEPPENWOLF

"Wasn't Born to Follow" – GERRY GOFFIN and CAROLE KING; THE BYRDS

"The Weight" – JAIME ROBBIE ROBERTSON; THE BAND

"If You Want to be a Bird" – ANTONIA DUREN; THE HOLY MODAL ROUNDERS

"Don't Bogart Me" – ELLIOTT INGBER and LARRY WAGNER; FRATERNITY OF MAN

"If Six Was Nine" – JIMI HENDRIX; THE JIMI HENDRIX EXPERIENCE

"Let's Turkey Trot" – GERRY GOFFIN and JACK KELLER; LITTLE EVA

"Kyrie Eleison" – DAVID AXELROD; THE ELECTRIC PRUNES

"Flash, Bam, Pow" – MIKE BLOOMFIELD; THE ELECTRIC FLAG, an American Music Band

"It's Alright Ma (I'm Only Bleeding)" – BOB DYLAN; ROGER MCGUINN

"Ballad of Easy Rider" – ROGER MCGUINN; ROGER MCGUINN

NATIONAL GUARD KILLS FOUR STUDENTS AT KENT STATE UNIVERSITY IN OHIO —May 4, 1970

TWO BLACK STUDENTS KILLED BY POLICE AT JACKSON STATE COLLEGE IN MISSISSIPPI —May 14, 1970

GENERAL DE GAULLE DIES —November 9, 1970

In 1971, 12,000 arrested in anti-Vietnam war demonstration in Washington . . . The *New York Times* publishes Pentagon papers . . . Eighteen-year-olds in US get right to vote . . . Forty-three die, many wounded, as New York State troopers storm Attica prison.

PRESIDENT NIXON VISITS CHINA —February 20, 1972

GOVERNOR GEORGE WALLACE SHOT —May 15, 1972

FIVE BURGLARS CAUGHT BREAKING INTO DEMOCRATIC HEADQUARTERS AT WATERGATE —June 17, 1972

NIXON DEFEATS McGOVERN —November 7, 1972

In 1973, US-Vietnam peace agreements signed . . . Pablo Picasso dies . . . Chilean President Salvador Allende killed in coup by CIA-backed forces . . . New Israeli–Arab war erupts . . . Spiro Agnew pleads no contest to tax evasion, resigns as Vice President . . . Nixon names Gerald Ford as replacement . . . Oil embargo decreed by Arab countries.

AARON TOPS RUTH WITH 715TH HOMER —April 8, 1974

HOUSE JUDICIARY COMMITTEE STARTS NIXON IMPEACHMENT HEARINGS —May 9, 1974

DR. MARTIN LUTHER KING'S MOTHER KILLED BY ASSASSIN IN CHURCH —June 30, 1974

1970-1979

NIXON FIRST PRESIDENT IN US HISTORY TO RESIGN
—August 9, 1974

PRESIDENT FORD PARDONS NIXON —September 8, 1974

In 1975, unemployment in US reaches 6.5 million, highest in thirteen years . . . Haldeman, Ehrlichman, Mitchell, Mardian convicted in Watergate cover-up . . . Justice William O. Douglas resigns from Supreme Court because of illness . . . Patricia Hearst captured in San Francisco . . . Franco dies. . . . Evidence of CIA and FBI abuses mounts.

CHOU EN-LAI DIES IN PEKING AT 78 —January 8, 1976

JIMMY CARTER ELECTED —November 2, 1976

In 1977, South African black leader Stephen Biko dies in police custody . . . Sadat makes historic visit to Israel to talk peace with Begin . . . In 1978, world's first baby conceived outside womb born in Britain . . . Polish-born Pope John Paul II is first non-Italian Pope in 455 years . . . Over 900 cultists die in Jonestown, Guyana, commune in mass suicide ordered by leader . . . President Carter announces US and China to establish diplomatic relations.

SHAH LEAVES IRAN ON VACATION —January 16, 1979

CHINA INVADES VIETNAM —February 17, 1979

EGYPT, ISRAEL SIGN PEACE TREATY —March 26, 1979

PENNSYLVANIA NUCLEAR POWER ACCIDENT POSES GRAVE RISKS FOR POPULATION —March 28, 1979

TORY MARGARET THATCHER WINS IN BRITAIN; FIRST WOMAN VOTED HEAD OF EUROPEAN COUNTRY
—May 3, 1979

HOUSE PANEL FINDS PLOT IN JFK KILLING
—June 2, 1979

1970

The Sorrow and the Pity

German soldiers patrol Paris.

Documentaries in Depth

OF THE MANY ADVANCES in the documentary form since *Nanook of the North, The Sorrow and the Pity* is its first significant extension as a historical method for comprehensive, in-depth probing of momentous issues and the intricacies of human behavior. Although it is possible to cite various pre-1970 film and television documentaries as substantial and provocative, none begins to approach the profundity of Marcel Ophuls's overwhelming study of France during the Nazi occupation. The film, four hours and twenty-five minutes long, demonstrates how the documentary can be freed from the customary time brackets of television and theatrical formats, and be dedicated to fulfilling intellectual challenge rather than to meeting the requirements of fast-paced drama.

"*The Sorrow and the Pity* is at the opposite end of the spectrum to *Nanook of the North*," Ophuls said to me in a 1976 conversation. "What still gives *Nanook of the North* that icy-pure, polar sparkle is that it is marvelously simple, straightforward, and direct. *The Sorrow and the Pity* is very complex, a sign of the times in many ways. It tries to use the documentary form of expression to show how complicated and confusing things are. You can drown in the complexity. The degree to which you get into it makes it a nightmare for the person doing the film. You end up wallowing in a pit and can go mad. I think I have come to a point where I have to switch off or I will go bananas. There are several reasons why more filmmakers don't do such pictures. For one thing, they may not be worth doing as they are extremely hard to market. Because I was successful once, I've been in a position where there are various solutions for financing from people willing to let me go that way, but financing is difficult for those who have not had that experience.

"Another reason is that I don't know how many of my colleagues would want to follow in the direction of *The Sorrow and the Pity*. In France, some directors have done so more or less, but not too successfully. Probably, it takes the tortured mind, the kind of intellect I have – very pluralistic. I rejoice in complexities and take pleasure in the fact that life is not simple. Most people do not. I'm more tolerant of complexity than some of my colleagues."

Precisely this fascination with complexity elevates *The Sorrow and the Pity* above documentaries that attempt either to forcefully project a particular viewpoint, or to mechanically offer a neatly balanced presentation that merely gives equal time in a surface way. Neither approach seizes the opportunity for the widest possible exploration. In sharp contrast, Ophuls pursues the threads of his subject wherever they may lead, the more contradictory, the better. Instead of coming away with tidy impressions, the viewer lives through an all-embracing intellectual and emotional experience and accumulates a wealth of information, opinions, insights, contradictions, and further questions, even an appreciation that there may be no definitive answers on some points. The method used by Ophuls includes lengthy interviews recorded in 1969 with persons on many sides of an issue detailing their experiences or giving their opinions. To illustrate their conversations, or perhaps to contradict them, he employs clips from newsreels and German propaganda films. The method itself is scarcely new. The difference lies in the subject matter, the questions he poses, the length of time he devotes to the explorations, and the editing of the film to allow the broadest range of experience rather than to condense it to the nitty-gritty. Underlying the construction of the film is Ophuls's commitment to seeking the truth regardless of how uncomfortable this may be for his audience or for the participants. He does this, not with a sensation-monger's desire to trap or embarrass, but with a historian's determination to comprehend.

Ophuls, assisted by André Harris, shot fifty hours of footage for the production, which was financed by Swiss and West German television networks. The desire to bury the unpalatable past was so ingrained in the national psyche that French television would not broadcast *The Sorrow and the Pity*. It was shown instead at the Studio Saint-Séverin, a Left Bank art theater, where it was received with such enthusiasm that it was also booked into a cinema on the Champs-Elysées. Before long, the film had achieved international acclaim.

The epoch is one of particular personal recollection for Ophuls, who was born in Frankfurt. At five, he was taken to live in Paris, his parents having had the foresight to leave Germany after the Reichstag fire of 1933. His father, the celebrated filmmaker Max Ophüls (*La Ronde*, 1950; *Le Plaisir*, 1951; *Lola Montès*, 1955), became a French citizen and broadcast anti-Nazi programs. Goebbels vowed to "get the Jew Oppenheimer" (Ophüls's real name) when the Nazis took Paris. When the Germans invaded in 1940, the family joined the exodus to the unoccupied zone, where they lived surreptitiously for a year until, by way of Spain and Portugal, they were able to reach the United States. In Hollywood, the young Ophuls played some bit parts in films and finished high school, before being drafted into the United States Army and sent to Japan. In 1950, he returned to France where he eventually became an assistant to John Huston on *Moulin Rouge* and to his father on *Lola Montès*; he also worked in German television, directed a section of the film *Love at Twenty*, made *Banana Peel*, starring Jean-Paul Belmondo and Jeanne Moreau, and later worked for the French television network ORTF.

He and André Harris were among those fired by the Gaullists after the student riots of 1968. The filming of *The Sorrow and the Pity* was for Ophuls a return to the scene of his youth, a study of the divided France he had to flee.

The documentary, subtitled "Chronicle of a French Town During The Occupation," is in two parts, the first "The Collapse," the second "The Choice." It is in French, and occasionally in English and German, with an English voice-over providing a running translation. The focal point is the industrial city of Clermont-Ferrand in the Auvergne near Vichy, 242 miles from Paris, which offers a microcosm of the crosscurrents existing in France during the ugly years of the German occupation and the collaboration of the Vichy government of Marshal Philippe Pétain and Pierre Laval. Pierre Mendès-France is the hero of the film in the sense that he vigorously personifies the integrity of those who opposed the Germans and the policy of collaboration. "Treason was spreading openly – the need to surrender, the desire to come to an understanding with the winners at any price. Anglophobia, which is traditional in France, surfaced quickly. All this was flaunted with a sort of dreadful cynicism. No one mentioned the misjudgments of the military chiefs. No, instead all the mistakes were attributed to Léon Blum, to the Popular Front. . . . Many people accepted the country's misfortunes and consoled themselves by seeking revenge in internal politics," he says in his fascinating reminiscence that includes an account of his trial, which was permeated with anti-Semitism. "Anti-Semitism and Anglophobia are two things that can always be easily revived in France. . . . People who would not have dared admit their anti-Semitism before were suddenly beginning to proclaim it. Since they were beginning to absorb German principles and to seek a closer understanding with Hitler . . . it was obvious that anti-Semitism provided a bond between certain German elements and certain French elements. . . ."

Mendès-France was tried and sentenced to six years in prison on a trumped-up charge of desertion. After two years he managed to escape, reaching London via Switzerland to join the Free French. In London he met Charles de Gaulle, and recalls the occasion as an "overwhelming experience." Mendès-France's description of his flight from prison provides a genial personal touch: "I was on top of the wall. . . . Just as I was about to jump, . . . I heard an unexpected noise. . . . There was a couple under the tree. . . . He had a very definite goal in mind; she couldn't decide. . . . It took a very long time. She finally did say yes. Then they left, and I jumped. And I swear that at that moment I was happier than he was."

British statesman Lord Avon (Anthony Eden) talks about the defeatism of Pétain, but is reluctant to castigate the French, contending that one who has not been through the horrors of occupation has no right to pronounce moral judgment on those who have. Nevertheless, when Pétain asked the Germans for an armistice, Eden recalled sending Churchill a note: "If France cannot go on with fighting, that is one thing; but if she ever collaborates with the enemy, that is something else." He justifies Britain's attack on the French navy: "What we didn't dare to risk happening was that those ships should pass at any foreseeable stage under German control . . . that would have had the most deplorable consequences for the whole of our chance of winning the war. . . ."

Others who give their reminiscences include Georges Bidault, former president of the National Resistance Council; Emmanuel d'Astier de la Vigerie, founder of the Liberation movement; Emile Coulaudon, the head of the Auvergne maquis, then known as Colonel Gaspard; and Jacques Duclos, leader of the underground French Communist party. Especially interesting are the Grave brothers, stalwart farmers who served in the Resistance; they convey the stubborn pride of those who chose to fight rather than accommodate to Vichy or Hitler. Louis Grave was denounced by a neighbor and sent to Buchenwald. He knows the informer's identity, but refuses to take revenge, because "then I would be the same as they are."

Choice – individual and collective – emerges as the unifying theme of the film. While Ophuls pays scrupulous attention to the heroism of the Resistance, he also dwells on the alternatives exercised. A shopkeeper named Klein admits that he took out a newspaper advertisement to announce publicly that, despite his name, he was not Jewish. In retrospect, he sees nothing wrong with his action. Teachers continued with their usual routines when students and colleagues disappeared. Ophuls presses the point: "What was it like when there was an empty seat in the classroom?" "I don't remember," is the response. Biologist and writer Dr. Claude Lévy claims that French officials outdid the Gestapo in seizing French Jews for deportation. He cites the infamous Vélodrome d'Hiver roundup in Paris on July 16, 1942. Although the Germans had not planned at that time to arrest children under sixteen, Lévy says, the French police abducted over four thousand youngsters. Laval, asked by a Protestant minister to intervene, replied that he was practicing prophylaxis. (Only five percent of French Jews survived the deportations.)

Renowned French actress Danielle Darrieux is among those shown leaving to perform in Germany. "It feels so good, it's France," sings Maurice Chevalier in 1942. At the conclusion of the film, his television broadcast to America has a hollow ring. In it, Chevalier cheerfully denies having made a tour of Germany during the German occupation of France. All he did, he says, was sing there once at a camp for French prisoners of war. The clip is a further illustration of the problem of confronting the past. In 1942, the Germans occupied all of France. One person queried insists that he never saw any Germans in Clermont-Ferrand. Another saw too many – "nothing but Germans!" Comte René de Chambrun, Laval's son-in-law, arrogantly and uncompromisingly defends the collaborationist policy. Aristocratic

Christian de la Mazière remembers with candor the youthful pro-Nazi enthusiasm that led him to join the French Waffen S.S., which fought on the Russian front. Of seven thousand, only three hundred returned. Mazière makes the point that members of the aristocracy naturally leaned toward fascism because of their virulent anti-Semitism, their fear of Marxism, and the divisiveness in France over the Spanish Civil War. On the other hand, British underground fighter Denis Rake, who speaks frankly of his homosexuality and his desire to prove that he could be as heroic as anyone else, lauds the support he received from the French working-class, even though helping him entailed the risk of being shot.

The horror of what the Germans represented is effectively brought to mind by a segment from Veit Harlan's notorious *Jud Süss* (1940), to which many French people flocked as if it were merely another entertainment. In *Jud Süss*, set in 1738, the Württemberg Council decrees that all Jews must leave within three days, and exhorts future generations to "preserve the purity of their blood from the blemishes of this accursed race." Its climactic scene is the hanging of a Jew, as a purge of all that is evil.

Ophuls provides a further dimension through conversations with Helmut Tausend, a former Wehrmacht captain who had been stationed in Clermont-Ferrand and who is in a talkative mood at the wedding of his daughter. For the occasion, Tausend proudly wears medals earned in Hitler's service. Portly and self-satisfied, enjoying his cigar, he complains about the unfairness of partisan attacks on German soldiers and fondly recalls his little flirtations with French women while his dowdy wife looks on with benign men-will-be-men tolerance. It is clear that Tausend would rather Germany had not lost the war. When reminded that some look disapprovingly upon the sporting of war decorations, he attributes such comments to those who did not earn any. Another former member of the German occupation forces speculates that having lost may be all for the best: "If Hitler had won, maybe we'd still be doing occupation duty in Africa or America, or somewhere."

Post-liberation scenes of women having their heads shaved in retaliation for consorting with the Germans generate questions as to the propriety of vigilante justice. Were all of them guilty? Were all those in the hostile crowd totally innocent? And what about those whose collaboration may have been far more serious, but not so obvious? *The Sorrow and the Pity* permits no easy responses and leaves little room for self-righteousness, but rather compels one to ponder one's own possible actions in similar circumstances. What if the United States were occupied by an enemy power? Who would collaborate? Who would resist? One does not have to take such an extreme situation. The United States under the "occupation" of McCarthyism offers subject matter for studying how Americans collaborated, resisted, or ignored the menace. The experience of Vietnam is also germane to the question of choice in Ophuls's film.

Ophuls next brought his methodology to bear upon the strife in Northern Ireland. *A Sense of Loss* (1972) is less successful than *The Sorrow and the Pity*, in that it lacks comparable sweep and perspective. The director does, however, succeed in etching a vivid portrait of the hatred, dismay, endless slaughter, and seemingly insoluble situation. *The Memory of Justice*, first shown out of competition at the 1976 Cannes Film Festival, is Ophuls's masterly exploration of justice and guilt through in-depth analysis of the Nuremberg war crime trials; it goes beyond Nuremberg to reflect on morality in other situations, such as Vietnam. A fascinating, provocative document that should endure as a major work of our time, *The Memory of Justice* had a stormy history before its release. Its original producers, against Ophuls's wishes, edited the film drastically, and Ophuls, charging that his work had been butchered, broke with them. An original print was smuggled out of Europe, support grew for circulation of the film as Ophuls had made it, and Paramount took over its distribution. *The Memory of Justice* runs four hours and thirty-eight minutes, employing techniques similar to *The Sorrow and the Pity*.

The Sorrow and the Pity has had the effect of opening up the subject of the Occupation to discussion, further stimulated by other films, both documentary and fiction. One documentary is *Frenchmen, If You Knew . . .* (1973), made by André Harris and Alain de Sédouy. Another, *Singing under the Occupation* (1976), by André Halimi, exposes those who continued to perform, write, and make films under the Nazis. Fictional treatment of factual situations can be found in Louis Malle's *Lacombe, Lucien* (1974), and Costa-Gavras's *Section Spéciale* (1974).

Peter Davis, in his disturbing film about Vietnam, *Hearts and Minds* (1975), uses a method similar to that of Ophuls, but does not achieve the latter's complexity. However, considering that the film was made without the advantage of some three decades of perspective, *Hearts and Minds* excels in its comprehensive survey of the ramifications of the United States's involvement, searching for the strains in American life that could give rise to a Vietnam. While less objective than *The Sorrow and the Pity*, *Hearts and Minds* approaches its subject with scope, intelligence, originality, and uncompromising frankness. Susan Sontag, critic and filmmaker, also manages more than usual depth in her documentary *Promised Lands* (1974), which captures the anguish, pain, and uncertainties inherent in the Arab-Israeli confrontation.

The evolution of the documentary form includes the CBS broadcasts of Edward Murrow in the 1950s. Some were hardhitting and extremely informative, and Murrow's close-up of the havoc wrought by Joseph McCarthy helped bring about the latter's downfall. Later controversial programs, such as *The Selling of the Pentagon,* by Peter Davis, further realized the potential of television documentaries, but nothing measures

In 1969, former Wehrmacht officer Helmut Tausend recalls the German occupation of Clermont-Ferrand

up to the totality and power of what Ophuls has achieved.

Another development has been the practice of photographing people in particular situations in the hope of extracting larger truths from these intimate observations. Frederick Wiseman has made such films, including *Titicut Follies, Law and Order, High School, Hospital,* and *Primate*. Family life and various forms of psychotherapy have frequently come before the camera eye in this cinéma vérité fashion. David and Albert Maysles use a variation of this approach; in *Salesman,* the audience virtually accompanies Bible salesmen on their territorial rounds, and in *Grey Gardens,* the turbulent, eccentric existence of the Beales, relatives of Jacqueline Kennedy Onassis, is painfully but intriguingly explored.

"Wiseman, the Maysles, and I are only part of the same movement in a technical way – the use of 16mm and direct sound," Ophuls said. "In every other way we're probably different from each other in what we look for and in our attitudes. Fred Wiseman is a little closer to me in his interests, but his means is the microcosm – finding a single police squad, a wing in a hospital, or an office in a welfare department, and just staying there. The Maysles are part of the cinema-direct movement, with the mythology and holier-than-thou attitude toward truth. For them going into homes and photographing reality is getting at the truth. I do not think it is very artistic or has much content value. The danger of that method as compared with mine is that they have to collaborate in being accomplices to the exhibitionism of the people they work with, whether the Rolling Stones [*Gimme Shelter*] or the Beales. I find it rather disgusting, although perhaps I shouldn't say that."

That is a harsh judgment of the Maysles. *Grey Gardens,* while sensational, also presents a portrait as poignant as one Tennessee Williams might create for the stage. By focusing a camera on the Beales, the Maysles extract much that is fascinating about two individuals of interest as inhabitants of our society. However, regardless of the effect, such a film can in no way be even remotely compared with the depth of an Ophuls documentary that strives to illuminate moral issues, public attitudes and involvements, and major historical events. Nor can it match the importance of such socially conscious documentaries as Barbara Kopple's *Harlan County, U.S.A.* (1976) or David Helpern's *Hollywood on Trial* (1976).

It is regrettable that more has not been done with the documentary form to increase our self-knowledge. Admittedly, the public has shown few signs of rushing to documentaries in lieu of feature entertainment. The very word is anathema commercially, and distributors are not averse to pleading with critics to avoid calling a film a documentary. It is essential to change this attitude rather than succumb to it. Ophuls shows the way toward far more enlightened use of this art form. The further development of video-discs and cassettes might make available works such as his for the study of history in high schools and universities. Many subjects are waiting, but it takes a filmmaker with the perception, tenacity, and inquisitiveness of Marcel Ophuls to pursue them and the willingness of television executives, sponsors, and film companies to finance controversial ventures and ensure that they are scheduled on the air or given proper theatrical distribution.

THE SORROW AND THE PITY
(Le Chagrin et la Pitié)

FRANCE-SWITZERLAND-GERMANY 1970

With

EMMANUEL D'ASTIER DE LA VIGERIE, founder of the Liberation movement of the Resistance; later secretary of the interior under de Gaulle.

GEORGES BIDAULT, president of the National Resistance Council; prime minister 1949–50.

COMTE RENÉ DE CHAMBRUN, lawyer, son-in-law of Pierre Laval.

EMILE COULAUDON, called Colonel Gaspard, head of the Auvergne maquis.

JACQUES DUCLOS, head of the then clandestine French Communist party.

MARCEL FOUCHE-DEGLIAME, director of the Combat movement of the Resistance.

LOUIS AND ALEXIS GRAVE, farmers in Yronde, a village near Clermont-Ferrand; active in the Resistance.

CHRISTIAN DE LA MAZIÈRE, volunteer Charlemagne company (French division of the Waffen S.S.).

GEORGES LAMIRAND, former minister of youth under Marshall Pétain; later mayor of La Bourboule, near Clermont-Ferrand.

MARCEL VERDIER, pharmacist, Clermont-Ferrand.

MME. SOLANGE, hairdresser, from Châteaugué, a village near Clermont-Ferrand.

CHARLES BRAUN, restaurant owner, Clermont-Ferrand.

PIERRE LE CALVEZ, cinema owner, Clermont-Ferrand.

M. DANTON, lycée teacher, Clermont-Ferrand.

M. DIONNET, lycée librarian, Clermont-Ferrand.

RAPHAEL GEMINIANI, champion professional cyclist from Clermont-Ferrand.

COLONEL R. DU JONCHAY, active in the Resistance – regional leader for Limoges.

MARIUS KLEIN, shopkeeper, Clermont-Ferrand.
M. LEIRIS, former mayor of Combronde, near Clermont-Ferrand; Resistance fighter.
COMMANDANT MENUT, army officer, active in the Resistance, from Clermont-Ferrand.
M. MIOCHE, owner of hotel in Royat, village near Clermont-Ferrand.
MAÎTRE HENRI ROCHAT, lawyer, defended Pierre Mendès-France in Clermont-Ferrand.
ROGER TOUNZE, editor *La Montagne*, newspaper in Clermont-Ferrand.
DR. CLAUDE LÉVY, biologist and writer formerly active in Franc-Tireurs movement of the Resistance.
PIERRE MENDÈS-FRANCE, captain of Lorraine unit of Royal Air Force; prime minister 1954–55.
MAURICE J. BUCKMASTER, head of British espionage group.
ANTHONY EDEN (LORD AVON), British foreign secretary 1940–45; prime minister 1955–57.
DENIS RAKE, British secret agent in occupied France.
GENERAL SPEARS, liaison between Churchill and de Gaulle.
FLIGHT SERGEANT EVANS, British pilot shot down in the Auvergne.
CORPORAL BLEIBINGER, soldier of the Wehrmacht, prisoner of the Auvergne maquis.
DR. ELMAR MICHEL, chairman of Salamander Shoes; economic advisor to German military command in France.
DR. PAUL SCHMIDT, Hitler's chief interpreter.
GENERAL WALTER WARLIMONT, chief of National Defense, Supreme Command of the Wehrmacht.
CAPT. HELMUT TAUSEND, of the German Wehrmacht, stationed in Clermont-Ferrand.

Running time.................................265 minutes
Production companies...........TÉLÉVISION RENCONTRE, SOCIÉTÉ SUISSE DE RADIODIFFUSION, NORDDEUTSCHER RUNDFUNK
Production....................ANDRÉ HARRIS, ALAIN DE SÉDOUY
Production Director ....WOLFGANG THIELE
Directed by...............................MARCEL OPHULS
Scenario by ....MARCEL OPHULS, ANDRÉ HARRIS
Interviews by ....MARCEL OPHULS, ANDRÉ HARRIS
Photography by................ANDRÉ GAZUT, JÜRGEN THIEME
Sound ....BERNARD MIGY
Edited by ....CLAUDE VAJDA
Assistant Director..........................CLAUDE VAJDA
Editing Assistants............HEIDI ENDRUWELT, WIEBKE VOGLER
Assistant Cameraman....................ALAIN DEMARTINES
Mixing ....WOLFGANG SCHROETER
Documentarists......................ELAINE FILIPPI (France)
CHRISTOPH DERSHAU (Germany)
SUZY BENHIAT (Great Britain)

1971

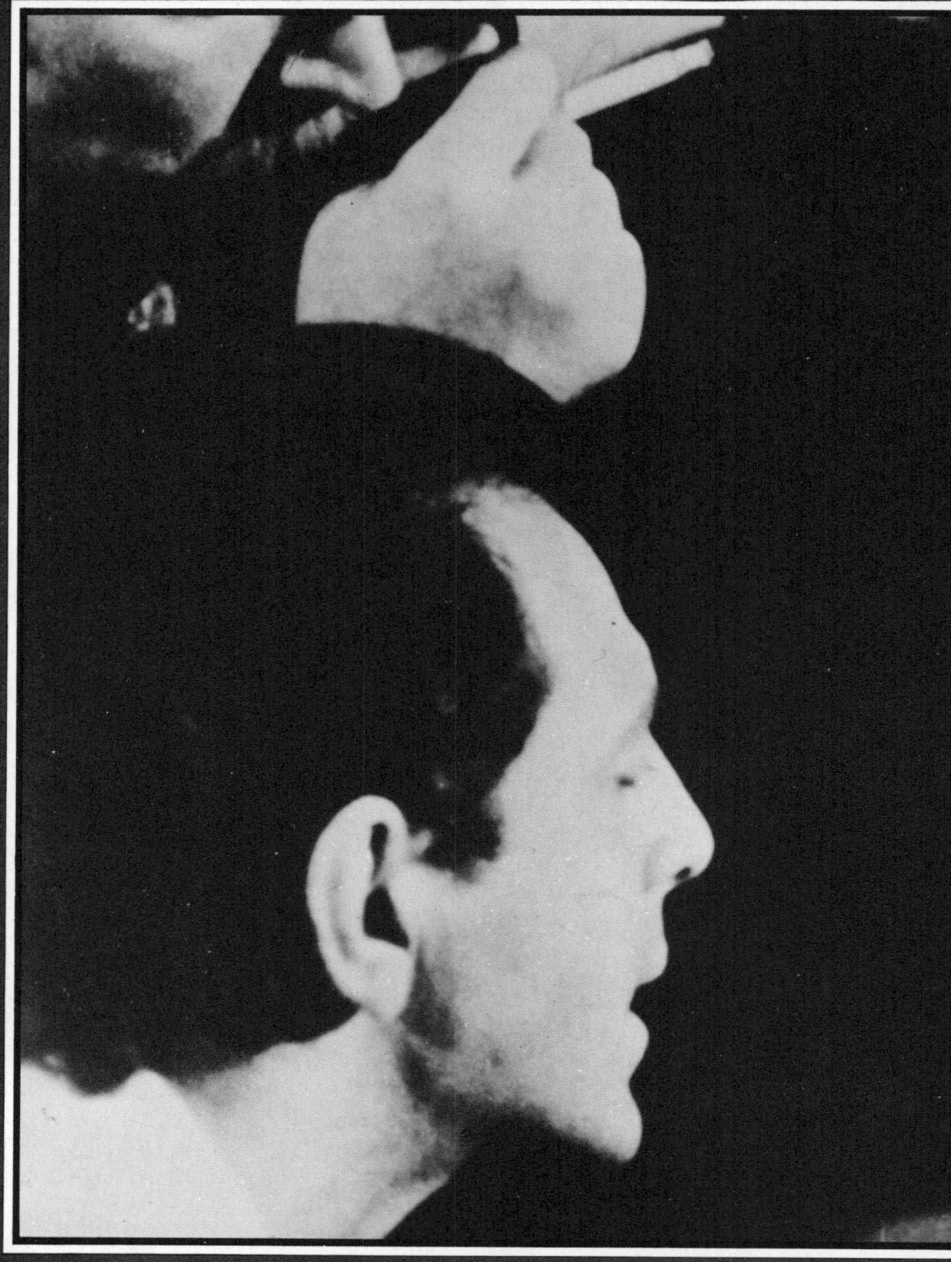

Sweet Sweetback's Baadassss Song

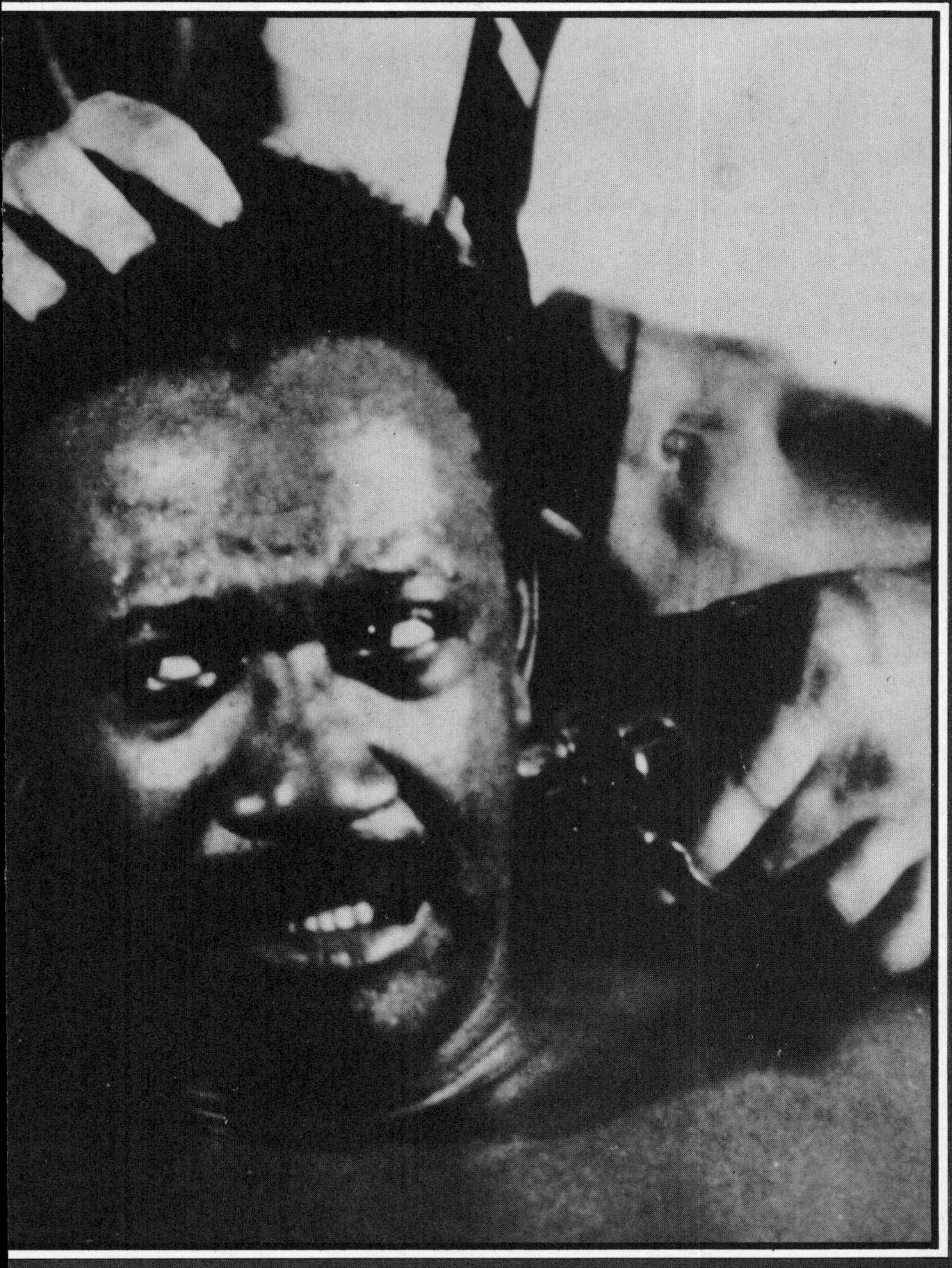

Beatle (Simon Chuckster) is pressured to inform on Sweetback.

The Black Experience

The more glamorous publicity went to *Shaft* and *Super Fly*. Indeed, many may not have heard of *Sweet Sweetback's Baadasssss Song* with its strange title and excess of s's, but the film became a milestone. As historians look back to the relationship between blacks and filmmaking in the 1970s, *Sweetback* will stand out as a force to be appreciated, partly because of content, but mainly because of the breakthrough it achieved and the consequences. Written, directed, scored, and produced by Melvin Van Peebles, who also starred in it, *Sweetback* was truly a film created for blacks by blacks. The nearly $12 million box-office gross claimed by Van Peebles dramatized in terms the film industry understands best, hard cash, that there was a market for black films. The lesson was not lost on others more interested in exploiting the market than in advancing the cause of black progress in the cinema.

Blacks (as well as Orientals, Indians, Hispanics) have long been ignored or stereotyped, or denied equal employment opportunities by the movie establishment. To comprehend *Sweetback*'s significance fully, one must take at least a cursory look at the shabby record with respect to black talent and black audiences. The racism inherent in *The Birth of a Nation* was a barometer of the film climate that would prevail for many years. Black roles, where they existed at all, were primarily those of maids, buffoons, and other stereotypes. Some actors became successful playing these characters. Willie Best was an expert at feigning fright; Stepin Fetchit became a millionaire as a shuffling lazybones; talented dancer Bill Robinson showed how much rhythm he had as a foil for Shirley Temple. There were exceptions, such as Paul Robeson in *Emperor Jones* in 1933. Well-meant but patronizing efforts at change included pictures like *The Green Pastures* (1936), starring Rex Ingram as De Lawd, and the musical *Cabin in the Sky* (1943), with Ethel Waters and Lena Horne. Hattie McDaniel became the first black to win an Oscar for her stereotyped Mammy role in *Gone With the Wind*.

After World War II, in the wake of changes taking place in America there were a number of films condemning racial prejudice. They represented movement, but hardly enough to justify the self-congratulations of the filmmakers. Elia Kazan's *Pinky* (1949) dealt with problems encountered by a light-skinned black woman who has passed up North but confronts the truth when she returns to the South. Timid 20th Century-Fox cast white actress Jeanne Crain to pass as black in Hollywood. *Home of the Brave,* a Stanley Kramer film released in 1949, traced the mental crisis and paralysis of a black soldier to a moment on a mission when his white buddy called him "nigger." In another Kramer film, *The Defiant Ones* (1958), progress was represented by the relationship of Tony Curtis and Sidney Poitier as escaped convicts chained together and forced into mutual respect. Later, in 1967, Kramer's *Guess Who's Coming to Dinner* starred Poitier, by then a black superstar, as the superman the daughter of white liberals wants to marry and brings home to meet mom and dad, Katharine Hepburn and Spencer Tracy. Kramer was busy making a feeble statement about a side issue at a time when American cities were seething with violent protests by blacks angered at official indifference to appalling ghetto living conditions. Also in 1967, *In the Heat of the Night,* starring Poitier and Rod Steiger, caused comment because a black man slaps a white man on screen. That this could be so noteworthy shows how short a distance Hollywood films had traveled.

There is little awareness, even among film enthusiasts, that a period of filmmaking by blacks existed in the past. Films were created for black audiences as a reaction to the dearth of product that could offer them character identification. One thinks of all the years in which black filmgoers, attending segregated theaters or compelled to sit in balconies known as "nigger heaven," saw only white stars with white problems. In the 1920s, partly in response to *The Birth of a Nation,* black-financed films appeared. They were made for distribution on a ghetto circuit (one estimate places the number of theaters at 700) and occasionally for special late-night showings in the white theaters.

The best known of these filmmakers was Oscar Micheaux, who between 1918 and 1948 made at least thirty films, among them *Body and Soul* (1924), in which Paul Robeson first appeared on screen. Once major studios, in the post-war period, began to deal in some form with racial prejudice, and more roles were available for black performers, the opportunities for black-produced films diminished. Hollywood had coopted some of the functions.

With the militant black activity of the 1960s and the gains made in civil rights, new changes occurred in the film world. They could be discerned in such films as *Nothing But a Man* (1964), starring Abbey Lincoln, Ivan Dixon, and Gloria Foster, and directed by Michael Roemer; *Uptight* (1968), Jules Dassin's black militant updating of *The Informer,* now set in Cleveland and starring Raymond St. Jacques, Ruby Dee, Julian Mayfield, Frank Silvera, and Roscoe Lee Browne; and *The Learning Tree* (1969), directed by Gordon Parks and based on his autobiographical novel about growing up in 1920s Kansas. Actor Ossie Davis was becoming active as a director (*Gone Are the Days,* 1963; *Cotton Comes to Harlem,* 1970 – a United

Artists release that was also important in demonstrating the commercial potential of black films), and as a force for black filmmaking. Whether directed by blacks or whites, some films were attempting to go deeper into aspects of black life.

Ambitious, rebellious, talented, and versatile Melvin Van Peebles felt there was a need for a black hero who could best his white adversaries and represent black defiance triumphant. He believed black audiences would identify with such a protagonist and was resolved not to whittle away the idea under the pressure of white financiers. Independence was a key aspect of Van Peebles's lifestyle, and when he finally achieved recognition, he often astonished those who met him. Wearing his hair in braids, he spoke with pride of his tattoos: "They express the real me. People used to assign to me the reputation of being just a loud-mouthed, bragging brawler. Now they label me as more refined. Now that they have to take me, they're trying to put sugar on me. But my tattoos express it all. On this dotted line around my neck it says 'lynch here,' and down here [he pointed to his buttocks] it says in an African dialect 'if you can.' That sums up in a nutshell where I'm at." In the same season that *Sweetback* became a hit, he staged two of his own Broadway musicals, *Ain't Supposed to Die a Natural Death* and *Don't Play Us Cheap,* and his firm, YEAH, Inc., was distributing a paperback on the making of *Sweetback* and the soundtrack album from the film, and promoting other tie-ins.

Van Peebles, who grew up in Chicago, has avoided discussing his biographical data, contending that the only important thing about him was his blackness. In 1960, he went to live in France, learned the language, and wrote four novels in French. He became a reporter for *France Observateur* and received attention for a scoop while covering a murder trial. His reputation in France led to his making *The Story of a Three Day Pass,* about a black GI on leave who falls in love with a white Frenchwoman, which won an award at the 1967 San Francisco Film Festival. As a result Columbia asked him to direct *Watermelon Man,* a satire starring Godfrey Cambridge made up as a white man who awakens one morning to find that he has turned black. Van Peebles took the money he earned on that assignment and borrowed $50,000 from entertainer Bill Cosby to put *Sweetback* into production.

A major problem to overcome in the California shooting was the union situation. "I was determined to have Third World technicians on my film," Van Peebles told me, "and I knew that the unions weren't ready to have them in their ranks. My position was that since the unions didn't know black people, it made perfect sense for black people not to know the unions. So I shot my film without them. I didn't get picketed. I shot it in the black communities and no one was too ready to come and make trouble."

The film's hero, Sweetback, who works in Los Angeles as a sex show stud, is arrested in a routine harassment and witnesses two white cops pummeling a black brother mercilessly. In desperation he attacks the police, beats them brutally, and flees, becoming the object of an intensive manhunt in Southern California. His escape takes him through the black community, which befriends him, and on a harrowing odyssey during which he is forced to turn to further violence for self-protection. The film is sometimes ragged artistically, but has tremendous driving force. It is also boldly explicit, with deliberate efforts to shock and portray black life as Van Peebles knows it. His son, then twelve, plays a youngster initiated into sex by a prostitute. In another candid sequence, Sweetback is confronted by a white motorcycle gang about to assault him. He is given a chance to defend himself and told to choose his weapon. He had not been a stud all those years to no purpose. Announcing sex as his weapon, he takes on the woman gang-leader, Big Sadie, for a marathon bout and wins.

Sweetback triumphs improbably over all obstacles and reaches safety across the Mexican border, but not before brutal ordeals. Starving, he eats a frog to stay alive; when a sheriff unleashes a vicious dog near the border, he battles the dog and kills it. With Sweetback safe, the film ends with the promise, "A BAADASSSSS NIGGER IS COMING BACK TO COLLECT SOME DUES."

Van Peebles explained that the use of the word "Baadasssss" in the title was to alert black audiences that "this picture would not be another one of those rip-off pictures in which, no matter how brave the black hero is, he has to lose in the end. I was saying that this man was really trouble and here was something different going to happen in my movie."

Sweetback had a special showing at the Museum of Modern Art in New York. Subsequently, Van Peebles made a distribution deal with Cinemation and the trade was astonished by early gross figures that foretold the success the film would have. He also became embroiled in several hassles. He went to court to compel a Boston theater operator to restore nine minutes that he charged had been deleted. He protested the X rating by the Motion Picture Association of America, and when it refused to retreat, advertised the picture as "rated X by an all-white jury." In a letter to Jack Valenti, president of the MPAA, Van Peebles asserted: "Should the rest of the community submit to your censorship that is its business, but White standards shall no longer be imposed on the Black community."

The film drew divided reactions from blacks as well as whites. Black detractors complained that Van Peebles was perpetuating derogatory images of blacks while purporting to do otherwise. But critic Clayton Riley, in an article in the *New York Times,* called *Sweetback* a "cinematic triumph." The enormous business the film did excited others, who now saw profit in a market hitherto largely ignored. *Sweetback,* coupled with the success of *Shaft* (starring Richard Roundtree as the black private eye created by white writer Ernest Tidyman), led to a spate of other pictures, including the lucrative *Super Fly,* starring Ron O'Neal. Various white-financed companies rushed to exploit the potential, quickly producing films that glorified the black hero, usually with a "get whitey" theme. From American International Pictures there was even a *Blacula* about a black Dracula, and a black exorcist film called *Abby,* in which a black woman is possessed by the devil. What Van Peebles hoped would be a positive development quickly degenerated into a scramble for fast profits.

At least more jobs opened up for black actors and actresses, and occasionally, some worthwhile projects. Certainly, there has been no shortage of talent or personalities, among them actors James Earl Jones, Brock Peters, Lou Gossett, Raymond St. Jacques, Billy Dee Williams, Richard Pryor, Bill Cosby, Calvin Lockhart, Bernie Casey; actresses Ruby Dee, Diana Ross, Vonetta McGee; macho types Jim Brown and Fred Williamson, and their female counterparts Pam Grier and Tamara Dobson. Cicely Tyson and co-star Paul Winfield won Academy Award nominations for *Sounder* (1972), a strong, moving drama of a black family struggling for survival in the South during the Depression. A severe loss occurred with the death of Diana Sands when her film and stage career looked brightest.

Among efforts to raise the level of films about black life was *Black Girl* (1972), which, while contrived and overwrought, was an absorbing, sincere story of family relationships. Motown, the record industry giant, produced *Lady Sings the Blues* (1972), released by Paramount and starring Diana Ross as the late Billie Holiday. It was glossy, Hollywood-style biography, but entertaining, and an excellent vehicle for Ross, who fared less well when she again co-starred with Billy Dee Williams in the insipid, clichéd *Mahogany. Claudine* (1974), teaming James Earl Jones and Diahann Carroll, told a heartwarming story of a young woman with six children who is on welfare and doing her best to cope. Unfortunately, attempts to make films more worthwhile than the crass exploitation pictures or imitations of second-rate Hollywood too often did not live up to the good intentions. An important exception was the uncompromising *Brothers* (1977), fictionalizing the George Jackson and Angela Davis cases. On television "Roots" (1977), the series based on Alex Haley's book, broke all records for video audiences and raised new hopes.

Still to come, if that day ever arrives, is an industry that is thoroughly integrated, from producers to technicians, and films, whether made by blacks or others, that deal maturely with black life. Whatever happens, *Sweetback* is a landmark film that boldly sidestepped past patterns, offered a militant, victorious hero, and proved that there is a vast audience willing to pay to see the black experience portrayed on screen.

Will there be further development in this direction? Or will the events of the seventies turn out to have been another, although more advanced, stage in tokenism?

SWEET SWEETBACK'S BAADASSSSS SONG
USA (Cinemation) 1971

Cast

Brer Soul (Sweetback) .... MELVIN VAN PEEBLES
Beatle .... SIMON CHUCKSTER

and HUBERT SCALES, JOHN DULLAGHAN, WEST GALE, NÍVA ROCHELLE, RHETTA HUGHES, NICK FERRARI, ED RUE, JOHNNY AMOS, LAVELLE ROBY, TED HAYDEN, MARIO PEEBLES, SONJA DUNSON, MICHAEL AGUSTUS, PETER RUSSELL, NORMAN FIELDS, BRUCE ADAMS, RON PRINCE, STEVE COLE, MEGAN PEEBLES, JOE TORNATORE, MIKE ANGEL, THE COPELAND FAMILY, JEFF GOODMAN, CURT MATSON, MARRIA EVONEE, JON JACOBS, BILL KIRSCHNER, VINCENT BARBI, CHET NORRIS, JONI WATKINS, JERRY DAYS, JOHN ALLEN

Running time .... 97 minutes
Color
Produced by .... MELVIN VAN PEEBLES
Directed by .... MELVIN VAN PEEBLES
Written by .... MELVIN VAN PEEBLES
Edited by .... MELVIN VAN PEEBLES
Director of Photography .... BOB MAXWELL
Assistant Director .... CLYDE HOUSTON
Make-up Supervisor .... NORA MAXWELL
Sound .... CLARK WILL
2nd Unit Director .... JOSE GARCIA
Assistant Editor .... JERRY HOENACK
Special Effects .... CLIFF WENGER
Optical Effects .... MULLER-CURTIS-O'NEIL and CFI Laboratory
Sound Editors .... JOHN NEWMAN and LUKE WOLFRAM
Dubbing .... ART PIANTADOSI

Crew: PRISCILLA WATTS, TONY SCOTT, DIANNE JENKINS, CHICK BORLAND, JOHN MURPHY, GEORGE RUBINE, WINFRED TENNISON, SKIP KARNAS

Sweetback's Wardrobe by .... MR. B'S FASHIONS OF L.A.
Music Composed by .... MELVIN VAN PEEBLES
Orchestra & Orchestration .... EARTH, WIND & FIRE
"Come on Feet" Courtesy of A&M Records

1972

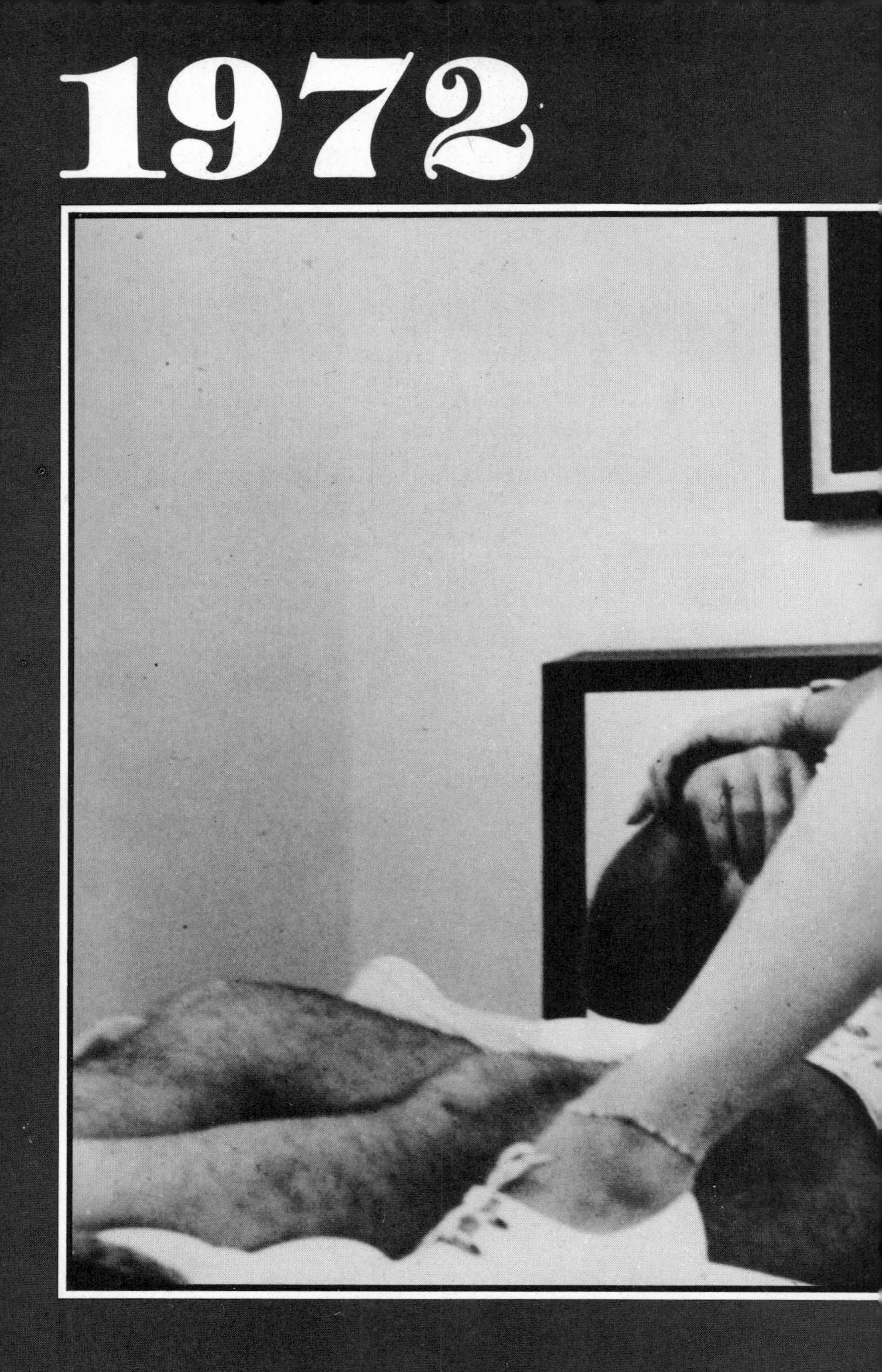

Deep Throat

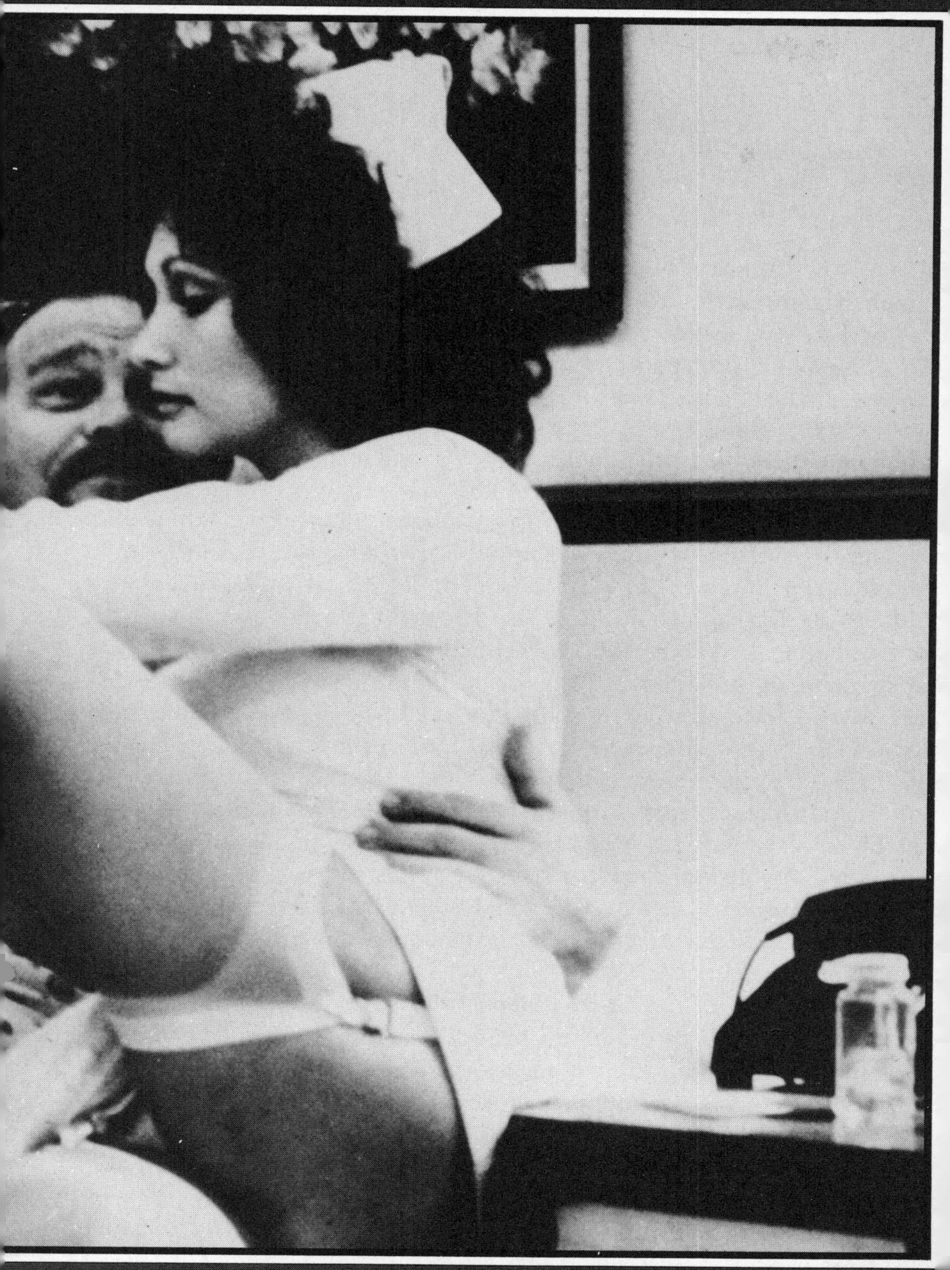

Nurse Linda Lovelace pays a motel call

Pornography at Large

LINDA LOVELACE HAD her clitoris in her throat and Woodward and Bernstein their source in the White House. That the intrepid reporters investigating the Watergate scandal referred to their mysterious news source as Deep Throat is an indication of how much attention this hardcore porno film had received. It became the landmark signifying the upheaval in sexual mores that made it possible for explicit sex acts to be seen by mixed audiences in public theaters in the United States.

For years the taboos had been eroding. The history of film has been spiced with a subplot involving the perpetual tug of war between those who consider themselves defenders of the public morality and those who urge more freedom on screen. The battles tend to define shifting attitudes, with films usually lagging behind behavior. All the arguments over "It" girls, vamps, flappers, Mae West, the Production Code of the 1930s, Hedy Lamarr running nude through the forest in *Extase* (1933), Jane Russell's cleavage in *The Outlaw* (1943), and other causes célèbres that excited the public from time to time were tame preludes to the swift changes of the 1960s. These changes were closely associated with the general tide of the tumultuous decade. Apart from the greater freedom manifest in films with higher aspirations, a ready market was waiting for purveyors of sexploitation. Softcore films were being made by Russ Meyer, Radley Metzger, and others. Authors Kenneth Turan and Stephen F. Zito reported in their 1974 book *Sinema* that five thousand sexploitation films had been made in the previous fifteen years.

The significance of *Deep Throat* reaches far beyond the porno genre. It must be viewed in the context of the history of sex on screen and of what the open appearance of pornography means with respect to the overall freedom to deal with explicit sex in motion pictures. The right to show pornography is inextricably linked to the right to present detailed sex acts in serious works. Thus the court cases that arise out of efforts to censor a hardcore film may yield decisions affecting other films. What is art to one person may be pornography in the eyes of another, which is why anyone who insists upon censorship cannot control where that censorship will lead once it takes a firm hold.

The Rating Board of the Motion Picture Association of America was established in 1968 as an outgrowth of the reaction against new freedoms in filmmaking. It was not formed to deal with pornography, but to categorize films and offer the public guidelines in the hope of avoiding the governmental censorship being sought in various states. Mores have been changing so fast that the MPAA ratings have been steadily eased; what would once have been branded X might today draw an R. A strong complaint against the board, apart from the central argument over whether films should be labeled at all (books are not), is that the X carries a stigma. The MPAA insists that this is not the intention and that the function of the X is to give producers the freedom to make an adult-only film. However, the label does reduce the number of theaters where the film can be shown, and some newspapers will not take ads for X films; the very choice of the letter, signifying a crossing out, carries a message of disapproval. The MPAA system of evaluating a script to advise a filmmaker in advance of the likely rating constituted a form of precensorship. Richard Heffner took steps to discourage this practice when he became the director of the rating board in 1974; he estimated that, by January 1979, only five percent of films rated had had scripts submitted for guidance. In such instances, he said, the filmmaker is told if his script contains specific language that would automatically determine its rating, but aside from that, it is impossible to predict the rating accurately until the finished film is screened. (According to Heffner, some filmmakers are angered by the board's reluctance to tell them what to expect on the basis of a script.) However, although theoretically a director can exercise his right to make any film, in reality – and here is where a built-in censorship operates – there are the dictates of contract commitments that depend on the avoidance of a more stringent rating, as well as the knowledge that an X or an R may lead to less money at the box office.

The rating system increasingly resembles a holding action in the face of continuing liberalization. At the time the board was founded, acceptance by at least a section of the public of actual sex on screen was predictable. In 1967, a major development occurred in Sweden – the release of Vilgot Sjöman's *I Am Curious (Yellow)*, a serious film exploring political and personal outlooks and containing scenes of simulated sex. (Because of the furor it engendered it is often unfairly called pornographic.) When I saw *I Am Curious (Yellow)* in Sweden, it was apparent that sex performed on screen would not be far off. In the United States, Customs officials seized the film and a court test developed. Critics were invited to see it and give testimony. A jury in New York upheld the action by Customs, but the decision was reversed on appeal. Before long this artistically intended work was followed by hardcore successors, crude at first but gradually becoming more ambitious. It was soon possible to walk into theaters and see wide-screen spectacles that a short while before would have been inconceivable.

The audiences were still mostly men, the briefcase and hat-in-the-lap set, furtively darting into porn houses to fantasize in the dark.

Deep Throat opened at the World Theatre on West 49th Street in New York City. "Business had already peaked and would have died in a few weeks had not the police decided to try to close us down," said Bob Sumner, then operating the World. "Attendance was average until the police handed us all that publicity. The legal action is what made *Deep Throat* take off the way it did." Sumner strove to exploit the publicity, and suddenly, with all the media attention, there was a qualitative change. Diplomats at the United Nations, writers, actors, actresses, businessmen, professors, students, and other solid citizens were openly lining up to pay $5 to see the film and then gossip about it. An article in the *New York Times* entitled "Porno chic," by reporter Ralph Blumenthal, listed among those who went to satisfy their curiosity Johnny Carson, Mike Nichols, Sandy Dennis, Ben Gazzara, Jack Nicholson, and Truman Capote.

Deep Throat was reviewed by some of the more serious film critics, and gained a reputation as a substantial improvement over run-of-the-mill hardcore, and as a film with a sense of humor and a virtuoso performer. Linda Lovelace became a star, interviewed by newspapers and magazines, and appeared on TV talk shows as the new celebrity about town. Comedians joked about her, and men lusted after her; she even turned up at the Cannes Film Festival wearing a white, Victorian-style, high-necked, lace-trimmed dress and a matching picture hat.

The protracted legal battle guaranteed steady attention. "The first week we opened we did $30,000 business," reported Sumner. "But at the time of the trial in December we did $14,000 in one day. The gross for the nine-month run at the World was $1.3 million." At the non-jury trial before Judge Joel J. Tyler in Manhattan Criminal Court, expert witnesses maintained that *Deep Throat* had redeeming social value. Dr. John W. Money, a professor of medical psychology at Johns Hopkins University, testified that watching explicit acts of fellatio, cunnilingus, and other sexual intercourse might help save marriages by removing Victorian inhibitions: "Couples would get so much joy in each other that they wouldn't keep discarding partners to seek pleasure in someone else." Judge Tyler was not convinced; he found the film obscene and it was banned in New York City. A fine of $100,000 was decreed, but was subsequently reduced to $10,000. Ironically, in Binghamton, New York, a jury did rule that *Deep Throat* had redeeming social value and was not obscene. Wicked New York City was apparently not as worldly as Binghamton.

The *Deep Throat* prosecution did not prevent other hardcore films from inundating the city. Meanwhile *Deep Throat* was booked elsewhere in the country. It was obvious that there would be many legal attacks against it and similar films, and that the entanglements would be prolonged, complex,

Linda (Linda Lovelace) and Dr. Young (Harry Reems)

costly, and possibly hazardous. But porno filmmakers, distributors, and theater operators, attracted by the high profit potential, were willing to take the risks. With the level of public response, many theaters that had never played hardcore films began to book them. In June 1973, the United States Supreme Court set forth new guidelines on obscenity, moving from the redeeming social value doctrine to a concept of local community standards determining what was obscene. Legal experts foresaw many complications, since the Court did not begin to define what constituted a community. One could envision decades of legal fights and attempts at censorship, but porno films appeared to have become a fact of life insofar as large sections of the public were concerned. With the vagueness of the Supreme Court's explanations in its five-to-four decision, the film community anguished over how non-pornographic films would be affected. In Georgia, *Carnal Knowledge* was banned as obscene, but the United States Supreme Court reversed the decision, which to some extent alleviated the fear that its 1973 obscenity rulings would automatically lead to open season on any film given an obscene label by local bluenoses.

Deep Throat, set in Florida, co-stars Linda Lovelace and Harry Reems in an absurd plot catering, as usual, to male fantasy. It seems Linda "felt no tingle" in her sex life. Alas, even orgies could not turn her on to the point of orgasm. Dr. Young (Reems) makes an astonishing discovery that will result in her sexual gratification (as well as his). Her clitoris has been misplaced by a caprice of nature – it is in her throat. Only through fellatio can she achieve climax. Linda loses no time in taking advantage of her new knowledge. With her deep throat specialty, akin to circus sword-swallowing, she devours every opportunity. Audiences marveled at her much-publicized technique. Linda's porno superstardom led to the publication of her autobiography, *Inside Linda Lovelace*. Harry Reems (real name Herbert Streicher), with the aid of writer Eugene Boe, produced his autobiography, *Here Comes Harry Reems*.

Gerard Damiano, the director of *Deep Throat*, explained how the project began: "I had done a film called *Changes*, about the sexual revolution, but with no hardcore sex in it. The people I was working with asked me to shoot some hardcore inserts. A young lady came into my office with Chuck Traynor, her husband, manager, and co-star. I thought they were right, and set up the filming for the next day. I fell in love with her immediately. She was not a glamour girl. She was more like the girl next door. People thought I was crazy to see something in her. She was wearing army-style boots and a pea jacket and was the least likely candidate to become a sex symbol, but I liked her naturalness.

"Well, we began to film, and when Linda started doing her deep throat it flipped me out. I said, 'Cut!' There was no way I wanted to waste something like that on inserts for a picture that had seen its day anyhow. So I decided to save the deep throat for a special picture. I wrote out the idea and then got the money to shoot the film in Miami. To us the big thing was a chance to get out of New York into the sun for six days. I insisted the film had to be made in a warm climate. For writing, producing, and directing, I got $150 a day, and I had an interest in the company. Linda got $100 a day and Reems $100 for one day's acting."

Figures vary as to *Deep Throat*'s box-office gross. Sumner estimated some $30 million; Damiano speculated that it was closer to $100 million, contending that there were so many pirated prints around that it was impossible to get an accurate count. The figures meant little to him at this point. After the picture became successful, he sold his share to his partner Louis Peraino for $25,000. Nicholas Gage in an article in the *New York Times* of October 12, 1975, titled "Organized Crime Reaps Huge Profits From Dealing in Pornographic Films," linked Peraino's father, Anthony Peraino, and his uncle, Joseph Peraino, with the Colombo family, and implied that Damiano might have sold his share out of fear. Damiano later insisted: "Nobody came to me and said I'd get my legs broken if I didn't sell. I was asked to stay on. But I couldn't make the kind of artistic pictures that I wanted to make. That's why I sold." Louis Peraino became president of Bryanston, a distributor of general films, and the *Times* article reported that he had used some of the profits from *Deep Throat* to help found the company, which, Gage noted, had a gross income of $20 million in 1974.

Louis, Anthony, and Joseph Peraino, Gerard Damiano Productions, and Harry Reems were among sixteen defendants convicted in April 1976, in a federal trial that promised to become a cornerstone case involving motion picture making and distribution. A jury in Memphis found *Deep Throat* obscene and the defendants guilty of a nationwide conspiracy to transport and distribute the film across state lines. The catch-all nature of the prosecution, undertaken at tremendous expense to the taxpayers (the first trial cost an estimated $4 million), was indicated by including Reems, merely an actor in the film, among the defendants. The message was clear: anyone having anything to do with a film judged obscene would be in jeopardy. Also, holding the trial in Tennessee meant that the United States Department of Justice could choose a location that afforded the probability of a guilty verdict. Linda Lovelace had been called as a prosecution witness and promised immunity, but she was reported to be in Latin America. *Variety* editorialized "there may also be a chilling effect on other filmmakers as well" and asked: "Will adventurous filmmakers now be willing to risk having their work judged by juries in places handpicked for their favorable climate for the prosecution? The Memphis trial was aimed at the hardcore pornographers who sought protection of the First Amendment right to freedom of expression. *Deep Throat* may have been an easy target. But what about tomorrow's targets for prosecutors zealous to protect local community standards? Is there a danger that serious films which challenge conventional morality will also be caught up in the dragnet?"

This prosecution tactic was developed on a wide scale by the Department of Justice, and Damiano's *The Devil in Miss Jones* was singled out as another target. (In April 1977, the conviction of Reems was reversed and the obscenity charges against him were dropped, but prosecution against others continued, with appeals where there were guilty verdicts.) It remained to be seen to what extent such trials would hamper hardcore films or interfere with other filmmaking. Experience indicates that once public attitudes have changed, a backlash may cause difficulties and hardships, but is not likely to stop the basic trend. Boredom might.

Other hardcore films that followed the appearance of *Deep Throat* included *Behind the Green Door,* starring Marilyn Chambers, who, it was learned, was the wholesome model on the Ivory Snow package. She promptly became another porno superstar, as did Georgina Spelvin in *The Devil in Miss Jones.* Satirical porn pictures also began appearing, including *S.O.S.*, in which a segment satirizing television talk shows featured Jody Maxwell and her specialty of singing while performing fellatio. *Pussy Talk,* an import from France, where pornographic films surfaced after having been illegal, had a plot with a talking vagina as the gimmick, a sort of lower-level *Exorcist.* Many theaters had begun to specialize in gay porn, as well as films featuring sadism and masochism. At the New York Film Festival in the fall of 1975, the selection of *Exhibition,* a porn film from France, gave it art status before its commercial opening.

Commenting on the audience observed watching *Exhibition* at the Fine Arts Theater in New York City, critic John Simon wrote in *New York* magazine:

> It is packed with matrons with their Bloomingdale's shopping bags, with couples and individuals of all ages, classes, and sexes. Though there may be no clear evidence that the audience is enjoying itself, neither is there the slightest sign of shock. Yet less than ten years ago such a thing would have been held impossible by most decent bag-carrying Bloomingdalians.

Not all audiences were ready for hardcore. But mindful of the desire for titillation, major companies were getting into the distribution of pseudo-porn films like *The Story of O,* a sado-masochistic saga presented in such a pretty package that it was more like whipped cream than whipped flesh, or *Emmanuelle,* a glossy picture about the sexual escapades of the wife of a French diplomat in Thailand. The situations could be explicit, the nudity flagrant, and the sexual preferences varied, but the films avoided close-ups of nerve endings. Both the soft and hardcore varieties were shown nationally, and suburban filmgoing patterns changed along with those in the cities.

The makers of hardcore films, at first content with the prospect of making huge grosses on low budgets, began to seek ways of infusing their films with better production values to make porn more respectable and professional. No matter what story lines were dreamed up or how attractive the photography and settings, the films still boiled down to repetitious body mechanics that became boring and degrading in the isolation of sex from psyche. Women in particular have found the films offensive, as their basis is usually the treatment of women as sex objects for the gratification of the male. Occasional attempts to produce porn from a woman's viewpoint have not been successful.

What happens if performers in the regular run of films decide to go all the way? Would the function of pornography be preempted? The idea might still seem somewhat farfetched, but we appear to be approaching that point. Marlon Brando and Maria Schneider flirted with the possibility in *Last Tango in Paris;* Donald Sutherland and Julie Christie were closer in *Don't Look Now.* The likelihood of major stars having sexual relations in films is intriguing. Of course, there would be new opportunities for stand-ins whenever a Burt Reynolds, Robert Redford, Paul Newman, or John Travolta could not match the dependability of a Harry Reems. We are a long way from the time when kissing on screen was considered daring.

Perhaps the momentum will be halted, but the combination of profit incentive and changing mores may prove mightier than backlash and obscenity prosecutions. *Deep Throat* is not only a landmark that dramatizes the social upheaval, but its position as a test case for free expression has reinforced its importance to the future of filmmaking as a whole.

DEEP THROAT
USA (Gerard Damiano Productions) 1972

Cast

Linda .... LINDA LOVELACE
Dr. Young .... HARRY REEMS

Running time .... 70 minutes
Color
Produced by .... JERRY GERARD (GERARD DAMIANO)
Directed by .... JERRY GERARD
Written by .... JERRY GERARD
Edited by .... JERRY GERARD
Set Design .... LEN CAMP

1973

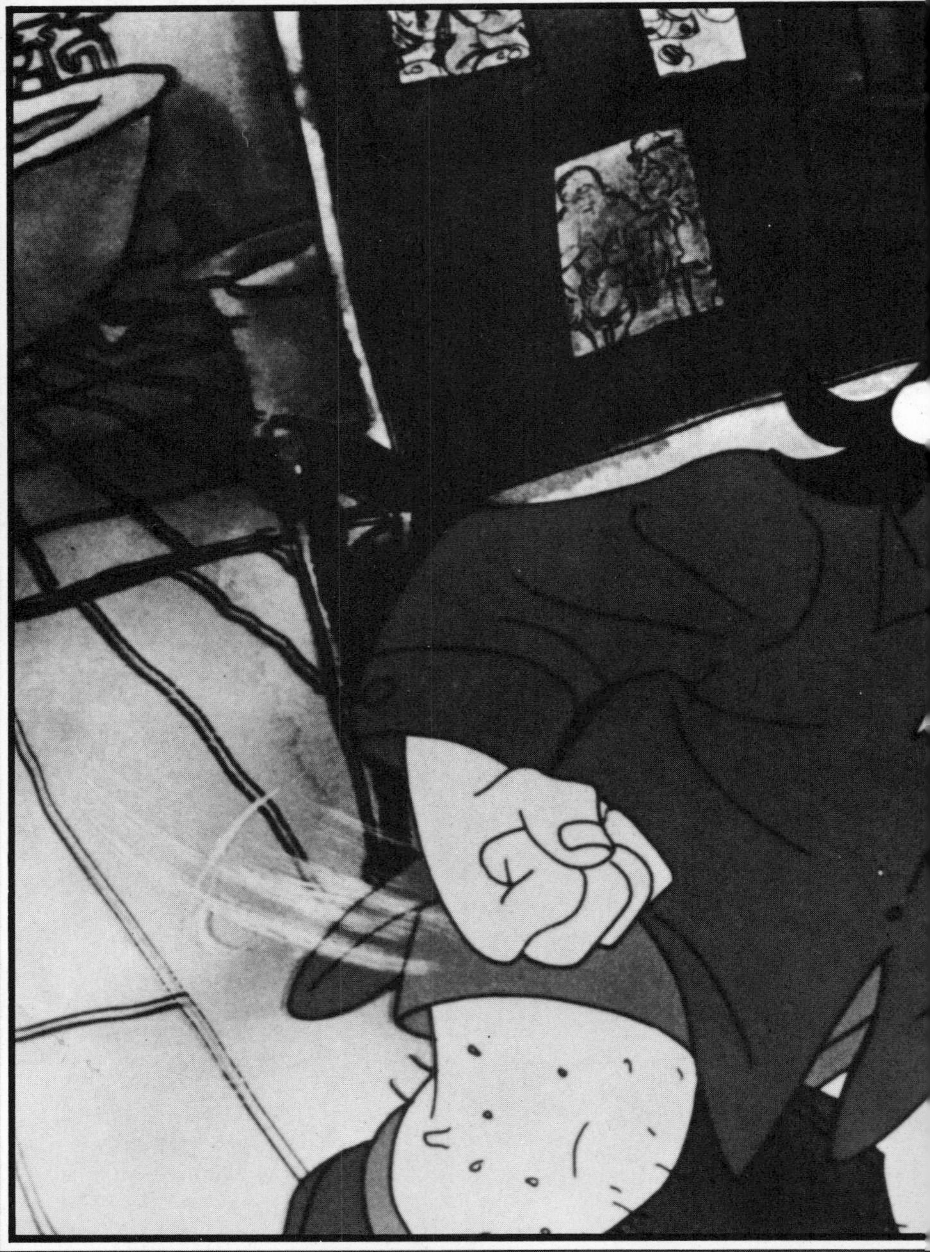

Angelo and Ida – a family quarrel

The New Animation

WALT DISNEY'S domination of animation both advanced the art and restrained it. Because Disney's success was such that he became a national institution, the public regards his films as synonymous with the entire process and use of animation. But why should the medium be reserved for bland entertainment? Ralph Bakshi had the audacity, talent, and vision to pose this question. He passionately wanted to use animation to express his viewpoint on life, and his *Heavy Traffic* stridently illustrates the art's potential for social comment. Bakshi was not universally welcomed for his daring. Hailed for his brilliance, he was also vilified as a heretic who had profaned the wholesome domain generally associated with cartoon characters. The situation was aggravated by the Motion Picture Association of America, which applied an X rating to the film, thereby debasing it in the public mind.

For Bakshi the issue was clear: "I believe in the right to use animation to make personal films. The feature film has been used by directors to express themselves emotionally, as Martin Scorsese did with *Mean Streets*. Why shouldn't the animator make a feature film for similar purposes? I did *Heavy Traffic* as an emotional experience. It obviously worked as a movie, and achieved a lot of recognition."

Bakshi, who was thirty-three when he made *Heavy Traffic,* grew up in ghetto conditions in Brownsville, Brooklyn. He attended the High School of Industrial Arts in Manhattan and then became an animator for CBS. Later, he obtained a job operating the cartoon studio for Paramount, and when he met writer, producer, and director Steve Krantz, who was working in television, they formed their own company and made *Fritz the Cat* (1972). Based on Robert Crumb's underground comic character, it outlandishly satirizes the political and social turbulence of the 1960s. The problem with *Fritz* is that it is funny in its pornographically tinged exploits but muddled in its sociology. However, the animation is provocative in concept, pointing to new use of the medium. Bakshi's work in *Heavy Traffic* is far more significant, meriting recognition as a pioneering step.

Among the first to recognize the film's brilliance was Willard Van Dyke, then director of the department of film at the Museum of Modern Art, who scheduled a special preview at the museum. Later, including *Heavy Traffic* in his ten best list that year, *New York Times* critic Vincent Canby judged it "by far the most original, far-out, imaginative, courageous, outrageous movie of 1973, a blend of animation and live action that extends the frontiers of filmmaking techniques in a way that no one else has done in years."

Bakshi created a world of funky characters in New York, born of his own experiences growing up in the city. Never had animation been used with so much cynicism. The humor is guaranteed to offend; the drawings are amusingly vulgar, with voices to match. The characters are gross, their lives a cauldron of disaster. The "cast" of *Heavy Traffic* includes Michael Collino, a young, introverted cartoonist, his orthodox Jewish mother (Ida), his Italian father (Angelo), a black barmaid (Carole), a neighborhood transvestite (Snowflake), Mafia types, and a further imaginative assortment. Their fate is to be buffeted by each other or by circumstances. They are peculiarly likable, funny, and human.

Michael is distracted from his drawing board by the battles between his mother and father, the latter a labor leader with Mafia connections and a mistress. Michael's mother, trying to kill her husband, bashes his skull with a frying pan, drags him to her oven, puts his head in, and turns on the gas. When Angelo regains consciousness because of the noise made by the escaping gas, he seeks help from Michael, who, exasperated by the family hostilities, retreats to the roof. There the boys on the block are taking turns with neighborly Rosalyn Schecter. In the excitement of his great opportunity, Michael, still a virgin, accidentally pushes her off the roof. She is left dangling on the clothesline that breaks her fall.

Ensuing plot developments include Michael's involvement with Carole, a dock strike, and Angelo's hiring of a legless bouncer named Shorty to kill Carole. Shorty has his own reasons for wanting to eliminate both Carole and Michael. Bakshi has two endings: in the cartoon finale, Michael is shot in the head when Shorty catches up with them. In a brief reprise, Michael and Carole, now played by live performers, meet in Union Square and face the future happily.

There are ironies in the charges of excessive violence and bad taste leveled at *Heavy Traffic*. Traditional animation has been saturated with violence. Cartoon shorts have featured incessant eye-for-an-eye battles between antagonists; the basic assumption is that it is amusing to watch cartoon characters do horrible things to each other. This does not seem to bother parents who deposit their youngsters in a theater for an afternoon, or permit them to watch violent animated – or live – programs on television.

Let the violence become more meaningful in a manner designed to make such behavior repugnant, and the furor begins. This is as true for Bakshi as it is for Stanley Kubrick, who made the violence of *A Clockwork Orange* an upsetting experience. *Heavy Traffic*'s greatest audacity was to challenge the myths that had been built around the animation of unreality and show that the medium could be used to express reality.

The controversy surrounding *Heavy Traffic* was minimal compared to that triggered by *Coonskin,* Bakshi's next film, in which he attempted to comment on the ordeal of being black in America. The Congress of Racial Equality attacked his film as racist. This seemed patently unfair and even absurd, a pressure group's mechanical response to the work of an artist who wanted to use caricature to illuminate injustice, instead of merely drawing pretty pictures. Understandably, all groups espousing causes want idealistic portrayals, but Bakshi is too free a spirit for that sort of conformity.

The campaign against *Coonskin* was effective in pressuring Paramount to withdraw as distributor, but the controversy only served to underscore the achievement of Bakshi in the field. That animation could arouse such passions confirmed that he had made a qualitative leap from Disneyism. As Stanley Kauffmann wrote in the *New Republic:*

> From the wry joke of the title on, this film is not against groups – it's against snarling, short-sighted, scrabbling, egocentric, murderous American city life, particularly as it beats up on blacks. Progressively through his three films Bakshi, who is white, has staked his territory– the American city as hell, racially torn hell, engulfing people who are learning how to live in hell. *Coonskin* is an obviously flawed but fierce little work of art, done at a high level of imaginative energy and with some touches of brilliance.

Critic Richard Eder also came to Bakshi's defense in the *New York Times:*

> *Coonskin* clearly is savage, and a cartoon clearly is a caricature. But it seems stupid and blind not to see that Bakshi is making a most serious and difficult kind of artistic commitment in trying to capture black Harlem's human condition by heightening rather than softening its miseries. The propriety of a white man's doing so is another matter. In recent attacks on Bakshi the suggestion is that he has committed an act of social effrontery. He has, of course. It has always been an act of effrontery to twist human life into art.

Although there are creative limitations on what Bakshi has attempted to do, the technology itself does not appear to be a problem to him. "My approach is basically a classical one technically," Bakshi said. "I use a staff of 150 to 200 in working on a picture. If anything, it is easier than a live feature in the sense that I know what I am going to get. I mean, I don't have to hire a Marlon Brando to do a part and then worry about his screwing it up. An actor is not going to change a character on me. Also, if something doesn't work the way you want it to, you can just redraw the scene, and

Father and son – Angelo a labor leader with Mafia connections, Michael a cartoonist

not be confronted with footage you have already shot and are stuck with. Six months later I can still redraw the scene." The budget can also be an advantage. Bakshi made *Heavy Traffic* for $850,000.

The difficulties stem from the dramatic limitations of animation. Bakshi disagreed with Steve Krantz, who, while enthusiastic about animation as an art form, saw a problem in realizing characters that, in two-dimensional drawings, can be sufficiently complex to reach the emotions deeply. Bakshi did not recognize this as a problem, but from this critic's viewpoint, it definitely does exist. Sustaining cartoon characters for a feature-length film is another burden. Bakshi has resorted to something others have done – combining live actors with animated characters. This is an uneasy mixture, since the appearance of a live performer accents the inadequacies of animation or is at best gratuitous. The live ending of *Heavy Traffic* does not work well as it undercuts what has gone before.

Bakshi acknowledged a shortcoming in his work. "I am not a writer and would like to collaborate with good writers," he said. He has usually done his own writing and scripts are the weakest components of his films. This is a serious handicap for a filmmaker attempting to make significant statements. Bakshi's ideas are extremely powerful and varied, but once he has introduced them, he is not always able to provide sufficient depth to give his films intellectual impact. Skillful writers attuned to his goals could increase his scope, and his awareness of this is in itself a hopeful sign.

The Bakshi achievement has not been the only animation advance since the predominance of Disney, although it is by far the most revolutionary. The UPA cartoons of the late 1940s and 1950s delighted audiences by displaying a sophisticated sense of humor. Ernest Pintoff's excellent satirical cartoons, such as *The Critic* (1963), and the body of work of John and Faith Hubley went far in delineating, often in a moving as well as an amusing manner, existence in the modern world. *The Yellow Submarine* (1968), revolving around The Beatles and their music, is a joyous, contemporary use of the medium, but still primarily for light entertainment. Interesting experiments have taken place throughout the world, including Czechoslovakia, the Soviet Union, Poland, Canada, Japan, and France. There is new technical and artistic potential in computer animation. By coordinating points of movement, a computer can be programmed to produce the multiple drawings needed to show motion between those points. A pioneer of this method, Peter Foldes, presented his work at the Cannes and New York film festivals. His *Hunger* is a particularly clever, entertaining short about compulsive eating.

Bakshi, elaborating on his philosophy, said: "I am not interested in much of what I see happening in animation because I think it is mainly art for art's sake. Animation for that purpose doesn't interest me. It is much too precious for that. The battle is still on. I see animation as a social force, and also as a director's medium as opposed to a producer's medium, the way it was in the days of Disney and Max Fleischer.

"But the problem is a big one. To get the financing is difficult, and to get an adult audience for animation is even more difficult, as is my battle with the people in the animation industry who are afraid to step out. They want to stay with what is safe and sure. In the long run it will probably defeat me. I find there is more of a respect for animation in Italy, France, Germany, and Belgium, where *Heavy Traffic* and *Fritz the Cat* did very well. In France, they have exhibited comic strips in the Louvre."

Despite Bakshi's pessimism, born of his lonely struggle to become an animation *auteur* with an uncompromising mission, he has already succeeded in changing previous conceptions of what animation can do. His futuristic *Wizards* (1977), an ambitious statement about survival, and his adaptation of J.R.R. Tolkien's *The Lord of the Rings* (1978), which he first filmed live as a guide for his animation, further demonstrate how far Bakshi has taken the art.

HEAVY TRAFFIC

USA (American International Pictures) 1973

Cast

Michael . . . . Joseph Kaufman
Carole . . . . Beverly Hope Atkinson
Angelo . . . . Frank De Kova
Ida . . . . Terri Haven
Molly . . . . Mary Dean Lauria
Rosalyn . . . . Jacqueline Mills
Rosa . . . . Lillian Adams
Also featuring the voices of . . . . Jim Bates, Jamie Farr, Robert Easton, Charles Gordone, Michael Brandon, Morton Lewis, Bill Strigolis, Jay Lawrence, Lee Weaver, Phyllis Thompson, Kim Hamilton, Carol Graham, Candy Candido, Helene Winston, William Keene, Peter Hobbs, John Bleifer
Characters created by . . . . Ralph Bakshi

Running time . . . . 76 minutes
Color by DeLuxe
Presented by . . . . Samuel Z. Arkoff
Produced by . . . . Steve Krantz
Directed by . . . . Ralph Bakshi
Written by . . . . Ralph Bakshi

Sleeper

Masquerading as a robot servant, Miles Monroe (Woody Allen) gets high from passing around an orb that turns people on when they fondle it.

Comedy for the Future

"COMEDIANS LIKE MYSELF have to find a new vocabulary," Woody Allen said one afternoon in a conversation about *Sleeper* and its relationship to the future of comedy. "Keaton worked on a railroad train, Chaplin worked in the setting of factories and technology. But now what's in the air all around us is much more cerebral and psychological. No one has yet really found a formula to express that in contemporary comedy." Allen has been in hot pursuit of that goal. *Sleeper* was his transition film – his leap from comedy writer and performer dabbling in film to accomplished director. It set him on the path that led to his great human comedies *Annie Hall* and *Manhattan*, which, together with his drama *Interiors*, solidified his reputation as a foremost American filmmaker.

Sleeper, in addition to being funny, offered evidence that Allen was developing in a direction that would propel film comedy forward substantially. Not since the Marx Brothers and Chaplin has there been a comic artist with the dimension of talent Allen exhibits. In *Sleeper* Allen's intent is clear. He is fusing earlier traditions of comedy with what he sees as contemporary requirements. "We were trying to do old-fashioned slapstick comedy, but we also gave it a more modern interpretation," Allen said of the film, which he wrote with his friend Marshall Brickman in the first of their brilliant series of screen collaborations. The sight gags depend on clever visual use of elaborate props, costumes, and sets. The misadventures of the hero are not merely comic incidents, but comments on living patterns, depersonalization, runaway technology, and control by a superstate. Allen, today's comic conscience among filmmakers, takes a contemporary character in the image of his own comedy persona and reaches for cinematic solutions to show the absurdities of man at odds with his environment. "It's very hard to do a contemporary comedy," Allen stressed, "because we're living in an intensely psychological era where what's funny between people is not really visual and interesting on the screen. In *Sleeper* we fake it by taking us out of the present and into the future."

The year is 2173 in an America that has become an authoritarian, lobotomized state ruled by The Leader. Members of an underground resistance group have found a capsule containing a man cryogenically preserved two hundred years earlier. They surreptitiously defrost the mummylike figure wrapped in aluminum foil to reveal Woody Allen, still wearing his glasses. In this society, where everyone is scrutinized and tabulated, they hope to enlist the alien, the only person without identification, to help them uncover the sinister Aires project. Woody, according to records found in the capsule, is Miles Monroe, an unsuccessful clarinet player who was part owner of the Happy Carrot Health Food Store in Greenwich Village. He thinks he is awakening in St. Vincent's Hospital, where he was admitted for a routine ulcer operation in 1973 expecting to be discharged in five days. Difficulties begin immediately when security police become suspicious.

The freeze-happy Miles, emerging from two centuries of unconsciousness, which he later describes as "like spending a weekend in Beverly Hills," goes through a lovely slapstick sequence of total disorientation. Still dazed, he is whisked away in a futuristic car to temporary safety. Miles learns that the world he knew was destroyed when Albert Shanker, president of the United Federation of Teachers, got hold of a nuclear warhead. Only a few artifacts remain. Shown some photographs in the hope that he can explain who the subjects were, he identifies Charles de Gaulle – a French chef; Norman Mailer – he donated his ego to the Harvard Medical School; President Richard Nixon – each time he left the White House the silverware was counted. From television clips of Howard Cosell the people of 2173 have deduced that watching him was a punishment devised for those who had committed crimes against the state. Miles's questioners are amazed at the craze for organic foods in his time, when people were ignorant of the healthful properties of deep fat and hot fudge.

The security police intrude again and Miles flees, masquerading as one of a group of robot servants he sees in a truck. He is delivered to a house to become the domestic of a pretty but vacuous poet, Luna Schlosser (Diane Keaton), who blithely writes poems about butterflies turning into caterpillars. Allen's world of robot servants is far more than a droll idea. While retaining the concept of depersonalization found in *Modern Times,* it also encompasses man's endeavor to harness technology to make living effortless by means of ultra-automation. Confronting Miles with the need to behave like a robot pits the human species against mechanization with hilarious consequences. An instant pudding he has mixed swells menacingly out of control and he beats it with a broom. During a party Luna's guests turn on by fondling a silver orb. Since Miles must pass the orb from guest to guest he becomes increasingly spaced out and lunges for one of the women. Although she wriggles free, the fact that she is not fazed by a robot's advances is an amusing comment on a society so entangled in mechanization. Even funnier than this chic group of dilettantes getting high with an orb is Allen's use of the orgasmatron, into which couples step for instant sexual gratification without the bother of intercourse.

Luna, delightfully and skillfully played by superb comedienne Keaton, thinks Miles ugly and takes him to a robot shop to have his head changed. He observes in terror the frightening process of heads being crushed and wrenched from their plastic bodies. A good sight gag, this is also a grimly comic forecast of human fate in a system that makes little differentiation between people and objects. Miles manages to escape and in desperation tells Luna who he is. When she tries to turn him in he kidnaps her. The sight jokes are never far from satire. Searching for food, Miles, in the role of the male hunter-provider, comes across a garden of gargantuan fruits and vegetables – horticulture triumphant – and a man leading a giant chicken. He removes the peel of a massive banana and keeps slipping on it. Luna is not satisfied with their repast. She is his prisoner but as she munches on a mammoth stalk of celery she berates him for not having any wine or dessert. The scene also ridicules the proverbial battle between man and woman, as well as people's penchant for dissatisfaction and complaint.

They stop at the house of homosexuals who have a gay robot. There Luna alerts the authorities, but is herself branded an enemy of the state because of her exposure to the alien. Now they are both fugitives and Allen stages a wild chase. Miles vainly tries to fly in an inflated, balloonlike suit. A hole is shot in it, and with Luna on his back, he jets across a lake. Another perfect illustration of Allen's ability to employ sight gags for satire is their discovery during their flight of a 200-year-old Volkswagen that starts instantly.

Miles is captured and put through a reorientation process. Luna joins the revolutionaries. They rescue an unwilling Miles and re-reorientate him by means of drama-therapy sessions that recreate the home environment in which he grew up. Luna struggles with a Yiddish accent; Miles lapses into an impersonation of Blanche DuBois in *A Streetcar Named Desire,* with Luna sustaining the mood by accurately imitating Marlon Brando as Stanley Kowalski. Subsequently, Miles and Luna inadvertently learn the details of the Aires project. A bomb has destroyed The Leader, except for his nose; the rest is to be restored by cloning. Miles and Luna, pretending to be doctors, are mistaken for the experts who are to accomplish the feat. They are soon found out, but Miles leads their escape by holding a fake gun to the sacred nose, which in the confusion is flattened by a steamroller.

A Woody Allen film is to be seen, not described. There are laughs at nearly every turn. Once having developed the robot idea, Allen carries it to further extremes. During his reorientation, Miles is given a robot dog. He goes to be measured for a suit by two robot tailors who look like ticker-tape machines but talk like quarreling business partners in New York's garment district. The lack of personal relationships is underscored beautifully in the one really intimate conversation between Miles and Luna. He tries to convince her that he can give her more sexual pleasure than the orgasmatron. She reminds him that he hasn't had sex for two hundred years. "Two hundred and four, if you count my marriage," he complains.

Will it fly?

Allen manages to convey the endless battle against repression, and the struggle for survival. That he can blend these and other elements into comedy laced with jokes, gadgets, chases, and slapstick is a tribute to his performing and creative skills. His acting style is a blend of Buster Keaton, Lloyd, Chaplin, the Marxes, and a touch of Bob Hope. He has the gift of thinking uninhibitedly in the spirit of *Duck Soup,* and his conceptions are more intellectually sophisticated than those of other director-comedians. Mel Brooks can also be satirical, uproarious, and exuberantly free, but Allen has the literary and philosophical dimension to further enrich his comedy without sacrificing its mass entertainment appeal. Even allowing for the cherished talents of Brooks, Jacques Tati in France, or the Monty Python contingent in Britain, Allen is unequaled as a comedy *auteur*.

"One of the two most difficult aspects of making *Sleeper,*" Allen recalled, "was getting futuristic locations for the budget we had. [The film was shot in Colorado and California.] It was not a big-budget picture, so it's not like Kubrick makes *2001* and spends $12 million. The budget was originally two million, but it went up to three, which is not a lot of money. For that we had to build automobiles and interior sets. The other difficulty was getting the physical jokes to work, having me able to fly in the suit, be shot through water, and hang from a ladder and from a building. The film was supposed to be shot in fifty days but it took me a hundred. Until this picture I had never gone a day over schedule.

"In a certain sense *Everything You've Always Wanted to Know About Sex* [1972] was a sort of turning point film for me. *Take the Money and Run* [1969] and *Bananas* [1971] were fun to make, but real crude in terms of the way they look. I shot them fast and inexpensively, and did the best I could. On the *Sex* picture I started to get more interested and more knowledgeable about how to work the camera, how to get the color, and how to work with sets and make that stuff effective. Some of this is reflected in that picture, although I hadn't really hit it. In *Sleeper* I felt I finally knew how to make a film, and consequently it cost me an extra million and another fifty days. United Artists got a little worried, but not very. They've always been very nice."

Allen began his career as a gag writer. (His parents had hoped he would become a pharmacist.) Born in Brooklyn in 1935 as Allen Stewart Konigsberg, he grew up as a shy person who hated school. By his senior year in high school, he began doing one-liners for a publicity agent, and was hired at $40 a week to write jokes for columnists. At New York University Allen managed to fail a course in motion picture production. NBC television offered him $175 a week in their Writers' Development Program and at eighteen, he was sent to Hollywood. His reputation for gag-writing spread, his earnings eventually climbing to $1,700 a week.

After watching Mort Sahl, Allen decided to try to perform his own material. His debut was in 1960 at the Blue Angel in New York, and he became a star performer in night clubs, on television, and on records. As Allen had long been a film buff, his turning to cinema was as logical as it was fortunate. He has had two plays on Broadway *(Don't Drink the Water* and *Play it Again, Sam);* he writes satirical articles for the *New Yorker,* the *New Republic*, and *Esquire*, and has published books *(Getting Even* and *Without Feathers)*. He is also a jazz clarinetist and is heard on the soundtrack of *Sleeper*. His film *Love and Death* (1975), rich in cinematic and literary parodies, further reflects the scope of his interests.

The perpetual challenge for any filmmaker is to advance and avoid making the same picture again and again. Allen is acutely aware of both the problems and the opportunities for the artist who moves ahead. "As Chaplin got older he started to try to say things with comedy. Most of the time he failed, but his instinct was correct. He wasn't stagnating. He was trying to grow, but not making it. He was better off than the Marx Brothers, who just did the same things. Whether *A Night at the Opera* or *The Big Store,* it was the same picture all the time. And great. That's fine, but Chaplin was a much more interesting artist. I feel a certain vague general ballpark similarity with him because, basically, I'm not really an aggressive comedian like Groucho, nor an insulter. I tend to be slightly more on the victim's side, like Chaplin, only occasionally aggressive. I'm talking very generally. And the same thing with Bob Hope. I think he shares those traits, too, a kind of vanity with women, a sort of cowardice, but in the end, he tries to be heroic. These things are shared by most comedians – Buster Keaton is like that, too – they are human-being comedians. The Marx Brothers aren't. They are a totally different phenomenon, just like some freakish force of nature let loose. They come in and they're just hilarious, but you never fear for Groucho's life, nor really feel very much, not even for Harpo in the so-called sentimental scenes. That's not what's great about Harpo; he's much funnier when he's not sentimental and not very moving when he is sentimental.

"It is impossible not to be influenced by earlier comedies, but you can't do the stuff that they did. You have to come up with a different kind of comedy that hasn't been done before, because those other forms are finished. The Marx Brothers were unique to themselves and begin and end with the Marx Brothers. You can't do a Marx Brothers-type film. The silent films are also over. You can put in some physical jokes, but what is needed is a new kind of screen comedy that takes into account the problems of today, when the whole playing area has become psychological. Somebody has got to come up with a form that works for now, where you can do a contemporary comedy about people living in New York or Texas or wherever, and it's a cinematic comedy, but it won't be in the antiquated slapstick style. It will be a style that expresses sort of a cerebral kind of lifestyle, but in physical terms.

"The closest example I can think of is that sometimes Ingmar Bergman experiments with the medium and does things that can only be done in cinema. They can't be done on the stage or anywhere else. They take advantage of the enormous complex subtlety of psychology between people. And it's cinematic, but the conflict between people is enormously internalized. You have to do that with comedy somehow. It's very difficult. That's why you don't see many comedies. I don't think even Mel Brooks or I have yet come up with a form that really defines what cinema comedy should be now. No one has come up with a way of expressing the contemporary person. That's why the contemporary sensibility has been more expressed in novels. You know, Philip Roth, Salinger, writers like that. They are very cerebral and introspective, and it's very hard to put that up on screen. There was a real effort in the film *Play It Again, Sam* [1972], a most commercial, lightweight attempt. I mean that, instinctively, without knowing what I was doing, or thinking about this, it was an attempt to show a guy's internal thought processes, his internal conflicts before he made the move to kiss his best friend's wife, things like that. The form wasn't really right at the time, but the instinct was correct.

"Fellini's *8½* is a very good example of a style reference. That's where the playing area is. If I do a comedy and I play someone remotely connected with myself, not a Russian in 1700 or someone lost in the future, you'll accept me as a contemporary, reasonably normal person living in rational circumstances, and what's funny is what happens to me. But I'm not a factory worker among machines that don't work. You can't cast me that way. No one would believe it. And those are not the problems that interest people now. It's an electronic world now, so if you showed a factory, it would not have the kind of machines they had in *Modern Times.* It would be enormously electronic and computerized. Everything has gone to electronics and the brain. No one has found a way to really show that on screen, to show the dilemma of the comedian as modern man interpreted comically in a way that's genuinely cinematic. *8½* is a good analogy. So are *Cries and Whispers* and *Persona*; they are very interesting because they can only be done in cinema. They illuminate the conflicts that we're involved in and are interesting to us today."

Allen agreed that his scene in *Everything You Always Wanted to Know About Sex* showing the physiological workings of an orgasm in a science-fiction manner was an illustration of his point. "That is one way of doing it, of in some way making photographic the internal conflict. The contemporary conflicts are within yourself. They're neurotic conflicts between you and your girl friend, or you and your parents. They're not the conflicts of the Depression, of having to make a living, or guys working in factories. They're much less clearly visual, much more subtle. They make you crazy. They're much harder to get a grip on, and very hard for a comedian to get a grip on without simply doing verbal comedy. The way of visualizing that would be something really worth working for. In *Sleeper* there was some attempt at that, of fusing visual jokes and more cerebral jokes, but it's a tough thing to do.

"Fellini tried in *Juliet of the Spirits* to deal with the inner state of a woman who was going through a life crisis. He wasn't completely successful at it, but he was trying to deal with that conflict in a visual way that could only be done in the movies. He didn't deal with it by talking about her husband cheating on her, or taking all those problems and making jokes about it. But you saw the world through her eyes, and it became very exaggerated and visual. The colors were very pronounced and the images were enormously bizarre and rococo. But this hasn't really been approached yet in comedy, although that is where I think it is going. However, it is much tougher to deal with primary experience because it is psychological. In the course of a day I don't get up in the morning and have a conveyer belt screwed on me. I get up and go to an analyst, I call some girl for a date, I have dinner, and I obsess over something. That's very hard to put on screen, so we get reduced to seeking content sources in secondary material.

"I am going to make an attempt. Otherwise, what happens is that you make the same film, and it's just a question of time before your films have no more importance. Nobody cares. They've seen it, they've enjoyed it, they've paid you money to make it, and then they want something from somebody else. But if the movie maintains that event quality so they can't predict what you're going to come out with next, it isn't just another Woody Allen movie. Conceivably it won't work, and then I'll feel bad, but there's nothing you can do about it. Sure, you have an enormous fear of not being successful that you have to fight against. But once success becomes the goal, I think you're dead. You must have the fun of working as a goal. It would be better if you just did the film and didn't care whether it succeeded, because then you'd be freer. Once you have an eye on 'will it succeed or not?' you start to sell yourself out. It's a real tough fight."

Allen has shown that it is possible to discover ways of using film for comedy parallel with the ways Fellini and Bergman approach drama. *Sleeper* was not internal enough to achieve such a lofty goal, but it was clearly a departure point in Allen's explorations and led to *Annie Hall* (1977), in which he put his theories to the test and further demonstrated his artistic growth. Allen's disciplined use of humor to comment on the joy and pain of human contact, and his heightened reflectiveness make this widely honored film serious and endearing as well as clever and hilarious. Next, he surprised fans with his Bergmanesque *Interiors* (1978); it was not a comedian's misguided fling at tragedy, but a powerful, haunting drama that showed his ability to apply his talents to difficult new terrain.

With *Manhattan* (1979), Allen comes closer to finding new "cerebral and psychological" film comedy levels. In it he displays the rare artistic gift of making us simultaneously roar with laughter and feel the nervous tension and open wounds of characters struggling to cope with their complex relationships. *Manhattan* is about many things – the pain we inflict, our own hurt, our missed opportunities. A wistful ending, reminiscent of Chaplin's *City Lights*, sums up the underlying sadness, but Allen's irrepressible comedy and his love-letter affection for New York also suggest what Chaplin was extolling in *Modern Times* – our indomitability. Allen's extraordinary body of work has solidly established him as the heir to the great comic traditions of the past and as a vital force for setting new standards in both comedy and drama. Perhaps in the real world of 2173 they will be looking at the films of Woody Allen in puzzling over this civilization's cultural artifacts.

SLEEPER
USA (United Artists) 1973

Cast

Miles Monroe .... Woody Allen
Luna Schlosser .... Diane Keaton
Erno Windt .... John Beck
Dr. Melik .... Mary Gregory
Dr. Tyron .... Don Keefer
Dr. Agon .... Don McLiam
Dr. Orva .... Bartlett Robinson
Rainer Krebs .... Chris Forbes
Dr. Nero .... Marya Small
Dr. Dean .... Peter Hobbs
Ellen Pogrebin .... Susan Miller
M.C. .... Lou Picetti
Woman in the Mirror .... Jessica Rains
Herald Cohen .... Brian Avery
Jeb .... Spencer Milligan
Sears Swiggles .... Spencer Ross

Running time .... 88 minutes
Color
A Jack Rollins-Charles H. Joffe Production
Executive Producer .... Charles H. Joffe
Produced by .... Jack Grossberg
Directed by .... Woody Allen
Written by .... Woody Allen and Marshall Brickman
1st Assistant Director .... Fred T. Gallo
2nd Assistant Director .... Henry J. Lange, Jr.
Director of Photography .... David M. Walsh
Camera Operator .... Roger Shearman
Production Designer .... Dale Hennesy
Set Designer .... Dianne Wager
Set Decorator .... Gary Moreno
Special Effects .... A.D. Flowers
Sound Mixer .... Jack Solomon
Location Special Effects .... Gerald Endler
Casting .... Lynn Stalmaster
Costume Designer .... Joel Schumacher
Make-up .... Del Acevedo
Hair Stylist .... Janice Brunson
Edited by .... Ralph Rosenblum
Music by .... Woody Allen with the Preservation Hall Jazz Band and The New Orleans Funeral and Ragtime Orchestra

1975

Nashville

Barbara Jean (Ronee Blakley) and Haven Hamilton (Henry Gibson) sing at a political rally.

New Forms

NASHVILLE is the most versatile American film since *Citizen Kane*. Orson Welles made his impact with startling technical virtuosity; the contribution of Robert Altman's colorful epic is the liberation of film from past forms, enabling it to become more free and expansive. *Nashville* is a gigantic happening that is comic, tragic, entertaining, jolting, spectacular, and contemplative. It is also a musical. Altman tapped his energy resources – script, acting, music, locale, ideas – to make a film somewhat Felliniesque, but peculiarly indigenous to the American scene. It is an inspired combination of semi-improvisation, showmanship, and a soundtrack emancipated from convention. The result is not only entertaining, but finally upsetting, for the film captures the smoldering contradictions of a troubled, assassination-prone society. Political columnist Tom Wicker, praising *Nashville* in the *New York Times,* called the film "a two-and-a-half hour cascade of minutely detailed vulgarity, greed, deceit, cruelty, barely contained hysteria, and the frantic lack of root and grace into which American life has been driven by its own heedless vitality."

"I think Stanley Kubrick and I are attempting to do the same thing, attempting to break form," Altman said in January 1976, the morning after being awarded plaques for best picture and best director by the New York Film Critics Circle. "Kubrick probably does it in a purer way than I do. I try it from a different level. I try to sneak into a viewer's mind in a conventional way, and do it from there out. I'm trying to tell everything backwards, to have the audience know when something happens but not know how they got into it. In the case of the assassination in *Nashville* I was constantly pointing arrows toward it."

Whereas Kubrick thrives on careful planning and total, almost obsessive, control of all components to transport his audience into his film atmosphere, Altman has moved steadily in the direction of overwhelming the viewer with films made in a spontaneous, cooperative manner. He moves into an area with his entourage, as he did in Nashville, the country and western music capital, and out of the total involvement and the collective talents of the group, inspired and forged by a director who treats the medium as a throbbing, living organism, a film emerges. Joan Tewkesbury wrote an environmental rather than a conventional script, and Altman expected his actors to flesh out characterizations by drawing upon their own backgrounds and instincts. Likewise, in contrast to the customary way of creating a musical by hiring professional composers, lyricists, and arrangers, Altman asked his performers, some of whom were experienced at composing but most of whom were not, to write their own songs. All the music was performed live, not post-synchronized. It was arranged and supervised by twenty-five-year-old Richard Baskin, who also wrote the music and the lyrics for many of the songs. A spectrum of talent is reflected in the twenty-seven numbers, and the Academy Award for best song of 1975, *Nashville*'s "I'm Easy," went to actor Keith Carradine.

An Altman soundtrack bears little resemblance to how sound is generally used in films. His multitrack concept is rooted in the recognition that the sounds we hear in life are not uniformly clear or on a single level; we hear noises and conversation around us without listening to everything. In many Altman films, some conversation is meant to be heard precisely, some is merely for background. Author Kurt Vonnegut joked at the New York Critics awards ceremony when presenting Altman with the best director plaque for *Nashville:* "Once you can understand the soundtrack for *McCabe and Mrs. Miller* you find that there's a pretty good story." Vonnegut was referring to the bewilderment many felt over the split-level sound in Altman's 1971 film challenging the myths of Western frontier days. Similarly, *California Split* (1974), about compulsive gamblers, relies heavily on this technique to evoke its gambling atmosphere.

Audiences are also puzzled by Altman's avoidance of linear storytelling. "To my mind," the director said, "a perfect film – a perfect use of the medium – would be one that would leave you amused by it but not able to articulate what it was about when you leave the theater. The only thing you could say walking out was 'wow,' but you could not say you didn't like the part where so and so did such and such. It would be a picture that enabled you to deal with your feelings along with what you were seeing." Not everyone says "wow." One young woman walked out of a *Nashville* preview in Boston, and recognizing Altman in the lobby, protested indignantly, "Are you making films for crazy people?" Altman retorted: "Well, you're here, aren't you?" Later he mellowed with second thoughts. Ever in search of new ideas, he pondered, "After all, what would be wrong with making films for crazy people?"

In *Nashville,* he has the audacity to juggle stories involving twenty-four characters, keeping the stories moving, not in a linear way but developing nonetheless, so that the characters contribute a strong, lasting impression of themselves and their relationship to the total mosaic. *Nashville* covers five days in their lives. The central theme is the preparation for an outdoor political rally for Hal Phillip Walker, the populist presidential candidate of the Replacement Party, who is denouncing existing politics and promising to straighten out the troubled nation. Leading Nashville singers are being pressed to participate.

Haven Hamilton (Henry Gibson), the king of country and western performers, composes sentimental and patriotic songs. Early in the film we find him recording "Two Hundred Years," a Bicentennial ode with the lyric, "We must be doin' somethin' right to last two hundred years." (Baskin wrote the music, Gibson the words.) With him is Lady Pearl (Barbara Baxley), owner of the Pickin' Parlor club; she is queen of the milieu, a Catholic, and a political activist disillusioned by the assassination of her idols, John and Robert Kennedy. Barbara Jean (Ronee Blakley), a new singing sensation, is emotionally tormented and headed for a breakdown. She is the key performer being sought for the rally. Barnett (Allen Garfield), her overbearing husband and manager, manipulates her life for greater glory and financial success. Connie White (Karen Black), a top singer of the Grand Ole Opry, envies Barbara Jean. Linnea (Lily Tomlin), a white lead singer in a black gospel choir, has two deaf children and is married to Delbert Reese (Ned Beatty), a lawyer for Nashville's stars and a local political fundraiser. She has a fling with Tom (Carradine), the promiscuous star of the disintegrating rock group Bill, Mary, and Tom.

Albuquerque (Barbara Harris) longs for her chance to become a superstar. So does the likable but pathetic waitress Sueleen Gay (Gwen Welles), who has no talent. Booked as a singer, she finds herself expected to do a striptease at a stag party and her performance is an affecting blend of humiliation and dignity. L.A. Joan (Shelley Duvall) is a gangling groupie following the music scene. Her elderly uncle, Mr. Green (Keenan Wynn), is having trouble coping with life and is deeply grieved because his wife is critically ill. He has taken in a boarder, Kenny (David Hayward), a loner dominated by his mother. Young soldier Glenn Kelly (Scott Glenn) worships Barbara Jean, whom his mother had saved from burning to death. Mysteriously popping up through the film is the Tricycle Man (Jeff Goldblum), who performs magic tricks and would appear to represent an all-knowing observer. Opal (Geraldine Chaplin), trying so hard to sound intellectual, purports to be a correspondent for the BBC doing a documentary on Nashville. Other characters add to Altman's potpourri.

The film drives toward its climax, the political rally and concert held in Nashville's replica of the Parthenon. While entertaining us with his sprawling, vigorous impression of the milieu and its foot-stomping culture, Altman has been leading us toward an imminent tragedy, presumably a political assassination at the rally. An assassination does occur, but the victim is not the populist candidate; Barbara Jean is the target of a senseless act, even more horrible because it reflects America's random violence. Albuquerque gets her chance to perform when, in an effort to calm the upset crowd, she leads the feverish singing of "It Don't Worry Me" ("You say that I ain't free/But it don't worry me").

Interpreting the ending, Altman said: "It can be taken as two sides of a coin, one saying, 'Look at these people – after a terrible tragedy they have gotten together and decided that they have to go on,' and the other saying, 'with something as terrible as this, they've forgotten it already.' " The film in its way faces the dynamics of a country that could experience in a decade the assassinations of John F. Kennedy, Robert Kennedy, Martin Luther King, and Malcolm X, and the crippling of presidential candidate George Wallace, followed by the attempts to kill Gerald Ford.

Made on location in Nashville, the film was shot on a budget of $2.2 million. United Artists was to have distributed it but dropped out, and Paramount took over. Altman originally wanted *Nashville* to be longer, but to satisfy Paramount had to cut it to two hours and thirty-nine minutes. He planned to expand it for a two-part television showing.

As might be expected, *Nashville* was praised and damned. It was denounced for mocking Middle-American values and using music that was not an accurate representation of the country and western genre. The complaints against its artistic merit also included the view that it was an incomprehensible jumble of characters and events, not a coherent story that could be understood and enjoyed.

"Any time you change a form," Altman shrugged, "you are going to lose the majority of your audience, because they are insecure about their own positions and are nervous because they want to know if they're behaving properly, and they are not free. As long as they can follow the form they are expecting, it is much simpler for them. With a picture like *Jaws* that everybody goes to see, the audience knows exactly what it is about – a shark. It's not really about anything else and there's no way they would ever be confused.

"Part of the reason *Nashville* was not as successful in the amount of audience it gathered or ever will gather is that it sounded, from a lot of what was written about it, as if it were a highly intelligent ripoff of a kind of people and an indictment of our society. It seemed that we weren't able to find a way to say in our advertising, 'Hey, you'll get this.' When you break form, you are not going to get a mass audience.

"The thing that I think makes *Nashville* different from most films," Altman continued, "is that it is kind of soap operaish. It doesn't really have a story line. It is just five days in the lives of these people. About five or ten years ago I started out with the idea of trying to get rid of the obligatory scene, and to see people in a circumstance, then go away and come back, and see that the circumstance has changed. You say, 'Oh, this must have happened.' You don't need any order. I look upon a film as being more like an essay."

Altman, who often casts the same actors and likes to include non-professionals, relies heavily on his offbeat choices to create the special freedom he is seeking. In this, he is like Fellini, who has had a major influence on him. "I find with casting," Altman explained, "that it is important for the actors to fit together in such a way that something happens between them. You can have excellent performers, but if they are abrasive it is not interesting from an audience standpoint."

A number of Altman's contemporaries have also been striving for screen flexibility according to their own theories. Andy Warhol has tried to do away with formal stories by basing films upon incident and atmosphere. John Cassavetes has achieved a naturalism in his work and encourages his actors to embellish specified situations. (Current filmmakers have no monopoly on nonconformity. Certainly, brilliant veteran director Luis Buñuel, who made his first film when Altman was three years old, has not been bound by convention.) Altman's *Nashville* coup depended upon the successful fusing of many ingredients on a scale every bit as ambitious as a huge Hollywood project, but with the kind of freedom that gives unusually full expression to the artist's creative imagination.

The film that first brought Altman to public notice was *M*A*S*H,* a rowdy satire set during the Korean War and released in 1970. Born in Kansas City, Missouri, in 1925, Altman served as a B-54 pilot in World War II, and then began making industrial films as well as writing scripts and magazine stories. After co-authoring *Bodyguard* (1948), writing and directing *The Delinquents* (1957), and co-directing a documentary, *The James Dean Story* (1957), he caught the attention of Hitchcock, who hired him to direct some "Alfred Hitchcock Hour" television shows. He spent a decade working in television before his career blossomed with *M*A*S*H*. Altman's other pre-*Nashville* films include *Brewster McCloud* (1970), *Images* (1972), *The Long Goodbye* (1973), and *Thieves Like Us* (1974).

While *Nashville* was receiving accolades, Altman was completing *Buffalo Bill and the Indians, or Sitting Bull's History Lesson* (1976), another venture uninhibited by traditional forms, and a film that punctures myths about America's heritage. His penchant for surprising audiences was further revealed by *3 Women* (1977), an alternately funny and harrowing conundrum that examines various facets of personality and projects ideas about relationships, attitudes, and realities. *A Wedding* (1978), in spoofing the wedding ritual, makes a sharp comment on the various strata of American life and on the hypocrisies that are perpetuated. *Quintet* (1979), a strange, demanding, many-layered allegory set amid snow and ice, suggests universal struggle against impending doom. After *A Perfect Couple* (1979), a story of mismatched lovers set to rock and classical music, and the ever-prolific director's fourteenth film in ten years, Altman set about filming *Health*.

Potentially significant was the idea of teaming Altman and E.L. Doctorow, author of *Ragtime* and *The Book of Daniel.* Doctorow's prose style and Altman's filmmaking style seemed made for each other. *Ragtime,* an entertaining but basically serious book about the fabric of America, mixes real historical figures and fanciful characters and situations. *The Book of Daniel,* a novel related to the case of Julius and Ethel Rosenberg, leads the son and daughter of a couple executed for an alleged espionage conspiracy on an odyssey to discover the truth about their parents and relate the era in which they lived to their own. Producer Dino de Laurentiis dismissed Altman as director of *Ragtime* in a rift over his refusal to drastically cut *Buffalo Bill,* but Altman still hoped to work with Doctorow on *The Book of Daniel* or another project.

Altman has extended his influence by producing the films of others, including his *Nashville* assistant director Alan Rudolph *(Welcome to L.A.,* 1977; *Remember My Name,* 1979), and Robert Benton *(The Late Show,* 1977). His success as a producer should ease his problems in obtaining financing and controlling his work. "There's so much commerce caught up in it," he lamented, even before the de Laurentiis dispute. "To paint a picture you have to have some paint, some canvas and some light. To make a movie you need a million dollars and those in the business of giving you that million want to get millions back – not merely another million, but one hundred million. They want the shark, King Kong, and sideshow material, and it is difficult to press them into something if they don't see much security in it. They're looking for *The Exorcist, The Godfather, Towering Inferno,* and *Jaws.* One reason I value the New York Critics award is that it not only pleases me but may help open the doors to other filmmakers who can say about the film they want to make, 'This will be like a *Nashville.*' Otherwise they wouldn't be listened to."

He was unable to count on such help from the Motion Picture Academy. Although *Nashville* was nominated, the best picture and best director awards went to *One Flew Over the Cuckoo's Nest,* itself a fine film. However, long after the memory of *Cuckoo's Nest* has faded into proper perspective, *Nashville* should grow in importance and significance. Films outside the realm of what the industry considers popular or safe at the time rarely acquire best picture or best director Oscars. Altman is a particular thorn as he is such an unregenerate individualist. You do not usually win Oscars by making films the way Altman does, but you may make a film that becomes a landmark.

NASHVILLE
USA (Paramount Pictures) 1975

Cast

Norman .... DAVID ARKIN
Lady Pearl .... BARBARA BAXLEY
Delbert Reese .... NED BEATTY
Connie White .... KAREN BLACK
Barbara Jean .... RONEE BLAKLEY
Tommy Brown .... TIMOTHY BROWN
Tom Frank .... KEITH CARRADINE
Opal .... GERALDINE CHAPLIN
Wade .... ROBERT DOQUI
L.A. Joan .... SHELLEY DUVALL
Barnett .... ALLEN GARFIELD
Haven Hamilton .... HENRY GIBSON
PFC. Glenn Kelly .... SCOTT GLENN
Tricycle Man .... JEFF GOLDBLUM
Albuquerque .... BARBARA HARRIS
Kenny Fraiser .... DAVID HAYWARD
John Triplette .... MICHAEL MURPHY
Bill .... ALLAN NICHOLLS
Bud Hamilton .... DAVE PEEL
Mary .... CRISTINA RAINES
Star .... BERT REMSEN
Linnea Reese .... LILY TOMLIN
Sueleen Gay .... GWEN WELLES
Mr. Green .... KEENAN WYNN
Jimmy Reese .... JAMES DAN CALVERT
Donna Reese .... DONNA DENTON
Trout .... MERLE KILGORE
Jewel .... CAROL MCGINNIS
Smokey Mountain Laurel .... SHEILA BAILEY, PATTI BRYANT
Frog .... RICHARD BASKIN
Themselves .... JONNIE BARNETT, VASSAR CLEMENTS, MISTY MOUNTAIN BOYS, SUE BARTON, ELLIOT GOULD, JULIE CHRISTIE

Running time .... 159 minutes
Panavision; Color by MGM Film Laboratories
Presented by .... ABC ENTERTAINMENT
A Jerry Weintraub Production
Executive Producers .... MARTIN STARGER and JERRY WEINTRAUB
Produced by .... ROBERT ALTMAN
Directed by .... ROBERT ALTMAN
Written by .... JOAN TEWKESBURY
Director of Photography .... PAUL LOHMANN
Music Arranged and Supervised by .... RICHARD BASKIN

Music and Lyrics by . . . . RICHARD BASKIN, HENRY GIBSON,
LILY TOMLIN, RONEE BLAKLEY, JOE RAPOSO,
DAVE PEEL, ROBERT ALTMAN, KAREN BLACK,
RICHARD REICHEG, KEITH CARRADINE,
BEN RALEIGH, ALLAN NICHOLLS, JUAN GRIZZLE,
JONNIE BARNETT, GARY BUSEY, ARLENE BARNETT,
MILLIE CLEMENTS (arrangements of
"Swing Low Sweet Chariot")
Edited by . . . . SIDNEY LEVIN, DENNIS HILL
Political Campaign . . . . THOMAS HAL PHILLIPS
Associate Producers . . . . ROBERT EGGENWEILER,
SCOTT BUSHNELL
Assistant Directors . . . . TOMMY THOMPSON, ALAN RUDOLPH
Production Coordinator . . . . KELLY MARSHALL
Assistant to the Producer . . . . JAC CASHIN
Sound . . . . JIM WEBB, CHRIS MCLAUGHLIN
Sound System . . . . LION'S GATE 8 TRACK SOUND
Rerecording Mixer . . . . RICHARD PORTMAN
Sound Editor . . . . WILLIAM A. SAWYER
Assistant . . . . RANDY KELLEY
Music Recorded by . . . . GENE EICHELBERGER and JOHNNY ROSEN
Camera Operator . . . . ED KOONS
Electrical Gaffers . . . . RANDY GLASS, MIKE MARLETT
Grips . . . . HARRY PEZ, EDDIE LARA
Assistant Editors . . . . TONY LOMBARDO, TOM WALLS
Script Supervision . . . . JOYCE KING
Property Master . . . . BOB ANDERSON
Hair Stylist . . . . ANN WADLINGTON
Make-up . . . . TOMMY THOMPSON
Wardrobe . . . . JULES MELILLO
Production Assistants . . . . ANGEL DOMINQUEZ, RON HECHT,
STEVE ALTMAN, MARK EGGENWEILER,
MAYSIE HOY, ALLAN HIGHFILL, ROGER FRAPPIER
Title Design . . . . DAN PERRI
Production Secretary . . . . ELAINE BRADISH

1975

Seven Beauties

Pasqualino's sisters in courtroom as his fate is being decided

A Leading Woman Director

THE CHERISHED NEO-REALIST period of Italian filmmaking emerged from the trauma of World War II; the vibrant talent of Lina Wertmüller from the political and economic chaos of Italy in the 1960s. Even cinemaphiles may not realize how many women directors there have been, but until Wertmüller none had merited inclusion in the high echelons. Wertmüller had been approaching special status for some time, and with her *Seven Beauties* among the great contemporary films, critics began to compare her with Bergman, Fellini, Antonioni, and others of international preeminence. There were, of course, dissenters.

The roster of women filmmakers includes such diverse talents as Alice Guy Blaché, Lois Weber, Germaine Dulac, Dorothy Arzner, Leni Riefenstahl, Ida Lupino, Maya Deren, Shirley Clarke, Elaine May, Barbara Loden, Joan Littlewood, Mai Zetterling, Nelly Kaplan, Nadine Trintignant, Agnès Varda, Marguerite Duras, Liliana Cavani, Shirley MacLaine, Susan Sontag, Joan Micklin Silver, Jeanne Moreau, Barbara Kopple, Claudia Weill, and many others with different degrees of experience and acclaim. Women editors and writers have been active, and there have been some women producers. Wertmüller, who has also worked in television and theater, directed a succession of outstanding films that had a cumulative impact. Her first film, *The Lizards* (1963), which she called "the last train of neo-realism," won fourteen international prizes. Her second, *This Time Let's Talk About Men* (1965), was a commercial success in Italy. *The Seduction of Mimi* (1972) is a comedy about a Sicilian who loses his political principles and throws away happiness by following his macho code; *Love and Anarchy* (1973), an imaginative story of a man who comes to Rome to assassinate Mussolini, and his relationship with the prostitutes who give him shelter; *Everything in Order, Nothing in Place* (1974, released in the United States under the shoddy title *All Screwed Up)*, a tragicomedy of young people who come to Milan to seek a better life but are ground down by the system; *Swept Away by an Unusual Destiny in the Blue Sea of August* (1974), a political-sexual fable concerning a spoiled upper-class woman and a working-class seaman who takes command and dominates her when they are stranded on an island. Wertmüller repeatedly casts two of her favorites, Mariangela Melato and Giancarlo Giannini, the latter giving a memorable performance as Pasqualino in *Seven Beauties*.

"I adore risks, if you take them in the right way," Wertmüller said in our talk on the crest of her New York triumph, when five of her films were showing in the city at the same time. "I have never felt, and I believe I never will feel, sure of myself. I make my films at the peak of confusion. Even if I think I will die of fear, I go exactly where I am most afraid. It is like walking a tightrope, the razor's edge."

This self-revelation does much to explain the distinction of her work: she consistently and successfully dares scenes that would be impossible achievements for lesser directors. Wertmüller communicates on film with fierce energy; she commingles tragedy and comedy, and fortified by her sympathies with anarchist philosophy, tends to see life in uninhibitedly expressed, brash conceptions, courageously endowing specific situations with the great themes confronting humanity. In *Seven Beauties,* she asks profound questions about survival. What must we do to survive? And to survive as what? If, to survive, a person must become corrupted and dehumanized, is the survivor's world worth living in? Some of the film's detractors, in the backlash against the unusual intensity of praise, have misunderstood the posing of such questions as a justification of survival at any cost.

Seven Beauties begins with a pop-style litany of contemporary values and crass preoccupations intoned against images of the modern world. Enter Pasqualino (Giannini), a deserter from the Italian army lost in Germany in World War II, who stumbles upon a massacre of civilians, probably Jews, by Nazi soldiers. What happens to him subsequently is interrupted by flashbacks. Pasqualino envisions himself as a Don Juan of Naples, but in truth he is a loser, a petty hustler steeped in machismo and consumed by the desire to be respected and feared. Pasqualino learns that the eldest of his seven sisters, an over-the-hill, untalented performer in a seedy music hall, has become a whore. Vowing manly revenge, he plans to kill her obnoxious pimp, whom she loves and who, she blindly believes, will keep his promise to marry her. Pasqualino summons up the courage to shoot him, but neglects to observe the hypocritical honor code requiring the pretense of offering a victim a chance for self-defense. To impress Don Raffaeli, the local Mafioso, he returns, chops up the body, puts the pieces in three suitcases, and dispatches them to different parts of Italy. Captured, "the butcher of Naples" is taken to court but spared prison when a deal is worked out. Instead, he is sent to an insane asylum, where, after intense suffering and electroshock punishment for raping a woman chained to her bed, he is released to fight for Mussolini in World War II.

His desertion leads to imprisonment in a concentration camp ruled by evil incarnate – a tyrannical, sadistic Bitch of Buchenwald-type (American actress Shirley Stoler) who orders prisoners beaten and shot at whim.

Pasqualino becomes a frenzied wreck. Here Wertmüller dares her riskiest sequence. Pasqualino, remembering his popularity with the ladies, conceives a wild scheme predicated on his belief that every woman, no matter how monstrous, needs love. He decides to attempt the seduction of the commandant as a way of saving himself, and plunges into a frantic, Faustian maneuver to lie down with the devil. This symbolic episode is stark and overwhelming, and propels the film toward its bitter, upsetting conclusion. To survive, Pasqualino must do the devil's handiwork, even carrying out an order to shoot his closest friend.

Another inmate, Pedro, a Spanish anarchist (Fernando Rey), refuses to continue in such a hell. In a conversation with Pasqualino, the anarchist laments the future he foresees, a world so overpopulated and desperate that families will fight each other for food. When Pasqualino is reduced to killing to stay alive, Pedro throws himself into a trough of excrement and is shot. After the war, Pasqualino returns home to an Italy busy concentrating on materialism, and finds that the innocent, adoring young girl he once said would be his fiancée has become a gaudy prostitute. Seizing upon Pedro's prediction, Pasqualino asks her to marry him and decrees that they must have a huge family to prepare for the vicious battle for survival that lies ahead.

"He has learned nothing," said Wertmüller, adding: "This is a true story. I heard it from the real Pasqualino, who worked as an extra in *The Seduction of Mimi* and also in this. He committed the murder; he was in the camp. Afterward he had three wives and eighteen sons. I can't tell you his name. I asked when we were making the film if he wanted credit. It was my plan to show him at the end and have him say that it was his true story. But he refused, saying, 'No, nobody knows about my life and it is better this way.' "

A simple plot outline cannot begin to convey the masterpiece that Wertmüller has shaped. Her scenes, so superbly photographed by Tonino delli Colli, have amazing visual power: some resemble paintings; some are suggestive of Fellini, an unmistakable influence. Her close-ups of faces are revealing, and just as de Sica was able to capture the soul of his characters in his close-ups, Wertmüller manages to touch our emotions with her intimate, unforgettable portraits. She is able to leap instantaneously from one mood to another and back again without being confusing. Her concentration camp scenes, with their casual grotesqueness, are devastating evocations of these human abattoirs. Contrastingly, her whirling shots of treetops have a majestic lyricism. Wertmüller knows the value of silence; she recounts the courtroom outcome by filming the glances between Pasqualino, his lawyer, his family, and the authorities. Whether conveying beauty, despair, hope, terror, sexuality, revenge, mass murder, madness, love, eroticism, or tenderness, Wertmüller confidently embraces her subject with a larger-than-life viewpoint that gives breadth to individual scenes and to her work as a whole. Her use of music is exceptionally forceful, either matching or counterpointing her imagery. Her choice of "The Ride of the Valkyries" for her concentration camp music might have been clichéd, but she succeeds with it because her prison is so gruesome that the blend creates a nightmarish mood.

Wertmüller is known for her tremendous energy, and has a reputation for wearing down her crew and her actors. She labors for long hours, with but a few stolen hours of sleep before she is ready for her next day at a similar pace. "There were many difficulties making *Seven Beauties,*" she recalled. "It was very expensive, about 3.8 million in dollars. I also should have had double the time because we had to shoot in so many places and had so many things to do." She begins a project by writing a voluminous script. "You should have seen the one for *Seven Beauties*," she exclaimed, holding her hands far apart. "I work from a complete screenplay. I write a lot, then I select, and I think while I write. There is a very big difference between a director and a film author. The author writes. There is nothing when an author begins, just a blank page. For the director, there can be a play, a comedy, something to which he can give his interpretation. Sometimes a director also becomes an author by taking what is not a very good screenplay and making it into a great movie."

Wertmüller is delightfully Roman – her name stems from a partly Swiss ancestry. Her full appellation is Arcangela Felice Assunta Wertmüller von Elgg Spanol von Brauchich-Job, which would be rather difficult to squeeze onto a marquee. Her husband, artist and designer Enrico Job, works on her films and was art director for *Seven Beauties*. Wertmüller, in her mid-forties when *Seven Beauties* was made, avoided citing particular filmmakers as influences upon her work, preferring to say: "All have influenced it; I learn from everybody. You will not get one name from me, even under torture. I like cinema very much, maybe too much, all of it. But no names." As a child she was fascinated by Hollywood films, and now looks upon them as realistic in an unintentional way. "They reflect the phony society. Whether that was intended doesn't matter. They gave the face of what was in fact American reality; even the sophisticated comedies did that. I saw the satin sheets, breakfasts in places like cathedrals, those blond women with their feathers – those fairy tales – as incredible documents that gave a realistic portrait of America, and therefore became realistic cinema."

Undoubtedly much of the attention paid Wertmüller results from the women's liberation movement's focus on the reluctance of the male-dominated industry to give women opportunities to make films. Activists expect women directors who do surmount the barriers to deal with subjects of special concern to women. Wertmüller has not recognized such an obligation. Her commitment is to filmmaking and humanity as a whole: "The woman director idea just doesn't interest me. I think of myself first as a person. My success in Europe comes from my movies. Afterward they realize I'm a woman." If there is any particular political leaning, it is toward anarchism, of which she said: "We Italians and the Spanish have a big tradition of anarchism, as there also is in America."

She is aware of the indignities suffered by women in trying to finance their films. "It took a lot of effort for me to get money. Do you want to know the method? The first rule of all is break balls a lot. The second rule – break balls again. The third rule – break more balls. Film is strictly related to business. After this, it may be many things, art, culture, politics. But if it doesn't look commercial, it isn't made. The relationship between art and finance through the years is very interesting; art and culture were always a kind of decoration for power. But popular art is more than just a decoration. It becomes political. Many stubborn directors don't work because they refuse to make commercial movies. There are compromises one must make, and I've compromised, but only functionally, not in terms of principle. I want to communicate with as many people as possible, and for that it is necessary to make compromises. By compromise I only mean that it is important for the public to understand a film. But I did not compromise at all in *Seven Beauties*. I'm not afraid of the obvious, the folkloristic; I'm not afraid of laughter. Movies are a popular art and a vast means of communication between people around the world. If we deal in universal problems the experience is a common one. People and countries are different, but the main problems are the same. I try to make pictures that I like and that have social commitment. But I want to keep in touch with a big audience, because I don't think quality is an elitist thing."

Predictably, when Wertmüller suddenly became fashionable, the new "in" director on the scene, Hollywood began wooing her, much to her delight. In New York for the première of *Seven Beauties*, she met with representatives who had flown from Hollywood to talk contracts. "One compromise I will not make," she insisted while in the throes of such negotiation, "is on total control of my work. Freedom. I will not lose that." Hollywood companies have not been known for generosity in that sphere. The winner in the Wertmüller bidding was Warner Bros., which signed a multi-picture deal with her. The first – in English – was *A Night Full of Rain* (1978), a comment on the problems of marriage starring Giannini and Candice Bergen; it turned out to be a disastrous misstep artistically and a failure at the box office. Wertmüller and Warner Bros. severed their relationship and she proceeded to work independently again.

"We'll see," she said warily, thinking of the many projects she has been nurturing through the years, including a film about the Roman emperor Caligula. Whatever her future, her work to date has already earned her international recognition, including the first Oscar nomination ever accorded a woman director – for *Seven Beauties*. (Ludicrously, she lost to

John Avildsen for *Rocky*. Her breakthrough may result in more opportunities for women. Perhaps producers, encouraged by Wertmüller's example, will think twice before rejecting someone with potential because of a reluctance to hazard large sums of money on a woman filmmaker. As Wertmüller said to critic John Simon, "If a woman can make you $20 million, there are no longer problems of uterus or testicles."

SEVEN BEAUTIES
(Pasqualino Settebellezza)
ITALY 1975

Cast

Pasqualino Frafuso .... Giancarlo Giannini
Pedro .... Fernando Rey
Commandant .... Shirley Stoler
Concettina .... Elena Fiore
Don Raffaele .... Enzo Vitale
Totonno .... Mario Conti
Francesco .... Piero di Orio
Mother .... Ermelinda de Felice
Carolina .... Francesca Marciano
Lawyer .... Lucio Amelio
Socialist .... Roberto Herlitzka
Doctor .... Doriglia Palmi

Running time .... 116 minutes
Technicolor
Produced by .... Lina Wertmüller, Giancarlo Giannini, and Arrigo Colombo
Directed by .... Lina Wertmüller
Screenplay by .... Lina Wertmüller
Director of Photography .... Tonino delli Colli
Film Editor .... Franco Fraticelli
Art Director .... Enrico Job
Original Music .... Enzo Iannacci

Bibliography

Agee, James. *Agee on Film: Volume One*. 1958. New York: Grosset & Dunlap, Universal Library Edition, 1969.
Agel, Jerome, ed. *The Making of Kubrick's "2001."* New York: New American Library, 1970.
Americana Annual, The. New York: Grolier. Published annually.
American Film Institute Catalog, The. Feature Films 1961–1970. Vol. F6. Richard P. Krafsur, Executive Editor. New York and London: R.R. Bowker Co., 1976.
American Film Institute Catalog of Motion Pictures Produced in the United States, The. Feature Films 1921–1930. Vol. F2. Kenneth W. Munden, Executive Editor. New York and London: R.R. Bowker Co., 1971.
Anobile, Richard, ed. *Buster Keaton's "The General."* New York: Avon Books, Film Classics Library, 1975.
Anobile, Richard, ed. *James Whale's "Frankenstein."* New York: Avon Books, Film Classics Library, 1974.
Anobile, Richard, ed. *John Ford's "Stagecoach."* New York: Avon Books, Film Classics Library, 1975.

Bakal, Carl. *The Right to Bear Arms*. New York: McGraw-Hill Book Co., 1966.
Barna, Yon. *Eisenstein*. Translated by Lise Hunter. Bloomington: Indiana University Press, 1973.
Barnouw, Eric and S. Krishnaswamy. *Indian Film*. New York and London: Columbia University Press, 1963.
Barry, Iris, *D.W. Griffith: American Film Master*. 1940. Rev. ed. with annotated list of films by Eileen Bowser. New York: Museum of Modern Art, 1965.
Barsam, Richard Meran. *Nonfiction Film: A Critical History*. New York: E.P. Dutton & Co., 1973.
Bazin, André. *Jean Renoir*. Edited by François Truffaut. Translated by W.W. Halsey II and William H. Simon. New York: Simon & Schuster, 1973.
Behlmer, Rudy, ed. *Memo From David O. Selznick*. New York: Viking Press, 1972.
Bergman, Andrew. *We're in the Money: Depression America and Its Films*. New York: New York University Press, 1971.
Biberman, Herbert. *"Salt of the Earth": The Story of a Film*. Boston: Beacon Press, 1965.
Bitzer, G.W. *Billy Bitzer: His Story*. New York: Farrar, Straus & Giroux, 1973.
Björkmann, Stig, Torsten Mannis, and Jonas Sima. *Bergman on Bergman: Interviews with Ingmar Bergman*. Translated by Paul Britten Austin. New York: Simon & Schuster, 1973.
Blesh, Rudi. *Keaton*. New York: Macmillan Co., 1966.
Bock, Audie. *Japanese Film Directors*. Tokyo, New York, and San Francisco: Kodansha International, 1978.
Braudy, Leo. *Jean Renoir: The World of His Films*. Garden City, N.Y.: Doubleday & Co., 1972.
Brownlow, Kevin. *The Parade's Gone By*. New York: Alfred A. Knopf, 1968.
Bucher, Felix, in collaboration with Leonhard H. Gmür. *Screen Series: Germany*. London: A. Zwemmer; New York: A.S. Barnes & Co., 1970.
Bullock, Alan, ed. *The Twentieth Century*. New York: McGraw-Hill Book Co., 1971.

Calder-Marshall, Arthur. *The Innocent Eye: The Life of Robert J. Flaherty*. New York: Harcourt, Brace & World, 1966.
Cameron, Ian, and Robin Wood. *Antonioni*. New York: Praeger, 1969.
Cameron, Ian, ed. *The Films of Jean-Luc Godard*. New York: Praeger, 1969
Capra, Frank. *The Name Above the Title*. New York: Macmillan Co., 1971.
Chaplin, Charles. *My Autobiography*. New York: Simon & Schuster, 1964.
Cawelti, John G., ed. *Focus on "Bonnie and Clyde."* Englewood Cliffs, N.J.: Prentice-Hall, Film Focus Series, 1973.
Clarke, Arthur C. *"2001: A Space Odyssey": Based on A Screenplay by Stanley Kubrick and Arthur C. Clarke*. New York: New American Library, 1968.
Collet, Jean. *Jean-Luc Godard*. 1963, 1968. Translated by Ciba Vaughan. New York: Crown Publishers, 1970.
Collier's Yearbook. New York: Macmillan Educational Corp. Published annually.
Concise Universal Encyclopedia, The. London: Amalgamated Press.
Corliss, Richard. *Talking Pictures: Screenwriters in the American Cinema 1927–1973*. Woodstock, N.Y.: The Overlook Press, 1974.
Cottrell, John. *Laurence Olivier*. Englewood Cliffs, N.J.: Prentice-Hall, 1975.
Cowie, Peter: *Seventy Years of Cinema*. South Brunswick and New York: A.S. Barnes & Co., 1969.
Crichton, Kyle. *The Marx Brothers*. Garden City, N.Y.: Doubleday & Co., 1950.
Crisp, C.G. *François Truffaut*. New York: Praeger, 1972.

De Sica, Vittorio. *Miracle in Milan*. New York: Grossman Publishers, Orion Press, 1968.
Dickinson, Thorold. *A Discovery of Cinema*. New York: Oxford University Press, 1971.
Donner, Jörn. *The Films of Ingmar Bergman: From "Torment" to "All Those Women."* Translated by Holger Lundbergh. New York: Dover Publications, 1972.
Donner, Jörn. "Three Scenes With Ingmar Bergman." Preliminary Dialogue List and Shot Description. Mimeographed.
Durgnat, Raymond. *A Mirror for England: British Movies from Austerity to Affluence*. New York, Washington: Praeger, 1971.

"Easy Rider": Original Screenplay by Peter Fonda; Dennis Hopper; Terry Southern. Edited by Nancy Hardin and Marilyn Schlossberg. New York: New American Library, Signet, 1969.
Eisenstein, Sergei. *Film Form*. Edited and translated by Jay Leyda. New York: Harcourt, Brace & World, 1949.
Eisenstein, Sergei. *Notes of a Film Director*. 1948. Translated by X. Danko. New York: Dover Publications, 1970.
Esslin, Martin. *The Theatre of the Absurd*. Rev. ed. Garden City, N.Y.: Doubleday & Co., Anchor Books, 1969.

Farber, Stephen. *The Movie Rating Game*. Washington: Public Affairs Press, 1972.
Fenin, George N., and William K. Everson. *The Western: From silents to the seventies*. Rev. ed. 1973. New York: Penguin Books, 1977.
Fellini on Fellini. Edited by Anna Keel and Christian Strich. Translated by Isabel Quigley. New York: Dell Publishing Co., 1977.
Film TV Daily 1970 Yearbook of Motion Pictures and Television. New York: Film TV Daily, 1970.
Flaherty, Frances Hubbard. *Odyssey of a Film-maker*. 1960. New York: Arno Press and The New York Times, 1972.
Flaherty, Robert J. *My Eskimo Friends*. Garden City, N.Y.: Doubleday, Page & Co., 1924.
Flamini, Roland. *Scarlett, Rhett, and a Cast of Thousands*. New York: Macmillan Publishing Co., 1975.
Florescu, Radu. *In Search of Frankenstein*. With Contributions by Alan Barbour and Matei Cazacu. Boston: New York Graphic Society, 1975.
Four Marx Brothers, The, in "Monkey Business" and "Duck Soup." New York: Simon & Schuster, Classic Film Scripts, 1972.
French, Warren. *Filmguide to "The Grapes of Wrath."* Bloomington and London: Indiana University Press, Filmguide Series, 1973.

Furhammer, Leif and Folke Isaksson. *Politics and Film*. 1968. Translated by Kersti French. New York, Washington: Praeger, 1971.

Garraty, John A. *The American Nation: A History of the United States*. 2nd. ed. New York: Harper & Row, American Heritage Publishing Co., 1971.
Geduld, Harry M. *The Birth of the Talkies: From Edison to Jolson*. Bloomington and London: Indiana University Press, 1975.
Gelmis, Joseph. *The Film Director as Superstar*. Garden City. N.Y.: Doubleday & Co., 1970.
Gifford, Denis. *The British Film Catalogue 1895–1970: A Reference Guide*. New York: McGraw-Hill Book Co., 1973.
Gifford, Denis. *Chaplin*. Garden City, N.Y.: Doubleday & Co., 1974.
Gifford, Denis. *Movie Monsters*. Reprint. London, New York: Studio Vista, Dutton Pictureback, 1974.
Gilliatt, Penelope. *Jean Renoir: Essays, Conversations, Reviews*. New York: McGraw-Hill Book Co., 1975.
Gish, Lillian. *The Movies, Mr. Griffith, and Me*. Englewood Cliffs, N.J.: Prentice-Hall, 1969.
Godard on Godard. 1968. With commentary and translation by Tom Milne. Edited by Jean Narboni and Tom Milne. New York: Viking Press, 1972.
Gottesman, Ronald, ed. *Focus on "Citizen Kane."* Englewood Cliffs, N.J.: Prentice-Hall, Film Focus Series, 1971.
Gottesman, Ronald, ed. *Focus on Orson Welles*. Englewood Cliffs, N.J.: Prentice-Hall, Film Focus Series, 1976.
Grierson on Documentary. Edited and compiled by Forsyth Hardy. 1947. Rev. ed. New York: Praeger Publishers, 1971.
Griffith, Richard. *The World of Robert Flaherty*. 1953. Westport, Conn.: Greenwood Press, 1970.
Guarner, José Luis. *Roberto Rossellini*. Translated by Elisabeth Cameron. New York: Praeger, 1970.
Gussow, Mel. *Don't Say Yes Until I Finish Talking: A Biography of Darryl F. Zanuck*. Garden City, N.Y.: Doubleday & Co., 1971.

Halliwell, Leslie. *The Filmgoer's Companion*. 4th rev. ed. New York: Avon, Flare Books, 1975.
Haskell, Molly. *From Reverence to Rape: The Treatment of Women in the Movies*. New York: Holt, Rinehart & Winston, 1974.
Henderson, Robert M. *D.W. Griffith: The Years at Biograph*. New York: Farrar, Straus & Giroux, 1970.
Houseman, John. *Run-through*. New York: Simon & Schuster, 1972.
Huff, Theodore. *A Shot Analysis of D.W. Griffith's "The Birth of a Nation."* New York: Museum of Modern Art, 1961.
Hughes, Robert, ed. *Film: Book One*. New York: Grove Press, 1959.
Hughes, Robert, ed. *Film: Book 2 – Films of Peace and War*. New York: Grove Press, 1962.

Insdorf, Annette. *François Truffaut*. Boston: Twayne Publishers, 1978.
Issari, M. Ali. *Cinéma Vérité*. Michigan State University Press, 1971.

Jacobs, Lewis, comp. *The Emergence of Film Art*. New York: Hopkinson & Blake, 1969.
Jacobs, Lewis. *The Rise of the American Film*. 1939. New York: Teachers College Press, 1969.
Joyce, James. *Ulysses*. 1934. With a foreword by Morris L. Ernst and the decision of the United States District Court rendered by Judge John M. Woolsey. New York: Vintage Books, 1961.

Kael, Pauline, Herman J. Mankiewicz, and Orson Welles. *The "Citizen Kane" Book*. Boston, Toronto: Little, Brown & Co., Atlantic Monthly Press, 1971.
Kanin, Garson. *Hollywood*. New York: Viking Press, 1974.

Kauffmann, Stanley, ed. *American Film Criticism: From the Beginnings to "Citizen Kane."* With Bruce Henstell. New York: Liveright, 1972.
Keaton, Buster, with Charles Samuels. *My Wonderful World of Slapstick.* Garden City, N.Y.: Doubleday & Co., 1960.
Kerr, Walter. *The Silent Clowns.* New York: Alfred A. Knopf, 1975.

Lambert, Gavin. *GWTW: The Making of "Gone With the Wind."* Boston, Toronto: Little, Brown & Co., Atlantic Monthly Press, 1973.
Lax, Eric. *On Being Funny: Woody Allen and Comedy.* New York: Charterhouse, 1975.
Leiser, Erwin. *Nazi Cinema.* New York, Macmillan Co., 1975.
Leprochon, Pierre. *The Italian Cinema.* 1966. Translated by Roger Greaves and Oliver Stallybrass. London: Secker & Warburg, 1972.
Levin, G. Roy. *Documentary Explorations: 15 interviews with Film-makers.* Garden City, N.Y.: Doubleday & Co., 1971.
Leyda, Jay. *Kino: A History of the Russian and Soviet Film.* London: George Allen & Unwin, 1960.
Lorenz, Pare. *Lorenz on Film: Movies 1927 to 1941.* New York: Hopkinson & Blake, 1975.

Maltin, Leonard. *The Disney Films.* New York: Crown Publishers, 1973.
Manvell, Roger, and Heinrich Fraenkel. *The German Cinema.* New York, Washington: Praeger Publishers, 1971.
Marx, Groucho, and Richard J. Anobile. *The Marx Bros. Scrapbook.* New York: Darien House, 1973.
Marx, Harpo, with Rowland Barber. *Harpo Speaks!* New York: Bernard Geis Associates, 1961.
Mast, Gerald. *A Short History of the Movies.* New York: Pegasus, 1971.
Mayer, David. *Sergei M. Eisenstein's "Potemkin": A shot-by-shot presentation.* New York: Grossman Publishers, 1972.
Mayer, Michael F. *Foreign Films on American Screens.* New York: Arco Publishing Co., 1965.
Maynard, Richard A., series ed. *The American West on Film.* Rochelle Park, N.J.: Hayden Book Co., 1974.
Mellen, Joan. *Voices From the Japanese Cinema.* New York: Liveright, 1975.
Metz, Christian. *Film Language: A Semiotics of the Cinema.* Translated by Michael Taylor. New York: Oxford University Press, 1974.
Monaco, James. *The New Wave: Truffaut, Godard, Chabrol, Rohmer, Rivette.* New York: Oxford University Press, 1976.
Montagu, Ivor. *With Eisenstein in Hollywood.* New York: International Publishers, 1969.
Moss, Robert F. *Karloff and Company: The Horror Film.* New York: Pyramid, 1974.
Moussinac, Léon. *Sergei Eisenstein.* 1964. Translated by D. Sandy Petrey. New York: Crown Publishers, 1970.
Murray, James P. *To Find an Image: Black Films From "Uncle Tom" to "Super Fly."* Indianapolis and New York: Bobbs-Merrill, 1973.
McBride, Joseph. *Orson Welles.* New York: Viking Press, 1972.

Nachbar, Jack, ed. *Focus on The Western.* Englewood Cliffs, N.J.: Prentice-Hall, 1974.
New Wave, The. Critical landmarks selected by Peter Graham. Garden City, N.Y.: Doubleday & Co., 1968.
"*New York Times, The.*" *Film Reviews.* New York: *The New York Times* & Arno Press, 1970, 1971.

Page One: Major Events 1920–1975 as Presented in "The New York Times." New York: Arno Press, 1975.
Pasolini on Pasolini. Interviews with Oswald Stack. Bloomington and London: Indiana University Press, 1969.
Patterson, Lindsay, ed. *Black Films and Film-makers: A Comprehensive Anthology From Stereotype to Superhero.* New York: Dodd, Mead & Co., 1975.
Perry, Ted. *Filmguide to "8½."* Bloomington, London: Indiana University Press, 1975.

Renan, Sheldon. *An Introduction to the American Underground Film*. New York: E.P. Dutton & Co., 1967.
Renoir, Jean. *My Life and My Films*. Translated by Norman Denny. New York: Atheneum, 1974.
Rhode, Eric. *A History of The Cinema From Its Origins to 1970*. New York: Hill & Wang, 1976.
Richie, Donald. *The Films of Akira Kurosawa*. Berkeley and Los Angeles: University of California Press, 1965.
Richie, Donald. *Japanese Cinema: Film Style and National Character*. Garden City, N.Y.: Doubleday & Co., Anchor Books, 1971.
Richie, Donald. Consulting ed. "*Rashomon*": *A Film by Akira Kurosawa*. New York: Grove Press, 1969.
Robinson, David. *Buster Keaton*. Bloomington and London: Indiana University Press.
Robinson, David. *Hollywood in the Twenties*. New York: A.S. Barnes & Co., 1968.
Rossellini, Roberto. *The War Trilogy: "Open City," "Paisan," "Germany – Year Zero."* Edited by Stefano Roncoroni. Translated by Judith Green. New York: Grossman Publishers, 1973.
Roud, Richard. *Jean-Luc Godard*. Garden City, N.Y.: Doubleday & Co., 1968.

Sadoul, Georges. *French Film*. 1953. New York: Arno Press and *The New York Times*, 1972.
Salachas, Gilbert. *Federico Fellini*. 1963. Translated by Rosalie Siegel. New York: Crown Publishers, 1969.
Sarris, Andrew. *Confessions of a Cultist: On the Cinema 1955/1969*. New York: Simon & Schuster, 1970.
Sarris, Andrew, ed. *Interviews with Film Directors*. New York: Bobbs Merrill, 1967.
Sarris, Andrew. *Politics and Cinema*. New York: Columbia University Press, 1978.
Schickel, Richard. *The Disney Version*. New York: Simon & Schuster, 1968.
Schickel, Richard. *Movies: The History of an Art and an Institution*. New York: Basic Books, 1964.
Schickel, Richard. *The Men Who Made the Movies*. New York: Atheneum, 1975.
Seldes, Gilbert. *The 7 Lively Arts*. 1924. Rev. ed. New York: Sagamore Press, 1957.
Seton, Marie. *Sergei M. Eisenstein: A Biography*. New York: A.A. Wyn, 1952.
Shelley, Mary Wollstonecraft. *Frankenstein*. 1831. Reprint. New York: Oxford University Press, 1971.
Sherwood, Robert E. *The Best Moving Pictures of 1922–23*. Boston: Small, Maynard & Co., 1923.
Silva, Fred, ed. *Focus on "The Birth of a Nation."* Englewood Cliffs, N.J.: Prentice-Hall, 1971.
Simon, John. *Ingmar Bergman directs*. New York: Harcourt Brace Jovanovich, 1972.
Sklar, Robert. *Movie-Made America: A Cultural History of American Movies*. New York: Random House, 1975.
Smith, John M. *Jean Vigo*. New York: Praeger Publishers, 1972.
Smith, Sharon. *Women Who Make Movies*. New York: Hopkinson & Blake, 1975.
"*Sorrow and the Pity, The.*" *A Film by Marcel Ophuls*. Filmscript translated by Mireille Johnston. New York: Berkeley Windhover, 1975.
Springer, John. *All Talking! All Singing! All Dancing!: A Pictorial History of the Movie Musical*. New York: Citadel Press, 1966.
Springer, John. *The Fondas: The Films and Careers of Henry, Jane and Peter Fonda*. New York: Citadel Press, 1970.
Sussex, Elizabeth. *Lindsay Anderson*. New York: Praeger Publishers, 1970.

Taylor, John Russell. *Cinema Eye, Cinema Ear: Some key film-makers of the sixties*. New York: Hill & Wang, 1964.
Taylor, John Russell. *Directors and Directions: Cinema for the Seventies*. New York: Hill & Wang, 1975.
Thomas, Bob, ed. *Directors in "Action": Selections from "Action," the Official Magazine of the Directors Guild of America*. Indianapolis, New York: The Bobbs-Merrill Co., 1973.

Thomas, Tony. *The Films of Gene Kelly, Song and Dance Man*. Secaucus, N.J.: Citadel Press, 1974.
Truffaut, François. *Hitchcock*. With the Collaboration of Helen G. Scott. New York: Simon & Schuster, 1967.
Turan, Kenneth, and Stephen F. Zito. *Sinema: American pornographic films and the people who make them*. New York: Praeger Publishers, 1974.
Tyler, Parker. *Underground Film: A Critical History*. New York: Grove Press, 1969.

Van Peebles, Melvin. "*Sweet Sweetback's Baadasssss Song*." New York: Lancer Books, 1971.
Vogel, Amos. *Film as a Subversive Art*. New York: Random House, 1974.

Walker, Alexander. *Hollywood UK: The British Film Industry in the Sixties*. New York: Stein & Day, 1974.
Walker, Alexander. *Stanley Kubrick directs*. New York: Harcourt Brace Jovanovich, 1971.
Wallechinsky, David, and Irving Wallace. *The People's Almanac*. Garden City, N.Y.: Doubleday & Co., 1975.
Warner, Jack. *My First Hundred Years in Hollywood*. With Dean Jennings. New York: Random House, 1964.
Wilson, Robert, ed. *The Film Criticism of Otis Ferguson*. Philadelphia: Temple University Press, 1971.
Wood, Robin. *The "Apu" Trilogy*. New York: Praeger Publishers, 1971.
Wood, Robin. *Hitchcock's Films*. 2nd enlarged ed. New York: A.S. Barnes, 1969.
Wolf, William. *The Marx Brothers*. New York: Pyramid, 1975.
Wright, Basil. *The Long View*. New York: Alfred A. Knopf, 1974.

Newspapers and Periodicals
The Amsterdam News, Asbury Park Press, The Atlanta Constitution, The Atlanta Journal, The Boston Globe, The Bulletin of the Atomic Scientists, The Chicago Tribune, The Cleveland Plain Dealer, Cue New York, Esquire, Life, The Listener, The Los Angeles Times, The Miami Herald, The Miami News, Le Monde, McCall's, The Nation, The New Republic, New York, The New York Daily Column, The New York Daily News, The New York Evening Journal, The New York Evening Post, The New York Herald Tribune, The New York Journal American, The New York Post, The New York Review of Books, The New York Sun, The New York Times, The New York Times Magazine, The New York World Telegram and Sun, The New Yorker, The Newark Evening News, Newsweek, The Observer, PM, Playboy, Popular Mechanics, The Providence Sunday Journal, Ramparts, The Rochester Democrat and Chronicle, The Rochester Times-Union, Rolling Stone, The San Francisco Sunday Chronicle, Saturday Review, Show, The Sunday Times, The Sunday Telegraph Magazine, Time, The Village Voice, The Wall Street Journal, The Washington Post, Women's Wear Daily.

Action, American Film, Arts, Boxoffice, Cahiers du Cinéma, Daily Variety, Ecran Français, Film Comment, Film Culture, Film Daily, Film Heritage, Hollywood Reporter, Independent Film Journal, Journal of the Society of Film and Television Arts, Motion Picture Daily, Motion Picture Exhibitor, The New York Film Bulletin, Positif, Screen Director, Sight and Sound, Take One, Theatre Arts, Variety.

Index

Page numbers in *italics* refer to illustrations